REDEFINING STUDENT LEARNING:
ROOTS OF EDUCATIONAL CHANGE

edited by

Hermine H. Marshall

ABLEX PUBLISHING CORPORATION
NORWOOD, NJ

Cover design by Deb Hoelfner.
Cover photograph from *Researching Patterns of Culture in Ancient History: The Sixth Grade Curriculum* (McKinley School, Santa Barbara, California). Photographer: Hongpen Liao. Reprinted by permission.

Copyright © 1992 by Ablex Publishing Corporation

All rights reserved. No part of this publication may be reproduced, stored in a retrieval system, or transmitted, in any form or by any means, electronic, mechanical, photocopying, microfilming, recording, or otherwise, without permission of the publisher.

Printed in the United States of America

Library of Congress Cataloging-in-Publication Data

Redefining student learning : roots of educational change / edited by
  Hermine H. Marshall.
    p. cm.
  Includes bibliographical references (p.) and index.
  ISBN 0-89391-854-7.—ISBN 0-89391-917-9 (pbk.)
  1. Learning. 2. Educational change—United States.
LB1060.R36 1992
370.15′23—dc20   92-3161
                                                                                     CIP

Ablex Publishing Corporation
355 Chestnut Street
Norwood, New Jersey 07648

For Hannah and Trevor, their siblings, cousins, and peers

Table of Contents

1. Seeing, Redefining, and Support Student Learning
   Hermine H. Marshall — **1**

2. Learning for What Purpose? Questions When Viewing Classroom Learning from a Sociocultural Curriculum Perspective
   Susanne Chandler — **33**

3. Learning in Classroom Settings: Making or Breaking a Culture
   Elaine Collins and Judith L. Green — **59**

4. Locating Learning in the Times and Spaces of Teaching
   Ginger Weade — **87**

5. Constructing Literacy in Classrooms: Literate Action as Social Accomplishment
   Santa Barbara Classroom Discourse Group — **119**

6. Revising Their Thinking: Keisha Coleman and her Third-Grade Mathematics Class
   Penelope L. Peterson — **151**

7. Change in Learning Mathematics: Change in Teaching Mathematics
   Terry Wood, Paul Cobb, and Erna Yackel — **177**

8. Translating Motivation into Thoughtfulness
   Phyllis C. Blumenfeld, Pamelo Puro, and John R. Mergendoller — **207**

9. Assessment in the Context of Schools and School Change
   Roberta Camp — **241**

10. Organizational Design and Teaching for Student Learning
    William A. Firestone — **265**

11 Beginning with The Classroom: Implications for Redesigning   *293*
    Schools
       Carolyn M. Evertson and Joseph Murphy

    Author Index   *321*

    Subject Index   *327*

Acknowledgments

Many colleagues have contributed to the thinking that led to this book. A special word of thanks, however, goes to Judith L. Green for asking the hard questions and for serving as a catalyst in the continuing refinement of my own understanding of learning processes.

Preface

Hermine H. Marshall

The need to center educational reform on new conceptualizations of learning—and thus the impetus for this volume—derives from several sources. One source springs from my research on differences between what I termed "work-oriented" and "learning-oriented" classrooms (Marshall, 1987a, 1987b, 1988a). In work-oriented classrooms, the teacher's role is to transmit a relatively fixed body of knowledge to the students in the most efficient manner possible. In this type of classroom, the emphasis is on students completing their work to receive an external reward. Work-oriented classrooms are congruent with traditional behaviorist views of learning. In contrast, in learning-oriented classrooms, the teacher's role is to facilitate students' active construction of knowledge by helping them build on what they already know in meaningful and relevant ways. The emphasis in these classrooms is on learning for purposes of understanding and solving new problems. In this type of classroom, knowledge is seen as dynamic and rapidly changing rather than fixed and easily transmitted. In these classrooms, there are more options in the ways students can engage in learning and in the ways they come to new understandings.

The distinction between these two types of classrooms stimulated my interest in how the common use of a classroom-as-a-workplace metaphor influences the way classroom learning is perceived and investigated and the conclusions that are made. Different consequences might become apparent if the classroom was viewed as a "learning place" (Marshall, 1988b, 1990). My hypotheses about qualities of classrooms that emphasize learning for understanding rather than completing work for external reasons led to a search for other classroom research that might provide additional clues about these types of classrooms. This search sparked a dialogue with researchers involved in intensive studies of classrooms where teachers were creating opportunities for students to construct knowledge actively based on what the students bring to the situation—rather than following the traditional workplace model.

As this dialogue expanded to include additional participants, questions were raised about the meaning of the term "learning," particularly as it was being used to describe "learning-oriented" classrooms. Indeed, I was reminded it would be hard to find a teacher who did not believe that the students in her or his classroom were learning. We needed, therefore, to shift our focus to different types and purposes of learning rather than assume that classrooms vary along dimensions of work or learning orientations. Classrooms vary on many interacting dimensions that need to be considered together to gain a picture of what it is that students are learning and for what purpose.

As the participants in the dialogue widened and as both the criticism of our educational system and attempts at reform became more prevalent, an additional concern surfaced: How could our knowledge about how students learn for purposes of understanding reach those who might be able to support this type of learning? As the movement to restructure schools gained momentum, we observed attempts at changing structural elements of the educational system without considering the learner and newer knowledge of how students learn. What has become apparent is that too often teachers, administrators, policymakers, and educational researchers in different fields lack opportunities to communicate with others in related fields. As a consequence, they miss opportunities to broaden their perspectives and build deeper understandings that have the potential for serving as a more substantial foundation for improving education. Consequently, a major catalyst for this volume has been the need to provide a vehicle for bringing together new research on classroom learning with notions of assessment and policymaking. Our goal is to increase the awareness of educators and educational researchers about the ways students learn for different purposes and about the implications of this knowledge for decision making to improve schools. This volume, therefore, addresses multiple audiences.

Over a period of years, the participants in this dialogue have continued to grow as we encountered research that is related to our concerns in the areas of learning and teaching, curriculum and instruction, assessment, and administration and policy planning. We know that there are other researchers who are working on similar types of problems. This volume represents a deliberate attempt to include a sampling of research from a variety of fields to address common concerns.

The first chapter begins by articulating the need to redefine learning and increase awareness of the relationship between how students learn for understanding and efforts to improve schools. The next seven chapters present examples of classroom research to provide a glimpse of what happens in classrooms as teachers attempt to implement newer views of learning that are based on knowledge of how students actively construct knowledge in meaningful and multiply connected networks. These examples serve not only to provide clues about what learning may look like in classrooms with these learning goals, but also to raise questions about factors that support and/or constrain teachers in providing opportunities for students to extend their understandings and solve complex problems. More specifically, these examples provide a basis for attempting to identify and analyze critical elements that need to be understood to create the conditions for educating students for the rapidly changing world of the 21st century. Following these examples, attention focuses on issues of assessment and the implications that the critical elements identified in the preceding chapters reveal for restructuring education to support student learning. These chapters are more specifically outlined below.

The classroom research presented here is from different theoretical perspectives, different content domains, different levels of school, and different socioeconomic, ethnic, and ability groups. However, although the chapters represent different content domains, the particular subject matter content is not the significant factor for our purposes. It is rather that the search for factors that influence different types of classroom learning, particularly where students can extend and deepen their understandings, has led to research in different content domains. Learning in subject matter domains is beyond the scope of this book.

In contrast with much previous research on classroom learning that has examined differences between types of classrooms, some of the studies described here investigate a single classroom through intensive observations and interviews to gain a sense of what it means to be a student/learner within the context of a particular classroom (Collins & Green, Chapter 3; Peterson, Chapter 6; Wood et al., Chapter 7). Some of the studies compare classes, but also use narrative records and/or interviews to make the differences and sources of differences more visible (Blumenfeld et al., Chapter 8; Chandler, Chapter 2). Some of these studies focus on changes in teachers over the school year or years and on the consequences for students of these changes (Peterson, Chapter 6; Wood et al., Chapter 7). As teachers come to deepen their understanding of learning processes and modify their teaching practices, shifts can be observed in what it means to be a student and how students see and do learning. The methodology of these studies facilitates a greater understanding of these changes.

OVERVIEW OF CHAPTERS

Chapter 1, *Seeing, Redefining, and Supporting Student Learning*, frames and examines the issues on which this book is centered: the definitions and purposes of learning, what counts as evidence of learning, what it means to be a student in different types of classrooms, what the consequences are of being a student in different types of classrooms, what factors support or constrain the provision of opportunities for learning—particularly opportunities for students to actively construct knowledge in meaningful and interrelated networks so that they come to deeper understandings of the world. Familiarity with these issues as well as with the learning theories, practices, metaphors, and methodologies that influence views of learning are central to understanding that the learner and how students learn are essential starting points for educational reform.

One of the central issues in Chapter 2, *Learning for What Purpose: Questions When Viewing Classroom Learning from a Sociocultural Curriculum Perspective*, is the purposes of learning. Through a study of three seventh-grade reading classes taught by the same teacher, Susanne Chandler demonstrates that the curriculum as planned is different from the curriculum as enacted and consequently that the planned learning purposes may not be perceived or accomplished by the students. What is actually enacted may constrain student learning. Moreover, the organizational structure and demands of the school and district may contribute to these constraints. The chapter shows that as curriculum was constructed through the particular face-to-face social interactions in each of the three classes, what was learned and the meaning of being a student in each class was also constructed and consequently did not always match teacher intentions. What was learned varied across classes as well—despite a common planned curriculum.

Chapter 3, *Learning in Classroom Settings: Making or Breaking a Culture*, by Elaine Collins and Judith L. Green, further describes the "situated" nature of learning through a methodology of investigating classrooms as culture. This chapter demonstrates how roles and relationships, norms and expectations, rights and obligations are constructed in the classroom through everyday interactions over time. The meaning of how students see and "do" learning and how to be a student during science and social studies in a fourth–fifth-grade classroom are constructed through ongoing teacher–student interactions. These meanings are made visible when substitute teachers with different orientations breached the previously established rules for participation and learning. The meanings of learning, what counts as learning, and how to be a student changed with the entry of the substitutes. As a consequence, students completed activities (assigned by substitutes with different frameworks) without learning academic content. These changes raise issues of "when is learning?" and "what counts as evidence of learning?" as well as how the nature of the activity and procedures can constrain and/or support learning.

In Chapter 4, *Locating Learning in Times and Spaces of Teaching*, Ginger Weade continues to explore the issues raised in the preceding two chapters concerning the nature and purposes of learning and what counts as evidence of learning. Using a social constructivist/interactional sociolinguistic perspective, she discusses a series of implicit beliefs or myths about the relationship between teaching and learning: that teaching causes learning, that learning is visible, and that learning occurs in a "teachable moment." She develops a model of the multiple moments of teaching, in which teaching/learning processes are seen as interactive, recursive, and embedded rather than as isolated and unidirectional. Weade's study of a thematically focused, integrated math/science program for fourth-and fifth-grade gifted classes shows how teachers' conceptions of learners and learning processes are reflected in and influence their reasoning about, planning for, and implementation of the program. This chapter shows how teacher beliefs, willingness to take risks, and collaboration can support the translation of instructional intentions into and ongoing program where the teaching of skills is integrated into larger interdisciplinary concepts.

Using interactional sociolinguistics, the authors of *Constructing Literacy in Classrooms: Literate Action as Social Accomplishment* (Chapter 5) describe how a common perspective on literacy is constructed by teachers and students as they participate in a high school summer English class. The notion of what counts as learning and, in particular, the meaning of literate action are considered in this chapter as well. The Santa Barbara Classroom Discourse Group shows how an "action research" professional development program, where teachers began by investigating their own questions, led two teachers to establish a student-centered, seminar-type of classroom environment where student justification of reasoning was an important element in arriving at a variety of acceptable answers. This chapter provides a sense of how the transformation of teachers' thinking and practices regarding literacy in the classroom continues over time. The chapter also suggests how external forces can either support or constrain what happens in classrooms.

Chapter 6, *Revising their Thinking: Keisha Coleman and her Third-grade Mathematics Class*, by Penelope L. Peterson, shows how a third-grade teacher's thinking about mathematics teaching changes as she acquires a deeper understanding of how children learn mathematics. As she changes how she teaches, new norms and expectations for what it means to learn math and what counts as evidence of learning are constructed by the participants in this ethnically and socioeconomically diverse classroom. New roles are created for students as they attempt to "prove" their answers to their peers. Support from the principal and opportunities to observe colleagues and reflect on practice facilitate her growing understanding of learning processes and her ability to provide opportunities for students to gain a deeper understanding of mathematics.

Terry Wood, Paul Cobb, and Erna Yackel present another view of conditions that can support changes in a teacher's understandings of mathematics and contribute to changes in students' understanding of what it means to learn math—this time in second grade—in *Change in Learning Mathematics: Change in Teaching Mathematics* (Chapter 7). From a framework where learning is seen as a coordination of psychological and sociological perspectives in which activity, problematic situations, and social interaction are crucial, classrooms are seen as learning settings for teachers as well as for children. The researchers provided problem-centered activities that encouraged students to exchange ideas and the teacher to listen, probe, and learn about mathematical thinking (as opposed to the provision of opportunities for teachers to observe colleagues). The provision of these activities together with support and guidance fostered the teacher's understanding of mathematics teaching and learning. Alleviating the teachers' responsibility for the district's testing program in math also facilitated new learning and consequently new understanding of mathematics within a mathematical community on the part of both teacher and students. This change is vividly portrayed with examples of how the teacher deals with the tensions between children's personal constructions and the mathematics of the wider society.

Chapter 8, *Translating Motivation into Thoughtfulness*, is written from a somewhat different framework. In this chapter, Phyllis Blumenfeld, Pamela Puro, and John Mergendoller portray differences between two fifth-grade science teachers: Teacher A whose students reported high levels of motivation and cognitive engagement, and Teacher B whose students reported high levels of motivation but low levels of cognitive engagement. The contrast between these two teachers demonstrates how the teaching strategies that Teacher A used helped students maintain their motivation as well as learn for understanding; whereas the strategies that Teacher B used motivated students to enjoy science, but failed to engage them in deeper understandings. The meaning of learning and what was considered evidence of learning was quite different in the classrooms of these two teachers.

Chapter 9 moves on to the implications for assessment practices of the views of learning exemplified in the preceding chapters. Like some of the preceding chapters, however, *Assessment in the Context of Schools and School Change* explores further the issues of what is considered evidence of learning and what factors support change. Roberta Camp points out that traditional assessment practices that are based on the belief that learning can be judged at one point in time are inconsistent with views of learning as ongoing and interrelated. Camp describes assessment practices that are not only congruent with the goals of learning, but are also integrated into the school context (in contrast with being externally imposed). This type of assessment can be used as a tool for change toward deeper understandings of learning processes and can serve to encourage the enactment of practices that facilitate greater understanding. Camp explains the collaborative development of a meaningful writing assessment program that serves to improve teaching/learning processes in grades six through twelve. Camp further demonstrates how the accountability needs of all concerned parties are being met through assessment practices that are consistent with the newer views of learning.

Chapter 10 is the first of the two chapters that centers on the relationship between types of student learning and changing organizational structures. In this chapter, *Organizational Design and Teaching for Student Learning*, William A. Firestone picks up on how views of learning and teaching are linked to conceptions of bureaucratic and professional organizations. Similar to visions of work-oriented classrooms, bureaucratic organizations see teachers as workers who carry out decisions made by supervisory authorities toward the goal of turning out a standard product. In contrast, organizations that encourage teachers to see themselves as professionals with special knowledge of students and of learning processes allow them to reflect on their practice and share in the decision making. Such organizations are more likely to be supportive of learning for understanding. Firestone provides case studies to illustrate the link between structural change and teachers' behavior and attitudes. He shows how even with a reform effort that followed a more professional design, other factors may hinder change.

Chapter 11, *Beginning with Classrooms: Implications for Restructuring Schools* by Carolyn M. Evertson and Joseph Murphy, brings together two bodies of literature: that on classroom teaching/learning processes, and that on school organization and administration. These authors present the notion that in order for reform efforts to succeed in changing the definition of learning to one where students actively construct their knowledge in meaningful and interrelated networks, one must "backward map" from the student and how students learn outward to the conditions required to teach for meaningful understanding. The need for coherence within the district is brought out by an example of a reform attempt that failed due in part to conflicting district policies.

The authors draw on examples from the preceding chapters and from related work to point out the need for redefining learning, redefining teaching, and redefining how students carry out their roles within the classroom for real change to occur. They argue for the establishment of a professional work culture to support teaching for meaningful understanding. They also call for a new vision of how classrooms and the roles, relationships, and responsibilities of those involved in education will look under restructured schools.

This brief overview has outlined the sequence and some of the themes in the chapters. However, it cannot do justice to the richness of the material and the vividness with which classrooms and issues are portrayed. Although a sense of what classrooms are like where the goals are learning with understanding is depicted, there is no attempt in these chapters to prescribe what is needed. It is not a "how to" book. Rather we hope to raise questions, such as:

- What can be learned from these theory- and research-based examples of selected classrooms that will facilitate understanding the meaning and purposes of learning?
- What types of learning result from different strategies and different tasks? How do various teaching strategies and learning opportunities influence students' beliefs about the nature of learning, about themselves as learners, as well as their knowledge of the subject matter content? What factors support and/or constrain achieving the various purposes of learning? How can this help us understand what is happening in other classrooms?
- What can be learned from these classrooms about how to look at what is happening in classrooms that will help in analyzing and aligning teaching with particular purposes of learning?
- What types of understandings about how students learn help teachers extend and deepen their students' knowledge of the world, of specific content areas, and of themselves as learners?
- What kinds of teacher development and support help teachers gain greater understanding of factors that enhance and/or constrain the type of learning that focuses on students' extending understandings of the world, of specific content areas, and of themselves?
- What kinds of organizational structures support teachers engaging students successfully in the types of learning processes that extend understandings of world and self?

REFERENCES

Marshall, H. H. (1987a). Building a learning orientation. *Theory into Practice*, 26, 8–14.

Marshall, H. H. (1987b). Motivational strategies of three fifth-grade teachers. *Elementary School Journal*, 88, 137–152.

Marshall, H. H. (1988a). In pursuit of learning-oriented classrooms. *Teaching and Teacher Education*, 4, 85–98.

Marshall, H. H. (1988b). Work or learning: Implications of classroom metaphors. *Educational Researcher*, 17, 9–16.

Marshall, H. H. (1990). Beyond the workplace metaphor: Toward conceptualizing the classroom as a learning setting. *Theory into Practice*, 29, 94–101.

Chapter 1
Seeing, Redefining, and Supporting Student Learning

Hermine H. Marshall

School of Education
San Francisco State University
and
Division of Educational Psychology
Graduate School of Education
University of California, Berkeley

Critiques of American education and prescriptions for educational reform abounded during the 1970s and 1980s. Many of the reform efforts focused on school-wide or system-wide structural elements usually pertaining to standards or incentives, such as higher standards for graduation, merit pay, career ladders, and mentor teachers. Many reform movements, like the educational problems that the reforms attempted to overcome, have been based on traditional behaviorist views of learning and a workplace metaphor for classrooms. Behaviorists assume that knowledge is comprised of hierarchically arranged facts and skills that can be transferred from book or teacher to passive students. Many common teaching and management strategies reflecting behaviorist views of learning are congruent with the metaphor of "the classroom as a workplace."[1] Teachers/managers reward students/workers with praise or grades for producing worksheets/products

---
[1] The factory model of the workplace most closely fits this metaphor.

as evidence that they have acquired the basic facts and skills that teachers have provided (Marshall, 1988b, 1990).

Some reform efforts within this behaviorist framework have centered on rewarding teachers for improved performance. Some have aimed at increasing the amount of content required without altering the mode of teaching. Others, such as those that have attempted to increase higher-order thinking or problem solving, have often been co-opted by the educational system as a product-oriented workplace. The result has been that the same types of tasks and worksheets that lead to lower-level thinking and a "right-answer" orientation are often used for higher-order thinking and problem-solving strategies.

The most recent reform effort has centered on "restructuring" the educational system. Restructuring efforts include modifying governance and control at various levels from the school site to the district and state levels, new roles for teachers, different scheduling and grouping arrangements, and so on. However, these restructuring attempts, like most of the preceding reforms, overlook the central role played by the learner as well as alternative conceptions of how students learn as starting places for improving education. In contrast to the notion of learning as the transmission of discrete elements from a static body of knowledge to passive students, several alternative views of how students learn center on students actively constructing knowledge in meaningful, multiply connected, contextually relevant networks that allow for deeper and interrelated understandings of a rapidly changing world. These alternative views, which will be elaborated below and exemplified in the following chapters, require a different way of looking at learners, learning, and the context for learning from the traditional behaviorist-derived perspective. Although there is a range of beliefs within both behaviorist and alternative conceptions of learning, I will highlight the contrast between these views—sometimes taking a "strong" or extreme view of behaviorism—to increase the visibility of unexamined assumptions about learners and learning and the consequences for learners of these different beliefs. To move beyond "reforming again, again, and again" (Cuban, 1990), these unexamined assumptions and the consequences for learners of these beliefs need to be analyzed together with alternative conceptualizations of how students learn and the conditions that support various types of learning.

The purpose of bringing together the chapters in this volume, therefore, is to stimulate understanding of an alternative view of where reform must begin: Rather than beginning by modifying the structures of the educational system, we contend that we must *begin* with rethinking the *nature of learning* and with newer *knowledge about how students learn*. Only then can the conditions and structures that support or constrain the type of learning that will create productive citizens for the 21st century be considered. The starting place selected for restructuring has important implications for the process and consequences of reform (Elmore & Associates, 1990). To this end, this volume presents (1) new research on classroom learning and (2) new notions of how assessment can support change in the types of opportunities provided for learning as well as (3) responses from the fields of administration and policy regarding the implications of these newer views. In a world where specialization has led educators and researchers to talk mainly to those in their own fields of expertise, the goal in pulling these areas together is to bridge the gap between new knowledge about how students learn and decision making about improving schools.

The purpose of this chapter is to examine the issues and themes on which this book is centered: the need to redefine learning, to rethink the purposes of learning and the consequences for learners of different conceptualizations of learning, and to reconsider elements essential to educational reform. The first section of this chapter briefly examines how theory and research methodology can constrain or enlighten what is observed and what can be concluded about classroom learning, the meaning of learning, and the consequences to individuals. The potential of more qualitative methods for richer understandings is highlighted. Second, two views of learning are contrasted: those derived from behaviorism, and alternative views derived from constructivism. In examining definitions of learning, some of the factors that influence common beliefs and unexamined assumptions about classroom learning are explored. A picture is sketched of what happens in classrooms where this alternative view frames how teachers create the conditions for learning, where multiple opportunities are provided for learners to construct knowledge in an interrelated manner for purposes of expanded understandings of the world. Third, evidence is presented from more experimental research traditions that supports this alternative view of learning. Problems in applying various labels to different types of classrooms are also pointed out. And fourth, a number of factors that appear to support and/or constrain teachers' implementation of opportunities for students to learn in deeper and multiply connected ways are examined.

The ideas that form the basis for this chapter have evolved from discussions with educational researchers from various fields, from the chapters in this volume, as well as from a larger body of research from a variety of traditions and methodologies. The ideas presented here are not intended as a comprehensive review. Although others have done extensive research that parallels what is included in this volume, this chapter draws heavily on examples from the subsequent chapters to integrate the ideas underlying alternative views of learning. The subsequent chapters elaborate in greater depth the elements presented here and refer to additional sources.

OBSERVING AND UNDERSTANDING
CLASSROOM LEARNING

What can be understood about the nature of learning and the conclusions that can be made are determined to a large extent by the lens that is used to view what is happening in classrooms. Classrooms have commonly been examined through behaviorist lenses. Investigators have concentrated on specifically defined, observable behaviors that can be counted, correlated with performance outcomes, and compared across classrooms. Outcomes are averaged across individual students and assumed to represent the "learning" that has occurred in the classroom. Recommendations based on this type of research are made with the goal of increasing or decreasing specific teacher behaviors. Those who evaluate teachers are often supplied with checklists of "effective" behaviors to observe (cf. Evertson & Murphy, Chapter 11, this volume). These observers are able to look for and "see" isolated behaviors believed to have positive or negative effects.

Overlooked by this approach, however, is the totality of the classroom context, where the meaning of behaviors has been constructed over time and is apparent to those who have participated in its construction (cf. Collins & Green, Chapter 3, this volume). Also neglected by this methodology is the possibility that other behaviors may in fact undermine the effects of the advocated behaviors (Marshall & Weinstein, 1984). For example, an observer may see that a teacher is calling on students of different ability levels and waiting the appropriate amount of time as prescribed by the advocates of "effective instruction." But this observer may not understand that from the *students' perspective*, some students are called on only to get their attention, whereas others are called on because the teacher knows they know the right answer and the material can be "covered"—regardless of whether learning occurs (Blumenfeld, Puro, & Mergendoller, Chapter 8, this volume; Marshall & Weinstein, 1984). Likewise counting questioning behavior may not reveal that the questions the teacher asks center on superficial information rather than deeper understanding (Blumenfeld et al., Chapter 8, this volume), or that the teacher may ask the students to think, but test them only on factual information. An observer watching for student on-task behavior may observe silent reading in the seventh-grade classes described by Chandler (Chapter 2, this volume), but may not realize that from the perspective of some students, the purpose was to quiet the students and allow the teacher time for paper work rather than to support a love of reading as the teacher intended. Similarly, observers counting motivational strategies may notice recommended motivational practices, but may not realize that these practices are not well integrated throughout instruction or may actually fail to engage students for purposes of understanding (Blumenfeld et al., Chapter 8, this volume).

In contrast to the surface behaviors that are revealed by more traditional behaviorist research, the qualitative methodologies and constructivist frameworks used by most of the researchers represented in this volume provide a deeper perspective on the complex interactions within actual classrooms. These methods provide a better sense of the quality of the interactions and processes that may or may not support meaningful understanding. Although the perspective of outside observers (even most participant observers) is somewhat occluded when they have not been a part of the construction of the classroom norms and expectations from the beginning, it is possible to gain a greater understanding and come closer to "seeing" the classroom and the meanings of events from the perspective of the participants by soliciting the views of the participants (Blumenfeld et al., Chapter 8; Chandler, Chapter 2; Collins & Green, Chapter 3; Peterson, Chapter 6; Santa Barbara Classroom Discourse Group, Chapter 5, this volume). It is the quality and meaning of these interactions and processes that are generally hidden by frequency counts of observable behaviors.

Thus, to learn about the different meanings of learning and classroom processes that support or constrain different types of learning, especially students' constructing their own knowledge, educators and investigators need to spend time closely observing in classrooms and talking with the participants about their perceptions. At the same time, educators and researchers need to be open to receiving new information and to asking new questions about what is happening and what factors influence learning processes. These methods of seeing what is happening in classrooms can shed new light on the nature of learning and on the basis for change.

SEEING, EXAMINING, AND REDEFINING CLASSROOM LEARNING: MAKING THE ORDINARY EXTRAORDINARY

As Weade (Chapter 4) vividly describes, learning is elusive, difficult to observe and pinpoint. What is taken as evidence of learning may be determined by beliefs and assumptions about the nature of learning. Beliefs and assumptions about the nature of classroom learning have important consequences for opportunities that are provided for learning, for what is learned, for the kind of knowledge that individuals will be able to deal with, for how knowledge is used, and for how students view themselves. The consequences of different beliefs and assumptions about the nature of classroom learning become increasingly salient in a society where knowledge is changing so rapidly that it becomes more important to know how to create, to deal with new knowledge, and to meet new challenges than to be able to transmit a fixed body of knowledge.

Common Definitions of and Assumptions about Learning

When the word *learning* is used, it is assumed that others have a common understanding of the term. On closer examination, however, learning can be seen to have many different meanings depending on the theoretical framework and the context in which its use is embedded. As noted earlier, within a behaviorist framework, learning is generally defined as the passive acquisition of facts, skills, and concepts often through drill and guided practice, rewards, and punishments.

Learning can also refer to the acquisition of strategies to perform a task to the teacher's satisfaction—what Bloome, Puro, and Theodorou (1989) have called "procedural display" (see also Edwards & Mercer, 1987)—but without deeper understanding of the underlying substantive content (Collins & Green, Chapter 3). For example, students can learn to fill in the blanks on a worksheet by clues or patterns in the questions without having to think about or process the intended substantive content. These surface types of knowledge are often retained for particular purposes, such as passing a test.[2] On the other hand, learning can refer to meaningful lessons that have been learned, such as the "aha" experience when things fall into place and new insights dawn.

Alternatively, learning can mean the active construction of knowledge in gradually expanding networks of ideas through interactions with others and materials in the environment. It can refer to building strategies that allow information to be processed on deeper levels, to be connected in multiple meaningful ways with relevant experiences, to solve complex problems, and to extend understandings of the world and self. This alternative type of learning has been referred to as "learning for meaningful understanding" (cf. Anderson, 1989; Brophy, 1989). This definition seems to come closest to the type of learning that is elaborated in this volume; but it requires further development and contextualization.

Additional assumptions about learning that need to be foregrounded to come to a better understanding of conceptions of learning concern what causes learning and where and when learning is believed to occur. Learning is assumed to be caused by teaching (usually teaching-as-telling) (cf. Peterson, Chapter 6; Weade, Chapter 4). This assumption may be related to research showing a correlation between so-called "effective teaching practices" and "time-on-task" (cf. Brophy & Good, 1986). In this research, observed behaviors are assumed to produce learning. Yet what it is that is

---

[2] Although worksheets are commonly limited to factual and superficial information, carefully constructed worksheets or more open-ended written responses (such as journals) may provide evidence of deeper understanding as is shown in the chapters by Camp, by Blumenfeld and her associates, and by Peterson.

learned and how learning occurs are not considered. Furthermore, the erroneous assumption that correlation indicates causality is not questioned.

Moreover, learning is traditionally assumed to occur within an individual's head and at a particular point in time (cf. Weade, Chapter 4). Learning is generally believed to occur when an individual completes "work." This assumption does not consider that the work or performance taken as verification of learning may, in fact, be a result of "procedural display" or of content previously learned (cf. Collins & Green, Chapter 3). In contrast, alternative conceptions of the nature of learning processes suggest that learning is constructed, not only in an individual's head, but in interactions *among individuals* or *between individuals and materials* as these occur *over time* (Bruner, 1986; Vygotsky, 1978; Wertsch, 1985). Actual learning may not be visible (Weade, Chapter 4). These alternative views of learning will be amplified after examining reasons for the persistence of the dominant views of learning.

Roots of Dominant Views of Learning

Awareness of the different meanings of learning facilitates a more careful analysis of just what type of learning may be occurring in classrooms. Variations on behaviorist-derived definitions of learning are most common in the vast majority of classrooms in this country. This type of classroom is the familiar one, the one in which most of us have been socialized. Although alternative views of learning can be traced in part to Dewey (e.g., 1902) and his predecessors (Farnham-Diggory, 1990), and although research on these alternative views has increased in recent years, the question of why it is that behaviorist views of learning seem to have such a hold in today's schools must be raised. Where do these beliefs come from and why are they so prevalent and so difficult to change?

Among the factors that influence conceptions of classroom learning and practices of schooling are (1) theories of learning, (2) "ordinary" practice, and (3) the metaphors used to think about learning (Marshall, 1988b). These factors are interrelated and mutually reinforcing.

Although many learning theories had been proposed by the middle of this century (see, for example, Hilgard, 1956), Thorndike's version of behaviorism has dominated the field of education (Farnham-Diggory, 1990). According to this theory, complex tasks need to be broken down into their components so that they can be taught separately, rewarded or punished appropriately, and scientifically measured as evidence of achievement (Thorndike, 1932). One reason for the predominance of this theory is its compatibility with the classroom-as-workplace metaphor and the "cult of efficiency" that had moved from business and industry into the schools early in this century (Johnson & Brooks, 1979). Efficient management of large numbers of students has contributed to the stability of teaching practices (Cuban, 1984). Second, this conception of learning was no doubt widely disseminated by the long line of educators trained at Teachers College where Thorndike taught. By 1940, nearly one-tenth of the teachers, more than one-half of big-city superintendents, and nearly one-third of the deans of colleges of education in the United States had attended Teachers College (Farnham-Diggory, 1990). It is no wonder then that educators and those educated in our schools tend to see learning as "stamping in" decontextualized correct responses and "stamping out" incorrect ones and to consider responses on achievement tests as evidence of learning. Unexamined is whether what commonly occurs in classrooms is what we want to occur. Also not considered is whether these are the types of learning and learners that will be needed for the 21st century—as contrasted with the uniformity, obedience, and productivity required in earlier bureaucratic and industrial societies (cf. Cuban, 1984).

Over the years, a number of cognitive approaches to learning have been recognized as alternatives to behaviorism. These alternatives vary in the degree to which the learner is seen as active and in the role attributed to social interaction in the learning process. The information-processing approach to learning appears to have received the greatest attention, at least as determined by the amount of space received in textbooks for teachers (e.g., Slavin, 1986; Woolfolk, 1990). This approach reflects a model of the mind as a computer. According to this view, the mind actively operates on information (input) and produces responses (output). Information-processing research has suggested ways to make the acquisition of certain types of information and behavior more efficient. Yet the mechanistic flavor of this model and its emphasis on individual learning remains close to behaviorism. The adequacy of this model has also been questioned (e.g., Bereiter, 1991; Prawat, 1991).

Other cognitive approaches to learning, such as cognitive constructivist views, have received less attention. Although textbook writers describe Piaget's theory, it is generally portrayed as a theory of cognitive *development*, rather than elaborated as a basis for cognitive constructivist approaches to learning. More recently, brief mention has been made of Vygotsky, particularly of his notion of the "zone of proximal development." Yet the larger issues of the construction of knowledge in interaction with others and of social constructivist conceptions of the nature of learning and learners (which stems in large part from Vygotsky) is unacknowledged. Given the brief textbook treatment of cognitive and social constructivist approaches to learning and the tenacity of behaviorist-derived approaches, it is unlikely that alternative conceptions are incorporated into classroom teaching.

Despite the drawbacks of praise and other external rewards (e.g., Brophy, 1981; Lepper & Green, 1978), practices derived from behaviorism remain strong. These practices appear to be accepted as normal, standard, customary, ordinary, often routinized practice. These accepted practices are so ingrained that they have become invisible to most of those within the culture of the school; and therefore the practices, the assumptions on which they are based, and the consequences for students remain largely unexamined. Even where teachers have had different experiences and hold divergent beliefs, they often feel compelled to conduct school in the accepted manner.

Like the influence of behaviorist theories and "ordinary" practices derived from them, the metaphorical nature of our language (Lakoff & Johnson, 1980) also contributes to beliefs about classroom learning. Metaphors frame our thinking, our understanding of problems, events, and concepts, and our proposed solutions to problems. The pervasiveness of the workplace metaphor of classroom learning reinforces the persistence of traditional classroom practice (see also Marshall, 1988b). Nevertheless, by changing ways of thinking about a problem and the metaphors for these problems, more effective solutions are often stimulated (cf. Schön, 1979). Hence, alternatives to metaphors of the classroom as a workplace and learning as the transmission of knowledge are essential to rethinking educational reform.

A Preliminary Sketch of Differences in Classroom Learning

My own thinking about these assumptions and alternative metaphors for perceiving and interpreting what goes on in classrooms began with a series of studies of teachers' motivational orientations. These studies highlight differences in types and purposes of learning as well as the life worlds and understandings of students between traditional work-oriented classrooms and classrooms where the focus is on thinking and deeper-level learning processes. The first two of these studies compared transcripts of classroom observations and teacher interviews from fifth-grade teachers who had participated in a larger study of 12 first-, third-, and fifth-grade teachers (Marshall, 1987a, 1987b). Teacher I emphasized work completion. Her lesson introductions and management statements centered on getting the work done, on completing the product. Students were motivated to complete their work by comments about losing recess or calls home. Errors were corrected as a routine part of the students' work. The workplace metaphor seemed to fit this classroom.

In contrast, Teacher K's emphasis was on thinking and the challenge of learning. She introduced lessons by challenging students to use their minds. More of the tasks were open-ended rather than right-answer and work-oriented, such as a decision-making lesson where there were "no right or wrong answer(s)." Students were told, "Just think. What will happen? What else might you do and what will happen? There're a lot of choices.... You'll be graded for ideas. I'm interested in what you say" (Marshall, 1987a, p. 9). Motivation for learning (rather than ritually performing the task) was based on challenge, links to the real world, and student interest. Less off-task behavior was observed in this class, but when redirection was necessary, students were reminded of the need to think. Errors were not evidence of a poor product, but of a way to "figure out what went wrong" and as a source of new learning. In thinking about this classroom, I used the term "learning place" rather than workplace (see Marshall, 1988b).[3]

Teacher K used different language and articulated different beliefs and assumptions about learning from Teacher I. She believed part of her role was to motivate students so "they want to" learn and to help them learn enough skills so that they can "find the joy" in learning. She maintained that students can take responsibility for evaluating their own learning and gave them opportunities to do so. Clearly, she saw learning as more than the acquisition of facts and skills evidenced by worksheets of the traditional behaviorist view. She attempted to involve students on a broader and deeper level in what they were learning. The types of tasks she provided, her teaching strategies, and the expectations she conveyed to students seemed to support the type of learning where students' ideas and understandings of the world are important and where students build on what they already know. The consequences for being a student in this type of classroom are more likely to be a sense of being able to think, to meet new challenges, to see errors as the means of rethinking understanding—in contrast to being able to fill in the blanks appropriately.

Questions about differences between what was going on in these classrooms led me first to search the transcripts from the other classrooms in the original study for additional classrooms where the emphasis was on thinking and the challenge of learning (see Marshall, 1988a, for the results of this search), and second to seek other classroom research that could extend these beginning clues about alternative views of learning and factors that support and/or constrain the type of learning that focuses on deeper and multiply connected meaningful understandings of the world. The quest for other classroom research that went beyond a workplace metaphor as well as for the implications for educational improvement of these alternative views of learning served as the primary impetus for this volume.[4]

---

[3] The other fifth-grade teachers and other patterns, including a "work-avoidance" pattern, are not described here.

[4] At the same time, other researchers seemed to be stimulated by the classroom as a learning place metaphor. For example, Roth and Rosaen (1991; Literacy in Science and Social Studies Project, 1991) used the postulated essential qualities of learning settings as differentiated from work settings (Marshall, 1988b, 1990) with a group of teachers and researchers to collaboratively construct a chart reflecting the ways in which teaching in the Literacy in Science and Social Studies Project differs from traditional teaching as well as the ways that they work together contrasts with typical in-service education.

Building the Picture: Elaborating on Views of Learning

The major set of beliefs that are exemplified in much of this research and in many of the following chapters are those derived from variations of cognitive and/or social constructivism (Newman, Griffin, & Cole, 1989; Vygotsky, 1978; Wertsch, 1985). Very briefly, constructivists believe that individuals *actively* construct knowledge and understanding (cf. Piaget), rather than passively receive information in response to external forces, such as rewards. According to constructivist views, learning consists of building on what the learner brings to the situation and restructuring initial knowledge in widening and intersecting spirals of increasingly complex understanding. Because learners come with different background knowledge, experience, and interests, they make different connections in building their knowledge over time. Therefore, classrooms within this framework stimulate multiple opportunities for coming to understandings. Diverse processes and ways to build knowledge are encouraged. Within a constructivist framework, learning of skills and concepts is not seen as occurring in an isolated and hierarchical manner, but rather within meaningful and integrated contexts. Learning does not occur all at once, but is built over time as initial knowledge is revised when new questions arise and old knowledge is challenged (Collins & Green, Chapter 3; Peterson, Chapter 6; Weade, Chapter 4; Wood, Cobb, & Yackel, Chapter 7). The teacher does not serve as the main source of knowledge-transmission; both students and teachers assume multiple roles. Students, too, can generate knowledge, challenge the thinking of others, and assume responsibility for their continued learning (Edwards & Mercer, 1987; Collins & Green, Chapter 3; Peterson, Chapter 6; Santa Barbara Classroom Discourse Group, Chapter 5). The chapters by Peterson and by Wood and her associates provide vivid examples of how students come to a clearer understanding of mathematical concepts as they present, challenge, and attempt to justify their ideas with their peers.

Although constructivists believe that learning is an active process, social and cognitive constructivists vary regarding the nature and influence of the social world in the process of knowledge construction. Whereas cognitive constructivist views of learning suggest that the *learner* constructs knowledge—although often with the guidance of an expert—social constructivists place greater emphasis on the role of the *social interaction* through which contexts, knowledge, and meanings in everyday life are constructed and reconstructed. According to a social constructivist framework, learning and thinking are situated in social contexts rather than occurring solely in an individual's mind (e.g., Newman et al., 1989; Wertsch, 1985; Vygotsky, 1978). Through interpersonal communication, new levels of conceptual understanding can be reached (Edwards & Mercer, 1987; Vygotsky, 1978). Although cognitive constructivists recognize the social context as a given background factor, social constructivists see the social context itself as being continually constructed in dynamic and ongoing interactions among the participants. The social context as constructed influences norms and expectations—such as whether teacher or students initiate actions, what types of questions and answers are acceptable, how learning activities are carried out. The social context, including the interactions of the particular teacher and group of students in a class, therefore, influence the opportunities students have for learning as well as what it means to learn and to be a student in a particular class. An example of differences in the constructed meaning of "a good student" can be seen by comparing classes that have the same teacher, goals, and curriculum (Chandler, Chapter 2). In one class, being a good student meant "asking a lot of questions" and "participating in discussions a lot;" whereas to students in the other class, it meant "being on time" and "keeping your daily log up to date."

The constructed meaning of learning can also change when a new teacher alters the social context of a class. For example, the teacher described by Collins and Green emphasized deeper understanding by encouraging students to "think through" questions and answers. The teacher and students in this classroom had constructed procedures for doing school that included expressing their understanding and demonstrating their learning from an assignment informally. With the entry of one substitute, the rules for "doing school" changed to emphasize what he thought were "proper" procedures for assignments, such as writing out complete sentences. This difference in emphasis imposed by the substitute reflected a change in the meaning of how learning was to be displayed. It may also have reflected a move from learning as understanding to learning as following proper procedures.

Thus, what counts as learning in a particular setting—whether it is the process or the product and whether it is understanding the concepts or memorizing the procedure (e.g., Blumenfeld et al., Chapter 8; Collins & Green, Chapter 2)—is constructed through the everyday interactions among teacher and students (Collins & Green, Chapter 2; Santa Barbara Classroom Discourse Group, Chapter 5; Green & Harker, 1982; Green, Kantor, & Rogers, in press). Whether students come to see themselves as "sense makers" and problem solvers or "rememberers and forgetters" (Lampert, 1986) is a function of this social construction. Whether students are willing to believe that they can contribute to their own knowledge and whether they can analyze and solve complex problems develops through a series of interactions in classrooms over years of schooling, and as a consequence, may be difficult to change. The opportunities created for learning and the meaning of learning in this socially constructed context thus have important consequences for students and for the future.

Viewing and creating classrooms with a constructivist perspective requires changing one's frame of reference from the ordinary—although there may be some as yet undetermined overlap. Because constructivist views of learning are less familiar, some of the chapters in this volume elaborate further elements of a social constructivist framework (e.g., Chandler, Chapter 2; Collins and Green, Chapter 3; Santa Barbara Classroom Discourse Group, Chapter 5; Weade, Chapter 4) and present examples of actual classrooms that implement these views of learning to varying degrees.

As teachers expand their knowledge of how children actively and often collaboratively construct their own knowledge, they modify their teaching practices (Peterson, Chapter 6; Wood, Cobb, & Yackel, Chapter 7). With increased knowledge, their goals include acquiring deeper understanding of what children know and understand (Peterson). New expectations regarding the meaning and purpose of assigned tasks and consequently the meaning of learning are constructed in the ongoing interactions among teachers and students (Chandler, Chapter 2; Collins & Green, Chapter 3; Peterson, Chapter 6; Wood et al., Chapter 7; Weade, Chapter 4, this volume). Peterson graphically portrays how Keisha Coleman gradually moved from the notion of teaching as telling toward a belief in encouraging students to explain their thinking to others, to question others' meanings, and to revise their own understandings as new insights arose. As her expectations and requirements moved away from the ordinary toward an emphasis on each student's expressing and discussing how each knew, new roles and responsibilities, norms and expectations of teachers and students evolved. The students gradually began to see that having the correct answer was no longer sufficient evidence of learning. Like the high school English students described by the Santa Barbara Classroom Discourse Group, these third graders had to know how to justify their answers and their thinking publicly. They were in the process of realizing that they, not the teacher, were in charge of revising their own thinking. The meaning of learning in these classrooms evolved toward understanding and expressing their understanding of content in ways not represented by the bits of information reflected on traditional worksheets and achievement tests.

Similarly, Blumenfeld and her associates contrast Teacher B, who often did most of the thinking for the students and whose students were not engaged on a higher cognitive level, with Teacher A, who created a "press" for student thinking and justification. Teacher A's focus was on understanding content and concepts rather than on facts and following procedures. Teacher A routinely checked for students' understanding in a variety of ways, such as waiting and soliciting opinions from many students or allowing them to express their understanding through journal writing or diagrams. In contrast, the students in Teacher B's classroom seemed to have learned that if they waited, the teacher would supply the answer, thereby reducing the cognitive demands on them as well as the opportunities for learning (cf. Doyle, 1983). Although the students in Teacher B's classroom enjoyed the lesson activities, the emphasis was on facts, rather than on understanding the content. In contrast to Teacher A's class where "to learn" meant to be thoughtfully engaged, the message conveyed in Teacher B's class was that "to learn" meant to remember facts (see also Wood et al., Chapter 7).

Important understandings that shine through several chapters are thus new views of what it means to "know" and "learn" in classrooms. Basic to these alternative views of classroom learning and knowing is linking knowledge, especially key ideas, in multiple ways to foster conceptual understanding (cf. Prawat, 1989). When students discuss their ideas, they are more likely to become more aware of the links between these ideas and their own prior knowledge as well as other new ideas. Although learning remains elusive, these chapters suggest that clues about the nature and location of learning may be found by observing how individuals are "making sense" of experiences and how they are using materials and the contributions of others to make sense over a period of time (Weade, Chapter 4). It may be that this "sense making" type of learning is more visible in classrooms where teachers require their students to make their reasoning public (Blumenfeld et al., Chapter 8; Evertson & Murphy, Chapter 11; Peterson, Chapter 6; Santa Barbara Classroom Discourse Group, Chapter 5; Wood et al., Chapter 7, this volume) than in classrooms where teachers accept "right answers" as evidence of learning.

Clearly, there are multiple ways of conceptualizing learning and multiple ways of encouraging different forms of learning for different purposes (cf. Bruner, 1985). Because of the multiple meanings connoted by the term, learning cannot be referred to in a generic sense. Questions must also be raised: Learning for what purpose? And what are the consequences of different forms of learning? What type of learner will become the thoughtful citizen needed in the future? Given these judgments, what conditions need to be provided to nurture these types of learning and learners? Consequences for learners of different views of learning are the focus of the next section. In the final section of the chapter, the last question will be revisited.

CONSEQUENCES FOR STUDENTS OF ALTERNATIVE VIEWS OF LEARNING: SUPPORT FROM OTHER RESEARCH PERSPECTIVES

The chapters in this volume illuminate the different meanings of learning and the consequences for students of alternative views of learning mainly through qualitative methods. Although qualitative methods paint a vivid picture, evidence from more experimental and quantitative methodologies supports aspects of the qualitative findings concerning the effects of different classroom processes without contradicting any of these findings. Research concerning the effects of different learning goals on persistence and self-perceptions is summarized first, with some cautions noted as well. Effects of alternative views of learning on achievement are then presented.

Goals, Strategies, Persistence, and Self-perceptions

Most of the research presented in this section focuses on the consequences to individuals of different learning goals. Different researchers have applied different labels to essentially the same sets of contrasting goals. Like my contrast between a "learning orientation" and a "work orientation," Dweck (1985, 1986) has contrasted "learning goals" with "performance goals." Similar comparisons have been made between a "task orientation" and an "ego orientation" (Nicholls, 1983; Nicholls, Cobb, Wood, Yackel, & Patashnick, 1990) and between a "mastery orientation" and a "performance orientation" (Ames, 1990; Ames & Ames, 1984; Ames & Archer, 1988). The first term in each of these comparisons refers to students seeking to understand and master something new or to gain insight or skill in something that is personally challenging. These students are "intentional learners" (Bereiter, 1990). Their goals reflect the type of learning on which this volume centers. The opposing term refers to attempts at "looking smart," protecting one's ego, and learning only as a means to display superiority or avoid looking stupid.

Research contrasting the effects of these goals has demonstrated that students who have learning goals and a task-mastery pattern tend to choose challenging tasks over easy ones regardless of how they see their ability, because their concern is with understanding and mastering something new rather than being able to perform well. When faced with obstacles, students with learning goals are likely to try harder or vary their strategies. These students "explore, initiate, and pursue tasks that promote intellectual growth" (Dweck, 1986, p. 1043). In contrast, students with performance goals avoid challenge, particularly in contexts that focus on ability, thereby decreasing chances for increased understanding. Students with learning goals are more likely to use deep-processing strategies (Nolen, 1988), including "trying to figure out how new information fits with what one already knows, and monitoring comprehension" (p. 271). Deep-processing strategies are believed to be more likely than surface-level processing strategies to result in understanding. In contrast, performance goals are detrimental to the deeper levels of processing (Graham & Golan, 1991) that are fundamental to constructivist approaches. Additional support for the benefits of the types of learning opportunities described in this volume for students' attitudes toward learning, self-concept, and creativity is provided by a meta-analysis of research on open education (Giaconia & Hedges, 1982).

Many children enter school with learning goals or the desire to master something new, but due to traditional behaviorist-derived classroom practices, such as extrinsic rewards, public comparative evaluation, ability grouping, and the emphasis on visible products, performance goals become dominant (Ames, 1990; Marshall & Weinstein, 1984). Bereiter (1990) points out that children rapidly adapt to schoolwork routines. When "doing school" is seen as completing work, students develop strategies that get the teacher to lower the cognitive demands of the task or to do the difficult parts for them rather than attempting to learn what the task is intended to teach. Students who acquire this mode may not interact as intentional learners. Such students may never come to think for themselves as learners, in contrast with more serious learners for whom learning is a part of their self-concepts.

In brief, these lines of research demonstrate that students enter school with goals that have potential consequences for the type of learner students become. What type of learner they actually become is influenced in large part by the classroom environment (Ames, 1990). These lines of research provide insights into elements within classrooms that seem essential to the type of learning on which this volume is centered. These elements include challenging tasks that require active involvement, use of diverse processes, provision of options, and establishing opportunities for shared responsibility.

Some cautions. Although this body of research demonstrates the consequences of the type of classroom learning espoused here and supports the findings in this volume, this work has a number of limitations. First, it is not able to explain *how* these features are built through dynamic interactions among participants in particular classrooms—as can social construction. That is, research in these traditions looks at the social context of learning as a background factor rather than recognizing the complex interactions among participants that occur in the construction of shared goals and meanings of learning.

Second, the multiple and interrelated factors that contribute to classroom learning may be too complex to be captured either on a single bi-polar dimension or on two dimensions (such as learning/performance). However, as the chapters in this volume illustrate, the complex interrelationships among elements can be made evident through detailed studies. Without this detailed study, knowledge will remain at the level of generalities and superficial labels.

Third, the use of labels to describe these dichotomies may be misleading. This becomes apparent when considering the labels "learning orientation" and "learning goals." Without the contrast to "work orientation" and "performance goals," these labels may not be sufficiently meaningful. It would be rare to find a teacher who did not believe his or her goals were learning (cf. Peterson, Chapter 6). What labels mask are the issues of types and purposes of learning.

Similarly, the term "mastery" implies that something has been "mastered" once and for all in a static sense, as opposed to a more dynamic conception of knowledge where ideas are revisited and modified as new knowledge expands or deepens prior knowledge. In addition, mastery may be perceived by some as retaining a behaviorist flavor, where what is to be mastered has been broken into small segments of skills or facts, in contrast to an emphasis on interrelationships and key ideas. This term may also be confused with "mastery learning programs" that generally call for high average success rates and consequently minimal failure. In contrast, an important feature of the environment is the constructive or adaptive use of errors and failure (Marshall, 1988b; Rohrkemper, 1989). In the classrooms described here, mistakes provide an opportunity for the construction of new learning, not something that must be extinguished. Consequently, "mastery" and other labels may carry unintended meaning.

Furthermore, teachers with an incomplete or superficial understanding of the underlying meaning of a label may implement only a few elements of the type of classroom that the label describes. On the surface, the classroom may appear to fit the label; but without complete understanding, the type of learning intended may not materialize—as was the case for many "open classrooms" (Marshall, 1981). Because of the problems with labels and their potential misinterpretations and inadequate implementations, we have chosen to avoid their use as much as possible. Instead, our goal is to let the classroom examples speak for themselves in depicting configurations of classrooms and learning.

Assessment and Achievement

New views of assessment contend that assessment should be compatible with theories of learning and related to the educational context—in this case, meaningful tasks that are closely related to needed real-world knowledge and skills rather than standardized achievement tests (Camp, Chapter 9). Camp also describes how alternative forms of assessment can be used to provide accountability information as well as to support educational improvement.

At this point in time, however, some individuals are only convinced of program effectiveness by achievement test data. Research related to some of the work reported in these chapters provides evidence that students who are provided opportunities and guidance for constructing their own knowledge, in fact, perform better on standardized achievement tests. Wood and her co-authors report that students in their project exceeded the control group on tests of mathematical concepts and applications and were not at a disadvantage on tests of computations. Similarly, Peterson and her associates found that students in the classes of first-grade teachers who were given access to findings about how children learn mathematics showed greater gains on math achievement test word problems and did as well or better on computation problems than a control group (Carpenter, Fennema, Peterson, Chiang, & Loef, 1989). The type of cognitive engagement and motivation seen in Teacher A's classroom (Blumenfeld et al., Chapter 8), too, has been linked to achievement. For example, seventh graders who were more motivated to learn the material in science and English classes rather than to get a good grade and who believed that their work was interesting and important were more cognitively engaged; and this cognitive engagement was related to actual performance (Pintrich & DeGroot, 1990). Cognitive engagement has also been shown to be related to math and reading achievement in elementary school (Skinner, Wellborn, & Connell, 1990). (Constraints imposed by traditional achievement testing on multiple opportunities for learning are considered in the next section.)

FACTORS THAT SUPPORT AND CONSTRAIN LEARNING FOR MEANINGFUL UNDERSTANDING

To change what goes on in classrooms so that students will develop deeper understandings of the world and will be able to solve new problems as the 21st century approaches, factors that have the effect of constraining or supporting teachers' ability to implement this type of learning need to be examined. The factors that are highlighted here are not meant to be exhaustive, but only indicative of some of the conditions that need to be considered in attempting reforms. Readers will, no doubt, be aware of or be stimulated to think about additional factors from their own experiences. First, some factors that constrain teachers—sometimes inadvertently—from providing students with opportunities for learning with deeper understanding are presented. Then some factors that support teachers in these attempts are discussed.

Factors that Constrain Teachers' Implementing Opportunities for Multiply Connected Meaningful Understandings of the World

Teachers' beliefs about the nature of knowledge and the nature of teaching/learning processes—either their own beliefs or beliefs imposed by school administrators or the community—influence the types of opportunities they provide for learning (cf. Cuban, 1984; Newman et al., 1989). A number of interrelated factors that constrain teachers from creating conditions that allow for meaningful understandings of the world seem to derive from behaviorist conceptions of the nature of knowledge and teaching. These include (a) an emphasis on factual and procedural knowledge; (b) pressures of content coverage, time, and assessment; and (c) beliefs about the effectiveness of controlling strategies.

Emphasis on factual and procedural knowledge. An emphasis on isolated facts and procedures derived from common behaviorist views of learning seems to constrain conceptual understanding (Cobb, 1988; Collins & Green, Chapter 3; Evertson & Murphy, Chapter 11; Prawat, 1989; Wood et al., Chapter 7). This is particularly evident in traditional, teacher-directed notions of "effective teaching." These approaches are based on the assumption that specific teacher-directed strategies that emphasize facts and procedures and have been correlated with time-on-task cause learning. Firestone, for example, describes a bureaucratic reform movement where in-service training centered on an "effective teaching" model. The main effect of this training was to focus teachers' attention on the major criterion of teacher evaluation: time-on-task—rather than learning in meaningful networks for purposes of understanding. The side effect of the training and of the district's accountability system was to increase the stress on the teachers. A similar effect is described by Evertson and Murphy. Like the opportunities that teachers provide for students, the types of learning experiences administrators provide for teachers also influence the meanings constructed and what is taken as evidence of learning.

Pressures of content coverage, time, and assessment. Pressures that teachers feel to "cover" the required curriculum stem from curriculum guides, textbooks, standardized achievement tests, administration, and parents. Lessons derived from textbooks and curriculum guides generally include many different topics, as can be discovered by observation or by listening to teachers like Keisha Coleman (Peterson, Chapter 6) or the teacher described by Collins and Green. Deeper understanding requires time and freedom to delve into and discuss a single topic. Talks with teachers often reveal that they must cut out an elaboration or discussion which would deepen understanding because they are "behind" other classes or not as far as they should be at this time of year. Restructuring efforts that increase the amount of content required are likely to exacerbate this problem.

Prawat (1989) cites a graphic example of the pressures of time and content coverage. He describes a fifth-grade teacher who responds to a student's lack of understanding that multiplication (by 0.5) can result in a smaller number. The teacher first repeats the problem on the board, including how to figure out where to place the decimal point—believing that she had made a computational mistake. When students still do not understand, she repeats the algorithm and explains "I'm just teaching the computational way. What I'm looking for now is for everyone to understand where to place the decimals" (p. 317). When she was asked later about her decision to move on despite the confusion of some students, she responded in terms of how much material she had to cover and how far behind her class was in the book. Content coverage rather than understanding was her guide.

Other research, too, demonstrates how time pressures constrain opportunities for learning with understanding (e.g., Knapp & Peterson, 1991; Neale, Smith, & Johnson, 1990). The customary 40–50-minute period and mandates about the number of minutes per day that must be spent on particular content domains limit the opportunities that teachers can provide for exploration, problem solving, and in-depth study of meaningful and interrelated topics. These types of learning require larger blocks of time.

In a similar way, items on standardized achievement tests have long been blamed for the limited and superficial nature of teaching. Smith (1991) documents the "narrowing of possible curriculum and a reduction of teachers' ability to adapt, create, or diverge" (p. 10) in the face of testing programs. Some teachers rejected the district's writing process curriculum because it did not correspond with the tests. Others reduced or eliminated hands-on science and math and critical thinking in the face of the demands of time for test preparation. One teacher in another study expressed her concern and conflict over the limiting effect of the district's assessment policy:

> No big ahas! Only trivial pursuit knowledge!... Assessment supports this.... The district wants me to give these assessments, and that's how I design what I do.... Or I can start to say 'Okay.' I can smile and play that role or do what I know is right and be a risk taker. (Peterman, 1991, p. 11)

Evertson and Murphy report that the frequent objective assessments required by the Basic Skills First curriculum constrained teachers' willingness to diverge from the state curriculum and find new ways of teaching in smaller classes. Wood and her co-authors, too, point out that in contrast to their math program, the emphasis in the reading program on the assessment of facts and skills through standardized achievement tests rather than on understanding may have prevented the teacher from using the same types of teaching strategies that enhanced conceptual understanding when she taught reading. These researchers speculate that their goals of helping teachers change their method of teaching toward students gaining deeper understanding of mathematics in a mathematics community were supported by relieving the pressure for test results.

In contrast to the emphasis on content coverage and outcomes measured by standardized achievement tests, some teachers described in this volume have found alternative ways for students to demonstrate their understanding. Peterson reports on the records teachers keep of students' thinking. Teacher A required students to record "What I learned in science" each day (Blumenfeld et al., Chapter 8). This type of formative assessment has the advantage of providing the teacher with information about student misconceptions and partial conceptions that facilitate planning opportunities for building more complete understandings. Camp's chapter enlightens us as to how an assessment program can support students' deeper understandings rather than constrain them.

Educators' and lay beliefs about the effectiveness of controlling strategies. The belief in the effectiveness of controlling strategies, such as rewards and lack of choice, as well as scripted lessons and the prescribed strategies of direct instruction, are pervasive in our culture—among educators as well as among the lay public. The negative effects of controlling strategies have been shown in a number of studies. In classrooms where teachers were pressured to have their students perform well and where they used controlling strategies and did not allow their students choice, students performed more poorly than those in classrooms of nonpressured, noncontrolling teachers (Flink, Boggiano, & Barrett, 1990). Surprisingly, observers who were unaware of the students' poorer performance rated these controlling teachers as more competent than the nonpressured and noncontrolling teachers. Parents, too, believe that more controlling strategies are more effective than less controlling ones for promoting learning (Barrett & Boggiano, 1988). It appears that when teachers are observed to push their students, they are, unfortunately, perceived by many as effective teachers.

Texts and curriculum guides that provide scripts or model dialogues, as well as mandated tests, likewise serve as a means of control and at the same time limit expectations for acceptable answers and inhibit students' construction of their own understanding. The chapters by Peterson (Chapter 6) and by Wood, Cobb, and Yackel (Chapter 7) present examples of how closely following the teacher's manual and scripted lessons constrains teachers' ability to understand and build on students' own understanding. In addition, Wood and her associates describe how the directions from the teacher's manual can contradict a developmental view of literacy—where students are encouraged to express their thinking—and thus inhibit change.

On the other hand, teachers who are overly concerned about the negative effects of controlling strategies may not provide sufficient guidance for sustained learning and understanding to occur. It may be that, like Teacher B (Blumenfeld et al., Chapter 8), some teachers' beliefs in the effectiveness of motivational strategies that are fun and noncontrolling override concerns for students' cognitive engagement and in-depth understanding.

Unfortunately, a control ideology seems to be relatively pervasive among administrators (Blase, 1990) as well as the general public. Although many principals may be unaware of the negative effects of their controlling behaviors on teachers, teachers report these practices actually discourage concern for improvement, change, effort, and involvement. The consequences of controlling strategies—whether they come from teachers, administrators, or the community—are limited opportunities for the type of learning that requires diverse processes and results in deeper and more meaningful understandings.

Cumulative effects. The factors that constrain teachers obviously place constraints on students' ways of learning and ability to solve complex problems. Consideration needs to be given as well to the cumulative effects on students over the years of schooling of having been in classrooms where the purpose of learning has been to acquire discrete facts and skills from a static body of knowledge, where the repertoire of strategies for solving complex problems is algorithmic and limited, and where completed worksheets and multiple-choice tests items are taken as evidence of learning. How will these students be able to respond in situations where independent judgment and higher-level thinking are necessary—in situations, that is, where the right answers are not in the back of the book? This scenario highlights the need to seek conditions that support alternative views of classroom learning.

Factors that Support Teachers' Implementing Opportunities for Multiply Connected Meaningful Understandings of the World

Factors that support learning for understanding are addressed in this section and are illustrated mainly through examples from the chapters that follow. Other research undoubtedly will point to additional factors that facilitate this type of learning. In considering these supportive factors, it is important to begin with those factors that are closest to the learner and then move outward to consider the next layer of supporting factors. Initial conditions that promote students constructing meaningful understandings of the world are those that help people who are involved with educating children—teachers, administrators, parents—understand these types of learning processes. After considering these conditions, factors within classrooms that facilitate change will be examined. Finally, some factors that pertain to the organizational system will be summarized.

Teachers' Knowledge of How Students Construct Meaningful Understanding

A number of ways to help teachers understand how students learn for meaningful understanding have been successful. One example is found in a study by Peterson, Fennema, and Carpenter (1988/1989) in which first-grade teachers were given access to *how children learn* mathematics (as opposed to how to teach mathematics). As a consequence of this experience, the teachers spent more time listening to the process of children's solving problems, built on students' prior knowledge, and encouraged students to use multiple strategies.

The chapter by the Santa Barbara Classroom Discourse Group (Chapter 5) provides an example of the results of another professional development program, where the teachers involved in an "action research" project raised their own questions. Investigating how questioning strategies played out in their own classrooms led them to pursue a more student-centered approach to literacy learning.

Other ways of helping teachers understand how students construct their own knowledge include providing opportunities for teachers to observe peers who teach from this basis, along with support for making a change. Opportunities for observing her colleagues and reflecting on their practice helped Keisha Coleman change her strategies and the opportunities she provided for learning as she came to have a better understanding of how children learn (Peterson, Chapter 6).

A different approach to helping teachers discover how children learn is to provide them with problem-centered activities that furnish students with opportunities to learn with understanding and to express their thinking. This appears to be the case, in part, in the project described by Wood and her associates.

These and other ways of beginning are only a part of the story. Other supporting factors are necessary for change to occur. Some of these factors are described below.

Factors Within Classrooms That Support Student Understanding

An alternative to beginning by helping teachers learn how students construct meaningful knowledge is to identify interrelated factors that support learning for understanding and help teachers consider how these practices might be applied in their own classrooms. However, there may be a number of problems with this alternative. First, attempting to apply these practices may be ineffective without a change in teachers' beliefs and understandings about the nature of learning and without support within and beyond the school. Cuban (1984) documents changes that occurred because teachers developed different beliefs about classrooms and learning and often received support in translating their beliefs into practice. With a change in administrators, support often erodes (Santa Barbara Classroom Discourse Group, Chapter 5).

Second, if educators attempt to implement a few of the identified practices without a real understanding of the theoretical rationale, the selected practices may be undermined by other practices that may operate in an opposite direction (cf. Marshall, 1981; Marshall & Weinstein, 1984). For example, probing students' understanding may help students to come to understand; but if the same teacher publicly compares different students' knowledge, pursuit of knowledge may be inhibited. The challenge is for teachers to think through and come to their own understanding of whether and how these practices can be used within the context of particular classrooms to enable particular types of learning.

Blumenfeld and her associates identify four types of teacher practices found in classrooms where students are thoughtfully engaged in learning for understanding—although teachers' underlying beliefs and understandings, as noted above, may be a prerequisite for adequately implementing these practices. Because these factors are so interdependent, they are discussed in an interrelated manner below. They are listed separately here only for purposes of identification. These practices, elaborated in greater detail in their chapter, include (a) constructing opportunities for learning where key ideas and the relationships among them are highlighted and where guidance is provided toward higher-level understandings; (b) creating the press (and expectations) for understanding through reframing questions and probing for understanding as well as soliciting justification for reasoning from all students rather than from just a target group; (c) supporting/scaffolding students' attempts at understanding through such techniques as modeling, providing examples, and allowing time for student planning; and (d) using evaluation systems that emphasize understanding rather than isolated right answers and peer comparison. Other supportive factors that emerge in other chapters include (e) establishing norms and expectations for psychological safety in expressing thinking and understanding and in questioning other students' explanations—as well as norms and expectations for students to share responsibility for knowledge-generation so that the teacher is not the sole source of knowledge (Blumenfeld et al., Chapter 8; Collins & Green, Chapter 3; Peterson, Chapter 6; Santa Barbara Classroom Discourse Group, Chapter 5; Wood et al., Chapter 7); (f) providing the time needed for deeper understanding—rather than pressure toward an expected outcome or to move on to new content (Peterson, Chapter 6); and (g) integrating curriculum in meaningful relationships and for the purpose of solving social problems (Weade, Chapter 4).

Opportunities for learning that focus on understanding key ideas and their interrelationships. As teachers move beyond traditional ways of teaching and following a script or text filled with material to "cover," they come to realize that meaningful understanding requires time to focus attention on a few main problems or ideas and the interrelationships among ideas. Perhaps because of the myth of children's short attention span, Keisha

Coleman is initially amazed as she realizes that students in her colleague's class were involved for the entire period on four problems (Peterson, Chapter 6). Main ideas rather than a great number of facts were emphasized by Teacher A as well (Blumenfeld et al., Chapter 8). She spent time making explicit connections among new ideas and between new ideas and previously learned concepts. Teacher A specifically allowed for student planning time, emphasizing a clear understanding of what the students were doing rather than just getting the task done. The collaborating teachers described by the Santa Barbara Classroom Discourse Group, too, linked students' life experiences with the development of ways of being literate in this classroom.

Weade's example suggests how the curriculum can be integrated for meaningful understandings. Her teachers demonstrate how even district-mandated math skills and concepts can be integrated with and serve to solve real problems and support science concepts and how both of these can, in turn, serve as a basis for considering larger social problems (e.g., should we colonize outer space?).

Teachers' expectations and press for understanding. Peterson shows how, as Keisha Coleman's expectations changed from (a) the traditional dyadic student–teacher interchange focused on answers consistent with the script to (b) discussions where students were required to explain the reasons for their answers directly to their peers, students' thinking and understandings (as well as misunderstandings and partial understandings) became the focus. As Ms. Coleman's demands for making sense became apparent, a new definition of and expectations for learning began to surface. The teachers described by Wood, Cobb, and Yackel and one of those described by Blumenfeld, Puro, and Mergendoller seem to have already made this transition to expecting greater understanding. The questions posed and feedback provided by Teacher A created opportunities for student thinking, not simply repetition of facts. She modified text-based worksheets with questions geared for deeper understanding. The students in this class kept journals in which they recorded their *learning* in science as well.

Sharing responsibility for knowledge-generation and for assessment of learning. Several chapters demonstrate a variety of ways that teachers encourage students to assume responsibility for their own learning and thereby create broader opportunities for learning. For example, Collins and Green describe a classroom where both students and teacher play the role of "facilitator and generator" of knowledge. Opportunities created for students to question each other's understanding, too, help hand over responsibility for understanding to the students (Peterson, Chapter 6; Santa Barbara Classroom Discourse Group, Chapter 5; Wood et al., Chapter 7). Interestingly, the type of assessment described by Camp provides an additional tool for helping students assume responsibility for their learning. Students become involved in the selection of materials they wish to have included in their "portfolio" and reflect on why it is of value.

Organizational Factors That Support Teachers' Implementing Opportunities for Multiply Connected Understandings of the World

With some understanding of factors within the classroom that promote learning for understanding, some of the organizational factors that support teachers in their attempts to create opportunities for students to develop deeper and multiply connected understandings of the world can now be considered. McLaughlin (1990) cautions that removing constraints alone does not mean that practices that support meaningful understanding will follow. Others have described challenges in enacting educational reform (e.g., Cuban, 1984, 1990; Edwards & Mercer, 1987; Goodlad, 1984; Sarason, 1990) and indeed the immense problems should not be minimized. Here, we focus mainly on organizational factors that support teachers' abilities to implement opportunities for interrelated understandings of the world that are described in the following chapters: (a) providing time and security for both students and teachers to learn, (b) professionalism in organizational design and coherence in professional development, and (c) a supportive school atmosphere and opportunities for questioning, feedback and collaboration. In considering these factors, it is important to be aware of the interrelatedness of elements that support and constrain both learning and change. All aspects and levels of the educational system need to work together to support change. Altering only one or two elements will not only be ineffective, but will also tend to cause some kind of counterreaction which may impede change (cf. Elmore, 1991). Teachers, like students, are a part of the larger social system. Teachers, like students (and other adult learners), need similar types of support to construct new knowledge and thus for change to occur.

Providing the time and security for both students and teachers to learn. The perceptive question raised by Weade's teachers of "Do we trust our students and ourselves to learn together about subjects and concepts where our prior knowledge is limited?" highlights the risks that teachers must take in venturing into new ways of providing opportunities for learning. Like their students, teachers need a safe environment to question, pose problems, and learn. They, too, must feel comfortable enough and be willing to reflect on practice, to consider and construct new knowledge, to meet the challenge of attempting something not previously experienced, and to actually take the risk (cf. Camp, Chapter 9). The security required for risk taking is reflected in the earlier quote from the teacher describing the district's assessment driving what she teaches. Organizational structures that allow teachers to be professional decision makers support the risk taking required to tune in to how students learn for understanding and to create the opportunities for this type of learning (Evertson & Murphy, Chapter 11; Firestone, Chapter 10). Many teachers already have some understanding of these views of student learning but need institutional support for them to create new learning opportunities for students.

Professionalism in organizational design and coherence in professional development. Firestone as well as Evertson and Murphy postulate that school organizational designs that are based on professionalism rather than on bureaucracy are compatible with conceptions of the student's role as a learner and have the potential for supporting learning as the process of extending understandings of the world in deeper and increasingly complex networks. Firestone points out that in professional as opposed to bureaucratic organizational designs, teachers (as well as students) are reflective problem solvers rather than controlling (and controlled) managers. Teachers in such communities would be more likely than teachers in districts with more top-down structures to be able to implement teaching strategies that allow students to construct their own knowledge and assume greater control of their own learning (cf., e.g., Blase, 1990).

Evertson and Murphy argue as well for the need for coherence across elements in any professional development model. They show how the potential effects of reducing class size were curtailed by district policies that espoused a limited model of learning that inhibited change and risk taking (where the emphasis was on teaching isolated skills and frequent multiple-choice tests). Reports of other contradictory mandates are not uncommon. For example, in one school where teachers and researchers were working to develop strategies that minimize competition and extrinsic rewards for products, the principal announced that the school would participate in the Pizza Hut program where students earn pizzas according to the number of books they read (Maehr, 1991). This pizza program had the counterproductive effect of increasing competition as well as encouraging students to read short, easy books rather than those where they would be challenged and exposed to new ideas.

Coherence must also endure. Transformation is likely to take years—as the superintendent cited by the Santa Barbara Classroom Discourse Group predicted. But his departure two years after he initiated an innovative professional development program undercut this transformation for most teachers.

Supportive school atmosphere and opportunities for observation, questioning, feedback, reflection, and collaboration. In the same way that opportunities to question, discuss, and challenge ideas and practices contribute to students' construction of knowledge, a supportive school atmosphere and opportunities for exploring, questioning, feedback, reflection, and collaboration can enhance the development of new knowledge for teachers. However, it may be that for these opportunities to have an enduring effect, teachers must first want to make the change.

Keisha Coleman attributes the evolution in her teaching in part to the supportiveness of her school atmosphere, principal, and colleagues as well as to opportunities to observe colleagues and reflect on practice, both theirs and her own (Peterson, Chapter 6; see also Evertson & Murphy, Chapter 11). Other research points to the value of experts' concrete feedback based on observations of teachers making changes in their teaching (Neale et al., 1990; Wood et al., Chapter 7). It is interesting that interviews by classroom researchers, especially if they are periodic and focused on teachers' actual practice may also serve as catalysts for teachers to reflect on their practice (Peterson; Weade; Wood et al.).

Collaboration on development of curriculum ideas enhances ownership and consequently implementation of these ideas. DeCharms (1976) attributes the failure of an attempt to disseminate a curriculum to enhance the motivation and learning of inner-city students developed by one group of teachers to the fact that the second group of teachers did not participate in the development and therefore did not have a sense of ownership of this otherwise successful program. Cuban (1984) also points to the importance of active collaboration. Camp, too, describes how teacher participation in the process of developing an assessment system consistent with the goals of instruction can help teachers reflect on their practice and inform them about how to support student learning. Likewise, opportunities for collaboration between teachers from different subject matter areas can result in opportunities for students to learn in more meaningful and connected ways (Weade, Chapter 4).

NEW DEFINITIONS OF CLASSROOM LEARNING

It is clear, as Evertson and Murphy conclude, that where restructuring begins with redefining classroom learning to account for how students construct knowledge, "student learning will 'look' different in restructured schools" from the way it looks in most classrooms today. The same is true for assessment of learning. For readers familiar only with traditional classrooms or with poorly implemented "open" or "alternative" approaches (cf. Marshall, 1981), this volume provides a glimpse of what learning will look like in classrooms where the learning goals center on deeper and extended understandings. It provides new images of how changes are brought about over time and how with increased understanding, students can be helped to establish new norms of what it means to learn. These pictures are not meant to be prescriptive. Rather, they are intended to help practitioners examine and reflect on their own practice. Moreover, further research is necessary to extend the picture. Perhaps a critical guiding question centers on the *kind of student/learner* we want rather than the kind of answer. The kind of student will depend not on ability or on what the teacher alone does, but on the types of opportunities provided for learning and what is constructed as evidence of learning (Santa Barbara Classroom Discourse Group, Chapter 5).

As teachers examine and reflect on their practice, they will need support in taking the necessary small steps toward change. The chapters also suggest needed elements of support for this type of learning. Because the conceptions of learning and classrooms are so different from what most educators and lay people have experienced, not only will teachers need to be educated to create the conditions for this type of learning, but administrators, parents, politicians and the lay public will also need to be informed regarding the meaning and implications of these new visions of classrooms and learning.

REFERENCES

Ames, C. (1990). Motivation: What teachers need to know. *Teachers College Record, 91*, 409–421.

Ames, C., & Ames, R. (1984). Systems of student and teacher motivation: Toward a qualitative definition. *Journal of Educational Psychology, 76*, 535–556.

Ames, C., & Archer, J. (1988). Achievement goals in the classroom: Students' learning strategies and motivation processes. *Journal of Educational Psychology, 80*, 260–267.

Anderson, L. M. (1989). Implementing instructional programs to promote meaningful, self-regulated learning. In J. Brophy (Ed.), *Advances in research on teaching* (Vol. 1, pp. 311–344). Greenwich, CT: JAI Press.

Barrett, M., & Boggiano, A. K. (1988). Fostering extrinsic orientations: Use of reward strategies to motivate children. *Journal of Social and Clinical Psychology, 6*, 293–309.

Bereiter, C. (1990). Aspects of an educational learning theory. *Review of Educational Research, 60*, 603–624.

Bereiter, C. (1991). Implications of connectionism for thinking about rules. *Educational Researcher, 20*, 10–16.

Blase, J. (1990). Some negative effects of principals' control-oriented and protective behavior. *American Educational Research Journal, 27*, 727–754.

Bloome, D., Puro, P., & Theodorou, E. (1989). Procedural display and classrooms. *Curriculum Inquiry, 19*, 265–291.

Brophy, J. (1981). Teacher praise: A functional analysis. *Review of Educational Research, 51*, 5–21.

Brophy, J. (Ed.). (1989). *Advances in research on teaching* (Vol. 1). Greenwich, CT: JAI Press.

Brophy, J., & Good, T. (1986). Teacher behavior and student achievement. In M. Wittrock (Ed.), *Handbook of research on teaching* (3rd ed., pp. 328–375). New York: Macmillan.

Bruner, J. (1985). Models of the learner. *Educational Researcher, 14*, 5–8.

Bruner, J. (1986). *Actual minds, possible worlds.* Cambridge, MA: Harvard University Press.

Carpenter, T. P., Fennema, E., Peterson, P. L., Chiang, C., & Loef, M. (1989). Using children's mathematics thinking in classroom teaching: An experimental study. *American Educational Research Journal, 26*, 499–531.

Cobb, P. (1988). The tension between theories of learning and instruction in mathematics education. *Educational Psychologist, 23*, 87–104.

Cuban, L. (1984). *How teachers taught: Constancy and change in American classrooms 1890–1980.* New York: Longman.

Cuban, L. (1990). Reforming again, again, and again. *Educational Researcher, 19*, 3–13.

DeCharms, R. (1976). *Enhancing motivation: Change in the classroom.* New York: Irvington.

Dewey, J. (1902). *The child and the curriculum.* Chicago: University of Chicago Press.

Doyle, W. (1983). Academic work. *Review of Educational Research, 53*, 159–200.

Dweck, C. (1985). Intrinsic motivation, perceived control, and self-evaluation maintenance: An achievement goal analysis. In C. Ames & R. Ames (Eds.), *Research on motivation in education, Volume 2: The classroom milieu* (pp. 289–305). New York: Academic Press.

Dweck, C. S. (1986). Motivational processes affecting learning. *American Psychologist, 41*, 1040–1048.

Edwards, D., & Mercer, N. (1987). *Common knowledge: The development of understanding in the classroom.* New York: Methuen.

Elmore, R. (1991, April). *Teaching learning, and school organization: School restructuring and the recurring dilemmas of policy and practice.* Paper presented at the annual meeting of the American Educational Association, Chicago.

Elmore, R., & Associates. (1990). *Restructuring schools: The next generation of education reform.* San Francisco: Jossey-Bass.

Farnham-Diggory, S. (1990). *Schooling.* Cambridge, MA: Harvard University Press.

Flink, C., Boggiano, A., & Barrett, M. (1990). Controlling teaching strategies: Undermining children's self-determination and performance. *Journal of Personality and Social Psychology, 59*, 916–924.

Giaconia, R., & Hedges, L. (1982). Identifying features of effective open education. *Review of Educational Research,* pp. 579–602.

Graham, S., & Golan, S. (1991). Motivational influences on cognition: Task involvement, ego involvement, and depth of information processing. *Journal of Educational Psychology, 83*, 187–194.

Green, J., & Harker, J. (1982). Gaining access to learning: Conversational, social, and cognitive demands of group participation. In L. C. Wilkinson (Ed.), *Communicating in the classroom.* New York: Academic Press.

Green, J., Kantor, R., & Rogers, T. (in press). Exploring the complexity of language and learning in the classroom. In B. Jones & L. Idol (Eds.), *Educational values and cognitive instruction: Implications for reform* (Vol. 2). Hillsdale, NJ: Erlbaum.

Goodlad, J. (1984). *A place called school.* New York: McGraw-Hill.
Hilgard, E. (1956). *Theories of learning* (2nd ed.). New York: Appleton-Century-Crofts, Inc.
Johnson, M., & Brooks, H. (1979). Conceptualizing classroom management. In D. Duke (Ed.), *Classroom management* (78th Yearbook of the National Society for the Study of Education. Part II, pp. 1–43). Chicago: University of Chicago Press.
Knapp, N., & Peterson, P. (1991, April). *What does CGI mean to you? Teachers' ideas of a research-based intervention four years later.* Paper presented at the American Educational Research Association Meeting, Chicago.
Lakoff, G., & Johnson, M. (1980). *Metaphors we live by.* Chicago: University of Chicago Press.
Lampert, M. (1986). Knowing, doing, and teaching mathematics. *Cognition and Instruction, 3,* 305–342.
Lepper, M., & Greene, D. (1978). *The hidden costs of rewards: New perspectives on the psychology of human motivation.* Hillsdale, NJ: Erlbaum.
Literacy in Science and Social Studies Project. (1991, March). *Qualities of learning vs. work-oriented classrooms: Reflections on our collaboration in LISSS Project and on our teaching at Elliott Elementary.* East Lansing and Holt, MI: MSU-Elliott Professional Development School.
Maehr, M. (1991, April). *Changing the schools: A word to school leaders about enhancing student investment in learning.* Paper presented at the American Educational Research Association Meeting, Chicago.
Marshall, H. H. (1981). Open classrooms: Has the term outlived its usefulness? *Review of Educational Research, 51,* 181–192.
Marshall, H. H. (1987a). Building a learning orientation. *Theory into Practice, 26,* 8–14.
Marshall, H. H. (1987b). Motivational strategies of three fifth-grade teachers. *Elementary School Journal, 88,* 137–152.
Marshall, H. H. (1988a). In pursuit of learning-oriented classrooms. *Teaching and Teacher Education, 4,* 85–98.
Marshall, H. H. (1988b). Work or learning: Implications of classroom metaphors. *Educational Researcher, 17,* 9–16.
Marshall, H. H. (1990). Beyond the workplace metaphor: Toward conceptualizing the classroom as a learning setting. *Theory into Practice, 29,* 94–101.
Marshall, H. H., & Weinstein, R. S. (1984). Classroom factors affecting students' self-evaluations: An interactional model. *Review of Educational Research, 54,* 301–327.
McLaughlin, J. (1990). The Rand change agent study revisited: Macro perspectives and micro realities. *Educational Researcher, 19,* 11–16.
Neale, D. C., Smith, D., & Johnson, V. G. (1990). Implementing conceptual change teaching in primary science. *Elementary School Journal, 91,* 109–131.
Newman, D., Griffith, P., & Cole, M. (1989). *The construction zone: Working for cognitive change in school.* Cambridge: Cambridge University Press.
Nicholls, J. G. (1983). Conceptions of ability and achievement motivation: A theory and its implications for education. In S. Paris, G. Olson, & H. Stevenson (Eds.), *Learning and motivation in the classroom.* Hillsdale, NJ: Erlbaum.

Nicholls, J., Cobb, P., Wood, T., Yackel, E., & Patashnick, M. (1990). Assessing students' theories of success in mathematics: Individual and classroom differences. *Journal of Research in Mathematics Education, 21,* 109–122.

Nolen, S. (1988). Reasons for studying: Motivational orientations and study strategies. *Cognition and Instruction, 5,* 267–287.

Peterman, F. (1991, April). *An experienced teacher's emerging constructivist beliefs about teaching and learning.* Paper presented at the American Educational Research Association Meeting, Chicago.

Peterson, P., Fennema, E., & Carpenter, T. (1988/1989, December/January). Using knowledge of students' cognitions in classroom teaching. *Educational Leadership,* pp. 42–46.

Prawat, R. S. (1989). Teaching for understanding: Three key attributes. *Teaching & Teacher Education, 5,* 315–328.

Prawat, R. S. (1991). The value of ideas: The immersion approach to the development of thinking. *Educational Researcher, 20,* 3–10, 30.

Pintrich, P., & DeGroot, E. (1990). Motivational and self-regulated learning components of classroom academic performance. *Journal of Educational Psychology, 82,* 33–40.

Rohrkemper, M. (1989). Self-regulated learning and academic achievement: A Vygotskian view. In B. Zimmerman & D. Schunk (Eds.), *Self-regulated learning and academic achievement* (pp. 143–168). New York: Springer-Verlag.

Roth, K., & Rosean, C. (1991, April). *Writing activities in a conceptual change science learning community: Two perspectives.* Paper presented at the American Educational Research Association Meeting, Chicago.

Sarason, S. (1990). *The predictable failure of educational reform.* San Francisco: Jossey-Bass.

Schön, D. (1979). Generative metaphor: A perspective on problem-setting in social policy. In A. Ortony (Ed.), *Metaphor and thought* (pp. 254–283). Cambridge, UK: Cambridge University Press.

Slavin, R. (1986). *Educational psychology: Theory into practice.* Englewood Cliffs, NJ: Prentice-Hall.

Skinner, E., Wellborn, J., & Connell, J. (1990). What it takes to do well in school and whether I've go it: A process model of perceived control and children's engagement and achievement in school. *Journal of Educational Psychology, 82,* 22–32.

Smith, M. L. (1991). Put to the test: The effects of external testing on teachers. *Educational Researcher, 20,* 8–11.

Thorndike, E. (1932) *Fundamentals of learning.* New York: Teachers College.

Vygotsky, L. (1978). *Mind in society: The development of higher psychological processes.* London: Harvard University Press.

Wertsch, J. (1985). *Vygotsky and the social formation of mind.* Cambridge, MA: Harvard University Press.

Woolfolk, A. (1990). *Educational psychology* (4th ed.). Englewood Cliffs, NJ: Prentice-Hall.

Chapter 2
Learning For What Purpose? Questions When Viewing Classroom Learning From A Sociocultural Curriculum Perspective

Susanne Chandler

North Adams State College
Education Department
North Adams, MA

This chapter explores the question of learning in classroom contexts from a sociocultural curriculum perspective. From this perspective, learning is not assumed to be a general phenomenon but rather a context-specific one that can be made visible by asking three questions: (a) What type of learning is occurring, and what knowledge is of most worth? (b) What is the purpose of learning in this situation, and whose knowledge is being taught? and (c) What are the influences on the learning environment? These three questions typify the types of questions addressed when considering the notion of curriculum and are the questions this chapter addresses. The need to consider the way in which curriculum and learning are related is captured in the following adaption of Peddiwell's *The Saber-Tooth Curriculum* (1939). It illustrates that, due to individual differences, the delivered (enacted) curriculum differs from that which is planned (in outcomes, levels of participation), even though the planned curriculum was to be uniform for each student.

> Once upon a time the animals had a school. The curriculum consisted of running, climbing, flying, and swimming, and all the animals took all the subjects.
> The Duck was good in swimming, better in fact than her instructor; and she made passing grades in flying, but was practically hopeless in running. Because she was low in this subject, she was made to stay in after school and drop her swimming class in order to practice running. She kept this up until she was only average in swimming. But average is acceptable, so nobody worried about that except the Duck.
> The Eagle was considered a problem pupil and was disciplined severely. He beat all the others to the top of the tree in climbing class, but he had used his own way of getting there.
> The Rabbit started out at the top of his class in running, but he had a nervous breakdown and had to drop out of school on account of so much make-up work in swimming.
> The Squirrel led the climbing class but her flying teacher made her start her flying lessons from the ground up instead of from the top of the tree down, and she developed charley horses from over-exertion at the take-off and began getting C's in climbing and D's in running.
> The practical Prairie Dogs apprenticed their offspring to a Badger when the school authorities refused to add digging to the curriculum.
> At the end of the school year, an abnormal Eel that could swim well, run, climb, and fly a little was made valedictorian.[1]

This example, while showing the inherent notion of learning from a sociocultural curriculum perspective, helps to illustrate how the above questions can help guide a perspective and narrow a focus. This example, and the study which follows, also help to raise questions about both the purpose of the curriculum and what is learned through participation in that curriculum. This perspective, or focus, thus makes visible what consequences the "planned" and the "enacted" curriculum has for each student.

The relationship of student learning and the planned and/or enacted curriculum is an area of concern to curricular theorists. From Tyler's (1949) perspective, for example, learning is an assumed activity in the classroom context and is also a purpose of education. The questions that are considered from this perspective deal with the types of learning that may be occurring

---

[1] This is an adaptation taken from *The Saber-Tooth Curriculum* by J. Abner Peddiwell (1939). The adaption was done by Hugh C. Black for his curriculum classes at the University of California, Davis, in which I was lucky enough to be a student.

(e.g., developing thinking skills, acquiring information, developing social attitudes). This type of focus is important in that it helps to dispel the misconception that all learning is worthwhile or of equal value.

OVERVIEW OF THE CHAPTER

This chapter explores the issue of learning from a sociocultural curriculum perspective in three seventh-grade reading classes taught by one teacher. The curricula foci thus presented serve to ground this exploration of the relationship of classroom curriculum and student learning in this chapter. By exploring the opportunities for learning that occurred within and across the three class periods, the factors that influence student learning are illustrated through the examination of three questions explored in this study: (a) what knowledge is of most worth in these classes (i.e., types of learning opportunities such as activities); (b) the purpose for learning in these classes, and whose knowledge is being taught; and (c) the influences on the learning environment.

The following points are also illustrated and help to dispel misconceptions that delivered (enacted) curricula can look the same as planned curricula:

- The curriculum that is planned and perceived by the teacher is not necessarily what is constructed in each class, or what is perceived by the student(s).
- The curriculum is constructed within each class; and it therefore varies across classes, even with the same planned curriculum and same teacher.
- The students are an active part of the constructive learning process. Students have their own perceptions, needs, etc., that they bring to the class to be negotiated with the teacher and other students.
- Because the curriculum is constructed through this interactive process, consideration needs to be given to the students' perceptions of learning opportunities in order to identify supports and constraints on learning.

The data used for this chapter were taken for a sustained, observational, comparative study of classroom curriculum done in a large suburban school district in central Ohio, over a period of one school semester. The school district is in an upper-middle-class socioeconomic community, and the population is predominantly white anglo-saxon American; very few minorities live in the community.

Data collection involved the use of multiple methods: (a) participant observation; (b) interviews of the students and teacher; (c) video- and audio-recordings of classroom life and talk; (d) fieldnotes; (e) triangulation[2] with the teacher and students of data, method, theory, and findings; and (f) classroom documents. Fifty-one periods were observed and analyzed.

In the first section of this chapter, some general conceptualizations and assumptions from a sociocultural constructivist perspective are described in order to provide the theoretical perspective that backgrounded this study. In the next section (Conceptualizations of and Assumptions about the Curriculum from a Sociocultural Constructivist Perspective), examples are provided on how the sociocultural constructivist conceptualizations and assumptions are applied to the area of curriculum within this study. In the concluding section, the study itself is described, the results of the study are used to answer the three curricular questions posed at the beginning, and the findings are identified in regards to the influences on the learning environment.

CONCEPTUALIZATIONS OF AND ASSUMPTIONS ABOUT EVERYDAY LIFE IN CLASSROOMS

A Sociocultural Constructivist Perspective

The purpose of this section is to provide the conceptualizations and assumptions of classroom life from a sociocultural constructivist perspective that illustrate the theoretical framework that guided this study. Within this social constructivist perspective, meanings are constructed and influenced through the interaction of the participants and materials in the classroom setting (Cochran-Smith, 1984; Green, 1983a, b; Green & Wallat, 1981; Green & Harker, 1982; Kantor, 1988; Puro & Bloome, 1987). These meanings, then, can shape behaviors in the classroom setting.

In this study, the students in each of the three classes constructed the meaning and "look" of the silent reading time event through over-time

---

[2] *Triangulation* is a term typically used by sociologists indicating the use of multiple methods (Denzin, 1989; Polkinghorne, 1983). The purpose of using triangulation in this study is that the data collected in one way (e.g., interview, video tape, audio tape) can be used to cross-check the accuracy of data gathered in another way. Triangulation can also be done with the theories, data, or investigators of a study, as well as the use of multiple methods (Denzin, 1989; Polkinghorne, 1983). The word *triangulation* originates from the Greek and continues on into our modern mathematics, as well as from geological survey and navigational methods of finding an unknown point by forming a triangle that has the two known points and the one unknown point as vertices (Denzin, 1989; Polkinghorne, 1983).

Triangulation allows for assessing the accuracy of conclusions drawn by triangulation with several sources of data, and assists in correcting observer biases that result when the observer and/or ethnographer is the only observer of the phenomenon under investigation. For further elaboration, see Lather (1986).

participation in that activity. In other words, while silent reading time is often viewed as an activity that occurs in similar ways across classes, silent reading time became constructed differently in each of these classes, and consequently the behaviors of the students differed in each class. In one class, for example, students sat at their desks to read, whereas in another class, students sat in their desks and on the floor.

This example illustrates that through interactions and communication (verbal/nonverbal), classroom behavior is socially constructed. And as classroom cultures have patterned ways of acting, perceiving, believing, and evaluating (Goodenough, 1971), the ways in which people perceive and act in specific situations are also constructed through the interactions occurring in a particular setting.

As multilayered meanings are constantly being interpreted and reconstructed (Berman, 1986) in the classroom setting, curriculum and instruction are integrated through dynamic and interactive constructed learning. From this perspective, *curriculum* is defined as the resulting aspects of the classroom participants' interactions and engagements with the environment and each other (King, 1986).

Interpretive constructivist studies done in the area of curriculum have also demonstrated that the curriculum, as well as the type of class itself, holds particular meanings for the participants in the setting. Burgess (1984), for instance, illustrated that students in a nonacademic class perceived the class as unimportant. As a result of their perceptions and interpretations that the class was unimportant, the students became discipline problems. The assumption that classroom behavior is socially constructed thus considers that participation in different learning environments (i.e., the resulting or enacted curriculum) has consequences for students in terms of perception of knowledge.

Included in these assumptions of constructed meanings and socially constructed behavior is the idea that there is a history, or historicity (Bloome & Bailey, 1990) to any given event. What this means for classrooms is that the teacher, the students, and the materials all have prior histories before being integrated in the process of classroom life. The teacher enters with already preconceived expectations, beliefs, and attitudes about classroom life. The teacher also enters with certain prior cognitive, physical, linguistic, and evaluative abilities.

The students, like the teacher, also enter with certain preconceived expectations, beliefs, and attitudes, as well as with certain cognitive, physical, linguistic, and evaluative abilities. Likewise, the materials that will be used in the class setting enter with certain features such as content, structure, language, and vocabulary. These features influence the curriculum and gained (constructed) meanings.

As a result, students enter into a classroom with preconceived notions of what classroom life is like and what will be expected of them. Students expect the classroom to contain a bulletin board, a blackboard, and desks. The students will be expected to be on time, remain quiet when the teacher talks, and stay in their seats (Green & Harker, 1988).

These assumptions lay the foundation for the notion that everyday life also builds up socially over time. Over time, norms and expectations, rights and obligations, and roles and relationships (i.e., Goodenough, 1971; Gumperz, 1981) of students and teacher become established as well: how class begins; the rights and obligations, and roles and relationships; the ways in which time will be scheduled (the rituals and routines of life in classroom); the ways in which space becomes organized; the types of events that can and will occur; and the types of outcomes that will be generated (Spradley, 1980).

This suggests that one way to view classrooms is as a culture (Green et al., 1990; Spindler, 1982). Classes can be viewed as cultures due to the social participation structures, rights and obligations, norms and expectations, and roles and relationships that are placed on students and teacher. For example, the ways in which the teacher and students interact, what they use and how they use it, how they communicate, and what they communicate are all instances of life in a culture (Green & Wallat, 1979) that become learned and shared as in any other culture (Goodenough, 1971; Zaharlick & Green, 1991).

This leads to the assumption that each class becomes a unique culture as the norms and expectations, rights and obligations, and roles and relationships become constructed over time. In this study, the way in which the students in one period constructed "question asking" differed from those of the other two periods. Period 1 students raised their hands and waited to be called on by the teacher before asking their questions. Period 2 students seldom raised their hands to ask questions; rather, they usually stated the teacher's name and then asked the question. Period 3 students generally raised their hands, but did not wait to be called on by the teacher before asking the questions.

Cultures are learned and shared (Goodenough, 1971; Zaharlick & Green, 1991) and are also always changing and variable (Heath, 1982; Hymes, 1982). Interpreting the occurrences within any given class requires an understanding of class as a separate miniculture within the context of a larger school culture with norms and expectations, rights and obligations, and roles and relationships for its group members.

When classes are viewed as cultures, teacher roles can be seen as constructed through interactions with students and materials. Likewise, student roles are constructed, not given. In each classroom, being a student means something different. According to student interviews, being a good student in Period 1 meant following the rules overtly, without question. Thus, whenever students whispered during Silent Reading Time, they were quickly quieted by their classmates. Being a good student in Period 2, on the other hand, meant "asking a lot of questions" and "participating in discussions a lot." In contrast, being a good student in Period 3 meant "being on time," "handing in your homework on time," and "keeping your daily log up to date."

How each class plays out over time is established in the interactions of the group members but is never a given. Relationships are built in the context of the classroom. Small groups may form, alter, grow, or reduce, but are not static or unchanging. This verbal and nonverbal participation in class is also influenced not only by what students and teacher learn to expect and do in that setting, but also by the expectations they bring from other settings (Erickson & Mohatt, 1982; Green et al., 1990; Philips, 1972; Shultz, Florio, & Erickson, 1982). As small groups change over time, roles and relationships, rights and obligations, and norms and expectations become constructed and reconstructed.

The interactions that occur with materials, such as reading, are also constructed, not given (e.g., Green & Meyer, 1990). In this study, reading silently every day from self-selected books (nontext) was a student obligation. The teacher had the expectation that students brought their reading books to class and were reading silently from them, although how this was done varied from class to class. Silent reading did not occur in Period 1 until the teacher made the announcement that it was reading time. In contrast, silent reading began when the bell rang in Period 2 with no mention of it by the teacher. What these examples suggest is that what gets created and constructed by the group members interacting with each other and the materials within the class is the curriculum.

Classroom life is made up of a set of events which are linked together in some way (Green & Meyer, 1990; Barr, 1987). Although some aspects of life in classrooms become stable over time, other aspects evolve in the doing. While participants cannot know what events will specifically look like or require until they occur, there are general predictable elements of classroom life.

Implications of the Social Constructivist Perspective for Student Learning

Everyday life is not random and chaotic, but more or less patterned (Gumperz, 1986). Some events of classroom life occur daily (i.e., announcements, roll taking), whereas some may occur weekly (i.e., pep rallies). This perspective considers the need to understand the kinds of learning opportunities in which students can participate. We need to understand how, over time, the norms and expectations, and so on, become interpreted, defined, and constructed in the classroom setting. By looking at these roles and relationships, norms and expectations, and rights and obligations in the classroom setting, the elements that influence student learning (i.e., the supports and constraints) can come to be understood.

Studies from socioconstructivist perspectives have provided foundational premises from which everyday life in schools and classrooms can be conceptualized. An abbreviated version of the assumptions discussed above and the foundational knowledge from research studies is provided in Table A1 and A2 in the Appendix. The premises and assumptions are presented in Table A1 and lead to the assumptions on which the study in this chapter is based (Table A2).

CONCEPTUALIZATIONS AND ASSUMPTIONS ABOUT THE CURRICULUM FROM A SOCIOCULTURAL CONSTRUCTIVIST PERSPECTIVE

Conceptualization of the Curriculum

Teachers and school districts conceptualize educational goals and purposes in many ways. Accordingly, this section provides a brief overview of general assumptions of curriculum and learning so that the supports and constraints of student learning within this study and perspective can be better understood.

Similar to the variety and diversity of metaphors on learning and classrooms (e.g., Marshall, 1990) such as classrooms-as-places-of-work (Doyle, 1986) and teacher-as-executive (Berliner, 1984, 1990), curriculum has also been conceptualized with different metaphors. Traditionally, curriculum has been viewed as a document that guides what teachers do with and to students. In this context, curriculum content is often seen as existing in the books, materials, and/or plans that are provided by districts to meet the goals of the course of study (Beauchamp, 1975).

Curriculum can also be seen as: (a) a set of planned learning activities (e.g., Bobbitt, 1918; Snedden, 1921; Taylor, 1970); (b) intended learning outcomes (Adler, 1982; Gagne, 1977); (c) content or subject matter (Bloom, 1987; Boyer, 1983; Smith, Stanley, & Shores, 1957); and (d) constructed in the interactions between the teacher, students, and texts (Berman, 1986; King, 1986; Measor, 1984).

Analysis of fieldnotes and interviews with the teacher and various school district administrators indicated that the school district in this study viewed curriculum as a document that guides what teachers do with and to students, and as a set of intended learning outcomes. Because the teacher had been on the curriculum development committee for the reading program, the teacher also viewed the curriculum as document and intended learning outcomes.

During the study, the specific content/subject matter was not prescribed for teachers in the document. Instead, the curriculum document provided the outcomes to be reached, but did not provide the means to reach them. Shortly after the study was completed, however, the school district moved to a more specific content/subject matter document that dictated to teachers how, as well as what, to teach, much like a set of planned learning activities (e.g., Bobbit & Snedden, above).

The Curriculum Agenda in Context: The Purpose of Education

The purpose of education as stated in the curriculum guide, and thus the agenda of the curriculum, can also be viewed from various perspectives. For example, the purpose of education has been seen as presenting a curriculum to: (a) prepare individual students for the position they would assume as adults[3] (Bobbitt, 1924; Finney, 1928; Ross, 1901; Snedden, 1921) (b) consider social reconstruction (Kliebard, 1987) (also known as a *curriculum for social meliorism*) or to provide students with an orientation to improve society (Counts, 1932; Kandal, 1941), (c) reproduce the culture and maintain the status quo (Broudy, 1982), and (d) provide knowledge that liberates people in a society attempting to maintain the status quo (known as the *reconceptualists*—i.e., Anyon, 1980; Apple, 1979a; Freire, 1970; Giroux, Penna & Pinar, 1981; MacDonald, 1988), among other goals (e.g., education for the liberally educated person, socialization, achievement, vocational training, and for personal growth).

Part of the school district's educational purpose can be seen as reproducing the culture and maintaining the status quo in light of the fact that the academic content was limited to a western-Eurocentric philosophy. The teacher, however, held her own purpose of education: to provide students with the abilities and incentives to promote a lifelong learning.

The purpose of education (or at least a particular type of education), however, is the idea, or goal, that guides a *curriculum development* (the conceptualization of what a curriculum looks like). Yet the curricular goals and statements, as Eisner (1985) notes, "are the most general statements that proclaim to the world the values that some group holds for an educational program" (p. 136). Curriculum is indeed a value-laden enterprise; for in an issue such as what knowledge *should* be taught, *should* is a value-based

---

[3] This was labeled the *social efficiency movement* or *social control* in order to stabilize a seemingly out-of-control society during the beginning of the 1900s.

decision (Reid, 1978; Schubert, 1986). Knowledge, in this case, is that which is considered worthwhile knowledge within a particular context. All the decisions that get made are based on sociocultural values and are interrelated with curriculum (i.e., Apple, 1979a, b; Freire, 1970; Klein, 1990; Shor, 1987; Shor & Freire, 1987; Schubert, 1986).

THE CLASSROOM STUDY

In the previous sections, segments of the study have illustrated issues of curriculum, teaching, and learning. In this section I describe the study of classroom curriculum, placing the above curricular concepts and concerns in context while examining what elements support and constrain student learning. The first two questions in this section provide a descriptive setting of classroom occurrences as correlated with time spent on classroom activities and are thus general in nature. They are provided here, however, to help place the lived reality of the classrooms into context.

I. What Knowledge is of Most Worth in These Classes?

In order to answer the question of what knowledge is of most worth in these classes, the element of time from Spradley's (1980) cultural domains was examined. Time, in this case, helps to focus on what activities occurred and for what length of time. This is important because curriculum activities provide opportunities to learn and define what students can do in the class. Length of time can indicate one way in which a teacher can demonstrate the importance of an activity. In this study and within the context and boundary of cultural domains, two elements of time were explored: (a) What activities was time spent on in these classes? and (b) On the basis of these activities, what kind of knowledge was time spent on in these classes? These elements are illustrated summatively across the three class periods.

(1) What activities was time spent on within and across these three classes?

Curriculum activities that time was spent on in these classes, on a general level, were classified by the teacher as: (a) Academic Events and (b) Nonacademic Events. The Academic Events were further divided into: (a) Reading Related Events, and (b) Graded Events. The Nonacademic Events were divided into: (a) rules, (b) announcements, and (c) paper shuffle. Seventh-six percent of the average daily classtime we spent on Academic Events (summed across the three classes), of which 69% was spent on Reading Related Events, and 24% of the average daily classtime was spent on Nonacademic Events (see Table 2.1).

Table 2.1. The Classroom Curriculum: How Class Time Was Spent

Classroom Events	Time Spent In Academic vs. Nonacademic Events	Time Spent in Academic Events	Time In All Events
1. **Academic Events**	76%		
Reading Related Events		69%	
SRT/SSR			55%
Classwork			10%
Review			4%
Reading Preparation			9%
T-reads aloud			19%
Reports			3%
Graded Events		31%	
Homework			48%
Quizzes/Tests			11%
Reports			41%
2. **Nonacademic Events**	24%		
Rules			64%
Announcements			6%
Paper Shuffle			30%

(2) On what kind of knowledge was time spent in these classes?

In order to answer the question of what kind of knowledge was time spent on in these classes, two types of data were explored: (a) time spent on each classroom event (Reading Related Events, Graded Events, Nonacademic Events), on a general level; and, (b) topics covered during each class period, thus time spent on a single activity, on a specific level.

Classroom events were further divided into categories within each of the major subcategories (see Table 2.1 for categories). This further reduction of the categories into events illustrates what type of events (versus knowledge) time was spent on in these classes. Table 2.1 also illustrates how time spent was spent during the Reading Related Events, Graded Events, and Nonacademic Events. Fifty-five percent of the Reading Related Event time was spent on Sustained Silent Reading, 48% of the Graded Event time was spent on Homework, and 64% of the Nonacademic time was spent on Rules and Expectations time. From this breakdown, and in answering what knowledge is of most worth in these classes, made visible is that the majority of the time spent in class was spent on Reading Related Events (52%). Within the Reading Related Event category, the majority (55%) of class time was spent on Sustained Silent Reading. The knowledge of most worth in these classes, assuming that amount of time spent can equate with subject worth, is that knowledge which directly related to reading. This conclusion was also supported by the goals of the teacher.

On a specific level, time spent on a single activity varied from period to period, thus changing the planned curriculum as it becomes constructed and/or enacted as well as opportunities for learning, within and across the three class periods. In the activity of the teacher explaining the components to consider when preparing visual aids for an oral report, the notion of time spent differed from that above. On this specific level, time spent considered which components became included in the explanation of the assignment, rather than the amount of time spent on an event as discussed above.

As indicated in Table 2.2, the topics covered by the teacher in the explanation of the assignment varied extensively across the three class periods. Period 3 was the only period in which a discussion of "spelling" was included, while this same period was excluded from a discussion of how to make the visual aids "understandable." When asked about this wide variance of topic inclusion and/or exclusion, the teacher explained that, by third period, she could no longer remember what topic had been covered in which period. Although these topics varied widely across the three periods, the grading criteria for these visual aids remained the same across the periods. Thus, the curriculum, opportunities for learning, and opportunities for grade achievement varied across the three class periods.

The next section explores the nature of the Sustained Silent Reading event. This event was selected for exploration because the majority of the class time was spent on this activity.

II. What is the Purpose for Learning in These Classes, and Whose Knowledge is Being Taught?

Two sets of learning purposes were evident in these classes. One set of purposes for learning was taken directly from the curriculum goals listed in the 1989 *Graded Course of Study* for the school district.[4] These learning purposes stated by the school district were to:

- foster a love of reading
- promote lifelong reading

---

[4] For purposes of anonymity, the names of the students, teacher, school, and school district are not given. This, of course, encompasses the site for this *Graded Course of Study.*

Table 2.2. Assignment Explanation of Visual Aids for Oral Presentation

	Per. 1	Per. 2	Per. 3
Visibility:			
Size/large	X	X	X
Mounting of pictures	X	X	X
Colorful	X	X	X
Use Borders	X		
Interesting	X		
Attention getting			X
Eye appealing		X	
Understandable:			
Related to topic	X		
People can look & read it		X	
Helps people understand topic		X	
Spelling:			
Titles			X
Wording			X
Examples:			
Title	X		
Illustrations	X	X	
Colorful	X		
Large enough	X		
Models	X		
Lists		X	X
Pictures			X

- increase knowledge of the world
- extend concepts of print
- develop literary awareness
- improve comprehension
- stimulate language development within all areas of the curriculum

The teacher's ideas for purposes for learning in these classes were obtained from: (a) interviews with the teacher, (b) records of what time was spent on in these classes, (c) the teacher's planned curriculum, and (d) the district's curriculum document that the teacher had helped develop. An analysis of these four areas indicated that the teacher's idea for learning in this classroom was to build reading comprehension so that the students could successfully interact with the text and to gain a lifelong enjoyment of reading. The teacher's goals also included consideration given to a classroom environment that was conducive for student learning and comprehension.

Student interview data illustrated varying viewpoints when contrasting their views with the teacher's and district's learning goals of the class. In agreement with one of the goals, 52% of the interviewed students stated that in allowing them to read the types of books they most wanted to read, their enjoyment (love) of reading was fostered. In contrast to this, 11% of the interviewed students stated that, by being required to read every day, they did no recreational reading during their spare time, nor did they agree with the goal of lifelong reading. In overwhelming agreement (97%), the students reported that their knowledge of the world was increased through their reading and reporting on historical fiction novels and the teacher's slide shows, discussions, and presentations on the same.

Thus purposeful goal-directed activity does not always become implemented in ways that support student learning or provide an environment conducive for learning, even within the teacher's definition of a supported learning environment and/or activity. In order to further illustrate how student learning is supported as well as constrained within a goal-directed activity aimed at improving student learning and comprehension, the next section describes, through the use of the students' and the teacher's voices, the nature of the Sustained Silent Reading event. Elements that support and constrain student learning within this event are then explored and illustrated.

III. The Influences on the Learning Environment

Out of 51 class periods, *Silent Reading Time* (SRT) occurred 46 times (90%). In other words, SRT occurred almost every class day and period. The SRT event was selected for further analysis because: (a) the teacher considered SRT the most important daily activity, and (b) the SRT event covered more class time than any other regular occurring event. Due to the importance of SRT in these classes, the next section focuses on how SRT is defined, what happens during this time, and what teacher activities support and/or constrain student learning processes.

1. How is Silent Reading Time defined in these classes?

The first part of this examination provides a picture, or an interpretive format of transcribed interviews, of what SRT is like from the teacher's and students' perspectives [T = Teacher; S = Student/s]. The student voice, as represented, is an aggregate of various student voices.[5]

T: I see Silent Reading Time as an opportunity for students to interact with the text. I have Silent Reading Time [in class] and which I really do think is valuable...interaction. This is leisure reading stuff, anything but textbook, and hopefully something they provide.

S: Silent Reading lasts about 15 minutes. You need to read a novel that you choose. You have a book and you have to read it during the time she says you have to read and it has to be a novel, it can't be a magazine. It has to be something with a story to it. The purpose [of Silent Reading Time] is to finish your novel in class so you don't have to read at home, and to put books in your reading record for extra credit. Right now we're reading the *Iceberg Hermit* in class—historical fiction. [So, in our Silent Reading Time], we're reading those kinds of books.

T: I think it's real important to give them time to practice what it is we're suppose to be doing, and so I put a big priority on us reading...like silent reading time. I'm suppose to be reading, too, but sometimes there are questions. But silent reading is markedly different when I read a book as opposed to when I do paperwork or housekeeping chores. We have better silent reading when I read with them than when I do desk work.

S: We can get out of our seats if we need to borrow a book or to ask her a question.

T: I do bookchecks to make sure that they bring in their reading books for Silent Reading Time.

S: If you didn't bring your book, she can loan you one. Like if I didn't bring my [silent reading] book in, *Gentle Ben,* she has extra *Gentle Bens* that I can read. But if she does a book check and you borrowed a book from her, she'll take off points, and you don't know when she'll give a book check. She just comes around and sees if you brought your book and if you didn't you lose five points.

T: I try to do silent reading with them. I try to sit in the student desk area and read while they are reading, but it doesn't always work out.

S: Usually like during reading time she either grades papers or does some work while we're reading or sometimes she reads too.

2. What occurred during the Silent Reading Time event?

As mentioned in the students' and the teachers' voices, there was more to the SRT event than just students and teacher *doing* silent reading. In fact, an

---

[5] All the collected data from this study were shared with the teacher in the study. The only part changed/altered was that the students were given codes in order to prevent recognition by the teacher. When triangulating student interview findings with the students, many students expressed fear at being recognized because their ways of talking were distinct—at least to them. In order to alleviate their fears and honor the initial agreement, the student voices are presented, generally, in aggregated form.

observation of the 46 class periods in which SRT occurred (out of 51), illustrated that 17 different subevents occurred within the SRT event.

In order to understand what occurred during the SRT event, subevents engaged in by the teacher and/or students were observed and established. Table 2.3 illustrates these subevents, which occurred during the larger SRT event. According to the teacher's definition, all the subevents are defined as Housekeeping Events, such as events that related to paper shuffle (e.g., collecting and/or returning homework), clean-up, an individual student's make-up work, or choosing individual report topics and/or presentation order; or in other words, nonacademic events.

After the observation of subevent occurrences during SRT, the frequency of the subevent occurrences was examined. This type of analysis helps illustrate which type of subevent occurred more frequently and consistently

Table 2.3. Silent Reading Time Subevent Occurrence Across 46 Class Periods (By # of Periods and Percent)

	# of Class Periods	(%)
*T. hands out loaners	32	70
T. checks out new books	16	35
T. checks in books	8	17
T. calls st† to T. desk	18	39
T. takes roll	19	41
Book check	16	35
T. sits to read	18	39
T. answers student's question at T's desk	30	65
T. walks around class	11	24
T. walks to student's desk to talk w/st.	18	39
T. writes on blackboard	5	11
T. answers student's question at st's desk	5	11
T. reminds sts. to read	17	37
Selection of report topic	2	4
Individual collection of h/work	7	15
T. overtly disciplines St	7	15
Class interruption	4	9

*T. = Teacher
† st/s = student/s

over time, in relation to each of the other subevents. On the average, five different subevents occurred daily that did or did not relate to the SRT event. Table 2.3 shows that a book check occurred at least once per day in 35% (16) of the class periods, out of the total 46 class periods observed.

Although this table does not provide the number of occurrences of each subevent during a given period, it illustrates, however, that out of the 46 class periods, the teacher:

- handed out book loaners at least once daily during 32 of the 46 periods (or 70% of the 46 periods)
- answered students' questions at her desk at least once daily during 30 of the 46 periods (or 65%)
- sat to "do" silent reading with the students (as well as modeled the procedure and expected behavior) for a portion (but never during the entire event) of the SRT event occurrence during 18 of the 46 periods (or 39%).

3. What activities during the Silent Reading Time event supported and/or constrained student learning?

On one level, this type of research and data analysis demonstrate the supports and constraints on a general, or more group/macro level. For example, as defined by the teacher and the students, all of the listed subevents/activities constrained student learning in that the subevents disturbed the SRT environment (i.e., created distraction).[6] According to the interviews, the students and the teacher complained that there was too much noise in the classroom for "real reading to occur."

The teacher also felt that much mock participation (e.g., pretending to read, nodding head in agreement to text while not really reading) occurred during those SRT events in which she did not participate. As illustrated in the above definition of SRT, the teacher knew that more "real reading" occurred during those moments that she also read. The students agreed with this assessment by stating that, during the times the teacher read, the classroom was quiet so they were better able to concentrate.

ST: I don't like reading time cause I'm reading this really good book but some people just goof around and stuff and it bothers me.

In the teacher's analysis of the data, silent reading was often used, albeit inadvertently, as a control device to keep the students busy while the teacher caught up on housekeeping chores. Since so many of the subevents that occurred during the SRT event were housekeeping chores, it became evident

---

[6] This is with the one exception during the 18 periods in which the teacher participated in the SRT activity for a portion of the event time.

that the external forces (e.g., required paperwork) placed pressure on the teacher, and thus influenced (constrained) the student learning environment. The student interviews support the finding that the SRT event was merely a control device through their definitions of SRT:

ST: Silent Reading Time is to make us kids quiet down. Like, she has us do silent reading so that we don't come in and act like animals—we have to come in, sit down, and read quietly. When she's done taking roll, we go on to our lesson.

Supports and Constraints for Learning

Before the data were analyzed, the teacher stated that SRT, as well as the time allotted to it, were important elements in the reading classes. Thus, the teacher assumed that, since the majority of the class time was spent on reading and/or reading related activities, students were actively engaged in reading practice. In other words, the teacher had equated the amount of time spent on the SRT event as a support for student learning. The data were able to make visible, however, the fact that the time spent and/or given to the SRT event was often determined by the number of housekeeping chores to be done, and thus constrained learning. Like the differences in the topics discussed in each period, these teacher actions may inadvertently have influenced what became the curriculum as different from what was planned, and may have created different events for students depending on whether or how they defined these teacher actions.

On the other hand, the data indicated that the teacher supported student learning by modeling the SRT event and behavior. When the teacher was engaged with reading, the students became more engaged with the reading. When the teacher modeled quiet behavior, the students became more quiet and thus engaged more with their text, or at least appeared more task focused.

Staying at this general group level across the three periods, and/or within class, rather than focusing on the individual, however, is problematic in that it can give the impression that a given support and/or constraint (such as modeling a behavior, SRT as a control device) holds across the entire class rather than being specific to the individual student. Consequently, as we examine the supports and constraints of student learning, we must understand that, while, on a group level, the teacher may constrain student learning, covertly or overtly (as with the 16 housekeeping activities as discussed above), the situation may be a different reality on an individual level. Whereas, for example, the students generally complained about distractions and interruptions during SRT, one student stated that she never was distracted from her silent reading and felt the class to be a quiet environment.

CONCLUSION

This perspective and method of analyzing what happens in classrooms can reveal the nature of learning in particular classrooms. It also demonstrates that learning, what counts as learning, and opportunities for learning vary among classes, even with the same planned curriculum and the same teacher.

The teacher in this study had a clear purpose for learning in her classroom: to increase reading comprehension in order to inspire a lifelong enjoyment of reading and interacting with text. While this overarching purpose impacted what the teacher chose as learning activities in her classroom (i.e., silent reading time/reading practice, topics covered), the way in which the teacher implemented the activity generally constrained the students' opportunities for focused participation. The way in which the teacher implemented the planned curriculum influenced students' perceptions of the curriculum/activity, and thus how the curriculum/activity came to be defined. Also, the way in which the teacher planned, but did not cover, the same specific topics across periods constrained opportunities for learning and gaining needed information.

How teachers view and/or define learning influences what types of learning activities that can occur. In this case, the teacher viewed time for SRT (reading practice) as an important element to accomplishing a successful student interaction with text ("real reading"). This was indicated not only in her philosophy of learning but in the daily and overall amount of time she allocated to this SRT/reading practice, maintaining that student learning was supported as justified by time spent on the activity. From the teacher's perspective, and based on analysis of time allotted on valued knowledge to be learned, enjoyment of reading was the primary concern. But planning the curriculum with the goal of "learning" is not enough; clear opportunities must be created for the types of learning to occur without inadvertently constraining the learning opportunities.

This study illustrates some supports and/or constraints of student learning at a macro/group level from a curriculum/constructivist perspective. The findings identified in this study concerning the influences on the learning environment are:

- How the teacher defines curriculum (in this case, SRT/reading practice as a support of student learning) and classroom goals influences what become the opportunities for learning (i.e., SRT and topics covered).
- The way in which a teacher implements a learning opportunity/activity can simultaneously support and constrain student learning at both a group and an individual level.
- The way in which a teacher implements a learning activity can influence how students' come to perceive and define the nature of the activity.

- Although the time a teacher allocates to learning activities influences what can get accomplished by the teacher and students and what type of accomplishments occur, the concept of time as a support of learning does not necessarily manifest into quality of time.
- Although a teacher may know and understand how a learning activity/opportunity should occur (how SRT is best used and supported, topics to be covered), external classroom pressures may predominate. Thus, while the learning activity/opportunity occurs, it may not occur at an optimal level.
- Although supports and constraints of student learning can be viewed from a group, or macro, level (such as in this study), the context-specific situation of an individual within that group may have a different reality.

As this chapter closes, it should be noted that, within this discussion, no prescription is given to prevent constraints on student learning, as prescriptions do not consider the "whole picture," or situational context. Yet from the socioconstructivist/curricularist perspective, the greatest strength is perhaps in suggesting some pivotal questions (e.g., What knowledge is of most worth? Whose knowledge is being reproduced in the classroom? and For what purpose?). These questions, together with the perspective and focus outlined here, can be applied to other classes for purposes of analyzing the types and purposes of learning as well as the supports and constraints for goals of the curriculum.

APPENDIX

Table A1
Premises of Constructed Life in Schools

- School is a social setting where people construct and conduct daily life together (Green et al., 1990).
- A classroom must be conceived of as a social system in which life is constructed over time by members interacting with and building on each other's actions, intentions, and messages (Gumperz, 1981).
- Such life becomes patterned over time as routines and rituals develop, events recur, norms become established, and a common set of expectations and common language develops for doing life.
- Individuals within the classroom society are also simultaneously members of other social groups, each of which has its own ways of doing life (Erickson & Mohatt, 1982; Green et al., 1990; Philips, 1972; Shultz et al., 1982).

- Participation in classrooms, verbally and nonverbally, is influenced, not only by what students learn to expect and do in that setting, but also by the expectations they bring from other settings (Green et al., 1990).
- Culture in classrooms is not a predictable or given entity. It is a dynamic, unfolding, constructed product of the patterned ways of perceiving, believing, acting, and evaluating that develop over time (cf. Goodenough, 1971) in classrooms (Green et al., 1990).
- All classrooms have unique cultural characteristics as well as characteristics in common with other classrooms (Kantor, 1988).
- Different patterned ways of life develop and along with them different requirements for participation that lead to differences in learning (Kantor, 1988; Marshall, 1987; Marshall & Weinstein, 1988; Philips, 1972).
- In each classroom, language use will be elicited, supported, or constrained in different ways and these ways influence what teachers and observers see as "language or communicative competence" (Green et al., 1990).
- Language that is produced in these contexts, then, reflects the social life that has been constructed and may not reflect the "competencies of individuals" (DeStefano, Pepinsky, & Sanders, 1982).

Table A2
Assumptions Underlying a Social Interaction Perspective
(adapted from Green, 1983a, b)

CLASSROOMS ARE COMMUNICATIVE ENVIRONMENTS:
- Differentiation of roles exist between teachers and students
- Relationships between teachers and students are asymmetrical
- Differential perceptions of events exist between teachers and students
- Classrooms are differentiated communicative environments
- Communicative participation affects student achievement

CONTEXTS ARE CONSTRUCTED DURING INTERACTIONS:
- Activities have participation structures
- Contextualization cues signal meaning
- Rules for participation are implicit
- Behavior expectations are constructed as part of interaction

MEANING IS CONTEXT SPECIFIC:
- All instances of a behavior are not equal
- Meaning is signalled verbally and nonverbally
- Contexts constrain meaning

- Meaning is determined by and extracted from observed sequences of behavior
- Communicative competence is reflected in appropriate behavior

INFERENCING IS REQUIRED FOR CONVERSATIONAL COMPREHENSION:

- Frames of reference guide participation
- Frame clashes result from differences in perception
- Communication is a rule-governed activity
- Frames of references are developed over time
- Form and function in speech used in conversations do not always match

TEACHERS ORCHESTRATE DIFFERENT PARTICIPATION LEVELS:

- Teachers evaluate student ability by observing performance during interactions
- Demands for participation co-occur with academic demands
- Teachers signal their theory of pedagogy by their behavior (verbal and nonverbal)
- Teacher goals can be inferred from behaviors

STUDENTS HAVE AN ACTIVE ROLE IN KNOWLEDGE CONSTRUCTION:

- Students interpret academic and social requirements through observations of teacher-student, student-student, and student-group interactions (Collins, 1990).
- Students are simultaneously part of teacher-student culture and peer culture (Bloome & Theodorou, 1988).
- The ways in which students participate depends on their standing in the peer culture as well as the teacher demands (Green et al., 1990; Bloome & Theodorou, 1988).

REFERENCES

Adler, M. (1982). *The paideia proposal.* New York: Macmillan.
Anyon, J. (1980). Social class and the hidden curriculum of work. *Journal of Education, 162*(1), 67–92.
Apple, M. (1979a). *Ideology and curriculum.* London: Routledge & Kegan Paul.
Apple, M. (1979b). On analyzing hegemony. *The Journal of Curriculum Theorizing, 1*(1), 10–43.
Barr, R. (1987). Classroom interaction and curricular content. In D. Bloome (Ed.), *Literacy and schooling* (pp. 150–168). Norwood, NJ: Ablex Publishing Corp.
Beauchamp, G.A. (1975). *Curriculum theory* (3rd ed.). Wilmette, IL: The Kagg Press.

Berliner, D.C. (1984). The executive functions of teaching. In J. Osborn, P.T. Wilson, & R.C. Anderson (Eds.), *Reading education: Foundations for a literate America* (pp. 87–108). Lexington, MA: Lexington Books/D.C. Heath.

Berliner, D.C. (1990). If the metaphor fits, why not wear it? The teacher as executive. *Theory Into Practice, 29*(2), 85–93.

Berman, L. (1986). Perception, paradox, and passion: Curriculum for community. *Theory Into Practice, 25*(1), 41–45.

Bloom, A. (1987). *The closing of the American mind.* New York: Simon & Schuster.

Bloome, D., & Bailey, F. (1990, February). *Linguistics in education: A direction for the study of language and literacy.* Prepared for the National Council on Research on English and the NCTE assembly for Research Conference on Multiple Disciplinary Perspectives on Literacy Research.

Bloome, D., & Theodorou, E. (1988). Analyzing teacher–student and student–student discourse. In J.L. Green & J.O. Harker (Eds.), *Multiple perspective analyses of classroom discourse* (pp. 217–248). Norwood, NJ: Ablex Publishing Corp.

Bobbitt, F. (1918). *The curriculum.* Boston: Ablex Publishing Corp.

Bobbitt, F. (1924). *How to make a curriculum.* Boston: Houghton Mifflin.

Boyer, E., for the Carnegie Foundation for the Advancement of Teaching. (1983). *High school: A report on secondary education in America.* New York: Harper & Row.

Broudy, H.S. (1982). Challenge to the curriculum worker: Uses of knowledge. In W.H. Schubert & A.L. Schubert (Eds.), *Conceptions of curriculum knowledge: Focus on students and teachers* (pp. 3–8). University Park, PA: College of Education, Pennsylvania State University.

Burgess, R.G. (1984). It's not a proper subject: It's just Newsom. In I.F. Goodson & S.J. Ball (Eds.), *Defining the curriculum: Histories and ethnographies* (pp. 181–200). Philadelphia: The Falmer Press.

Cochran-Smith, M. (1984). *The making of a reader.* Norwood, NJ: Ablex Publishing Corp.

Collins, E.C. (1990). *Content as constructed: Two contrasting units of instruction in a fourth/fifth grade class.* Unpublished doctoral dissertation, The Ohio State University.

Counts, G.S. (1932). *Dare the schools build a new social order?* New York: John Day.

Denzin, N.K. (1989). *The research act: A theoretical introduction to sociological methods* (3rd ed.). Englewood Cliffs, NJ: Prentice Hall.

DeStephano, J.S., Pepinsky, H.B., & Sanders, T.S. (1982). Discourse rules for literacy learning in a classroom. In L.C. Wilkinson (Ed.), *Communicating in the classroom.* New York: Academic Press.

Doyle, W. (1986). Classroom organization and management. In M.C. Wittrock (Ed.), *Handbook of research on teaching* (3rd ed., pp. 392–433). New York: Macmillan.

Eisner, E. (1985). *The educational imagination* (2nd ed.). New York: Macmillan.

Erickson, F., & Mohatt, G. (1982). Cultural organization of participation structures in two classrooms of Indian students. In G. Spindler (Ed.), *Doing the ethnography of schooling.* New York: Holt, Rinehart & Winston.

Finney, R.L. (1928). *A sociological philosophy of education.* New York: Macmillan.

Freire, P. (1970). *Pedagogy of the oppressed.* New York: Continuum.

Gagne, R.M. (1977). *The conditions of learning.* New York: Holt, Rinehart & Winston.

Giroux, H., Penna, A., & Pinar, W. (Eds.). (1981). *Curriculum and instruction*. Berkeley, CA: McCutchan.
Goodenough, W. (1971). *Culture, language, and society*. Menlo Park, CA: Benjamin/Cummings.
Green, J.L. (1983a). Exploring classroom discourse: Linguistic perspectives on teaching-learning processes. *Educational Psychologist, 18*(3), 180–199.
Green, J.L. (1983b). Research on teaching as a linguistic process: A state of the art. In E.W. Gordon (Ed.), *Review of research in education, 10* (pp. 152–252). Washington, DC: American Educational Research Association.
Green, J.L., & Harker, J.O. (1982). Gaining access to learning: Conversational, social, and cognitive demands of group participation. In L. Cherry Wilkinson (Ed.), *Communicating in classrooms*. New York: Academic Press.
Green, J.L., & Harker, J.O. (1988). *Multiple perspective analyses of classroom discourse*. Norwood, NJ: Ablex Publishing Corp.
Green, J.L., Kantor, R.M., & Rogers, T. (1990). Exploring the complexity of language and learning in classroom contexts. In B. Jones & L. Idol (Eds.), *Educational values and cognitive instruction: Implications for reform, Vol. II*. Hillsdale, NJ: Erlbaum.
Green, J.L., & Meyer, L.A. (1990). The embeddedness of reading in classroom life: Reading as a situated process. In C. Baker & A. Luke (Eds.), *The sociology of reading*. Amsterdam: Benjamins.
Green, J.L., & Wallat, C. (1979). What is an instructional context? An exploratory analysis of conversational shifts over time. In O. Garnica & M. King (Eds.), *Language, children, and society* (pp. 159–174). New York: Pergamon Press.
Green, J.L., & Wallat, C. (1981). Mapping instructional conversations—A sociolinguistic ethnography. In J.L. Green & C. Wallat (Eds.), *Ethnography and language in educational settings*. Norwood, NJ: Ablex Publishing Corp.
Gumperz, J.J. (1981). Conversational inference and classroom learning. In J.L. Green & C. Wallat (Eds.), *Ethnography and language in educational settings* (pp. 3–24). Norwood, NJ: Ablex Publishing Corp.
Gumperz, J.J. (1986). Interactional sociolinguistics on the study of schooling. In J. Cook-Gumperz (Ed.), *The social construction of literacy* (pp. 45–68). New York: Cambridge University Press.
Heath, S.B. (1982). Ethnography in education: Defining the essentials. In P. Gilmore & A.A. Glatthorn (Eds.), *Children in and out of school*. Washington, DC: Center for Applied Linguistics.
Hymes, D. (1982). What is ethnography? In P. Gilmore & A. Glatthorn (Eds.), *Children in and out of school* (pp. 21–32). Washington, DC: Center for Applied Linguistics.
Kandal, I.L. (1941). The fantasia of current education. *The American Scholar, 10*, 287.
Kantor, R. (1988). Creating school meaning in preschool curriculum. *Theory Into Practice, 29*(1), 25–35.
King, N. (1986). Recontextualizing the curriculum. *Theory Into Practice, 25*(1), 36–40.
Klein, M. (1990). Approaches to curriculum theory and practice. In J.S. Sears & J.

Marshall (Eds.), *Teaching and thinking about curriculum: Critical inquiries* (pp. 3–14).
Kliebard, H. (1987). *The struggle for the American curriculum.* New York: Routledge & Kegan Paul.
Lather, P. (1986). Issues of validity in openly ideological research: Between a rock and soft place. *Interchange, 17*(4), 63–84.
MacDonald, J. B. (1988). Curriculum, consciousness, and social change. In W. Pinar's (Ed.), *Contemporary curriculum discourses* (pp. 156–174). Scottsdale, AZ: Gorsuch Scarisbrick Publishers. 156–174.
Marshall, H. (1987). Motivational strategies of three 5th grade teachers. *Elementary School Journal, 88,* 134–50.
Marshall, H. (Ed.). (1990). *Theory into Practice, 29,* 70–140.
Marshall, H., & Weinstein, R. (1988). Beyond qualitative analysis: Reconceptualization of classroom factors contributing to the communication of teacher expectations. In J.L. Green & J.O. Harker (Eds.), *Multiple perspective analyses of classroom discourse* (pp. 249–279). Norwood, NJ: Ablex Publishing Corp.
Measor, L. (1984). Pupil perceptions of subject status. In I. Goodson & S. Ball (Eds.), *Defining the curriculum* (pp. 201–218). Philadelphia: The Falmer Press.
Peddiwell, J.A. (1939). *The saber-tooth curriculum.* New York: McGraw-Hill.
Philips, S.U. (1972). Participation structures and communicative competence: Warm Springs children in community. In V. John & D. Hymes (Eds.), *Functions of language in the classroom.* New York: Teachers College Press.
Polkinghorne, D. (1983). *Methodology for the human sciences.* Albany, NY: State University of New York Press.
Puro, P., & Bloome, D. (1987). Understanding classroom communication. *Theory Into Practice, 26,* 26–31.
Reid, W.A. (1978). *Thinking about the curriculum.* Boston: Routledge & Kegan Paul.
Ross, E.A. (1901). *Social control: A survey of the foundations of order.* New York: Macmillan.
Schubert, W. (1986). *Curriculum: Perspective, paradigm, and possibility.* New York: Macmillan.
Shor, I. (Ed.) (1987). *Freire for the classroom.* Portsmouth, NH: Heinemann.
Shor, I., & Freire, P. (1987). *A pedagogy for liberation: Dialogues on transforming education.* South Hadley, MA: Bergin & Garvey Publishers, Inc.
Shultz, J.J., Florio, S., & Erickson, F. (1982). Where's the floor? In P. Gilmore & A.A. Glatthorn (Eds.), *Children in and out of school* (pp. 88–123). Washington, DC: Center for Applied Linguistics.
Smith, B.O., Stanley, W.O., & Shores, J.H. (1957). *Fundamentals of curriculum development.* New York: World Book Company.
Snedden, D. (1921). *Sociological determination of objectives in education.* Philadelphia: J.B. Lippincott.
Spencer, H. (1910). What knowledge is of most worth? *Works* (Vol. 6). New York: D. Appleton & Company. (Original work published 1860)
Spindler, G. (1982). *Doing the ethnography of schooling.* New York: Holt, Rinehart & Winston.
Spradley, J.P. (1980). *Participant observation.* New York: Holt, Rinehart & Winston.

Taylor, P.H. (1970). *How teachers plan their courses*. London: The National Foundation for Education Research in England & Wales.

Tyler, W. (1949). *Basic principles of curriculum and instruction*. Chicago: The University of Chicago Press.

Zaharlick, A., & Green, J.L. (1991). Ethnographic research. In J. Flood, J. Jensen, D. Lapp, & J. Squire (Eds.), *Handbook of research on teaching the English language* (pp. 205–225). New York: Macmillan.

Chapter 3
Learning in Classroom Settings: Making or Breaking a Culture

Elaine Collins

North Adams State College
Education Department
North Adams, MA

Judith L. Green

University of California, Santa Barbara
Graduate School of Education

Throughout schooling, children are faced with a myriad of complex areas of learning. The most obvious task facing students is that of learning the official content of schooling. Recent research from an interactional sociolinguistic perspective[1] has shown that this task is influenced by a series of other types of learning: learning how to be students (Fernie, Kantor, & Klein, 1990); how to participate in a peer culture (Fernie, Kantor, Klein, & Elgas, 1988; Bloome & Theodorou, 1988); how to receive help from teachers (Merritt & Humphrey, 1979), and how to interpret the norms and expectation, roles and relationships, and rights and obligations of everyday life in classrooms (Green & Harker, 1982).

What has become evident from this and related research is that the ways in which daily life in classrooms is conducted in and across years of

---

[1] Interactional sociolinguistics (Gumperz, 1986) combines ethnographic research with sociolinguistic research. The ethnographic phase enables the researcher to identify speech events that are marked and/or recurrent events within the life of a social group.

schooling supports as well as constrains the opportunities students have to learn school content. Opportunities, in turn, influence the presuppositions about learning that students bring to new learning situations in subsequent school years. Thus, across time, as children learn to be particular types of students in particular classrooms, they develop expectations and presuppositions about what counts as "being a student in their local schools." Learning, therefore, is situationally defined in the ways in which teachers and students construct the patterns of classroom life in each classroom. Learning to be a student, then, is continually being accomplished and reaccomplished across years of schooling in each and every classroom.[2]

In this chapter, we examine the situated nature of being a student and of learning in classroom situations from an interactional sociolinguistic perspective. The purpose of this examination is to illustrate how patterns of life lead to particular ways of engaging in learning in classrooms. The discussion in the chapter is presented in three parts. In the first part, we explore the relationship between theory and method involved in studying classrooms as cultures and learning in the cultural context of the classroom. In the second part, we present a series of theoretical concepts that help to define the classroom as culture. Data from a fourth–fifth-grade classroom are integrated with the discussion of the theoretical concepts. In the final section, we raise questions about how to "see" learning in everyday classroom events from other perspectives as well, and discuss factors that support and/or constrain "learning."

To examine this issue, we describe life in one fourth–fifth-grade classroom as it existed with the regular classroom teacher and with a series of eight substitute teachers. The school in which this class is found is located in a largely white, high socioeconomic community. The classroom is part of a parent-choice, informal alternative program serving kindergarten through eighth grade. Our exploration focuses on a three-month period in which daily observations were made during science and social studies instruction (approximately one hour daily).[3]

What is unique about this period of life in this classroom is that it was made problematic for students by the introduction of eight substitute teachers. The introduction of the substitutes into the ordinary pattern of classroom life led to "clashes" between students and the substitutes about ways of performing classroom tasks and ways of participating in classroom

---

[2] See Heap (1991) for a theoretical discussion of situated perspective. The cumulative effect of learning patterns is similar to the notion of classroom orientation that Marshall (1987) has discussed.

[3] The description of this classroom and the findings of the classroom study are presented in Collins (1990). The data on the substitutes were not presented as part of the earlier study. The substitute data were analyzed separately for presentation at AERA and for use in the present chapter.

life through which learning was expected to occur. Thus, the entry of the substitutes into the pattern of classroom life created a "natural experiment" in which factors were made visible that support and/or constrain what counted as "learning" in this particular classroom.

STUDYING CLASSROOMS AS CULTURES: THEORY-METHOD RELATIONSHIPS

As the members of this group (a culture) engage each other in the everyday events of classroom life, they develop common knowledge (Edwards & Mercer, 1987) and patterned ways of living together (Erickson, 1986; Green, 1983a). The patterns that are constructed include ways of: (1) *perceiving* the actions, objects, and social practices of others in the group; (2) *acting and interacting* with others across time and events of everyday life in this classroom; (3) *interpreting* the actions of members of the class and artifacts of the group; and (4) *evaluating* what is accomplished within and across the everyday events of classroom life of the group (cf., Goodenough, 1981).

Viewed in this way, every classroom is a setting in which a social group constructs and reconstructs a "class culture" within a "schooling culture" (Fernie, Kantor, & Klein, 1990). Teaching and learning, therefore, are viewed as social-communicative processes that must be explored within the situations of class life in which they occur (e.g., reading groups, peer groups, whole class time). Comparisons across situations as well as across different classes are possible once the situated dimensions of the life of each of the classes or groups within classes are understood. Such comparisons provide a basis for constructing an understanding of the relationship between participating in local cultures and student learning on a more general level.

To explore the situated nature of teaching-learning processes from an interactive sociolinguistic perspective, we had to explore what members needed to know, understand, interpret, perform, and produce in order to participate in socially and culturally appropriate ways (Gumperz, 1986; Heath, 1982) in the fourth–fifth-grade classroom. In addition, to understand how the interactions among members of the class influenced meaning construction and interpretation in and across events of everyday life, we had to examine the interplay of linguistic, social, and contextual presuppositions students brought to events (cf. Gumperz, 1986). These presuppositions contributed to the conditions for learning and were reflected in the actions and interactions of individual students with other members of the class. By considering the objects or persons toward which students oriented and the types of actions they accepted as appropriate and for which they held each other accountable (Erickson & Shultz, 1981), we were able to extract the norms and expectations for participation in the everyday events of classroom life.[4]

By combining ethnography and sociolinguistics, we were able to explore: who could do and say what to (and with) whom, under what conditions, in what ways, when, where, for what purpose(s), with what outcome(s). In other words, the combination of these perspectives provided a means of examining cultural demands of group membership as they were being constructed by teachers and students in their daily interactions. Specifically, we examined factors that supported and/or constrained construction of knowledge in this class and the consequences for members (e.g., access, learning) of participating in (or failing to participate in) life in the particular classroom. Finally, by considering what happened to the patterns of life and to individual members when a substitute was present in place of the regular teacher, we were able to identify how the conditions for learning changed when the patterns of everyday life became more and more problematic for the student members of the culture.

CONCEPTUALIZING CLASSROOMS AS CULTURES

The discussion above describes the theory-method relationship for studying classroom life. In this section, some key concepts are presented that build a framework for understanding how the classroom as a culture influences what is available to be learned and what is displayed as learning in the classroom:

- classroom as setting, class as social group
- life as holistic
- experience as continuous and intertextual
- referential systems of classroom communication
- breaking the culture

These concepts are different dimensions of a holistic process. Each draws on a common essential phenomenon—the social construction of knowledge within the lifeworld of a social group. For heuristic purposes, the concepts

---

[4] For examples of how this combined approach has been used successfully in the past to describe the patterns of classroom life and requirements for culturally and socially appropriate participation see: Bloome & Theodorou, 1988; Edwards & Furlong, 1979; Emihovich, 1989; Gilmore & Glatthorn, 1982; Green & Wallat, 1981; Collins, 1990; Spindler, 1982. For examples of how this approach has been used to explore the consequences of participating in classroom life, see Bloome & Theodorou, 1988; Cochran-Smith, 1984; Cook-Gumperz, 1986; Edwards & Mercer, 1987; Fernie, Kantor, Klein, & Elgas, 1988; Philips, 1982; Green, 1983a, 1983b; Green & Harker, 1988; Weade & Green, 1989.

are presented individually. In the lifeworld of a social group, these dimensions overlap and often cooccur. To contextualize these concepts, findings from the patterns of life in the fourth–fifth-grade classroom during social studies and science units are presented.

CLASSROOMS AS SETTINGS: CLASS AS SOCIAL GROUP

Before the people who will inhabit the space enter a classroom, this space is merely a room in the social institution called school. As such, it has only potential but serves no purpose unless used by people for particular purposes (e.g., education). Once a group of people enters and affiliates over time, this room becomes a purposeful environment for a social group or "class." Viewed in this way, classroom is a setting, and class is a social group constructed by individuals—a person called "teacher," individuals called "students," and other individuals such as teacher aides or student teachers. As these individuals affiliate over time, they develop ways of working together and interacting to meet societally determined goals (i.e., curriculum goals, instructional goals; Collins & Green, 1990; Green, Kantor, & Rogers, 1991). Each class can be distinguished from other classes by exploring its goals, purposes, and opportunities reflected in the patterned ways of engaging in daily life.

Three elements of the constructed culture can be used to identify the characteristics of group membership within a particular class: roles and relationships, norms and expectations, and rights and obligations.

Roles and Relationships/Rights and Obligations

The element of roles and relationships is central to understanding the social nature of the class. Role is a social and institutional entity, not an attribution of person. People in the class can assume a variety of roles within and across the various events and activity of life in the class. These roles have traditionally been defined by society as teacher, student, aide, student teacher, administrator, and peer. These predefined roles, however, do not provide adequate description of the roles and relationships possible for members of this social group. In addition, to know that someone is defined as teacher or as student merely tells us what the official status of these individuals is within the larger institution of school. These definitions do not provide information about what "teacher," "student," and "peer" mean in this context, or what roles and relationships are possible for these institutionally defined people.

Recent work by Fernie, Kantor, and Klein (1990) shows that "teacher" and "student" are constructed definitions within the first days of school. In a longitudinal, ethnographic study of preschool, Fernie et al. (1990) found that within the first three days of school for three- and four-year-olds, the patterns of interaction between teacher and students as well as among students changed as the schooling culture (i.e., the patterns of life of teachers and students) and the peer culture (i.e., the patterns of life among students) became established. In addition, knowing that someone was a member of a particular subgroup (e.g., a group of boys, a group of Korean girls) did not provide information about the requirements and demands for performing and participating in this group.

To label the adult and children in this preschool group as teacher and students, then, is to mask the complexity of roles that were constructed through the doing of life in this group and the varying possibilities in interrole relationship. To understand the specific meaning of teacher and student in a given classroom, we must ask what roles and relationships are possible, understand the conditions under which particular members may or may not assume a role or engage in a particular relationship, and explore the consequences of assuming or failing to assume a particular role or engage in a particular relationship (e.g., learning, failure to learn, ostracism, help).

In the fourth–fifth-grade class, consideration of the roles and relationships made visible the complexity of the requirements for participating in daily life. The analysis of roles and relationships indicated that the dichotomy of the label of "teacher and student" actually masked the range of roles and relationships that were possible in this class. In the class, members (the adult and the children) assumed a variety of roles and engaged in a diverse set of relationships both within and across the activities of daily life in the Science and Social Studies units. Among the roles assumed by teacher and students were: generator of knowledge (both teacher and students), monitor of knowledge (teacher), aligner of knowledge (teacher), and facilitator of knowledge (teacher and students) (Collins, 1990).

As *generators of knowledge*, teacher and students presented a certain body of knowledge to the group and set particular conditions for learning (e.g., films, student presentations in large and small groups, student individual activities). As a *monitor of knowledge*, the teacher examined knowledge at the group level as well as surveyed individual students by asking specific questions (e.g., "How many beetles did you finish with at the end of the science unit?"). As part of the monitoring process, the teacher often redirected individual student attention during work time (e.g., "What are you doing right now?"). As an *aligner of knowledge*, the teacher brought individual student knowledge together with particular information, signaled how earlier information was to be used in this event, made links between prior knowledge and new information, and helped students plan ways of exploring the topics they had chosen. Thus, the teacher signaled an expectation that students were to position themselves in relation to their own background knowledge and the knowledge at hand (e.g., reading textbook aloud in the meeting area, discussing a particular topic in group). Finally, as *facilitators of knowledge*, the teacher and students met on a one-to-one basis on the couch. Students were expected to engage in conversations with the teacher by either asking questions or answering questions about a specific topic. Analysis of these topics indicated that the most frequent topics included requests for resources, clarification of assignment, and future directions for individual projects. At such times, personal topics could also be discussed (Collins, 1990).

The aforementioned roles and relationships were not predefined but were constructed during the interactions of teacher and student across time. This set of findings does not negate the fact that the adult in this fourth–fifth-grade class was legally and morally responsible (considering both the rights and obligations of occupying a societally defined role) for the organization and functioning of the group within the larger culture of schooling. It does, however, indicate how the adult chose to construct the patterns of interactions with children that defined a particular way of being a student in this group.

The teacher elected to establish with the children a pattern of interaction in which he diminished the historical asymmetry between the roles of teacher and students at particular points in time. In such instances, he and the children shared the roles of "facilitator and generator" of knowledge. He accomplished this by "handing over" (Edwards & Mercer, 1987) responsibility for actions and knowledge to students and by constructing expectations of shared responsibility for learning. In such instances, students often initiated the topic of discussion, asked for resources, and introduced resources they had found. Students also provided resources for other students without consultation with the "teacher" and thus assumed the role of instructor for other students for particular periods of time.

Analysis of the other roles that the teacher assumed indicated that not all of these roles were open to students (e.g., aligner, monitor). The asymmetry of responsibility (rights and obligations of the societal role of teacher) for class direction was present but not always related to "role" within a specific event. Rather, roles were constructed to serve particular purposes and to reflect particular requirements for group membership. The ways in which class roles and relationships were constructed is only one of the features of classroom life that distinguishes this class from other classes and illustrates the situated nature of classroom life.

Norms and Expectations Entail Rights and Obligations

The construction of roles and relationships was associated with the construction of norms and expectations for daily life that entailed particular rights and obligations. For example, the adult and children in this class:

established expectations for how to interact with each other within and across the events of daily life; established expectations for use of time and space; constructed norms to guide participation within and across events; established common understandings of events; developed responsibilities for being members of the class; and established particular uses of objects (e.g., computers, library books).

In this class, students were permitted options during "work time" about where (i.e., classroom, hall, back room, library), and with whom (i.e., alone, with a partner, with the teacher), they would work. They were also given options within limits about what they would study. The teacher chose the *general theme*, the interrelatedness of plants, humans, animals, and insects. He initiated a *particular theme*, the lifecycle of mealworms (insects). The students, however, were able to determine which *specific topic* they would study and observe (e.g., physiological features of mealworms, behaviors of mealworms).

The teacher, therefore, established the parameters for study and set the conditions for learning. He engaged in interactions with students in large group sessions (public knowledge construction) and held individual conferences with students (private knowledge construction). In some instances, students worked alone, and in other instances, they worked in pairs. They shared observations with others and contributed resources and information to the work of others. The patterns of life, therefore, were guided by norms and expectations that were established, checked, maintained, suspended (at times), and reestablished in the daily interactions with members of the class (Wallat & Green, 1982). These norms, as demonstrated later, guided the ordinary activity of daily life and defined ways of participating as a member of the group.

CLASSROOM LIFE IS HOLISTIC

Another key concept is the view of the life of a social group as holistic. *Holism* refers to the "seamless" nature of everyday life and to the part-whole relationship among the events of everyday life. Life is not viewed as a series of discrete bits, but as a continuous ebb and flow of activity in which some events are recurrent, others are closely related or overlapping, and still others are separate. As events in classroom life evolve, so does a social history of life of the group. This history contains both a past and a future. Some events may build on previous ones (on the same day or other days), whereas other events may be discrete and nonrecurrent (a special speaker; a party) (Green & Meyer, 1991).

Class, as a social group, does not end on a given day of the week, but at the end of a specified period of time, the end of the school year when members of the social group disband. Viewed in this way, life in the classroom is holistic for members. Class is a dynamic entity (a social group), and not merely a setting (classroom).

EXPERIENCE IS CONTINUOUS AND INTERTEXTUAL

To understand the holistic nature of classroom life and what is learned from participating in this lifeworld, we must explore the interrelated nature of classroom events and the continuity of experience in which learning is embedded (Edwards & Mercer, 1987). Continuity of experience for learning in classrooms may be viewed in different ways. One way to examine the continuity of experience is to identify cycles of activity that form the substructure of classroom life (i.e., the boundaries of the units of instruction and classroom events; Green & Meyer, 1991).

In the fourth–fifth-grade classroom, experiences were related to units of instruction that occurred across time and focused on particular curriculum areas (e.g., science, social studies). From the end of Easter vacation in March to the end of school in June, two units of instruction occurred in this class. The units were a marked part of the day and occurred after "reading" period and before recess (approximately 45 minutes).

Figure 3.1. Science and Social Studies Units: Time of Occurrence

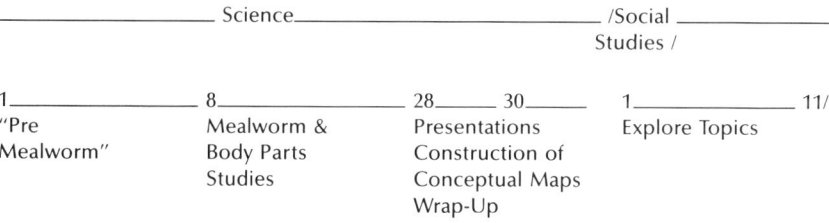

Figure 3.1 provides a graphic representation of the two units across time. As indicated in this figure, the science unit occurred across 31 days and the social studies unit across 11 days. The continuity of experience in these units was related to time spent, types of events and activity in which students engaged, and the opportunities for participation. Each unit had subevents that were interrelated. For example, the science unit was divided into four distinct phases of activity: "premealworms," mealworm and body parts studies, presentations, and wrap-up. The social studies unit had two phases: introduction of topics (settlement of Ohio for fourth graders and American Revolution for fifth graders), and discussion about how topics would be explored (e.g., book study, films, and discussions).

The units can be viewed as bounding particular types of continual experience. Within a unit, the teacher and students engaged in particular types of events that formed an "ever-expanding foundation of shared knowledge" (Edwards & Mercer, 1987, p. 5). Each phase within the unit, therefore, served a particular purpose in the construction of individual and common knowledge that culminated in presentations and construction of conceptual maps of knowledge about mealworms.[5] The "premealworm phase" established the general structure of the unit, introduced basic concepts, and established ties between this unit and previous units (basic needs of animals, humans, insects, and plants). In this way, the teacher established a continuity of experience between this unit and previous areas of study.

In the Mealworm and Body Parts Studies Phase, the teacher provided large blocks of time to establish a continuity of experience for students, and opportunities to extend and expand their prior knowledge and acquire new knowledge from the current projects. The last two phases, Presentations and Wrap-Up, provided a means for bringing common experiences to a close. Thus, the teacher used multiple ways of concluding the unit, a process that indicated to students that there were multiple ways of demonstrating knowledge about mealworms.

The social studies unit was markedly different from the science unit in the way it became structured, in requirements for participating, and in ways of constructing knowledge. For the science unit, the teacher used a whole class organization—all students participated in the same unit. In contrast, in the social studies unit, a distinction was made between fourth-grade and fifth-grade topics. This unit also involved more individual work and book-driven assignments (reading assignments, writing assignments). Although it might be argued that the difference in occurrence was due to the discipline (science vs. social studies), observation of the social studies unit through a second cycle of occurrence in the next year with another group of students revealed a unit with a structure that mirrored the science unit on mealworms in the previous year (Collins, 1990). Interviews with the teacher showed that the observed difference in the social studies unit across years was due to the lack of time at the end of the first year for completing the entire social studies unit as planned, and not to any notion of disciplinary differences. These examples suggest that continuity of experience exists within a unit of instruction in terms of the types of events and requirements that form the conditions for learning as well as across units in terms of themes.

---

[5] Conceptual maps were constructed by students. They could be drawn in any manner and were to reflect what students knew and what they saw as the relationship among elements on the map. Examples of these can be found in Collins and Green (1990). These maps were used by the teacher to examine prior knowledge as well as what each student understood as a result of participating in the opportunities to learn in given units. The mapping process often involved a discussion about the content by the teacher and the student.

Another way to view continuity of experience is as *intertextuality*. Intertextuality has been captured succinctly by Bloome (1989):

> Whenever people engage in a language event, whether it is a conversation, the reading of a book, diary writing, etc., they are engaged in intertextuality. Various conversational and written texts are being juxtaposed. Intertextuality can occur at many levels and in many ways.
>
> Juxtaposing texts, at whatever level, is not in itself sufficient for intertextuality. Intertextuality is a social construction. The juxtaposition must be interactionally recognized, acknowledged, and have social significance. In classrooms, teachers and students are continuously constructing intertextual relationships. The set of intertextual relationships they construct can be viewed as constituting a cultural ideology, a system for assigning meaning and significance to what is said and done and for socially defining participants. (pp. 1-12)

As reflected in this definition, the events of classroom life can be viewed as texts that are written by teacher and students in and through their actions and interactions (oral as well as written) (Green & Meyer, 1991; Weade & Green, 1989). Interpretations and understandings of one event serve as a basis for future events, and, at times, for the reinterpretation of past events.

In the fourth–fifth-grade classroom, classroom life involved "cycles of activity" not "lessons." Neither the teacher nor students referred to the events of classroom life as "lessons." By examining the intertextual web across events, the prior knowledge students needed to bring and brought to particular events was identified. Intertextual ties occurred across different types of interactions (e.g., Teacher–Group, Teacher–Student, Student–Student, and Student–Group). These ties helped to connect events within day, within unit, and across units, and to make visible the norms and expectations for participating in life in this class.

Intertextuality is a particular form of continuity of experience. In the fourth–fifth-grade classroom, for example, the teacher deliberately planned a series of events that built on each other to help students "learn" to write a science report. Some events were oral in nature (e.g., discussion), others were written (e.g., science notebooks), and still others involved interpretation of published texts (e.g., classroom resources). While each event appeared to have discrete boundaries, an examination of the potential relationships between and across events showed that the majority of the events in this classroom were interrelated and involved what Edwards and Mercer (1987) called an "ever-expanding foundation of shared knowledge." In addition, the ways in which the teacher constructed the conditions for learning enabled students to construct officially ever-expanding foundations of unique, individual knowledge, knowledge that was not shared by or with the group either in discussions or in presentations. Such knowledge was visible only by closely observing students as they worked on projects or interacted privately with other students.

REFERENTIAL SYSTEMS OF COMMUNICATION

The discussion of continuity of experience has focused on structural and textual issues that are visible in the life of the classroom. Another less visible but important element is the continuity of experience of communicating in daily life and of meaning construction. Edwards and Mercer (1987) capture communicative elements of continuity of experience in their notion of the establishment of shared understanding:

> There are some basic elements of the process of establishing a shared understanding, of building an ever-expanding foundation of shared knowledge which will carry the weight of future discourse (and action). These are the offering of new information, reference to existing past experience, requests for information, and tests or 'checks' on the validity of interpretations of information offered....
> By use of these elements, or mechanisms, two or more people can construct through discourse a continuity of experience which itself is greater than their individual experience. Its existence as a referential framework may become taken for granted by the participants, so that they do not strive to be as explicit as they might for an uninitiated newcomer. They may construct well, or badly. They may use this mutual knowledge to good effect, or squander it. (p. 6)

What Edwards and Mercer (1987) capture in this statement is the constructed and historical nature of the communicative life within a group.

One aspect of a communicative system that developed over time in the fourth–fifth-grade classroom was a "referential system" for the actions, objects, and events of daily life. That is, words in this culture developed specific meaning or represented particular concepts (Lakoff & Johnson, 1980). For example, the teacher and students held a particular set of meanings for library. Library was a place where students could go during science, just as they had done during previous units of instruction to obtain information about their topic and to work on projects. The students and teacher had a particular set of procedures that further defined library: Students had to ask permission; if permission was given, they had to sign out on the blackboard; and no specific limits were placed on the number of students who could go to the library at a particular point in time.

From this perspective, much of life in classrooms becomes taken for granted, invisible, and "ordinary." Outsiders to this life may *hear* particular words and *see* particular actions but may not *interpret* these in the ways that members of the social group do. In Figure 3.1, we used terms that members employed to refer to events—Mealworms & Body Part Studies, Presentations, and Wrap-Up. There was one phase that did not have an official label within this group—the "Premealworm" phase. This phase is indicated by the quotation marks around it to illustrate that this was a label we attached to this period of time within the unit. What each term means and the purpose it served cannot be defined by looking at the words, even in the context of use on a single day. These words and the purposes of these phases can be defined only within the continuity of experience of the group. Interpretation of meaning is especially problematic to outsiders since they do not "share the referential system" of members (e.g., observers, substitutes, administrators, parents).

An example of the problem of terms occurred during one of the days in which a substitute was assigned to the class. The substitute referred to the assignment as "mealie worms." The observed response of students showed that the students laughed at the substitute, snickered throughout the day about the term, and used the term in a derogatory manner. The substitute's "error" marked her as an outsider to the culture. The students' actions signaled group affiliation and set them apart from the substitute teacher in particular ways. The substitute's inadvertent error could not be anticipated, yet it had social consequences for her life with this group that could not be anticipated by her and that caused a mild disruption in the flow of life in this social group.

Similar cultural definitions were constructed for terms that designated classroom space (e.g., places in the room such as meeting area, back room, hall, work space), events (e.g., work time, presentations, class meetings), and activity (e.g., individual, partners, small group). Some of these concepts were held in common with substitutes. Others had meanings specific to the unit of instruction and group in this classroom.

In addition to a referential system for words, a system for communication develops (e.g., turn taking, topic initiation, requests for help). As Hymes (as cited in Gumperz, 1986) has argued:

> By applying the term competence to communication rather than to language as such, ethnographers of communication put forward the claim that there exists measurable regularities at the level of social structure and social interaction which are as much a matter of subconsciously internalized ability as are grammatical rules proper. Control of these regularities, they contend, is a precondition of effective communication. (p. 54)

This argument suggests that as teachers and students construct the ways of engaging in daily life, the meanings of classroom events, and the content of classroom lessons, they are also constructing a set of discourse rules for communicating. For example, in the fourth–fifth-grade classroom, norms and expectations developed for how to talk with whom, for what purpose, in what ways, under what conditions, when, where, and with what potential outcomes. In this classroom, during Mealworm and Body Parts studies, students did not have to raise their hands to receive help. They could approach the teacher or seek help from others. Norms also developed for when and about what the teacher would provide help. The teacher encouraged students to "think through" the questions and seek their own answers. He was a facilitator of resources and not the "giver" of information. The task of questioning and exploring was "handed over" to the students and supported by the teacher (Edwards & Mercer, 1987). Thus, students and teacher constructed a set of discourse conventions that guided members in their interactions across time.

BREAKING THE CULTURE: MAKING CONDITIONS FOR LEARNING VISIBLE

The discussion above has built an argument about the nature of life within a classroom. What we have argued is that life in classrooms becomes patterned as members construct a common language and set of experiences that influence their interpretations of future actions and interactions. Members of the class also develop roles and relationships, rights and obligations, and norms and expectations that influence the ways in which individual members and differing subgroups will participate and act as well as how the total class itself will conduct life.

This life can be viewed not merely as background for learning but as the conditions for "potential learning." What we argue is that the social system that is constructed and the flow of everyday life influence what opportunities members have to learn, how the opportunities will be accomplished, and what results from participating in the varying types of everyday events. Viewed in this way, participating in events does not equate with learning. It only forms a "potential condition for learning."

To further illustrate the importance of understanding the relationships of the social conditions of the group in the classroom and potentials for learning, we explore life in this classroom with the substitute teachers. By comparing the aspects of classroom life that became problematic (marked as different) when the substitutes were responsible for the class and then examining the ordinary (unmarked) ways of engaging in life when the teacher was responsible (Collins, 1990), we were able to identify factors that supported and/or constrained opportunities for learning in this classroom. What became evident is that when an outsider was responsible for classroom life, students had to shift requirements from "what was to be learned" to "how to do" school or academic tasks.

Table 3.1 presents a summary of the norms and expectations for engaging in classroom life that were problematic for students (members of the

Table 3.1. Comparison of Norms and Expectations for Life with the Teacher (T) and the Substitutes (Sub)

	Norms and Expectations	April 18	21	24	25	May 2	11	16	19	23	June 1
T	Students solve problems										
Sub	Sub uses assertive discipline			X	X				X	X	
T	T accepts student's private space										
Sub	Sub sits close in student's space							X	X	X	
T	T-S private display of knowledge										
Sub	Sub-Group public display of knowledge								X	X	
T	Collaborative assignments										
Sub	Individual assignments								X	X	
T	Answers–Not in complete sentences										
Sub	Answers in complete sentences								X	X	
T	Computer not used during "work time"										
Sub	Computer used during "work time							X	X	X	
T	Pre-lesson and lesson structure										
Sub	Pre-lesson, lesson, wrap-up structure	X	X	X					X		
T	Students need not raise hand for turn										
Sub	Students must raise hand for turn								X	X	
T	Students called ladies/gentlemen										
Sub	Students called boys/girls		X								
T	No confusion in assignments										
Sub	Confusion in assignments								X	X	X
T	No negative reinforcement										
Sub	Heads down as punishment									X	
T	No negative reinforcement										
Sub	Removal of privileges as punishment									X	
T	Student—thinks through questions										
Sub	Sub gives student answers									X	
T	Instructions given at students place										
Sub	Students move to meeting area										X
T	Mealworm changes recorded Friday										
Sub	Mealworm changes recorded Tuesday					X					
T	No "free" time										
Sub	Free time						X				X
T	Library opportunity in work time										
Sub	Library off bounds									X	
T	Work time less than 40 minutes										
Sub	Work time greater than 40 minutes							X			
T	Majority of students work in classroom										
Sub	Majority of students work elsewhere								X	X	
T	Familiar (Common) terms										
Sub	Unfamiliar terms (e.g., mealie worms)						X				

Table 3.1. Comparison of Norms and Expectations for Life with the Teacher (T) and the Substitutes (Sub)

Norms and Expectations	April 18	21	24	25	May 2	11	16	19	23	June 1
T Does not overtly record observations										
Sub Overtly records observations						X				
T Sends students to "lab"										
Sub Sends students to LD room				X						
T Students think through answers										
Sub Sub gives students answers									X	

continuing group). As indicated in this table, the eight substitutes adhered to or "broke" the norms in differing degrees. To make visible the issues raised by the "breaking" of the norms, we first consider the types of "norms" most often broken and then the patterns of actions of the individual substitutes and their impact on classroom life.

The most frequent pattern of life that was broken involved the structure of "events/lessons." Four of the eight substitutes used a three-part structure that included pre-lesson, lesson, and wrap-up phases. The teacher, on the other hand, used only a pre-lesson, lesson structure. The consequence of this change in structure is evident in the actions of students. When the substitutes told students to "put things away," the students did not attend to the request. They waited for the bell to signal the end of class and the beginning of recess. The substitutes repeated the directions multiple times but the students "cleaned-up" when the bell rang, not when requested to do so.

The students' actions might be defined as not listening, if the issues of continuity of experience and class as a culture are not considered. However, when we consider what the norms and expectations are for "doing" class with the teacher, the students' actions are understandable and even predictable. On ordinary days, with the teacher, students "wrapped-up" when the bell rang without teacher direction.

Two of the eight substitutes used assertive discipline techniques (e.g., broken record technique, names on board with warning checks). This approach makes visible individual student "misbehavior" and involves public sanctioning of negative behavior. The teacher's entire approach involved students in the acceptance of responsibility for actions, involved private conferences, and required positive interactions with others. The teacher did provide "negative" feedback about actions. His comments, however, suggested the consequences for students continuing the behavior (e.g., "you're keeping yourself from learning, your head is too good for that"). In addition, the teacher provided alternatives for students (e.g., "you can join the group or work by yourself").

The clash here reflects a difference in teachers' theories about discipline, responsibility, and authority. These two substitutes used techniques that placed the control in the teachers' hands, whereas the teacher used techniques that "handed over" the responsibility of choice of continued action to students. This clash becomes even more important when the issue of discipline is considered for the other substitute teachers. The six other substitutes did not have overt discipline problems. What may have contributed to this state of affairs is the fact that these substitutes maintained the ordinary way of engaging in classroom life. They told students what the events were and then permitted them to continue their work. Thus, these substitutes maintained the continuity of experience for the students. They did not change the norms for doing class.

An examination of Table 3.1 shows other patterns of life that were problematic. For example, three of the substitutes invaded student work space. These substitutes sat close to students and/or sat on students' desks. Although this set of actions may not appear problematic out of context, in the context of the culture of this class, these actions were problematic. The teacher provided individual space for students (a private zone of action) and interacted with them in a way that honored the existence of student space zones. The substitutes' attempts to close the distance broke the norms for physical and interactional space of this group. Observations of student reactions to this showed that the students physically withdrew from the substitutes. These substitutes may have thought they were being "friendly" or "supportive." Student actions, however, did not indicate that students perceived the actions in this manner.

The individual substitutes broke a series of individual norms and expectations. We do not argue that breaking a single norm is a problem. The issue is that norms do exist. When they are broken, they break the ordinary flow of life and bring attention to that aspect of life. This change in attention takes students away from learning and focuses them on doing. The cumulative effect of this process is that life becomes problematic for both students and substitute. The problematic nature of life can be seen clearly in two days (May 19 & 23—Friday and Monday) with one substitute. This substitute changed the discipline procedures (i.e., imposed assertive discipline), the use of space (encroachment into student space zones), ways of participating (i.e., whole group versus both whole group and individual/partners, raise hands to talk), the use of objects during work time (i.e., computers), and the ways of doing assignments (i.e., answers in whole sentences, types of assignments).

The cumulative result of these "breaks" in life was confusion, tension, and open conflict. One student crawled under a table and refused to come out. Another student closed his book and chose not to finish the daily assignment. Students who chose to participate perceived the academic tasks to be extremely difficult. Students complained that they could not do the tasks assigned. Students questioned the substitute as to why they were assigned such tasks. By the end of the substitute's second day, the principal had to intervene in the class. This is the only time that the principal became involved across the 10 days of substitutes.

On the subsequent day, the teacher returned and told the students the next day to ignore the assignment given to them by the substitute because it was not the one he had intended to assign. The students complained about having to write out answers in complete sentences. The teacher advised them to ignore the assignment and continue as usual. He told the students that this substitute would never be asked to take his class again.

What these data show is that those substitutes who intervened least in the ordinary ways of engaging in life in this classroom had little trouble, and life continued more or less as usual. The more that the substitutes intervened and brought their own theories into the classroom, the more problematic life became for students and, in turn, for the substitutes as well.

If we return to the discussion of culture presented above, we can identify factors that explain the problems facing the substitutes. Problems for the different substitutes arose because they did not share the referential system of the class, lacked the continuity of experience with the members of the group, and did not understand the ordinary patterned ways of engaging in daily life of the group. In other words, the substitutes entered an ongoing social group (a culture). They were the strangers and the students were the members of the social group.

The ways in which the substitutes entered this culture influenced the ways in which life was accomplished as well as what could be accomplished. Those substitutes who entered in ways that supported the extant culture caused few problems for the group. The substitute who attempted to impose his own way of teaching on the classroom, however, caused major frame clashes for students in terms of what to do and how to accomplish the tasks. These clashes interrupted the ordinary conditions for learning and caused problems for the group as a whole.

The discussion above explores the class as culture and raises questions about what occurs when cultural life is "broken" by the substitutes. The substitute data make visible a variety of elements that influence teaching and learning processes in the classroom that are often invisible elements of classroom life. In the final section, we revisit the previous discussion and consider factors that support and/or constrain "learning" from a cultural and communicative perspective (that of interactive sociolinguistics).

By viewing classrooms as cultures, we have defined a particular theoretical perspective to examine the conditions in which "learning" is assumed to occur. What we are attempting to show is that learning is an outcome of participation within and across the patterned events of classroom life. Within this framework, we define learning as both a group (social) and an individual process. In the final section, we take a closer look at issues involved in "seeing" and "locating" learning in classrooms.

LEARNING TO SEE LEARNING

In this chapter, we have provided both a theoretical and empirical description of the social and cultural nature of classroom life. Classroom life was defined as being marked by continuity of experience and patterned ways of engaging in everyday life. Patterns discussed include ways of using words (e.g., referential system; discourse system), and accomplishing particular events (e.g., wrap-up, library), constructing knowledge (private, public, alone, or in groups), and using time and space. The patterns, we argued, influence: the expectations people bring to new events of classroom and school life; the ways in which members of the social group interpret what is occurring; and the actions members take both within a particular event and across time and events.

Given this perspective on life in classrooms, what is meant by learning must be reconsidered. In the previous discussion, we used the term learning as if the definition was self-evident. In the remainder of this section, we reexamine the question of learning in classroom cultures. As part of this discussion, we draw on three traditions to raise questions of how learning might be defined in classrooms: cognitive anthropology, ethnomethodology, and interactive sociolinguistics.[6] These perspectives were selected as they share a concern for the study of everyday life of a group (Erickson, 1986; Green & Harker, 1988).[7]

From a cognitive anthropological perspective, the term *learning* has meaning only within a particular group. Learning is viewed as a socially constructed and situationally defined term that has meaning to members of a particular social group. For example, the very fact that the authors of articles in this volume ask questions about what constitutes learning and

---

[6] This discussion is illustrative of ways that learning might be defined. It is not inclusive. Other theoretical perspectives will raise additional questions about what counts as learning and what factors support and constrain its occurrence and its display. For discussions of factors from other perspectives see: Solsken (in press) who grounded her exploration of literacy learning at home and school in a poststructuralist perspective; Lemke (1990) who explored learning of science in classrooms from a social semiotic perspective; and Baker and Luke (1991), who brought together a group of researchers to explore reading pedagogy from a critical sociology perspective.

[7] Green and Harker (1988) have argued that constructing a multiple perspective approach is possible but requires perspectives that are conceptually compatible; that is, the perspectives share a common set of assumptions about the phenomenon being studied—for example, common views of participants as actors not subjects.

write articles on this subject marks them as members of a particular social group—educational researchers. The ways in which they ask the questions also marks them as members of subgroups (e.g., educational psychologists, sociolinguists, policy analysts). Learning, therefore, is not a term with a single definition; rather, learning can be thought of as a metaphor for a way of conceptualizing a particular type of cultural phenomenon (cf., Lakoff & Johnson, 1980).

The cognitive anthropologists would not assume that a group has a concept that educational researchers generally think of as learning. They would seek to understand whether a group has such a concept, and if so, what constitutes the concept and what terms are used by group members to refer to the concept. In addition, cognitive anthropologists would be interested in what the concept means to members of the group (cf., Goodenough, 1981; Spradley, 1980), what functions it serves, and who has access or fails to have access to the processes entailed by the term (e.g., learning).

From an ethnomethodogical perspective, the existence of the concept learning is also not assumed. However, if it is found to be relevant to the group members as part of their everyday interactions and social life, then the question that must be asked is—What counts as learning when learning counts? To examine what counts as learning, the ethnomethodologist examines for what members of a social group hold each other accountable, to what they orient, and how they accomplish learning within the ordinary events of everyday life (Baker, 1991; Heap, 1980; Paoletti, 1991). Consideration of these questions only provides part of the picture. The second aspect of interest to the ethnomethodologist is when and under what conditions does learning count to members of the group.

From an interactional sociolinguistic perspective, learning would be examined ethnographically from, for example, a cognitive (see above) or symbolic anthropological perspective (Geertz, 1983) to determine the events that count as learning events. Once the events that are marked as learning events, as opposed to other types of events, by members of the group are identified, these events are examined sociolinguistically to explore how learning is accomplished in and through the discourse of members within and across these events of everyday life (cf., Gumperz, 1986). The interactional sociolinguistic analysis might focus on one of a variety of issues: the social and communicative demands for appropriately participating in the events; the linguistic, social, and contextual presuppositions members bring to an event and use to frame their participation within the event; what is available to be learned; what knowledge is constructed; and social, linguistic, and contextual factors that support and constrain access to participation and thus learning. In addition, the question of what might be viewed as learning, or often the display of learning, would be explored.

The issues raised by the cognitive anthropological perspective are clear—determine whether or not members of the group being studied have a concept for "learning," and then, identify what members understand learning to mean and be. To illustrate the value of this way of defining learning in classrooms, we return to the fourth–fifth-grade class. Learning in this class was both personally and socially defined. Students in this class were able to explore areas of personal interest within the boundaries established by the teacher for the class. The teacher and students also defined learning together through their group interactions and through the topics that were discussed in group activity in this class. Finally, the teacher had differing personal definitions of learning—learning as information not previously known and learning as information to be shared.

These definitions are not operational definitions. They are situated definitions that served members of this class in the everyday events of classroom life. Such definitions may be problematic for researchers and other outsiders (i.e., policymakers, administrators, parents), but they are not generally problematic for most members of the class. The existence of such definitions of learning within a group does not, however, ensure that all members of the group have knowledge of the ways in which this term is being defined. Depending on the roles and relationships among members, some members may not access or construct the knowledge needed to participate appropriately in the social world of the group. In addition, given past experiences, a particular member may interpret the actions of others in ways that do not reflect an understanding of the definition held by other members of the group.[8]

The problem of seeing learning in action was faced by Collins in her initial study of social studies and science instruction in the fourth–fifth-grade class that has formed the empirical basis for this chapter. Collins (1990) was not certain what had been learned from the unit on mealworms even though she had been in the room daily since before the unit had begun (over 31 days). In interviews with the teacher, she asked questions about how he knew what the students had learned. The teacher suggested that Collins check student learning for herself rather than rely on his interpretations alone. She accepted his suggestions and constructed a 10-item test that focused on a variety of topics: physiology of mealworms and the life cycle of mealworms. The range of correct responses ranged from 7 to 10. The

---

[8] Cook-Gumperz and her colleagues (Collins, 1986; Cook-Gumperz & Michaels, 1979; Michaels, 1986, 1985) have shown that the ways students act in classrooms are often based on linguistic presuppositions they bring to an event that influences what actions they take, how they interpret the actions of others, and the assessment of the individual by others (e.g., linguistic minority students by teachers). Similar arguments have been made by Florio and Shultz (1979).

outcome of this test led Collins to conclude that on the items she valued as indicators of learning, the students had learned the content she tested.

The teacher was not surprised by these scores on the test administered by Collins. He had collected information on individual and group knowledge about mealworms during class discussion lessons, periods of monitoring of students' individual projects, one-to-one interviews with students, presentation of students to the class, and periods of observing small group projects. The problem for Collins was that while she observed and recorded life in this classroom on a daily basis, she was not a member of the class. Rather, she was a special outsider, an outsider who held a special role within this group—a researcher. She had entered the group in March and did not have access to all of the meanings that members of the group had for everyday life and did not share the history of the group prior to her point of entry. Her concern about what students had learned led to her discovery that even when you participate over time in a group, you may not always see or understand phenomena, such as learning, as members do. This problematic situation led her to ask a series of questions: When is learning? How can outsiders enter an ongoing lifeworld and see learning?

This example suggests that what an outsider sees and understands is often not what members see and understand. It also demonstrates that the short-term observations by administrators and others are always problematic for both members and for the observer. Finally, the example suggests that it may not be possible or even desirable to resolve the insider-outsider problem through observation. What is needed is a process through which members and outsiders can engage in a dialogue that generates further information about the phenomenon being studied.

If learning is problematic to see, just what do we see in classrooms when we observe teaching-learning processes. One way to explore this question is to turn to ethnomethodology and interactional sociolinguistics research to understand what is being accomplished in the face-to-face life of a social group. Heap (1980) explored what counts as reading and what contributes to our limits to certainty in assessment. In an exploration of reading in a second-grade class, he identified a series of barriers to certainty in assessing student learning. In one of the lessons he observed and analyzed, the teacher asked students to name the "little man" in the story they were reading. The students answered, Rumpelstiltskin. The teacher affirmed the answer but indicated that they did not know his name because they had not yet come to his name in the story. Heap found that the students had seen the film in the previous school year and knew the story. The teacher's actions showed that she "preferred" a different answer and did not acknowledge the prior knowledge students brought to the class.

This example demonstrates that the display of knowledge does not equate with learning. Students already knew the answer but did not display it in academically and socially expected ways. Heap's study, along with the study of making and breaking the culture described above, raises questions about whether what we see displayed can be defined as learning, or more appropriately, whether it should be defined as socially appropriate performance. This study, therefore, supports the need to ask—How do we know when and if what we are observing should be called learning or counts as learning in the group?

An example from an interactional sociolinguistic study by Weade and Green (1988) extends the questions about locating learning to include concerns about factors that must be considered as we seek to explore learning in classrooms. In an analysis of a grammar review lesson in an eighth-grade English class, Weade and Green (1988) examined how the teacher and students constructed a lesson called grammar review, and what factors supported and constrained student performance both on the test and in the review of the test. They also examined this lesson in light of prior and future lessons to identify topics and intertextual relations among lessons.

Their analysis showed that in reviewing Part I of the test, the teacher's comments indicated that the students had made two errors on items the teacher had expected them to get correct. A "puzzlement" expressed by the teacher led Green and Weade to examine the frames of reference that were potentially constructed as students worked on the test in an item-by-item manner. What they found was a structure in which the first 18 items on the test were irregular verbs. Only the last two items were regular verbs. The teacher's comments indicated that she was surprised that the students had missed these items, the regular verbs being "drown" and "raise."

Analysis of the topics the teacher emphasized in her talk about the items indicated two themes: spelling patterns of regular and irregular verbs; and meaning. The teacher indicated that irregular verbs are not formed by adding "ed" and that students needed to be careful to spell and use the correct form of the verbs. Analysis across the school year showed that spelling and meaning were recurrent themes.

If we now return to the errors the students made on "drown" and "raise," one potential interpretation can be offered. The students were to give the past and past participle for each verb. In giving the past participle for "drown" they constructed a form of the verb that did not end in "ed." In doing so, they were following the rule for forming an irregular verb. But "raise" is a regular verb, so why would students "misspell" this verb? The pattern of items on the test appears to have overridden student knowledge of verbs and led students to make the error. A similar explanation can be offered for "raise." The teacher indicated that many of the students had given the past and past participle of the verb "rise." This error can also be attributed to the format. Weade and Green argue that the structure of the test led students to anticipate an irregular verb so that when they came to regular verbs in the last two items, they acted accordingly and gave irregular forms for the given verbs. Thus, they argue, the format of the test and not student knowledge contributed to the error pattern the teacher and they observed.

The ways in which students participated and what they gave as answers were not simple reproductions of what was on their test papers. Students often attempted to renegotiate the answer they gave in the discussion phase if they had an incorrect one on their paper. An example of this can be seen in Weade and Green's analysis of this lesson. During the second phase of the review lesson, one student volunteers to answer an item that he had missed on the test. Although he does not publicly announce the earlier error, he attempts to repair the error by giving an alternative response when the teacher calls on him. His second attempt, however, is no more successful than the first. The teacher indicates this in her comments and asks students to help the student get it correct because he was still having trouble. The teacher's actions were based on her prior knowledge of the student's performance on the test and on her observations in the review lesson.

These examples indicate that learning may not be readily visible in the actions of students at particular moments. Rather, to see learning a teacher, a researcher, or other observer needs knowledge of the social and personal history of students and the class. Such knowledge requires exploration over time, understanding of local meanings, and insider knowledge of what counts.

If we now return to the fourth–fifth-grade class, we can explore one additional issue—the organization of this class involved group and individual activity. The concept of public and private knowledge was raised previously. Collins, in following individual students across time, found that individuals often displayed more knowledge about topics and themes in their individual and peer group actions than they displayed in large groups. A systematic analysis of topics across the 42 days also showed a differential pattern of information across types of events. Group events had a particular set of topics in contrast to one-to-one teacher–student conferences.

This analysis raises further questions about what counts as knowing. Both Collins (1990) and Heap (1980) challenge educators to consider the relationship between knowing something and displaying this knowledge. Several issues must be considered: What opportunities do students have to learn? What opportunities do students have to display what they know and/or have learned? When they display what they know, do we as observers see learning, or do we see socially negotiated performances and/or preferred ways of being seen by teachers and peers? These and related questions require exploration from multiple points of view. They also challenge the very base on which most of our assessment of teaching-learning processes is based. Future work needs to consider whose perspective counts, what counts, and what purpose(s) our questions and actions serve, both as teachers and as researchers.

REFERENCES

Baker, C. (1991). Literacy practices and social relations in classroom reading events. In C. Baker & A. Luke (Eds.), *Towards a critical sociology of reading pedagogy* (pp. 161–188). Philadelphia: John Benjamins.

Baker, C., & Luke, A. (Eds.). (1991). *Towards a critical sociology of reading pedagogy.* Philadelphia: John Benjamins.

Bloome, D. (1989). *The social construction of intertextuality on classroom literacy learning.* Unpublished paper presented at AERA, San Francisco.

Bloome, D., & Theodorou, E. (1988). Analyzing teacher-student and student-student discourse. In J.L. Green & J. O. Harker (Eds.), *Multiple perspective analyses of classroom discourse* (pp. 217–248). Norwood, NJ: Ablex.

Cochran-Smith, M. (1984). *The making of a reader.* Norwood, NJ: Ablex.

Collins, E. (1990). *Content as constructed: A study of two contrasting units of instruction in a 4th/5th grade class.* Unpublished doctoral dissertation, The Ohio State University, Columbus, OH.

Collins, E., & Green, J. (1990). Metaphors: The construction of a perspective. *Theory into Practice, 29*(2), 71–77.

Collins, J. (1986). Differential instruction in reading groups. In J. Cook-Gumperz (Ed.), *The social construction of literacy* (pp. 117–137). New York: Cambridge University Press.

Cook-Gumperz, J. (Ed.). (1986). *The social construction of literacy.* New York: Cambridge University Press.

Edwards, A.D., & Furlong, V.J. (1978). *The language of teaching.* London: Heinemann.

Edwards, A., & Mercer, N. (1987). *Common knowledge.* New York: Methuen.

Emihovich, C. (Ed.). (1989). *Locating learning: Ethnographic perspectives on classroom research.* Norwood, NJ: Ablex.

Erickson, F. (1986). Qualitative research. In M. Wittrock (Ed.), *The handbook of research on teaching* (3rd ed., pp. 119–161). New York: Macmillan.

Erickson, F., & Shultz, J. (1981). When is a context? Some issues and methods on the analysis of social competence. In J.L. Green & C. Wallat (Eds.), *Ethnography and language in educational settings* (pp. 147–160). Norwood, NJ: Ablex.

Fernie, D., Kantor, R., & Klein, E. (1990). *School culture and peer culture influences on adult and child roles in a preschool classroom.* Unpublished paper presented at AERA, Boston.

Fernie, D., Kantor, R., Klein, E., & Elgas, P. (1988). Becoming students and becoming ethnographers in a preschool. *Journal of Research in Early Childhood, 3*, 132–141.

Geertz, C. (1983). *Local knowledge: Further essays in interpretive anthropology.* New York: Basic Books.

Gilmore, P., & Glatthorn, A. (Eds.). (1982). *Children in and out of school*. Washington, DC: Center for Applied Linguistics.
Goodenough, W. (1981). *Culture, language, and society* (2nd ed.). Menlo Park, CA: The Benjamin/Cummings Publishing Co.
Green, J.L. (1983a). Research on teaching as a linguistic process: A state of the art. In E. Gordon (Ed.), *Review of research in education* (Vol. 10, pp. 152–252). Washington, DC: American Educational Research Association.
Green, J.L. (1983b). Exploring classroom discourse: Linguistic perspectives on teaching-learning processes. *Educational Psychologist, 18*(3), 180–199.
Green, J.L., & Harker, J.O. (1982). Gaining access to learning: Controversial, social, and cognitive demands of instructional conversation. In L.C. Wilkinson (Ed.), *Communicating in the classroom* (pp. 46–76). New York: Academic Press.
Green, J.L., & Harker, J.O. (Eds.). (1988). *Multiple perspective analyses of classroom discourse*. Norwood, NJ: Ablex.
Green, J., Kantor, R., & Rogers, T. (1991). Exploring the complexity of language and learning in the classroom. In B. Jones & L. Idol (Eds.), *Educational values and cognitive instruction: Implications for reform* (Vol. II, pp. 334–362), Hillsdale, NJ: Erlbaum.
Green, J.L., & Meyer, L.A. (1991). The embeddedness of reading in classroom life: Reading as a situated process. In C. Baker & A. Luke (Eds.), *Toward a critical sociology of reading pedagogy*. Amsterdam: Benjamins.
Green, J.L., & Wallat, C. (1981). Mapping instructional conversations. In J.L. Green & C. Wallat (Eds.), *Ethnography and language in educational settings* (pp. 161–205). Norwood, NJ: Ablex.
Gumperz, J. (1982). *Discourse strategies*. New York: Cambridge University Press.
Gumperz, J. (1986). Interactional sociolinguistics on the study of schooling. In J. Cook-Gumperz (Ed.), *The social construction of literacy* (pp. 45–68). New York: Cambridge University Press.
Heath, S. (1982). Ethnography in education: Defining the essentials. In P. Gilmore & A. Glatthorn (Eds.), *Children in and out of school* (pp. 33–55). Washington, DC: Center for Applied Linguistics.
Heap, J. (1991). A Situated perspective on what counts a reading. In C. Baker & A. Luke (Eds.), *Towards a critical sociology of reading pedagogy* (pp. 103–139). Philadelphia: John Benjamins.
Heap, J. (1980). What counts as reading: Units to certainty in assessment. *Curriculum Inquiry, 10*(3), 265–292.
Lakoff, G., & Johnson, M. (1980). *Metaphors we live by*. Chicago, IL: The University of Chicago Press.
Lemke, J. (1990). *Talking science*. Norwood, NJ: Ablex.
Marshall, H. (1987). Building a learning orientation. *Theory into Practice, 26*, 8–14.
Michaels, S. (1986). Narrative presentations: An oral presentation for literacy with first graders. In J. Cook-Gumperz (Ed.), *The social construction of literacy* (pp. 94–116). New York: Cambridge University Press.
Michaels, S., & Cook-Gumperz, J. (1979). A study of sharing time with first-grade students: Discourse narratives in the classroom. In C. Chiarello et al. (Eds.), *Proceedings of the Fifth Annual Meeting of the Berkeley Linguistics Society* (pp. 647–660). Berkeley, CA: Berkeley Linguistics Society.

Paoletti, I. (1990). *Social structure as collective imagery: Three studies in educational settings*. Unpublished dissertation, University of New England, New South Wales, Australia.

Philips, S. V. (1982). *The invisible culture: Communication in classroom and community on the Warm Springs Indian Reservation*. New York: Longman.

Solsken, J. (in press). *Literacy, gender and work at home and at school*. Norwood, NJ: Ablex.

Spindler, G. (Ed.). (1982). *Doing the ethnography of schooling: Educational anthropology in action*. New York: Holt, Rinehart & Winston.

Spradley, J. (1980). *Participant observation*. New York: Holt, Rinehart & Winston.

Wallat, C., & Green, J. (1982). Construction of social norms by teachers and children: The first year of school. In K. Borman (Ed.), *The social life of children in a changing society* (pp. 97–121), Norwood, NJ: Ablex.

Weade, R., & Green, J. (1989). Reading in the instructional context: An interactional sociolinguistic/ethnographic perspective. In C. Emihovich (Ed.), *Locating learning the curriculum: Ethnographic perspectives on classroom research* (pp. 17–56). Norwood, NJ: Ablex.

Zaharlick, A., & Green, J. (1991). Ethnographic research. In J. Flood, J. Jensen, D. Lapp, & J. Squire (Eds.), *Handbook of research on teaching the English language* (pp. 205–225), New York: Macmillan.

Chapter 4
Locating Learning in the Times and Spaces of Teaching

Ginger Weade

Associate Professor
University of Florida
Department of Instruction and Curriculum

> Teachers cannot simply transmit information to their students and assume that it will be learned. For students to understand new information, they must be given the opportunity to engage in the processes of *coming to know*—through problem solving, exploration, observation and practice—with direction and assistance from the teacher. They must become actively involved with the information they are attempting to learn, in ways that are most conducive to learning. (Reid, Forrestal, & Cook, 1989, p. 9)

The authors of this quotation are arguing for a particular view of learning—that it happens through "problem solving, exploration, observation and practice." Like Marshall (this volume), they are rejecting a transmission model of information transfer in favor of a more active role for the learner. In adopting an alternative, however, a problem becomes apparent. In order for teachers to be sure that students will learn, they are to engage them in "processes of *coming to know*...in ways that are most conducive to learning." Thus, the logic circles and the argument comes to a premature closure. The issue of what will constitute learning remains undefined. As various alternatives to a transmission model are explored, the question that must be raised is, "What will 'count' as learning?"

The ideas suggested by Reid and her colleagues are nonetheless compelling. Although they fail to articulate the assessment issue, they do begin to characterize learning as a phenomenon that occurs *in relation to* other factors. In the quotation, two models of interpersonal relationship between learners and teachers (e.g., a transmission model and an unnamed alternative) are compared to show extreme differences and to suggest that the unnamed alternative will bring about learning. However, it cannot be assumed that the transmission model will result in an absence of learning. Learning occurs in all classrooms, by all methods or by no method (Green & Weade, 1990). The question is *what* is being learned in different classrooms. Thus, as we examine particular illustrations of teaching/learning relationships, additional questions emerge to guide observation and description (e.g., "What is it that is being learned here?") or critical assessment (e.g., "What is the worth of what is being learned here?"). Whether answers to these open-ended questions are cast as processes, skills, subject matter knowledge, understandings, or simply ways of "being" in relation to others, decisions about value and relative worth need to be predicated on more adequate understandings of the complexities involved in accomplishing teaching/learning processes (cf. Chandler, this volume; Green, Kantor, & Rogers, 1991).

Unfortunately, our literature on teaching/learning processes is filled with examples of the failure to adequately define *learning*. We don't typically acknowledge the fact that learning is a tacit, elusive, and largely invisible act. As an assumed phenomenon that occurs *intra*personally (e.g., within the mind of the individual), learning is not amendable to direct observation (Bloome & Green, 1984; Weade & Evertson, 1991). Likewise, indications of learning based on some substitute or proximal sets of criteria, whether formally or nonformally assessed, frequently miss their mark (Taylor, 1989; Wexler-Sherman, Gardner, & Feldman, 1988). Theories of learning are abundant, but the bulk of these theories focus on a view of learning as a cognitive *intra*personal process. These theories rarely account for the social, interactive and *interpersonal* dimensions of learning processes (cf. Bloome & Green, 1984; Bloome & Phinney, in press). Context, if considered at all, is frequently treated as a static, isolated variable rather than as a dynamic, constructed set of conditions out of which opportunities for meaningful engagement emerge. Moreover, these theories tend to disregard the influence of learners' and teachers' historical, institutional, and cultural biographies on learning processes (Bernstein, 1990). As a consequence, evidence about how learning occurs in classrooms within the ordinary ebb and flow of classroom life, and in relation to learners', teachers', and outside observers' frames of reference, is scarce (see Bloome, 1987, 1988; Cochran-Smith, Paris, & Kahn, 1991; Kantor, 1988; Green, Weade, & Graham, 1988; Solsken, in press, for recent notable exceptions).

The primary purpose of this chapter is identify a range of elements that need to be considered in our attempts to better understand the complexities of teaching/learning processes. Data presented in what follows are taken from a study of teaching/learning processes in an innovative math/science program. Questions that guided the study, which are also explored in this chapter, include (a) how teachers' conceptions of learners and learning processes are reflected in their intentions for action and interaction in classrooms, and (b) how learning is "situated" in the times and spaces of teaching.

A secondary purpose in this chapter is to document the teaching/learning processes that evolve in an exemplary school program. Documentation is important for at least two reasons. First, the dominant tradition of research has produced an image of everyday life in classrooms that is based on observations collected across large aggregates of teachers, students, and school settings. Exemplary situations are defined as outliers, and when prescriptions for practice or policy are needed, the lessons that could be learned from them are lost to a law of averages. Theoretically at least, these oversights perpetuate a system of relation between research and practice that serves to maintain the status quo. Given recent methodological advances, illustrations of what occurs in exemplary programs can be used to more adequately inform deliberation, debate and policymaking. As Evertson and Murphy (this volume) suggest, learning will look different in a restructured school. This suggestion alone opens avenues for examining (a) a wide range of what can be seen by looking at learning, (b) what we can take to "count" as learning, and (c) what the consequences of the "counting" will imply for learners and for others concerned with the improvement of schooling.

A second reason that documentation is important is related to the selection of a criterion for inferring excellence. Measures of student learning outcomes were not collected. Rather, the program was selected for study on the basis of its reputation for excellence at community, state and, more recently, national levels.[1] Therefore, questions of the sort "but what happens to test scores?" cannot be entertained. The present case becomes one of an increasing number (see others in this volume) that begin to break a traditional precedent of need for standardized measures to validate teaching/learning effectiveness.

The remainder of this chapter is organized in two sections. First, a set of myths about teaching/learning processes is presented to reveal both a need and a focus for reexamining these processes. Selected features of a social

---

[1] Outside visitors to the program are frequent, including local and nationally syndicated news reporters, subject matter specialists, community business and industry representatives, and other researchers. The science teacher was recently named runner-up in a statewide Teacher-of-the-Year competition.

constructivist/interactional sociolinguistic perspective on the nature of everyday life in classrooms are outlined as a base for reformulating identified myths. In the second section of this chapter, representative findings from a study of math/science learning are used to illustrate the multiple points of connection that link processes of learning to processes of teaching. Finally, implications are drawn with an eye toward continuing the search for ways of uncovering additional patterns of mythology that may be lurking in our understandings of teaching/learning processes.

FINDING THE FOLKLORE OF TEACHING/LEARNINGPROCESSES: TOWARD A SOCIAL CONSTRUCTIVIST PERSPECTIVE

Recently, many teachers in the U.S. have taken on the challenges of transition into alternative forms of classroom practice. These practices, considered state-of-the-art by many, are more holistic and process oriented than those they replace, and the movement toward adoption is spreading quickly throughout North America (Bull, 1989; Pearson, 1990). The practices recommended to teachers can appear simple on the surface (e.g., use "Big Books," designate an "author's chair," and have "writing conferences"; plan long-term projects and thematic focus units), but the problems encountered in adopting innovations designed to radically alter students' opportunities for learning are also complex. Like fitting round pegs into square holes, implementation can reveal gaps between the philosophical or theoretical base that grounds a recommended practice and the ongoing system of norms, expectations, and characteristic reasons people have for doing things that exists in a local school setting.

Many teachers in transition have discovered new ways in which they function interdependently within complex systems. The changes they are seeking cannot be accomplished by simply "closing the classroom door." In some settings teachers are lauded for their efforts to initiate change—as long as they can continue to demonstrate satisfactory performance on mandated measurable outcomes. However, accountability by testing is not the only dilemma these teachers face. Parents, other teachers, building and district-level administrators, and even the students themselves demonstrate conflicting conceptions about what should occur in classrooms, and implementation of new practices can bring these conflicts to the fore (cf. Wood et al., Chapter 7, this volume). In effect, it seems that images of what "counts" as learning have not kept pace with what "counts" as state-of-the-art teaching. The dissonance that results is not yet fully understood (Edelsky, 1990; McKenna, Robinson, & Miller, 1990). Most importantly, the tensions created for students, teachers, and others who somehow manage to juggle the inherent contradictions in conflicting ideologies of classroom practice remain relatively unexplored (see Solsken, in press, for a notable exception).

Reexamination of our images of classroom practice is needed to better understand the intricate and complex relation that links processes of learning to processes of teaching.

Myths don't spring from nowhere. They are constructions of belief that follow from implicit orienting frameworks about how the world works. Myths are also typically rooted in earlier times when the beliefs they reflect were probably more functional than they are today. By definition, a belief becomes a myth when new evidence is brought forth to shake its foundation. What "counts" as evidence that is relevant and sufficient to discount a belief, however, is also open to question. Evidence, like belief, follows according to an implicit orienting framework, or theoretical perspective, that guides its identification. The challenge, then, is to make our orienting framework explicit and visible so that relevant evidence can be used to separate mythical thinking from reasoned and justifiable belief.

The identification of myths presented below is guided by a social constructivist perspective on the nature of teaching/learning processes. This perspective, grounded in principles and constructs from anthropology, educational research, linguistics, and sociology, among others, focuses on prominent features of everyday life in educational settings (e.g., classrooms, home, community), including: (a) how social and academic life is constructed and conducted through the social interaction of participants; (b) what is learned through participation; and (c) how participation influences performance and assessment of ability. Researchers guided by this perspective use analytic approaches such as discourse analysis and ethnography of communication to explore the nature of the classroom as a social system and to understand how teaching and learning are accomplished through face-to-face interactions among participants (Bloome, 1987; Green & Weade, 1987; Heap, 1985a; Lemke, 1990; Weade & Evertson, 1988). Constructs relevant to each myth are outlined in greater detail in what follows.

Myth #1: Teaching Causes Learning

Even though the general public may expect schooling to "cause" students to do certain things that they could not do before (e.g., read, write, do long division, play football, etc.), educational researchers have become increasingly dissatisfied with causal explanations of teacher effects (Schlechty, 1990). In shorthand form, the classic "equation" that an increasing number of education researchers are rejecting can be represented as:

Teaching

Learning

In general, the earliest efforts to revise this belief were to explore the reciprocal effects of students on teachers and direct vs. indirect channels of transmission (Fiedler, 1975). Simply stated, however, these explorations failed to probe the underlying assumptions of hierarchical distance and oppositional stance between teachers and learners. Although helpful in elaborating a model of reciprocal effects, new evidence was also reinforcing existing beliefs that were deeply rooted in a public press for causal explanations of teacher effects (Evertson, Weade, Green, & Crawford, 1985).

Fenstermacher (1986) provides one contribution toward reconfiguring the classic equation. He rejects a causal explanation by noting the lack of semantic equivalence in the expression "teachers teach and students learn." The argument is that one kind of thing (e.g., teaching) cannot cause another kind of thing (e.g., learning). Edited to achieve parallel structure, the expression becomes "teachers teach and students 'student,'" giving rise to the notion that what students are doing (e.g., "studenting") is a relatively unexplored capacity that students demonstrate as their teachers are teaching. In reformulating the classic equation, "studenting" serves as proxy for learning. Studenting and learning, which are also two different kinds of things, may not be causal in their relation either, but the adjustment brings the learning closer to those who are ultimately responsible for it, that is, the students (cf. Ericson & Ellett, 1990). Moreover, referring to individuals as teachers and students rather than as adults and children, or adults and learners, acknowledges the institutionally defined character of social roles taken on by actors in a social/cultural setting. Casting these roles in an active voice (e.g., the *-ing* forms) emphasizes the dynamic, fluid capacities of the individuals who carry out these roles; teachers and students do things with each other that affect each other. Revised to achieve parallel semantic structure, the classic equation becomes:

Teaching  Studenting

Nonetheless, questions remain about how the relationship between teaching and studenting leads to learning, and what forms of teaching and studenting lead to what forms of learning.

In a similar vein, Schlechty (1990) argues that a teacher's performance produces plans and subsequent actions that can be characterized as "knowledge-work." Teachers establish conditions and provide opportunities for knowledge-work in such a way that students will engage in knowledge-work. Thus, not unlike Fenstermacher's argument, both the process and outcome sides of a teaching/learning equation are represented by approximations of what social actors are doing in their respective social roles. The quality of the knowledge-work is viewed as dependent on its strategic design to meet students' needs for risk taking, achievement, and success in relation to what the school's constituencies value. Engagement in knowledge-work serves as proxy for learning, and the reformulated equation becomes:

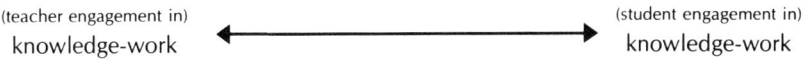

(teacher engagement in) knowledge-work ⟷ (student engagement in) knowledge-work

The assumption here is that learning is defined as engagement in knowledge-work.

Both contributions to revision of the classic cause–effect equation illustrate movement toward a social constructivist perspective in that they admit the plausibility of interaction and jointly contributing influences as central issues in defining the nature of teaching/learning processes. Nonetheless, the linear juxtaposition and oppositional stance that is based on distinctions, not similarities, between social roles is maintained. A synthesis that emphasizes the co-occurrence of teaching and learning as jointly constructed processes, yet preserves for the moment the linear format of the causal model, might be conceived as:

Teaching and studenting ⟶ participation in classroom events and activities

That is, teachers join together with students. The oppositional stance and hierarchical distance between them is reduced as they enter into processes of co-constructing classroom events and activities. Side by side, they pursue a joint, collaborative search for ways of proceeding and ways of interpreting, responding to, and making sense of the material and conceptual artifacts of their interactions. Together, they co-construct and co-investigate the questions, dilemmas, issues, and concerns that mark the substantive, topical character of these interactions. In doing so, they are co-participants and co-makers of dynamically evolving events and activities. These events, constructed through action and interaction, constitute the foundation in which all else (e.g., subject matter or topical substance) is embedded. Participation in the co-construction of these events and activities, represented here in the position of outcome, serves as proxy for learning. That is, participation supports and constrains what students (and, as co-participants, their teachers) have an opportunity to learn.

Nonetheless, a more dramatic departure from the linear format of the cause–effect equation is needed to adequately portray the full range of "participants" (e.g., both human and structural) that play their roles in co-constructing the events and activities of everyday life in classrooms. The model of teaching/learning processes depicted in Figure 4.1 is a synthesis that incorporates four "participants": the teacher, student(s), "group" (e.g., in various configurations such as whole class group, peer groups, math group, lab group, grade-level group, etc.), and the materials-in-use (e.g., reflecting a subject matter orientation, topical content, specialized language, etc.). Each "participant's" contributions are represented as one of four overlapping circles that come together to define what will occur and how it will evolve. (For a more complete description of the model, see Weade & Green, 1985.)

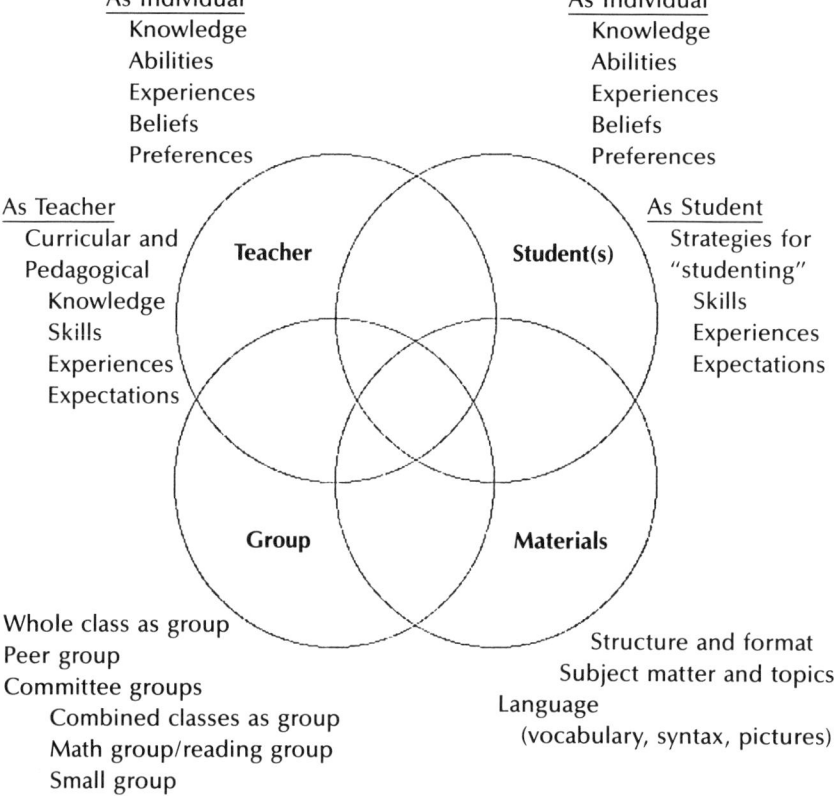

Figure 4.1. Model of lesson construction processes: The interaction of teacher, student(s), group, and materials.

From a social constructivist perspective, the classroom is viewed as a dynamic, evolving and differentiated communication environment. From their first encounters, the human participants in this environment (e.g., students *and* teacher) join together to construct and conduct the events and activities and the routines and rituals that define their daily lives. As individuals interact, they observe, monitor, and interpret the behaviors and actions of others. As patterns of events and activities evolve, participants also infer intentionality, reason, and purpose for what they are doing. They demonstrate their interpretations of what is intended, what is expected, and what is meant through their own behaviors and actions. Teachers may signal what they expect, but accomplishing an event requires cooperation and development of a jointly held perspective on what is occurring "now" and what will be needed "next." Thus, a classroom event is a "product" or outcome of these interactions (cf. Doyle, 1986; Erickson, 1986).

As the products of interaction, classroom events carry both social and academic significance (Collins & Green, Chapter 3, this volume; Doyle, 1986; Erickson, 1986). The structure and meaning of an evolving academic discourse is embedded within an evolving social structure. Simply put, the social structure mediates who can talk to (or act toward) whom, when, where, in what ways, for what purposes, under what conditions, and with what tangible or imagined outcomes. Interpretations, understandings, and academic meanings are socially constructed "in the doing" as participants contribute to and build on the contributions of others. The evolving pattern of classroom events and activities supports and constrains what will occur, what participants will have an opportunity to access (e.g., types of experiences, knowledge, meanings) (Weade & Evertson, 1988), and what abilities, understandings, and interpretations of meaning they will display for others to witness. Observations both within and across classrooms provide evidence that teachers with the same training, comparable groups of students, and the same text material do not deliver lessons in the same ways (Green, 1983; Green & Harker, 1988). Rather, there are patterns of both similarity and difference in the kinds of lesson events that get constructed and, consequently, what students have an opportunity to learn as a result— despite common materials and training (see Chandler, Chapter 2, this volume, Green, 1983, Green & Weade, 1987; Weade & Green, 1989, for a more complete elaboration of constructs underlying an interactional sociolinguistic perspective). These findings constitute evidence that refutes earlier, time-worn beliefs. The belief that teaching (with the same materials and training) causes learning (of the same concepts and skills) is a myth. Based on a social constructivist perspective, we will see more generally that it is not *just* teaching that brings about learning. Rather, opportunities for learning are embedded within a complex and dynamically evolving social context that is co-constructed by students and teacher as they affiliate over time in pursuit of instructional and curricular goals (Green et al., 1991; Lemke, 1990).

Myth # 2: Learning is Visible

Locating learning within the complex web of events and activities that make up everyday life in classrooms is like trying to catch a butterfly. The butterfly is elusive, moving erratically, flitting here and there, stopping only to start again, or so it seems. And if caught, the magic of momentum in its ordinary course is lost. So too with learning. We can only wonder where it might have gone over the years (e.g., what learners might have accomplished), had we not been so persistent in trying to "catch" it. In retrospect, what the "catch" has revealed is disappointing. It includes some of the more definable and measurable attributes of learning, usually in the form of simple, declarative "fact knowledge" that is valued less today than ever before. Accounting for learning of any higher cognitive complexity has generally eluded those who have pursued it. As Wolf, Bixby, Glenn, and Gardner (1991) suggest, one reason is that *we* have been caught in a narrow and constricted culture of testing, and that movement into a culture of assessment (e.g., one that monitors learning, but also uses assessments as occasions for social accomplishment and learning) will require dramatic changes in how we think about learning. In this case, the folklore to be abandoned is the belief that cognitive processes (of any form, type, level or sort) are observable. This belief is a myth; learning is invisible.

One way to check the validity of the assertion that learning is invisible is to go observe a group of learners, and to note the points at which learning is occurring. Obviously, such an exercise would also reveal the limits of looking. At one level, trying to observe learning helps to define a distinction between competence and performance. The latter is what we see; competence, or ability, remains invisible. That is, the patterns of behavior, talk, action, and interaction that are visible are at least partially dependent on what the learners make available for observing. What they display is public, socially mediated performance, and the dangers of inferring either competence or learning on the basis of performance are well documented (Wilkinson & Silliman, 1990).

From a social constructivist perspective, learning to see learning is learning to see "how one means," or "how another is making sense" and how various materials and tools, along with the contributions of other participants, are being used as resources for problem solving and problem posing. The meanings extracted as activity is being constructed, however, are rarely held by a single individual. They are always participatory, always shared. Meaning is part of the glue that unites individuals in relationships (cf. Tannen, 1989).

At another level, any prior knowledge we hold about the learners, the setting, or the situation will support and constrain interpretations of observed performance. In effect, such information extends the boundaries (e.g., the physical/spatial, beginning and ending boundaries, conceptual boundaries) of what can be seen; what is gathered from "out-of-bounds" enlarges the scope of patterns available for observing. In addition, observers themselves bring a frame of reference, biases, and value commitments that influence how they interpret what they see. Conclusions about what is being learned are, at best, inferences extracted from observed patterns of talk, action, and interaction that are filtered through the observer's frame of reference. It is these inferences that constitute what will "count" as learning. The exercise, however, does not end here. In a practical world, what "counts" as learning will also be mediated by the perceived consequences of the "counting." The consequences are never merely conceptual; they are also social and political (Cook-Gumperz, 1986; Solsken, in press). Even the learners will want to know who is doing the observing and for what purpose an observation is being conducted (Weade & Evertson, 1991).

When we acknowledge the fact that learning is invisible, we also add complexity to the task of understanding its relation to other factors, in particular, teaching. Although learning is publicly proclaimed to be the central purpose of schooling, an invisible construct is simply unavailable for explicit regulation or direct manipulation within the systems of schooling. A first point of recourse is to examine existing theories of learning (e.g., those based on a view of learning as an active process of acquiring increasingly complex understandings of self, others, things, and the world) in search of implications for teaching. Unfortunately, these theories generally reveal only a vague set of guidelines that are not as helpful as they could be: teachers are to facilitate, not dominate, and accommodate, not impose (Bernstein, 1990). Clearly, new directions are needed in order to complement, yet extend, the usefulness of the theory base that grounds our understandings of teaching/learning relationships.

Myth # 3: Learning Occurs in a "Teachable" Moment

Learning rarely happens all at once, yet the myth of the "teachable moment" lives on. As a colloquial expression, the "teachable moment" describes a point in time when conditions seem ripe for students to make an association between relevant elements of a problem, or when they recognize a discrepancy between new evidence and the way they had expected things to be. Partly because interpretations are being made visible through public display, resolution of dissonance seems especially near at hand. Explanations are needed and opportunities become available to extend, modify, adapt, and elaborate the reasoning that explains what is happening, what is meant and what can be understood.

The myth of the "teachable moment" is both boon and boondoggle. As boon, it captures important qualities of varying significance that take place within face-to-face interaction. All moments count, but those that mark points of progress in a long journey are looked forward to and worked toward with anticipation. For teachers, recognizing a "teachable moment" is one of the intrinsic rewards of conscientious investment in the learning potential of others, and these rewards should not be denied or dismissed as trivial. However, when the "teachable moment" is viewed as a merely serendipitous happening, or a fortuitous, random accident, the connotation is one of mythology and mysticism. Under these circumstances, students and teacher might not be purposely invested in the pursuit of curricular goals; they are just lucky. Thus, the notion of the "teachable moment" can be boondoggle.

Nonetheless, learning rarely occurs in a single moment. Neither does teaching. What is needed are ways to consider what *does not* occur in a single moment, yet simultaneously enables and enriches that moment. To describe a moment (e.g., a classroom event) by locating it within an ongoing stream of everyday life is to take what Bloome and Green (1984) refer to as a *situated perspective*. That is, the multiple layers and levels of context that give rise to a classroom event are explored in search of their relevance for better understanding the event. From a social constructivist perspective, the experiences, perceptions, and capacities that individuals have acquired elsewhere are brought forward to the point of face-to-face interaction where they help individuals define and interpret what is happening. Thus, the social, linguistic, cultural, political, and economic backgrounds of participants contribute to the formation of a context for communicating. Although participants continue to define and elaborate this context as they interact, their participation is also "situated" within the larger series of contexts that they draw upon as resources to guide interaction and interpretation of meaning. In other words, the "moment" of face-to-face interaction is constructed out of multiple "moments" brought forth from other times and other places.

"Moments" in time and space. Engaging in a search for what *doesn't* occur in a moment of face-to-face interaction requires consideration of various levels of dimensionality that can account for its evolution. Time is one of those dimensions. A "teachable moment" is dialectically embedded within various points of past, present, and future. What is occurring "now" is constituted and realized out of a prior set of conditions and historical realities, and in anticipation of what will occur "next." That is, as members of a classroom affiliate over time, they develop both a shared history and a shared set of expectations about whatever future they will spend together. They construct patterned ways of acting and interacting, perceiving the world, interpreting and evaluating what is occurring, and believing what can and will occur "next" (Green et al., 1991).

A "moment" of face-to-face interaction is also situated in physical space. In an immediate sense, the ways members of a social group utilize space can be examined as a nonverbal feature of interaction in classrooms. As teacher and students interact, they not only monitor and adjust the physical distance or closeness among themselves in relation to one another and to the materials they are using, they also interpret a multitude of proxemic, nonverbal cues that accompany what they say and do, and contribute to interpretations of meaning (Walker & Adelman, 1975).

Nonetheless, the conceivable dimensions of physical space go well beyond what is occurring in the immediate, local vicinity of the classroom. They extend into other sites of learning within the larger environments of the school and out into home and community settings. A search to locate learning cannot be satisfied by limiting investigation to what transpires in the classroom. Rather, what is being acquired in home and community settings, and how what is learned in these places supports and constrains what will occur in other sites of learning, needs to be considered. The assumption that instructional and curricular goals can be realized in the limited times and spaces of the school is an artifact of mythical thinking. Their accomplishment requires an openness and meshing of the boundaries that might otherwise segment different sites of learning, e.g., the classroom, the home and the community (cf. Bernstein, 1990; Bloome & Bailey, in press).

Figure 4.2 provides an illustration that represents both the historical and spatial dimensions of classroom life and simultaneously locates a "teachable moment" in this life (cf. Green, 1990). As indicated, a "teachable moment" is embedded within an observable event. As a point in time and space, this observed event is dynamically situated within a past and a future that are relatively immediate and local (e.g., within the same observed event). Simultaneously, however, the event is situated within more distant and far-ranging places, both inside and outside the classroom, that share selected features of similarity and difference with the observed event. For example, in joining together with students to organize an activity, a teacher might signal "the way we did this on Tuesday," such that an earlier experience shared by the group gets appropriated as a resource to facilitate what will occur today. The apparent similarities between "Tuesday's" event and "today's" event are in their social organization; differences in the academic focus of the event might be dramatic, or participants might simply be more "practiced" the second time around. Additional examples, selected on the basis of their relevance for illustrating the multiple "moments" that connect learning processes with teaching processes, are provided in what follows.

THE MULTIPLE "MOMENTS" OF TEACHING AND LEARNING: FINDINGS FROM AN ELEMENTARY MATH/SCIENCE PROGRAM

Data presented in what follows are taken from a study of teaching/learning processes that was conducted during the 1989–1990 school year and the following summer. Over the prior 7 years, two teachers had jointly defined and developed an innovative program in science and math for their

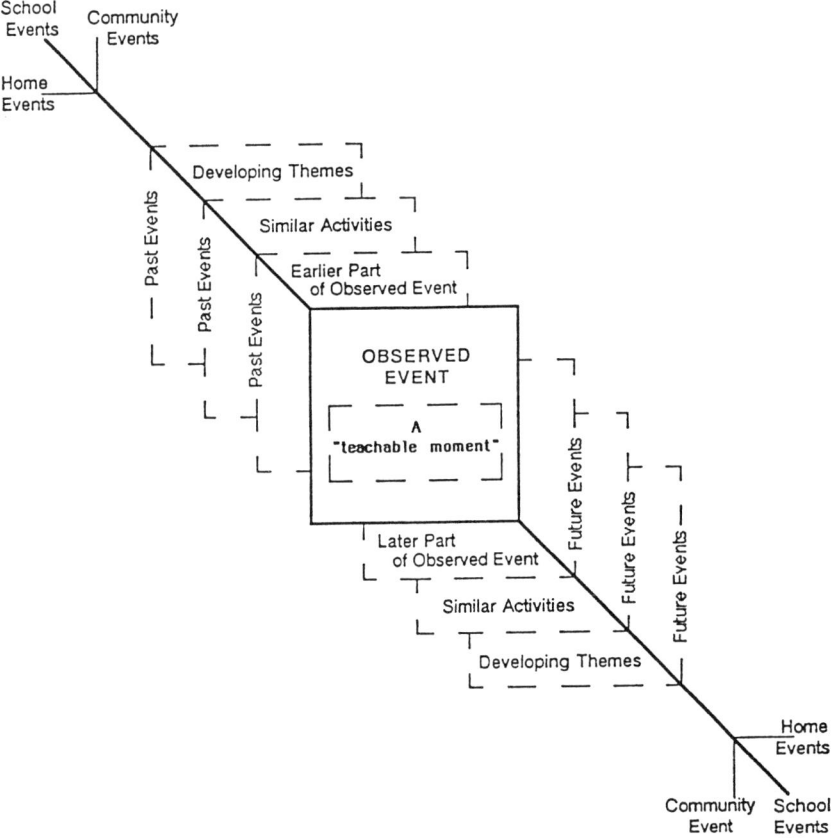

Figure 4.2. The times and spaces of a :"teachable moment."

combined classes of fourth and fifth graders. Following a type-case analytic framework (Erickson, 1986; Evertson et al., 1985), a series of bounded, recurrent events were identified to describe structural features of the program's organization. A brief sketch of these events provides an introductory "grand tour" of the program.

As illustrated in Figure 4.3, the program consists of eight thematically defined units of instruction distributed over a two-year sequence. As a new group of fourth graders enters each year, joining with a continuing group of fifth graders, they enter into an ongoing series—like jumping onto a merry-go-round that is already going around. Units carry titles that range from "Abracadabra" (on the "magic" of math and science, problem solving, and scientific processes) to "Ride a Lightwave" (on the "inner spaces" of 3-dimensional geometry and the far reaches of "outer space" as a habitat for future colonization). On some days, grade-level groups meet together for a double-length class period; on other days, they separate for single class periods in the respective subject matter classrooms.

Each unit is a "part" within the "whole" of the larger program, but each unit is also a bounded "whole" in its own right. Each unit, in turn, consists of component "parts" that share features of structural similarity and difference across units. For instance, units are typically launched with a "kick off" in which the thematic focus is introduced and expectations are set for one or more future events that will culminate the unit. During the "kick-off," which is typically marked by combined-group, double-period lessons that span 2–3 days, teachers display a projected calendar of events designed as preparation for the culminating event(s). Throughout the units, purposes and rationales are systematically "anchored" to the designated thematic focus (cf. Cognition and Technology Group, 1990). But the focus does not remain abstract. Concepts, skill learning, and problem-solving activities are strategically embedded in an action framework that is geared toward accomplishing the culminating event(s). Any given lesson in the framework is also a "whole" in its own right, but participation is simultaneously a component of multiple, larger "wholes" that are defined according to subject matter group (e.g., math or science), grade-level group, classroom space, and the evolving point in time within the designated thematic focus.

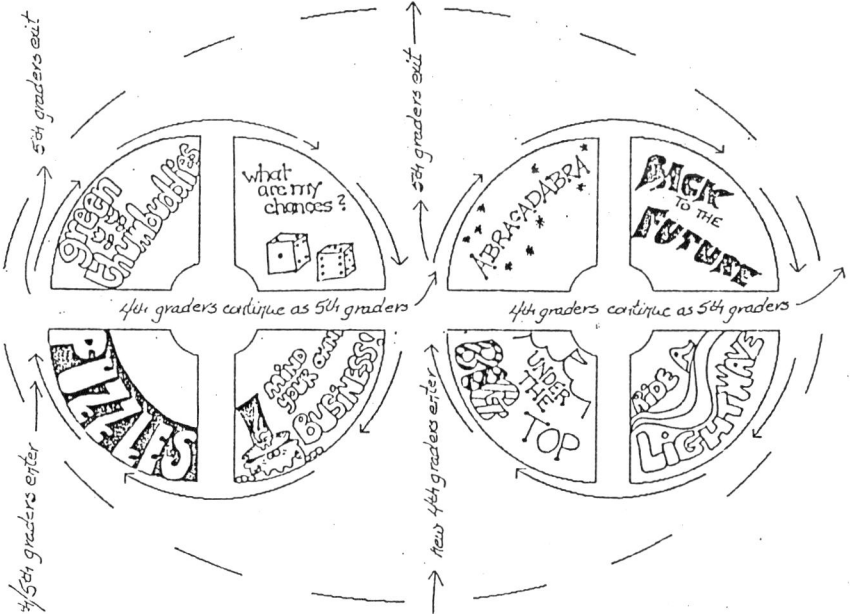

Figure 4.3. Thematic units in an integrated math/science program.

Teaching and learning are visibly situated within the variable times and spaces of a locally constructed, shared, and thematically defined social context.

Taking the broad scope of the program as background, we now turn to a series of examples that permit closer examination of classroom processes. The examples, one taken from a science lesson that is only loosely tied to the larger unit in which it is situated, and others from a combined group unit "kick off," illustrate a confluence of "moments" that connect processes of teaching with processes of learning.

"Moments" in Time and Space in a Math/Science Program

At the outset of an introductory fourth-grade science lesson on the skills of observing, the teacher distributed a peanut to each student in her class. Students were to observe their peanut and to record their observations on a paper that would be kept in their individual science folders. What happened next suggests an extreme variation across the dimensions of time and place that came together in the here-and-now of an otherwise "routine" science lesson. As they began observing their peanuts, the teacher asked the students to imagine the ways their mothers had first observed them when they were newborn infants. Amid initial, sporadic giggles, she continued to elaborate the analogy and students began talking to their peanuts and describing them as "bald headed," "wrinkled," and so forth. Together, they were appropriating an imagined scene out of a far distant past to generate involvement with each other (cf. Tannen, 1989) and with materials (e.g., the peanuts and assorted measuring devices that had been strategically placed on nearby tables), as well as engagement in the task of focused observation.

Students and teacher were also anticipating a future event that mediated the ways they carried out their observations. At the conclusion of the lesson, peanuts would be sent to the "nursery" (e.g., collected together on a paper plate) until the next day, when the "mothers" would use their recorded observations to claim their "infants." Thus, the teacher had established a criterion for students to use in judging the adequacy of their observations. At the same time, a more distant future was also being projected. The peanut lesson marked initiation of what subsequently became an established routine for science experiments: recording observations in a science folder and using what was recorded as evidence for drawing conclusions. In other words, as students and teacher moved forward over time into a sequential progression of science experiments, "today's" learning became "tomorrow's" routine. This suggests that what "counts" as learning does not remain static or fixed, and cannot be verified through random observation of isolated events. Rather, both the social and academic character of what is being learned is fluid and dynamic, and, in this case, it is embedded within a logical, sequential progression of lesson events (cf. Weade & Evertson, 1988, for illustrations of the relationship between sequential progression of evolving thematic systems, e.g., an oral "text," in classroom lessons and observed teaching effectiveness).

Additional examples, these drawn from a combined group/team teaching format, demonstrate convergence across the boundaries that separate different sites of learning (e.g., classroom, home and community) as "moments" in space. On their first encounter with the teachers at the beginning of the school year, the new fourth-grade students arrived in the classroom almost 15 minutes before fifth graders were released by their homeroom teachers. Although the delay was unanticipated, the teachers demonstrated minimal concern. They were circulating around the classroom, engaging in dialogue with each other and with individual students. As they did so, one of the teachers said, "I see a lot of faces that I don't know. I see a few that I know." She then proceeded to name individuals by last name only in a repetitive, "sing-song" rhythm: "I see a Davis face that I know; I see a Baker face that I know; I see a Wilkerson face that I know" (pseudonyms are used here). The pattern continued until several of the students in the room at that time had been named. At some points, the teacher signaled her memory of older siblings from prior years, or that she had enjoyed meeting a parent last week. Throughout, even though she appeared to know family names quite well, the teacher continued to insist that it would take a few days to learn all the names—and she added, "Because you know what? I'm the o-o-l-l-d-d-est person around here." The teacher was not merely conducting a "get acquainted" activity. She was establishing the fact that she already knew many of the students' families (but that she'd learn first names too), and that they already shared a social history in their community.

When the fifth graders finally joined, and after the teachers had briefly introduced their "Green Thumbuddie" unit (they were dressed as "old-time farmers"; "why do you suppose we're dressed this way?"), a more formal "get acquainted" activity was launched. In order to write labels on bingo cards, students first circulated to find out "something special" about each other. Then, as individuals introduced themselves by first name before the whole group, they used listening skills and memory to arrange beans on their cards. On the subsequent two days, fifth graders in small groups were assigned the task of teaching fourth graders about the rules and routines they remembered from last year (to be recorded on one large sheet of newsprint), and what was "fun to do in math and science" (for another sheet of newsprint). As the written products of this activity were subsequently displayed (by hanging from horizontal wires that spanned the room), students "reviewed," talked about, and "practiced" routines that were now remembered by fifth graders and increasingly familiar to fourth graders. Expectations for what would occur over the course of the year, both socially and academically, were being clarified throughout.

The ways participants in a classroom event interact with each other, with subject matter, and with the material artifacts of their interaction can never be predicted with certainty. Participation is always fluid, dynamic, and problematic. Whenever individuals join together in a classroom (e.g., for a reading lesson, a science experiment, the first day of school) they bring with them a mixture of social, linguistic, and culturally defined presuppositions about what will occur and what will be required to participate (Gumperz, 1986). These expectations are derived from the individuals' personal histories, a shared history of their affiliation as a group (Bloome & Bailey, in press; Green, Weade, & Graham, 1988), and as argued here, a range and progression of anticipated futures. What the interactional sociolinguistic perspective contributes is a way of viewing interactions as dynamically constructed events that are situated within in the multiple "moments" of past, present, and future that occur both inside the classroom and in other sites of learning. Consideration of these multiple "moments" enables exploration of the interpretations and expectations that individuals bring to, develop, and continue to construct by participating in classroom events, what "counts" as learning in these events, and what is accomplished by participating (Green & Harker, 1988; Weinstein, 1991).

"Moments" that Connect Teaching and Learning: Situated Intentions

To this point, our aim has been to locate learning by considering an observable classroom event as dynamically situated within other events that occur along the extended dimensions of *physical* time and space. Exploring these "moments" (e.g., past, present, future, home, school, community) reveals the multiple layers of social context that converge as participants' join together to establish conditions for learning. As members of a classroom affiliate over time, they weave these layers together in ways that support and constrain what will occur and what will be understood in the here-and-now "moments" of face-to-face interaction (Bloome & Bailey, in press). However, by limiting exploration to the physical dimensions of time and space, we run a risk of viewing teachers and students as individuals who merely cohabitate a given classroom space over a period of time. A third dimension is needed to account for the intentions that guide individuals' actions and interactions. Exploration of the "moments" along this dimension will reveal the intricate ways in which teachers' intentions are strategically situated within an ongoing stream of everyday life in classrooms.

Like learning, an individual teacher's beliefs about how students learn and what should "count" as learning, are largely invisible. In addition, any intentions a teacher may hold about what should occur in the classroom may not match what the teacher visibly signals to students about what should occur. Teachers act *as if* they hold certain beliefs about learning; and students, or outside observers, can only draw inferences on the basis of observed actions. As teachers state what they intend, they are also opening opportunities for negotiation (e.g., students may cooperate, fail to cooperate, or attempt to modify a teacher's expectations), but the beliefs that underlie a stated intention are not readily available for explicit manipulation. It is only through the teacher's departure from the immediate press of face-to-face interaction that beliefs can be articulated and examined. Moreover, the "space" that connects intention to action is a *conceptual* space, not a physical one. It is this third dimension (e.g., the dimension of situated intentions) that defines members of a classroom according to their institutionally sanctioned roles (e.g., as teacher and students, not merely individuals who happen to cohabitate a classroom), and that ultimately reveals the points of connection (e.g., the situated intentions) that link processes of teaching to processes of learning.

The dimension of situated intentions presented here is derived from a model developed by Carr and Kemmis (1983) to articulate a view of teaching as an active, inquiry process. Illustrated in Figure 4.4, the model designates four "moments" within a dynamic cycle: planning, acting, observing, and

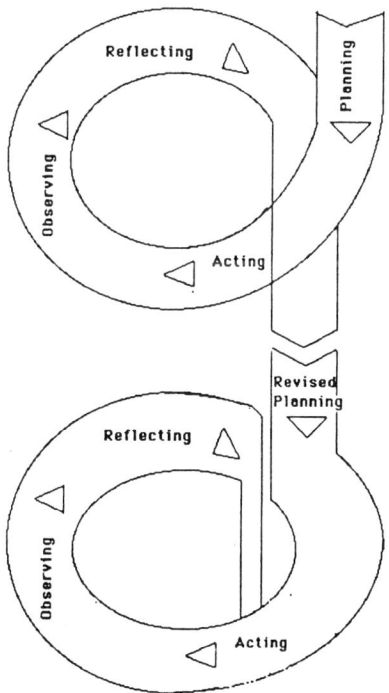

Figure 4.4. Four "moments" in a view of teaching processes (adapted from Carr & Kemmis, 1983).

reflecting. Although the model provides a useful tool or metaphor for understanding teaching processes, it does not characterize the substantive content of the process. Rather, the model provides a post hoc description of generically defined strategies that occupy various points in time and space, both within and outside the boundaries of face-to-face interaction. It does provide a framework for (a) accounting for the strategic intentions in a teacher's approach (e.g., the "moment" of planning, (b) raising questions about the focus of the teacher's observations (e.g., the "moment" of observing; is the focus on student learning?), and finally (c) adjusting or redefining intentions for subsequent plans and actions (e.g., the "moment" of reflecting).

In adopting the four strategies, a linear sequence is not prescribed. Rather, these four "moments" constitute nonreducible points in a dialectical relationship that defines processes of teaching. When a focus on learning can be assumed, the model is useful for representing the "conceptual space" that (a) connects a teacher's intentions to classroom actions and (b) links observation of and reflection on action to possibilities for adjustment and change in habitual beliefs and actions. The teacher's conception of what "counts" as learning is carried in these beliefs and, therein, a potential for relating processes of teaching as systematic, intentional action to processes of learning.

What follows is presented with two specific objectives in mind. The first is to illustrate what the teachers' plans (e.g., the "moment" of planning) reveal about their conceptions of learners and learning processes. A second objective focuses on the influence of subject matter as a dynamic and integral component of lesson construction processes (refer to Figure 4.1). Data are used to demonstrate how math and science concepts are strategically selected, integrated, and "situated" within a systematic, intentional plan of action to bring about student learning.

Locating learning in teachers' plans for action. Each summer typically brings the two teachers together for a series of 12–14 afternoons during which they either revitalize or replace one of their existing units. Thus, innovation and change are an integral part of their program's established system. Although they are responsive to district guidelines, the teachers are not content to merely "deliver" a "received" curriculum (cf. Chandler, Chapter 2, this volume). Rather, they act on an apparent need to craft their plans from the beginning by exploring the conceptual underpinnings of their respective subject matter domains in order to identify points of convergence that will support integrated instruction.

At the end of the academic year, several factors were coming together in ways that made planning data available for the present study. The teachers were voicing an interest in sharing what they do with other teachers who might wish to adopt their practices. In collaboration with the researcher, decisions were made to pursue a summer project in which they would systematically document the planning processes they use to develop and improve one of their existing thematic units. In so doing, they would be engaging in the retrospective "moments" of observation and reflection (e.g., looking back at past practice) in order to satisfy a prospective concern that improvements were needed in the selected unit (e.g., the "moment" of planning).[2] Material outcomes of the summer project would be developed with two "audiences" in mind. Plans would be implemented with students in the subsequent school year, but documentation of planning processes would yield supplementary materials for use in a statewide Teacher-of-the-Year competition in the fall. Presentation of the planning model would not replace artifacts such as lesson plans, calendars of events, and so forth that the teachers had typically used in conducting inservice workshops in the past. Rather, it would serve in tandem as background information that might enable others to see *how* as well as what is involved in their approach.

As they began their summer project, one of the challenges the teachers faced was how best to represent and display their practices to make the processes visible and accessible to others. Meeting this challenge would require a shift from the relatively private domain of their own classrooms (e.g., a context of purpose and discovery that had served these teachers well) into a more public domain that would be largely composed of anonymous others for whom teaching takes place in diverse school settings (e.g., a context of presentation aimed at helping others improve their practices; cf. Heap, 1985b). The risk they would run was one of inadvertently applying their own conceptions of practice to the diverse conditions other teacher face in their attempts to bring about learning. The design decisions that they had made about what is appropriate, what is feasible and what is best in their own setting might constitute inappropriate prescriptions for others. The problem would lie not in their plans, or in their desire to share, but in the temptation to prescribe.

Amid an array of flow charts, concept maps and gradually evolving lesson plans, the teachers articulated a series of questions that they pose to themselves, and systematically answer, as they develop a unit of instruction. Their attempt was to locate *perennial* questions, those that like the flowers in spring seem to crop up every time an occasion arises that call for systematic, intentional action.[3] The suitability of these questions in guiding other

---

[2] In formulating plans for the summer project, teachers were not enthusiastic about joining in data analysis on the research project. The dimension of situated intentions lends an interpretation to this response: to engage in the retrospective "moments" (e.g., observation and reflection; looking back at past practice) in isolation of their prospective counterparts (e.g., planning and action) was not viewed as useful (e.g., intentions would not be situated).

[3] At a midpoint in the summer project, teachers had outlined "steps" they had followed in planning. The researcher's response was to suggest that they transpose the "steps" into a set of guiding questions that other teachers might use in adopting their approach. With some skepticism, the teachers obliged. Later, audience response following the Teacher-in-of-the-Year

planning ventures on topically diverse units could be validated in future years. Table 4.1 provides a list of questions identified by the teachers.

Table 4.1. Questions used for planning a thematic unit in a 4th/5th-grade science/math classroom (Turner & Seymour, 1990).

Selecting a Theme
1. What are some high interest topics for kids? What is visible through television and newspapers?
2. What resources are available to support this theme?
3. What themes relate to several concepts we need to teach?
4. Which themes are conducive to integrating science and math?

Motivating Learners
1. How can we introduce the unit so students will be excited enough to talk about it at home?
2. What kinds of activities do kids enjoy doing? What hands-on experiences can we plan?
3. What props or costumes are available to display or to wear to arouse interest?
4. What BIG project could be the strong, culminating focus?

Integrating Math and Science
1. What possible applications of math fit into this theme?
2. What math objectives are we required to teach this year?
3. What are some possible connections for math and science?
4. What science topics relate to this theme?
5. Which science topics are most critical to the curriculum?
6. How available are the materials needed for these topics?
7. How available is information on the theme?
8. Who could provide expertise, supplies or support?

Integrating Other Subject Areas
1. What other subject areas can be integrated within this theme?
2. How can we meet the needs of creative students who may not be naturally oriented to math/science?
3. What media materials are available?
4. What community resources are available to enhance the theme (e.g., experts, field trips, equipment)?
5. What other teachers (in departmentalized subject areas) should be informed about this unit?
6. How can we involve the rest of the school?
7. How can we involve parents?

---

presentation was surprising to teachers and researcher alike. Although a high interest in lesson plans and other artifacts had been anticipated, teachers also wanted copies of the guiding questions. This response demonstrates their interest in using the questions to guide systematic development and adaptation for use in their own classrooms, not merely direct implementation.

Designing a Calendar
1. How can we fit everything within our unit time frame?
2. What is a logical sequence of activities?
3. How should we make allowances for combining groups for some activities?
4. What are the best times for special activities in the overall sequence?
5. What new connections appear as we organize the calendar?

Writing Lesson Plans
1. What format will be most helpful?
2. What directions should be given by the teacher? What dialogue should be thought about ahead of time?
3. How should we sequence the parts of an activity?
4. How do we motivate students?
5. What materials will we need?
6. What objectives will we teach?
7. How will we conclude?
8. How will we know students have met the objectives?

Logistics
1. What supplies, materials, equipment will be needed for the unit? What is available in the school? What needs to be ordered? Where will we get the money? What businesses might donate?
2. What media resources need to be ordered?
3. What letters and other papers need to be prepared in advance?
4. What resource speakers need to be contacted?
5. What parent volunteer committees do we need??
6. Where will we keep and manage equipment? Where will we display students' projects?

Content analysis of the planning document reveals a set of concerns that are presented here in a linear format. As they worked, however, the teachers noted constraints in the step-by-step appearance of what was evolving. They couldn't respond to one set of questions and then abandon that set altogether as they moved forward to the next. Rather, decisions made at one point would lead them recursively back to an earlier point for reframing and adjustment of earlier decisions. However, although the linear format belies an evolutionary progression, not a rigid, step-by-step procedure, it does reveal a progression in what these teachers considered important (e.g., in descending order from most important to less critical). In summary, the topical content of the questions ranges from an emphasis on motivation, to locating points of integration across subject matter domains, securing community support, resources, and parent involvement, and finally, to manipulation of logistical arrangements.

Surprisingly, there is no apparent question or category in the planning document that pertains to assessment of student performance during the unit. There was also no discussion of assessment or evaluation that was evident to the researcher during planning meetings. On the surface it appeared to the researcher that locating learning by exploring the "moment" of planning would be a formidable challenge. However, the omission of explicit criteria for assessing student learning is not an oversight. It simply points to a distinction between "program" (e.g., as a larger whole that defines the two-year sequence) and "unit" (e.g., one of eight component parts; assessment is one of several additional component parts). Formal evaluation for the schools' established system of grade reporting appears to be a component of program planning, not unit planning.[4]

The omission of explicit attention to issues of evaluation in the unit-planning document reflects an intentional loose coupling between participation in unit-defined classroom events and assignment of grades. This pattern suggests a deviation from traditional prescriptions that instructional planning should begin within decisions about how learning will be evaluated. It also raises questions about the wisdom of an increasingly rampant yet oversimplified belief that methods of evaluation "drive" curriculum. Emphasis in this case of unit planning is clearly and squarely allocated to designating and sequencing concepts and skills, and creating conditions for meaningful involvement in classroom events and activities—not on measuring student performance.

In the "moment" of planning, what "counts" as learning is more a matter of a prospective inquiry than a retrospective accounting. It is a search for ways of orchestrating multitask events within the ordinary ebb and flow of everyday activity that will provide opportunities for students to display actively what they are learning and what they know. Competence (e.g., the extent to which students are equal to and capable of accomplishing designated tasks) is, in fact, not a relevant question. Competence is assumed

---

[4] For example, a weekly homework assignment that spans the full course of the year constitutes 50% of the science grade. For "News and Views" (current events in science), each student receives a copy of a news article to read. They then respond to five questions (attached to the inside cover of a spiral-bound notebook) that range from designating the main point to making predictions about "next steps" in scientific investigation of the reported problem. The news article changes each week, but the five questions remain the same throughout the year. In the alternate year the assignment is called "Trivia." Students each receive a copy of designated terms or concepts; the task is to use at least five different resources (ranging from their own or others' knowledge to use of library reference materials). Like "News and Views," the topical content of "Trivia" changes weekly, but expectations for use of reference resources remain constant. Thus, students have extended opportunities for consistent practice and skill development; they "get good at" these assignments. When an announcement was made at the beginning of the school year that "Trivia" would be replaced with something else, several of the returning fifth graders responded with audible disappointment. The teacher later explained that they had enjoyed their early morning collaborations in the school's media center over "Trivia." The point of this example is twofold: to illustrate the relatively loose coupling between assessment as a component of program planning and co-occuring unit-defined activities, and (b) to show how an assessment system can also function as an extended series of occasions for motivated learning.

from the outset. In short, what "counts" as learning in the "moment" of planning resides in the prospective creation of occasions for learning (cf. Wolf et al., 1991). It is the quality and character of these occasions, subsequently constructed through interaction with students in the time and space of the classroom, that supports and/or constrains what students have an opportunity to learn, how they will display competence and performance, and how they will derive meaning out of schooling.

"Situating" subject matter within intentions for learning. The unit the teachers were developing as they documented their planning processes was entitled "Ride a Lightwave." "Space" had been chosen as a central, unifying concept that would support subject matter integration (e.g., the "inner spaces" of measurement and 3-dimensional geometry in math, and the far reaches of "outer space" in science). An action framework was achieved through a decision to simulate construction of a space colony in the science classroom. For culminating events, the students would take on roles as docents in conducting guided tours of their space colony for parents and students from other classrooms in the school. A student-produced play, "The Gathering of the Planets," would complete the bill of fare for invited guests.

A search for specific ways of integrating math and science came into play *after* decisions had been made about the thematic focus, the action plan, and ways of motivating and orienting students toward the general theme (see order of presentation in Table 4.1).[5] From the start, the teachers had confided that there were differences in their levels of accountability to district-level guidelines; the math teacher was more accountable for documentation of mastery than the science teacher. As the math teacher later revealed in her narrative account of the planning, the search for ways of integrating math and science objectives that would "fit" within the selected thematic focus became a process of discovery:

> Now at some point reality must set in for me. My dreaming must be put on hold while I remember the pace that I must keep up in order to cover all the county objectives and document mastery. Dot and I sat down together and *brainstormed* possible topics and math/science concepts that would fit under

---

[5] The "overlap chart" consisted of a hierarchically organized web of designated science and math concepts. In summary, science concepts included: cycles (life, oxygen, water, growth) solar system, energy (electrical, solar, heat, electromagnetic), force (balance, magnetic, centripical, gravitational), flight (lift, thrust, drag, gravity), gases (oxygen, hydrogen, heating and cooling, molecular movement), light and sound waves, and environmental control of space (climate, waste, recycling). Math concepts included: geometry (plane and solid figures, figure congruency, lines of symmetry, segments, parallel and perpendicular lines, graph coordinates, radius and diameter), metric measurement (conversions, estimation of liquid measure and weight), and decimals (identifying place values, rounding, performing operations, applying to real problems).

our SPACE theme. Dot began asking me questions such as "Can they measure in metrics yet? Have you taught them multiplying with decimals?".... and through this questioning, we made some exciting discoveries. There were many mathematical skills that were going to be *necessary* to construct the SPACE COLONY. What an incredible opportunity for me to teach metrics and decimals—when they will be using them to solve REAL PROBLEMS!!! We both agreed that this was a perfect time of year, through this unit, for me to teach metric measurement, decimals and geometry. We decided to go our separate ways to develop a list of more specific objectives that would help us to make more connections.... When we sat down after making individual math and science objectives, the very best part of our *collaboration* occurred.... We made a math/science overlap chart and we were able to find an application for almost every single math objective through a science concept or activity.... My reasons for teaching students these math skills were sitting fifty feet across the courtyard—right there in the SPACE COLONY! (Emphasis in original)

For the math teacher, the discoveries were not about which concepts should be taught. Freedom to choose had already been limited by decisions made at district levels, and compliance was mandated. Rather, the discoveries involved identification of strategically situated purposes and rationales for learning various math skills—"to solve REAL PROBLEMS!!!" Quite simply, the question of what should "count" as mathematics learning seemed to be a matter of "when" and "for what reason" math should "count." In the "moment" of planning, math concepts were being strategically situated in time, in space, and in the teachers' shared intentions for student learning.

As math and science were being integrated, one aspect of the teachers' planning processes was initially confusing to the researcher. Although negotiations about what could be done appeared to be open, and each teacher was highly responsive to the concerns and interests of her partner in the collaboration, the balance of power in decision making seemed to be uneven. Science typically took the lead and apparent control of the substantive agenda. Math, in contrast, was forever in search of "connections." At one level, math was responsive and compliant in relation to district requirements; at another level, its purposes were always being imported from elsewhere—"50 feet across the courtyard." Surface appearances suggested an uneven reciprocity in the planning relationship, but further exploration raised questions about why equal reciprocity should have been assumed in the first place.

Recourse to the literature on teaching/learning processes suggested that the observed pattern of relationship between the two teachers could not be interpreted on a solely interpersonal base. Rather, interpretation required recognition of the role played by the teachers' respective subject matter domains as well as their shared expertise in establishing conditions through which students could gain access to subject matter knowledge. A compelling argument about differences in subject matter areas, in particular the relationships between mathematics and science, is provided by Lemke (1990):

> Most people who use mathematics, even research scientists, statisticians, actuaries, and systems programmers know very little of what is called "abstract mathematics" or "pure mathematics," that is, the theoretical part. They get along very well without it because their uses of mathematics take place within well-known mathematical models and their motivations for performing manipulations are not pure mathematical ones but physical, chemical or statistical reasons. Asked why they performed a particular operation, they will give you a scientific answer, not a mathematical one. For most of us, mathematics is a tool to be used without understanding why it works, as we use most of our modern technology with only a vague understanding of how it does its tricks.... As it stands now, teaching abstract mathematics outside the context of familiar, concrete applications is an extreme... error.... it makes unfamiliar thematic patterns all the harder for students to learn, and the students are then labeled as stupid when they fail to learn them. (p. 165)

If math is a "tool" used in service to science, the math teacher's search for "connections" in the science curriculum is clearly warranted. As she subsequently explained, the "struggle" of the search reaps its own rewards—it leads to "discovering *even more* connections" (emphasis in original).

Science, nonetheless, is also a "tool." Its use cannot be justified as service to science (e.g., to itself; theoretical science). Rather, as illustrated in this case of subject matter integration, math and science are both viewed as "tools" used in service to larger purposes. These larger purposes involve the identification and movement toward resolution of human, social problems. For "Ride a Lightwave," the social problem being explored by students and teachers alike is, at root, a practical and a perennial one: Should we colonize outer space? In terms of the way the teachers orchestrated their plans, this question encompassed others, including: How can we think about what it would be like to live in a space colony?, and What systems of action will help us find out? A review of other units in the series of eight that make up the teachers' program reveals a similar pattern of situated intentions in some of the units (see Figure 4.2). For instance, although landscape architecture was billed as the thematic focus in "Green Thumbuddies," its social relevance carried a wider scope. Students walked an acre, tested soil, tended roses, and viewed "gardens of the world" (among other activities) as they prepared to draw plans and elevations to be used in landscaping an area of the school campus. At the same time, they also investigated the social-scientific problems of natural resource depletion and the pressing need for reforestation in the state of Florida.

As suggested earlier in this chapter, the established system of program improvement that these two teachers are perfecting is born out of a discontent with merely "delivering" a curriculum that has been "received" from somewhere else (cf. Weade, 1987). By exploring the conceptual underpinnings of their respective subject matter domains, they are searching for connections that will invite responsiveness among their students. The teachers' interests in motivation are not simplistic ones. And they don't merely organize content. Rather, they are disorganizing and reorganizing what will be taken by their students to count as common sense and refined reasoning—or in other words, what will "count" as *worth* learning, not only in the classroom but at the multiple levels of school, home and community as well. The regard for subject matter as "tools" in service to larger social purposes reveals a critically important aspect of the teachers' conceptions of learning and learning processes. That is, learners are viewed as active, socially responsive, and socially responsible reasoners whose engagement in learning processes, construed as participation in meaningful action, will yield inevitable consequences. These consequences are not simply cognitive, nor merely conceptual. Rather, they encompass a range of possibilities for further social action that are, at once, both local and global and both immediate and longer range. As teachers plan the events and activities that will constitute the fabric of life in their classrooms, their intentions are "situated" at the confluence of their understandings of student(s), subject matter, and social group (see Figure 4.1).

CONCLUSION

In this chapter, a series of implicit beliefs that underlie conventional thinking about the relationship between processes of learning and processes of teaching have been explored. These beliefs, that teaching causes learning, that learning is visible, and that learning occurs in a "teachable moment," have been cast as myths. They typify the folk wisdom that permeates both our understandings of teaching/learning processes and various systems of action that are currently directed toward the restructuring and improvement of schooling. They also suggest points of focus for reexamining beliefs in the light of new evidence about the nature of what occurs in classrooms as well as engaging in a continuing search for understanding what can and should "count" as learning.

A range of elements necessary for exploring the points of connection between processes of learning and processes of teaching has also been proposed in this chapter. These elements, which add up to 10 "moments" located in the times and spaces of a teaching/learning relationship, include: the past, the present, the future, home, classroom/school, community, planning, acting/interacting, observing and reflecting. Taken together, these "moments" constitute a dialectic of factors that support and constrain what students have an opportunity to learn in classrooms.

Nonetheless, consideration of 10 "moments" in their raw, abstract form will contribute little to the improvement of schooling. These "moments" take on meaning only in the contexts in which they are observed. Used as markers in tracing an outline, like connecting dots to reveal an image, they can be helpful in charting the evolution of a teaching/learning process. Understanding the process is a matter of examining how it is evolving in the ordinary ebb and flow of everyday life in classrooms, and how its "moments" are constituted in the lifeworlds of its participants. As we observe, the questions that need to be raised revolve around (a) where does what we see fit, either as myth or as reasoned action, in the lifeworlds of participants?, and (b) how can new evidence be introduced into that world so that it can be brought to bear on the ways decisions are being made and actions taken?

Examples drawn from an observational study of math/science learning in an exemplary school program have been used in this chapter to illustrate ways of locating 10 "moments" in a teaching/learning process. As the two teachers involved in the study were collating what they had developed in their summer project, they did some final editing. To make a title for the set of guiding questions that documented their planning processes, displayed here in Table 4.1, they superimposed an overarching question. Their question captures a central dilemma:

> Do we trust our students and ourselves to learn together about subjects and concepts where our prior knowledge is limited?

The issues of trust and of learning together with students by actively pursuing unknown territories and untested assumptions are keys. They unlock a range of possibilities. The question asserts a learning orientation (Marshall, Chapter 1, this volume) in which everybody is teaching and everybody is learning. It acknowledges an open-endedness within an established system of action and interaction that takes full advantage of opportunities for continuing dialogue and inquiry, and champions the potential for moving beyond the status quo in classrooms and in schools. The question also leads us back to the quotation that opened this chapter. There we can identify one additional myth—the myth of the transmission model. As a belief that is deeply rooted in our understandings of teaching/learning processes, and what "counts" as learning, the transmission model has outlived its usefulness. Time is well nigh to make it part of our history, not our future.

REFERENCES

Bernstein, B. (1990). *The structuring of pedagogic discourse.* London: Routledge.
Bloome, D. (1987). Reading as a social process in a middle school classroom. In D. Bloome (Ed.), *Literacy and schooling* (pp. 123-149). Norwood, NJ: Ablex Publishing Corp.
Bloome, D. (1988). *Literacy and classrooms.* Norwood, NJ: Ablex Publishing Corp.
Bloome, D., & Bailey, F. (in press). From linguistics and education, a direction for research on language and literacy: Events, particularity, intertexuality, history, material, dialectics. In R. Beach, J. Green, M. Kamil, & R. T. Shanahan (Eds.), *Multiple perspective approaches to the study of literacy.* Bloomington, IL: National Council for Research in English.
Bloome, D., & Green, J.L. (1984). Reading as an event: Situated perspectives. In R. Spiro (Ed.), *Reading research in the 1990's.* Hillsdale, NJ: Erlbaum.
Bloome, D., & Phinney, M.Y. (in press). Classroom writing as social events: Directions for conceptualizing related intellectual processes and development. In N. Spivey & R. Tierney (Eds.), *Writing, learning and knowing: Social and cognitive perspectives.*
Bull, G. (1989). *Reflective teaching.* Carlton South Victoria, Australia: Australian Reading Association.
Carr, W., & Kemmis, S. (1983). *Becoming critical: Knowing through action research.* Victoria, Australia: Deakin University Press.
Cochran-Smith, M., Paris, C.L., & Kahn, J.L. (1991). *Learning to write differently: Beginning writers and word processing.* Norwood, NJ: Ablex Publishing Corp.
Cognition and Technology Group at Vanderbilt. (1990). Anchored instruction and its relationship to situated cognition. *Educational Researcher, 19*(6), 2-10.
Cook-Gumperz, J. (1986). *The social construction of literacy.* New York: Cambridge University Press.
Doyle, W. (1986). Classroom organization and management. In M.C. Wittrock (Ed.), *Handbook of research on teaching* (3rd ed., pp. 392-431). New York: Macmillan.
Edelsky, C. (1990). Whose agenda is this anyway? A response to McKenna, Robinson, and Miller. *Educational Researcher, 19*(8), 7-11.
Erickson, F. (1986). Tasks in times: Objects of study in a natural history of teaching. In K.K. Zumwalt (Ed.), *Improving teaching* (pp. 131-148). Alexandria, VA: Association for Supervision and Curriculum Development.
Ericson, D. P., & Ellett, F.S. (1990). Taking student responsibility seriously. *Educational Researcher, 19*(9), 3-10.
Evertson, C.M., Weade, R., Green, J.L., & Crawford, J (1985). *Effective classroom management and instruction: An exploration of models* (Final Report, NIE G-83-0063). Washington, DC: National Institute of Education.
Fiedler, M. (1975). Bidirectionality of influence in classroom interaction. *Journal of Educational Psychology, 67,* 735-744.
Fenstermacher, G. (1986). Philosophy of research on teaching: Three aspects. In M.C. Wittrock (Ed.) *Handbook of research on teaching* (3rd ed., pp. 37-49). New York: Macmillan.

Green, J.L. (1990). Reading as a social process. In J. Howell, H. McNamara, & M. Clough (Eds.), *Social contexts of literacy* (pp. 104-123). Canberra, Australia: ACT Department of Education.

Green, J.L. (1983). Research on teaching as a linguistic process. A state of the art. In E. Gordon (Ed.), *Review of reserach in education* (pp. 151-252). Washington, DC: American Educational Research Association.

Green, J.L., & Harker, J.O. (Eds.). (1988). *Multiple perspective analysis of classroom discourse.* Norwood, NJ: Ablex Publishing Corp.

Green, J.L., Kantor, R., & Rogers, T. (1991). Exploring the complexity of language and learning in the classroom. In L. Idol & B.F. Jones (Eds.), *Educational values and cognitive instruction: Implications for reform, Volume 2*. Hillsdale, NJ: Erlbaum.

Green, J.L., & Weade, G. (1990). The social construction of classroom reading: Beyond method. *Australian Journal of Reading, 13*(4), 326-336.

Green, J.L., & Weade, R. (1987). In search of meaning: A sociolinguistic perspective on lesson construction and reading. In D. Bloome (Ed.) *Literacy and schooling* (pp. 3-34). Norwood, NJ: Ablex Publishing Corp.

Green, J.L., Weade, R., & Graham, K. (1988). Lesson construction and student participation. In J.L. Green & J.O. Harker (Eds.), *Multiple perspective analyses of classroom discourse* (pp. 11-47). Norwood, NJ: Ablex Publishing Corp.

Gumperz, J. (1986). Interactional sociolinguistics in the study of schooling. In J. Cook-Gumperz (Ed.), *The social construction of literacy* (pp. 45-68). Cambridge, UK: Cambridge University Press.

Heap, J. (1985a). Discourse in the production of classroom knowledge: Reading lessons. *Curriculum Inquiry, 15*(3), 245-279.

Heap, J. (1985b, April). *Getting there from here, in ethnomethodological research: Steps and maxims.* Address given at the annual meeting of the International Reading Association, New Orleans, LA.

Kantor, R. (1988). Creating school meaning in the preschool curriculum. *Theory into Practice, 27* (1), 25-35.

Lemke, J. (1990). *Talking science: Language, learning and values.* Norwood, NJ: Ablex Publishing Corp.

McKenna, M.C., Robinson, R.D., & Miller, J.W. (1990). Whole language: A research agenda for the nineties. *Educational Researcher, 19*(8), 3-6.

Pearson, P.D. (1990). Reading the whole-language movement. *Elementary School Journal, 90*(2), 231-242.

Reid, J., Forrestal, P., & Cook, J. (1989). *Small group learning in the classroom.* Scarborough, Western Australia: Chalkface Press.

Schlechty, P. (1990). *Schools for the twenty-first century: Leadership imperatives for educational reform.* San Francisco: Jossey-Bass.

Solsken, J. (in press). *Literacy, gender, and work: In families and in school.* Norwood, NJ: Ablex Publishing Corp.

Tannen, D. (1989). *Talking voices: Repetition, dialogue, and imagery in conversational discourse.* Cambridge, MA: Cambridge University Press.

Taylor, D. (1989). Toward a unified theory of literacy learning and instructional practices. *Phi Delta Kappan, 71*(3), 184-193.

Turner, D., & Seymour, B. (1990, October). *Ride a Lightwave*. Presentation at the annual meeting of the Florida Association for the Gifted.

Walker, R., & Adelman, C. (1975). *Classroom observation:* London: Methuen.

Weade, G., & Evertson, C.M. (1991). On what can be learned by observing teaching. *Theory into Practice, 30*(1), 37-45.

Weade, R. (1987). Curriculum'n'instruction: The construction of meaning. *Theory into Practice, 26*(1), 15-25.

Weade, R., & Evertson, C.M. (1988). The construction of lessons in effective and less effective classrooms. *Teaching and Teacher Education, 4*(3), 189-213.

Weade, R. & Green, J.L. (1985). Talking to learn: Social and academic requirements for classroom participation. *Peabody Journal of Education, 62*(3), 6-19.

Weade, R., & Green, J. (1989). Reading in the instructional context: An interactional sociolinguistic/ethnographic perspective. In C. Emihovich (Ed.), *Locating learning: Ethnographic perspectives on classroom research* (pp. 17-55). Norwood, NJ: Ablex Publishing Corp.

Wexler-Sherman, C., Gardner, H., & Feldman, D. (1988). A pluralistic view of early assessment: The Project Spectrum approach. *Theory into Practice, 27*(1), 77-83.

Weinstein, C.S. (1991). The classroom as a social context for learning. *Annual Review of Psychology, 42,* 493-525.

Wilkinson, L.C., & Silliman, E. (1990). Sociolinguistic analysis: Nonformal assessment of children's language and literacy skills. *Linguistics and Education, 2*(2), 109-125.

Wolf, D., Bixby, J., Glenn, J., III, & Gardner, H. (1991). To use their minds well: Investigating new forms of student assessment. *Review of Research in Education, 17,* 31-74.

Chapter 5
Constructing Literacy in Classrooms: Literate Action as Social Accomplishment

**Santa Barbara Classroom Discourse Group
(J. Green, C. Dixon, L. Lin, A. Floriani, M. Bradley
with
S. Paxton, C. Mattern & H. Bergamo, Columbus, OH)[1]**

The study of literacy and literacy learning in classrooms is generally viewed as the study of reading and writing processes that individuals use as they engage in interpreting or producing text. Recently, however, other views of literacy have been proposed in which literacy is conceptualized as a social accomplishment of a group (Baker & Luke, 1991; Bloome, 1986a, 1986c).

---

[1] Authorship within the Santa Barbara Classroom Discourse Group reflects co-authorship. S. Paxton and C. Mattern are the teachers of the class that was the site for the analysis of literacy construction that is reported in this study. H. Bergamo is one of the teacher leaders who developed the professional development project. She participated in the data analysis process for this chapter. J. Green was a participant in the larger professional development project. She was brought into the teacher-leader group to serve as critic-consultant on the process from the first year and participated in the project over a three-year period. She was present throughout the entire five weeks of this program. She participated in the project for five hours per day, five days a week, for the five weeks of the project. In addition, she taught two classes after school, for those teachers who wanted to work on action research and observation of teaching-learning processes. She continues to be in contact with members of the project and with the English teacher. This contact made possible additional interviews as questions arose in this analysis.

From this perspective, in every classroom, teachers and students are constructing particular models of literacy and particular understandings of what is involved in learning how to be literate (Cochran-Smith, 1984; Golden, 1988, 1990). That is, as teachers and students construct the norms and expectations, and roles and relationships that frame how they will engage in everyday life in classrooms, they are also defining what counts as literacy and literate action[2] in the local events of classroom life (Weade & Green, 1989).

Viewed in this way, literacy is a socially constructed phenomenon that is situationally defined and redefined within and across differing groups, including reading groups, classrooms, schools, communities, and professional groups (e.g., educators, lawyers, doctors, administrators, and plumbers). What counts as literacy in any group is visible in the actions members take, what they orient to, what they hold each other accountable for, what they accept or reject as preferred responses of others, and how they engage with text (Green & Harker, 1982; Heap, 1980, 1991).

Literacy, then, is not a generic process located solely within the heads of individuals, or a process that is the same for all people in all situations (cf., Baker & Luke, 1991; Bloome, 1986c; Cook-Gumperz, 1986; Street, 1984). Nor is literacy a state of being that one arrives at like a state of grace. Rather, it is a dynamic process in which what literate action means is continually being constructed and reconstructed by individuals as they become members of new social groups (e.g., classes, businesses, social groups, professions). Being a member of a class, then, means understanding and constructing literate actions that mark membership in that class (Chandler, Chapter 2, this volume), and that mark individuals as members of a particular group or subgroup (i.e., one person reads like a member of the top reading group and another like a member of the low reading group) (Allington, 1984; Collins, 1983, 1986). From this perspective, we must talk of literacies and not literacy, for no one definition can capture the range of

---

[2] The term *action* is used in this chapter rather than behavior. Action is viewed as an intentional act of a person who is participating in social interaction (Spradley, 1980). Social interaction is defined as goal-directed and participation is viewed as intentional. The intention of the act is observed by considering the actions and interactions of participants, by noting how they are orienting to each other and to objects within the interaction, and by considering on a post hoc basis what they accepted, how they responded, and to what they held each other accountable. Through a post hoc analysis of the acts of participants, we are able to examine the topics that are constructed, and identify norms and expectations for participation, roles and relationships, and rights and obligations of group membership in local events. In addition, we can examine the ways in which the norms and expectations are signaled by participants, and constructed and reconstructed through their interactions. From this view, intentional acts are viewed through performance and not through participants' perceptions of what they meant. This view of intention is akin to the notion of preferred ways of being visible in the actions of members of a group within a local event.

occurrence in everyday life in classrooms, the multiplicity of demands, or the ways of engaging in literacy within and across groups.

Bloome (1986b) captures the complexity and dynamic nature of this process succinctly:

> although members of a community have a shared framework for the use of reading and writing, this does not mean that the use of reading and writing within any specific situation is static or predetermined. As people come together and interact, they must establish a shared communicative context... Communicative contexts are established by how people act and react to each other's communicative efforts... Literacy is not monolithic; rather, it depends on the community for its definition... within a community the nature of literacy is not static... people are continuously building and rebuilding literacy.... On one hand, the nature of literacy has continuity across a community, while on the other, it is continuously evolving and situation-specific. (p. 72)

To understand what literacy is and how students learn to be literate in a particular classroom, we must examine how members of a particular social group (a culture)[3] construct and reconstruct literacy as part of everyday life. Literacy, therefore, involves more than reading and writing processes, it also involves the communicative processes through which it is constructed.

In this chapter, we show how adopting a social construction perspective on literacy can make visible factors involved in learning to be literate in classrooms that support the construction of student-centered models of literacy learning. As part of this discussion, we will examine two interrelated issues: (1) how a common perspective on literacy is constructed by teachers and students as part of the everyday activity of classroom life; and (2) what factors support and constrain the development of a nontraditional, student-centered model of literate action.

To illustrate how a situated definition of literacy is constructed, we will present a study of what counts as literacy in a summer high school English class. We argue that the study of individual classrooms leads to the identification of generic processes, processes that occur across groups. While generic, however, these processes must be situated in a group's life if we are to understand what, why, and how they occur and the consequences of their occurrence for what members can and do understand about literacy and literate action (Erickson, 1986).

This high school English class was selected as a site to study literacy construction and learning for three reasons. First, it was created as part of a

---

[3] See chapters by Collins and Green (Chapter 3), Weade (Chapter 4), and Chandler (Chapter 2), this volume, for a discussion of theoretical constructs related to classrooms as cultures and teaching-learning processes as sociocommunicative processes. These constructs are part of the framework for this chapter.

professional development program in which teachers were provided an opportunity to explore student-centered curriculum approaches and to engage in action research about these processes (Bergamo, Green, & Ridgeway, 1988, 1989). To accomplish this goal, the class and the larger professional development project were videotaped to permit teachers and participants to examine and reflect on the processes involved. Thus, a permanent record was available in the form of teacher-made videotapes that made possible the analysis of literacy presented in this chapter.

Second, the class was defined by the two teachers and students as different from their ordinary classes. It was also defined as successful by members of the professional development project and has been described by the teachers at national and local teacher conventions.

Third, the teachers who taught the class developed it as part of a long-range professional development process in which they transformed and continue to transform their thinking and practices related to literacy in the classroom. The videotape records which exist provide a unique basis for examining both the everyday actions of teachers and students and factors external to the class (e.g., other teachers, administrators, district policies) that support and constrain what can and does occur within and across time in their curriculum.

Given the range of data available, we conclude the chapter with a brief discussion of the implications of this study for understanding what factors support and constrain teacher exploration and implementation of new directions in literacy. As part of this discussion, we will examine: factors that contribute to the success and maintenance of educational innovations, and factors that influence research on learning in classroom settings.

RESEARCHING PRACTICE FROM AN INSIDER'S PERSPECTIVE

This examination of how literacy is constructed in the dynamics of everyday life in classrooms is predicated on the view that throughout the years of schooling, the range of opportunities students have to engage in literate actions can limit or expand students' literacy repertoires and what students count as appropriate literate actions in school settings (Green, Kantor, & Rogers, 1990). That is, if students are engaged with literate actions that are the same across all years of schooling, they will develop *a* particular model of literacy, not *the* model of literacy (Cochran-Smith, 1984). The model or models that are constructed may support or constrain how students will approach literacy in other situations (e.g., business, higher education, other grades of schooling), and what they view as counting in school settings (Green, Kantor, & Rogers, 1990). Thus, from the range of opportunities students have in school, they develop what has been called schooled literacy and not a generic literacy process (Cook-Gumperz, 1986).

If we are to understand how students develop literate actions from participating in schooling, then we need an approach that will provide a means of identifying and describing the range of opportunities students have, one that is responsive to the dynamic and variable nature of life in classrooms. Interactional sociolinguistics provides such an approach (Gumperz, 1986). Interactional sociolinguistics brings ethnographic study of class life together with sociolinguistic analysis of those key events of the life of the group that are identified by the ethnographic aspect of the research. Once the key events have been identified, the sociolinguistic aspect of this approach provides a means of examining how this "bit of life" is accomplished through the discourse strategies of participants. By using this approach, we are able to examine how common meanings as well as the patterns of literacy are constructed over time by members of the class (teachers and students), and how individual events are communicatively constituted.

The value of this approach can be illustrated in the following excerpts from the third day of school in the English class. These excerpts were part of a continuing lesson around a short story, a cycle of activity that took two days to complete (day 2 through day 3 of the 17 days of class). As will become evident, this segment illustrates the need to observe over time and to identify the range of sources of information available to members if we are to understand what counts as literacy and literate actions within the group.

Defining Literacy In and Across the Moments of Classroom Life

On the third day of school, the following statement was observed approximately 30 minutes into the class period.

EXCERPT 1[4]
DEFINING LITERATE ACTIONS

Scene:
The two teachers in this class are standing near the front of the room as students complete the transition from an interviewing task to a discussion task. The students are sitting at tables in seminar groups that were established on the previous day. They are preparing to share with other groups their group's response to two questions: How many characters are there and who are they? The groups have selected a reporter to share the group's negotiated response.

---

[4] The excerpts presented in this chapter were selected because they represent patterns identified throughout the 17 days of life in this high school English class. These are not individual occurrences but rather recur across time and events.

Excerpt from Transcript[5]

Teacher: Susan
We have some questions that you
want to talk about
since you did such a good job
yesterday talking in your groups
and Mrs. Mattern and I are only going
to be the question askers
and we're going to be the recorders
we're going to put your answers
on the board
if there's a discrepancy between what the
different groups have to report
then
you will probably want to question each
other
question the other groups
you know, why did you put that?
our group didn't agree
in other words,
you need to come up with a class answer
that we can all feel comfortable with
and we'll go around and try to ask all of the
groups to contribute something
obviously
and if you want to chime in and answer
you know, any portion
whoever the reporter is for your group
if you want to answer a question
or add to a question that another group is
answering
please feel free...

In this excerpt, the teacher's words paint the following picture. This is a class where:

students have questions they want to talk about
students talk in groups
there are two teachers
teachers ask questions

---

[5] The transcript is written to reflect the ways the teachers delivered the messages. This form of transcriptions is theoretically derived and is based on a unit called a message unit (cf. Green, 1977; Green & Wallat, 1981). To identify message units we consider contextualization cues (cf. Gumperz & Herasimchuk, 1973): pitch, stress, intonation, pause, juncture; how messages were heard in all of the bursts and hesitations, repetitions, and nonverbal elements (body movement, gesture, proxemics, and eye gaze).

teachers act as recorders of student answers
discrepancies in group reports are envisioned as a possibility
members of one group can question the interpretation of other groups
teachers and students will agree on a class answer that all in class feel
    comfortable with
every group is asked to contribute something
each group will have a group reporter
reporters for a group may "chime in" and add to the
    answer of another group

What these words do is define a range of actions that the teachers see as appropriate ways of interpreting text during group discussion. These ways of interpreting text distinguished members of this class from members of other classes with different views of what it means to discuss literature (Alvermann, 1989; Golden, 1986, 1990). As will be illustrated below, what is not visible to us as well as students at this point in time is: just what it means to work in groups; what counts as an answer in this class; what it means when the teacher says that they (the two teachers) will be recorders and question askers; what the content is in which differences in interpretation will occur; what it means to arrive at a class answer; or even who the referent is at particular points (e.g., you).

To understand what is meant by these words, we (researchers), like the students in this class, cannot depend on the words alone. Rather, we must seek further information that confirms, modifies, or disconfirms our interpretation of these words. Such information is available in the patterns of action as well as the words that members of the class use with each other across time. For example, later in this period, the teacher and students define further what it means to arrive at a class answer and thus to be literate.

EXCERPT 2
EXTENDING THE DEFINITION OF LITERATE ACTIONS

Scene: Approximately 15 minutes later as the teacher was recording information, a student suggested that the task was vague and that the vagueness led to the discrepancy in answers which was "bad." At this point the teacher defined further what she and the other teacher meant:

Excerpt from Transcript:

Teacher: Susan
if you justify your answer
that's all I'm asking
you to do
to think about it
and give me a reason

for your thinking...
so there's a lot of different ways of learning
and arriving at the same answer
there's no one right way
whatever works best for you
is what's right
as long as you arrive
at some sort of answer
as long as you arrive at
an understanding of what ever's being asked
so don't worry when you get into groups
if everybody doesn't want to do it exactly your way
negotiate as you very definitely did
very effectively yesterday
negotiate what you want to say
and how you want to go about saying it
and how you want to find the answers
so I'm really very pleased
with how well you are working
in a seminar structure

What is visible in this slice of life is that the teacher felt a need to define further how one arrives at a class answer and what a class answer means. The need for this clarification was prompted by a student comment that the task was vague. The teacher's response indicates that a class answer did not mean a single response required of all as is often the case in high school classrooms (Applebee, 1981). In this class, students were permitted to hold differing interpretations if they could provide support for their answers.

While the teacher's words provide further clarification of what counts as literate action (i.e., you need to justify your answer), these words do not provide a complete definition of what counted as a class answer or as literate actions. To understand what counted as literate actions in arriving at a class answer, we had to examine what occurred throughout this day and over the preceding and future days. The following summary of the sequence of activity that the students and teachers constructed as they worked together to define characters in the story on the third day of school illustrates the importance of considering how life is constructed within and across time. The sequence of activity around character is summarized in the following account:

An Account of the Sequence of Activity for Defining What Counts as A Character

Student Actions: The first group to report identified at least five characters. A second group immediately chimed in to challenge the first group's list arguing that there were really only two characters. This group's definition was then challenged by a third group who agreed with the first group.

Teacher actions that supported student alternative views: As groups reported, the teachers asked questions or made comments that invited agreement or disagreement with the group's response. Examples of these actions include: How do the rest of you want to respond to that? Does anyone else want to comment? We haven't heard from... What else could you do?

As groups reported the teachers asked students to give their reasons for their responses. One group (group 2) suggested that the way to define characters was to view only those people in the story who "talk or actually participate" as characters. This distinction would eliminate all others who were talked about but were not physically present. The students did not accept this and continued to argue positions.

Revisiting the answers to establish a common class answer: After all groups had reported, one of the teachers (Chris) points out that the groups are evenly divided: Three agreed with the first group and its list, and three agreed with the second group and its list. At this point, the teachers initiate a new phase of the negotiation: "And now we need to arrive at some decision, how can we go about that?"

After this statement, one student names the characters and indicates that they are main characters. The teachers *take up* (Collins, 1986) the student's suggestion about main characters, thus focusing the group on this idea and moving beyond individual positions of the groups.

After an extended discussion, the teachers build on the student idea of main character and introduce the idea of minor characters as a way of dealing with all characters. The students discuss this and then the teachers check with the individuals and groups who had differing views to determine whether this was a satisfactory way of establishing a class answer: "For discussion purposes we have to have something we subscribe to. Does that make sense to you?... There are these characters you really want to think about and there are these other characters. They're sort of on the outskirts." The students agree with this formulation and proceed to take notes from the board and to revise or add to their own lists.

Examination of the teacher reflection data (see Excerpt 3) indicates that some students did not make changes while others copied part and still others agree to all.

This sequence of activity shows that the teachers and students had to establish a referential system that defined both how a term would be defined (i.e., character) and how communication would occur within the class (i.e., arrive at a class answer). In addition, they had to establish a common basis for participating (Edwards & Mercer, 1989), while still permitting variation in answer to what appeared to be simple questions: How many characters are there? Who are the characters?

The actions of the teachers and students showed the range of actions preferred by the teachers and students in the discussion phase of this story (cf. Heap, 1980, 1991). By observing how the teachers responded to students, how students responded to teachers and to other students, what teachers and students signaled as important, and what they accepted or rejected, we were able to identify a consistent set of actions from which we constructed the meaning of literate action within this segment of class life. From the teachers' actions we see a particular model of instruction that entails a particular model of literacy: the teachers withheld their own interpretations, expected students to support their answers, supported student discussion within and across groups, followed student leads, elicited criteria from students, and helped students reach a common framework for response. These actions define for outside observers and for students what the teachers meant by a *student-centered curriculum* or what they meant by *this class is different*.

These examples show how the teachers and students collaboratively establish conditions under which an answer could be seen as counting within this classroom. In other words, the members of the social group established patterned ways of acting, interacting, and evaluating what counted as literate action. These patterns reflect a particular position on response to literature, a position associated with the particular school of thought about literary theory that framed the reading-writing-literature program these teachers were exploring (Bartholomae & Petrosky, 1986).[6]

LITERACY IN THE MAKING

In the examples above, we illustrated in part how teachers and students constructed conditions, definitions, and meanings of literacy through their words and actions. In the sections that follow, we will expand the discussion of what counts as literacy in this English class. As part of the discussion, we will introduce key concepts that frame our analysis and make visible how literacy is constructed and what literacy is constructed within and across the actions and interactions of members of this class.

What became evident in our analysis is that the teachers organized life in this classroom around three categories of activity: interactions with texts, interactions with others, and interactions through texts. These interactions are defined below. In addition, these activities were interwoven to create a web of meaning that led to the construction of an autobiography. The autobiography was the vehicle for formalizing what students learned about the overriding theme of the class, Coming of Age. What was also evident is that an individual event served a variety of learning purposes. As can be seen in the events described above, students had the opportunity to contribute to

---

[6] Different schools of literary theory and reader response posit differing views of text, and some question whether there is a text at all. For a discussion of these issues see Fish, 1980; Golden, 1984, 1989, 1990.

and explore content, meaning construction, and processes involved in literate actions. Thus, from participating in and across the events of classroom life, students were learning how to be literate as well as developing an understanding of the content of the texts.

Interactions With Text

One way of defining literacy and literate actions in this class is through the texts that were used. In this class, text varied in form, substance, and voice (personal, formal, distant, historical). Students had an opportunity to examine a concept, Coming of Age, through different types of text. The selection of certain texts provided particular opportunities for the students in this class. The nature and types of text, therefore, contributed to the development of a model of literacy; they did not define the model. Rather, a model is defined in the interactions people have with these texts. This is a model of literacy-in-action and suggests that any model of literacy is situated in the actions and interactions that members of groups have with texts within and across a variety of settings—home and school.

In this class students had the opportunity to interact with a range of text types: a novel, short stories, excerpts from longer pieces, fiction, psychological treatments, poems, and poem in song form (Coming Through the Rye). Ten texts formed the core around which the theme Coming of Age was constructed across the 17 days of this summer class. What counted as text, therefore, was varied. The importance of considering the range of interactions with text in defining literacy is reflected in the following brief history of one of the texts, the novel, *Catcher in the Rye* (Salinger, 1951).

A BRIEF HISTORY OF A TEXT

Catcher (the group's name for the novel) was read entirely outside of class. On the first day of class, the students were told to read the first half of the book by the next week. On the second day of class, the teacher elaborated the assignment and told students to write a long journal (30-minute) response on the first half of the book. The assignment was to be completed at home. This assignment came after the students and teachers had established the parameters for a short (10-minute) journal response in class. The journals were to be turned in on the following Monday, and the teachers would write comments on these responses. On day seven, the teachers told the students to read the remaining half of the book and to write a second long journal response. These responses formed the basis for a discussion of the book in the third week. The book was also used as a referent throughout the remaining days of this class as the teachers and students linked this text with others in an intertextual web that built a larger text that defined Coming of Age.

In this history, what becomes evident is that reading occurs in a variety of settings, under a variety of conditions (alone, in groups), and serves a variety of purposes. From this perspective, reading is not a unitary process but a differentiated one. This view contrasts markedly from the generally held view of reading as something an individual reader does with a text (see Singer & Ruddell, 1985).

While it might be argued that such a perspective is appropriate when the students read the novel at home, we argue that there are others involved in this reading, others who are not necessarily physically present. The text is being read for "school purposes" and therefore the teacher and other students are part of the reading. Students do not have free choice but must accomplish the reading in order to participate in socially and academically appropriate ways in the class. It can be argued, therefore, that the way in which the text is being read is mediated by what students anticipate others will say and do both with the text and with their responses. Thus, reading is a social process even when done alone in another setting.

In this class, reading frequently involved more than one person in the process of interacting with texts. Reading in this class involved a variety of organizational structures and purposes that helped to define what literate actions meant and the ways students were to interact with texts. In the following excerpt from the second day of class, an illustration of how the group engaged with text is visible.

EXCERPT 3
READING AS A GROUP ACTIVITY

Scene: On the second day of class the teachers and students have just completed a second round of the name game to include new students and are getting ready to "read" a short story that will form the core for a new cycle of activity.

Excerpt From The Transcript:

Teacher: Chris
Today we're going to start with the first short story
and it really is a short, short story
it's called the long, long journey and we
want you to listen again, you know,
we're using our listening skills you did
so well yesterday and you remembered
everything from yesterday for today
too as far as names and what people
like to do
we want you to listen
carefully because I'm going to stop in

the middle of this story, like I said
very, very short and we're going
to ask you some questions, your opinion
as to what might be happening and so on

Teacher: Susan
when Mrs. Mattern says stop, if you
are following along you don't have to
follow along with her
but when she says stop
if you are following along
and reading with her please stop
reading

Teacher: Chris
... because we have couple of
questions we're going to ask you
while I'm reading also you might be
thinking about why does this
what's the significance of this title
you know
where does this title the long journey
come from?
so be thinking about that
we can talk about that when we're done
okay, here we go.

In this excerpt, one teacher indicates that she will read to the class in a particular way. The words in advance of the reading are part of the definition of reading of this particular text and frame how the students are to take action: They may read along or listen, but must stop reading when she does. These actions not only indicate what students should do as readers/participants but what they should not do: *read ahead*. They also indicate that both teachers are framing this task and hold a common view of what actions are to occur. Just why the students are to stop reading and not read ahead can be understood only when the event is considered as a whole. When the teacher who is reading (Chris) stops reading, she and the other teacher (Susan) ask the students to write their prediction in their reading journals. After the students completed writing, Chris completed the story. Only after the students had heard and had had an opportunity to respond in writing did the teachers discuss the story.

Like the other examples described earlier, the ways in which the teachers engaged students with texts served a variety of purposes. In this instance, students were given an opportunity in class to experience writing responses to a text. This activity occurred on the second day of school and set a frame for how to do this task at home. In addition, this way of engaging students with text let students see that there were multiple ways of interpreting the text within the class and that these interpretations were appropriate if you could provide reasons for your interpretation. This activity precedes the one on characters that occurred on day three. Thus, the instructional patterns in this class were a form of text that was tied across time, task, and content.

Reading, viewed in this way, is a socially defined way of interacting with text that includes more than the physical text. It also includes the communicative patterns of participants through which definitions of literacy and literate actions are constructed. Reading, therefore, is not a generic process that occurs solely in the interaction of an individual reader with an individual text (e.g., Bloome, 1986a; Golden, 1990). In classrooms, reading is an instructionally defined process that is constructed in and through the interactions of teachers, students, and texts (Green & Harker, 1982). As indicated in the examples above, the teachers deliberately constructed conditions in this classroom that involved students in interactions with a series of texts in a wide variety of ways, with differing groups of people, in different settings.

Interactions About Text

In the activity that was established around text, the teachers constructed with the students particular definitions of what it means to interpret text and to interact with text. In this class, interactions about text involved students in discussing published texts, texts produced by other students, written texts produced by the individual student (e.g., editing, sharing response), and oral texts. All of these ways of interacting became part of the building of community norms and expectations for how to be literate in this class.

From this perspective, text is not a given or solely the published materials as is generally considered. Rather, text is also produced in the interactions of participants. Even when a written or published text exists, this text is merely a potential set of meanings. What becomes the text is constructed in the interactions of members with these cultural artifacts (Golden, 1990; Robinson, 1986). Thus, as readers read or speakers speak or writers write or listeners listen, they are participating in a process of text construction. Text, therefore, is constructed through the communication of members of a group, and meaning involves interpretation not mere extraction.

Underlying this view of text is the conceptualization of text as a bounded entity—oral, visual, or written, that an individual or group seeks to interpret. From this perspective, the events of everyday life are a form of text that is to be read and interpreted as members simultaneously construct the text (Green & Harker, 1982). Thus, events that are oral in nature and do not include formal published or written material can be viewed as texts.

An example of the textual nature of oral events can be seen in an earlier analysis of a sharing activity on days 11–14 of this class that involved students bringing an artifact from their lives that represented them to the class and sharing this with the class (Green & Meyer, 1991). Some students brought pictures, computer disks, and other objects to class and shared them. This activity was oral in form. Each student who elected to share had an opportunity to be the focal point of the group, to have their object and their comments provide the information to be interpreted, and to exchange information with others.

These oral texts were not isolated occurrences or fillers. They served to bring life experiences into the class and to help students identify elements that they might want to include in their autobiography. Thus, the oral texts were tied to future events (the writing of autobiography) and to past events (personal experience stories). In addition, as part of these oral conversations, the teachers included ties to published texts in this class. For example, the teachers asked the students what Holden (the main character in *Catcher in the Rye*) would bring to represent himself. Thus, oral texts are a means of linking life to text and text to life (cf. Cochran-Smith, 1984), and texts to text (Green & Meyer, 1991).

In this class, oral, written, and visual texts were not isolated objects in isolated events. They were part of an intertextual web that could be visited and revisited; defined and redefined in many ways for varying purposes. In this way the teachers linked ways of interacting about the texts across time and built text-to-text relationships. These interactions established a pattern of activity that defined interactions about text: students read the texts; wrote responses to each text; discussed the response in seminar group; discussed their responses with other groups to arrive at a class answer; responded to their own texts, texts of others students, and to published texts; and linked information obtained from one part of life to others through text. By considering the range of activity with and about text, we found that literate actions in this class were varied, dynamic, and interactive.

Bloome (1989) captures the constructed and tied nature of texts in his definition of intertextuality:

> Whenever people engage in a language event, whether it is a conversation, a reading of a book, diary writing, etc., they are engaging in intertextuality. Various conversational and written texts are being juxtaposed. Intertextuality can occur at many levels and in many ways.
>
> Juxtaposing texts, at whatever level, is not in itself sufficient for intertextuality. Intertextuality is a social construction. The juxtaposition must be interactionally recognized, acknowledged and have social significance.
>
> In classrooms, teachers and students are continuously constructing intertextual relationships. The set of intertextual relationships they construct can be

viewed as constructing a cultural ideology, a system for assigning meaning and significance to what is said and done and for socially defining participants. (pp. 1–2)

The socially sanctioned nature of this process can be illustrated by returning to the example in excerpts 1 and 2 and by considering additional information contained in the teacher reflection/planning tape that followed these excerpts. In responding to a question about how things were going, the teachers made visible the processes associated with literate action during the planning/reflection time—reading, interpreting, modifying, revising, and refining text. This example also illustrates how literacy involves social sanctions by members.

EXCERPT 4
SOCIALLY SANCTIONING TEXT AND LITERATE ACTIONS

Scene: The two teachers are talking after class about what occurred and planning what will happen in tomorrow's class. The professional development leader and one of the researchers (Green) enter the classroom. The professional development leader asks them how things are going.

Excerpt From Transcript

Teacher: Susan
you know what was interesting
we were discussing
they were reporting out of their groups
the answers they'd come up to the questions
and
as we were asking or eliciting their answers
their reports
we changed
Chris said that she could see
see my thinking

Teacher: Chris
I could see her thinking

Teacher: Susan
and see how it was changing
because instead of listing
what we ended up doing
was asking them to report out
we had somebody volunteer
to do the writing
and everything on the board
and we negotiated answers
(both point to answers on board)
and every time we did that

we asked them to justify what you want to say
and if anybody disagreed
what do you want
are you going to accept that answer
or how are you going to take that
so we left the answers
deliberately
you know everybody didn't have to accept
what we put on the board
and some people only copied part of what we did off the board
and others added to their notes

Teacher: Chris
whatever they could justify

Teacher: Susan
whatever they could justify
but what we stressed was
on a test
if I put this down
and I'm not going to give you a test on this
but if I were a regular classroom teacher
in a regular classroom situation
giving you this question
what would be the most important thing about this
and they
decided
being able to explain or justify my answer
that's what
that's what we came up with all the time
. . .
I didn't agree with all of them
but they all had a justification

Teacher: Chris
But you know it took an hour

Teacher: Susan
an hour
and we had allotted half an hour
but it was really...
We were really excited though
we were pleased...
We changed it
but it was fun
it was great

The teachers' spontaneous comments to the outsiders to this class make visible the social construction process, the social sanctions of what counts as literate actions (e.g., acceptance of answers by teachers), and the construction process of defining literate actions. In this example, the teachers show that they and the students linked this event to others, established a common understanding of possibilities, yet permitted individual selection of what was accepted. Thus, both teachers and students participated in developing a common view at the group level but they also had personal views.

What the discussion indicates to this point is that the interactions with text and about text are highly interrelated. It is possible to foreground one aspect for heuristic purposes, but in actuality they are intertextually tied and interdependent. This intertextual and interdependent relationship of person(s) and text are also central to the discussion of interactions through text that follows. In this section, what counts as literacy and literate action will be examined as we consider the texts written by students.

Interactions Through Text

The interactions through texts involved teachers and students in written conversations in the form of response journals and editing processes. Teachers and other students engaged the writer in a conversation through print about the text. These conversations focused on both response elements in journals and the formal papers in this class. Two types of written papers were required: personal experience papers (3) and the autobiography (rough drafts and final draft). The personal experience papers occurred in week 1 (day 2), week 2 (day 10), and week 3 (day 13).

The following statement from the plan constructed by the teachers captures the ways in which students interacted through text:

EXCERPT 5
INTERACTING THROUGH TEXTS AS REFLECTED IN TEACHER PLANS

Students will write three rough drafts in response to three writing prompts (one each week for the first three weeks). These prompts will be based upon one of the readings assigned in class. During week 4, the students will be writing, revising, and editing an autobiography. Thy are encouraged to incorporate all writings they have previously completed, as well as discussion notes and journal entries to help them write their essay. The basic focus of this autobiographical essay will be "Growing Into Adulthood." It might be wise to have the students complete their rough drafts over the weekend so that the class can be working on revision on Monday.

This example illustrates once again the intertextual and socially organized nature of literate action in this classroom. The interactions through text were not always visible to an observer since they often occurred after class (teachers wrote comments to students) or they were placed in materials that were not overtly discussed in class (in journals). While the act of editing was often visible in the actions of participants, the content of this type of text was not open to all members of the group. Learning through text, therefore, involved members in conversations that were not public, that is, open to the group. These conversations were more or less silent and generally private in nature. Thus, not all aspects of life were visible in the words and observed actions.

While we were able to identify the three categories of interactions discussed above, we also found that they were not discrete but rather three threads that were interwoven into a web of meanings and actions that formed intertextuality across events, actions, and content. This intertextual web was not a patchwork quilt, but rather a tapestry in which the individual dimensions worked together to create a picture and in which the boundaries of the individual components became blurred. Another way of thinking about this tapestry is that the parts contributed to a larger text, a text that involved members in differing ways with differing patterns of interaction.

HOW EXTERNAL DECISIONS INFLUENCE CLASSROOM LIFE

This view of class as text constructed by members through their actions and interactions may give the appearance of a self-contained unit or a closed system. In such a system, meanings and actions would be seen as generated solely by members with no influence from sources outside of the system. This is not the model that undergirds this discussion. Rather, classes are viewed as open systems in which sources of influence from outside the group can and often do influence what occurs and how life will occur (e.g., home, community, peer group, administrative influences).

In the remaining sections of this chapter, we step outside of this classroom to consider factors that supported and constrained both what occurred in this class and what the teachers had an opportunity to do with the knowledge gained from participating in the professional development program that supported this curriculum innovation. As will be illustrated, a focus on the actions and interactions of members of the group is necessary but not sufficient to define literate actions and to understand what counts as literacy.

Several sources of external influence always exist within a group, while others are brought into the group by members of other groups external to the class. Co-existing potential sources of influence exist within individual members of the group in the form of prior experiences; background knowledge; patterns of beliefs, actions, and expectations learned by participating in other groups (e.g., family, other classes, peer groups); and individual repertoires (cognitive, social, linguistic, psychomotor).

We have labeled these elements as potential sources because the individual may or may not approach the new situation in the way required in other situations, but rather, the individual may read the requirements of this new situation and participate in socially appropriate ways. For example, extensive work exists about the ways in which the language resources students bring from home influence their construction of meaning in the new situation and the ways in which they will participate through language (see Cazden, 1986; Cazden, John, & Hymes, 1972; Wells, 1986). Still other research shows how participation in peer group influences how students will interact with teachers and others in a class (Bloome & Theodorou, 1988; Fernie, Kantor, Klein, Meyer, & Elgar, 1988; Fernie, Kantor, Scott, Schwarz, Kesner, & Klein, 1990).

We acknowledge the importance of considering these sources of potential influence that individuals bring. This study, however, focused on what opportunities individuals had as a member of the group and not on individual performance. The concern for literacy and literate action, therefore, was a concern for what was possible at the level of community and not at the level of individual.

The need to consider external sources of influence at the group level arose from observed interactions between teachers and students on the third and fourth day of school. As members of the research team examined the requirements for participation across the first five days of school, we found that there were inconsistencies in statements about grading and credit. In juxtaposing the transcripts of the first and third days of the class, we identified a potential source of the change in statements. On the first day, students were told that they could take the course either for credit or pass/fail. On the third day, the teachers indicated that they would have to take the course for credit since it "does have to replace an actual credit of English."

The change alone did not define this inconsistency as a critical element to consider. What made this "bit of life" stand out as marked and important to examine further were the ways in which the teachers talked about it with the students.

EXCERPT 6
FORCED TO CHANGE

Scene: The teachers and students had been talking informally before school started. A new student had entered and the teachers had explained what was required in the class. It was 9:00 and they moved to the front of the class to begin class.

Excerpts From Transcript
Teacher: Susan
Before we go on
and um

get a little friendlier today
with each other
we want to make two announcements
and I think they are important announcements for you
you want the good news or the bad news first? which do you want?
... (Susan gives information that the course as to be graded)
so it is a graded course
I want you to understand that
we had to do that
we really had no choice about that
we really would have preferred to give you pass fail
but since it does have to be reflected in your
    grade point as a replacement course for an
    English course
    then it does have to be graded

The teacher's use of the terms "had to" and "we really had no choice about that" and "we really would have preferred to give you a pass fail" indicated that the decision to change this aspect of the class was an external one, one that was mandated by district policy. The teacher's choice of words indicated that this decision was not one that they agreed with but one they could not control.

This statement led us to examine all statements about credit and grades across the first five days of school and to review the planning/reflection session tapes made on the day in which the excerpt above occurred. Figure 5.1 traces the influence of grading across the five days.

As indicated in this figure, we identified four sites where members of the class came in contact with members of other groups (i.e., administration, policymakers, teacher leader in professional development project). These sites were labeled: within class, within team planning, within team interaction, and with external groups. In each location, the issue of credit and grading was discussed and decisions made that had potential influence on what occurred in the class.

The shift in action is visible in the trace across days represented by the arrows in Figure 5.1. The chain of activity associated with grading began with an unclear statement to parents and students about the credit for this class before school began. The need to clarify led to a policy decision which in turn led to teacher reconsideration of grading and planned actions. The teacher redefinition led to a consultation with a teacher leader from the professional development project which in turn led to further reconsideration.

At the point of contact with the teacher leader, what became visible was that factors other than policy constrained what occurred in the class. The teacher leader listened to the plan the teachers' had constructed for grading.

Figure 5.1. When Micro and Macro Contexts Interact: Making Cultural Patterns Visible:

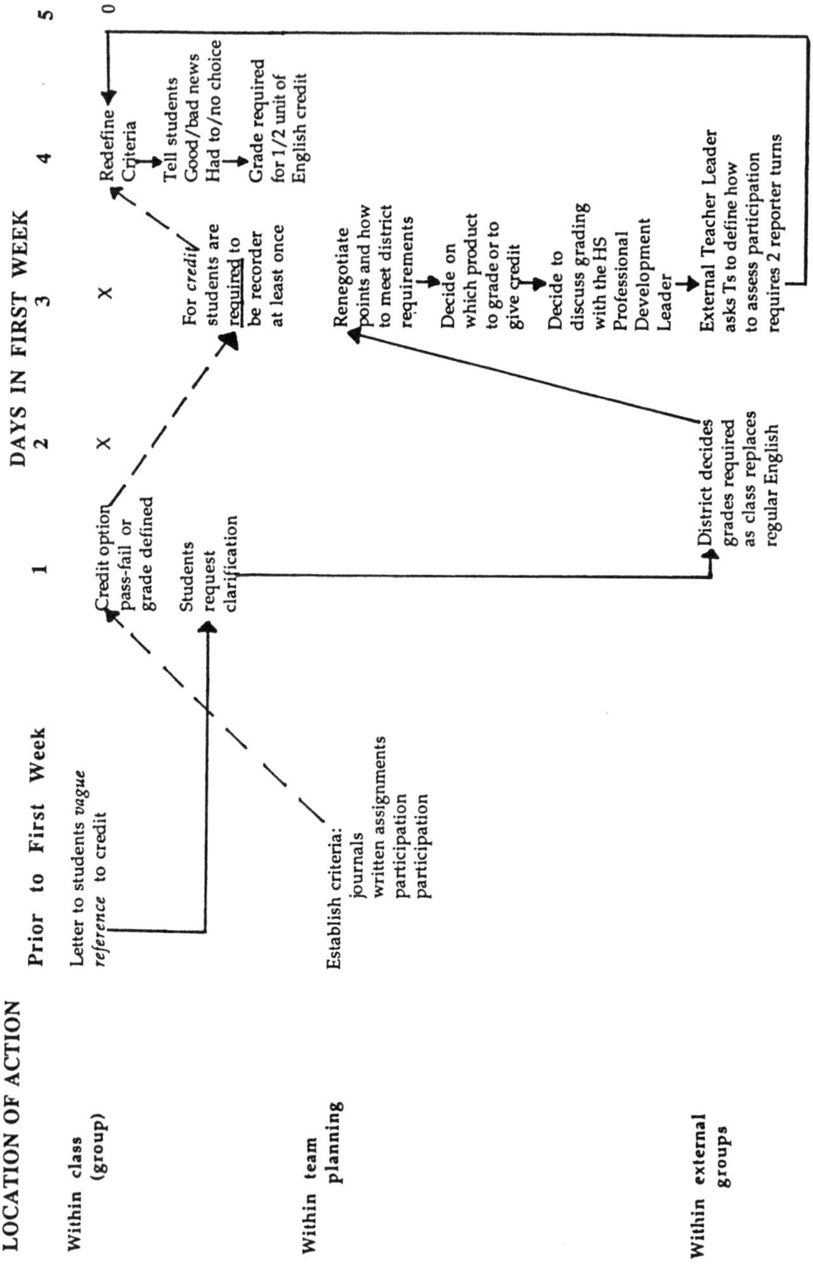

LOCATION OF ACTION

	Prior to First Week	DAYS IN FIRST WEEK				
		1	2	3	4	5
Within class (group)	Letter to students *vague reference* to credit	Credit option pass-fail or grade defined / Students request clarification	X	X	Redefine Criteria / Tell students / Good/bad news / Had to/no choice / Grade required for 1/2 unit of English credit	0
Within team planning	Establish criteria: journals / written assignments / participation / participation			For *credit* students are required to be recorder at least once / Renegotiate points and how to meet district requirements / Decide on which product to grade or to give credit / Decide to discuss grading with the HS Professional Development Leader / External Teacher Leader asks Ts to define how to assess participation requires 2 reporter turns		
Within external groups			District decides grades required as class replaces regular English			

She made no comments in support of the plan but focused on how the teachers would grade participation. She felt that participation should be counted and points given to different types of activity. The teachers had proposed a more global approach to point distribution. Observations made at this point of contact indicated that the teachers accepted her "requirement." Analysis of the shift in voice, body position, and body language of the teachers throughout their talk with the teacher leader indicated that they did not agree. That is, as she focused on the distribution of points in a more and more specific way, they physically moved away, changed eye gaze, stopped interacting, and generally signaled their discomfort with this approach to grading participation.

What is significant is that the teachers had used global measures for other aspects—personal experience papers, journal entries, rough drafts. That is, students received full points if the papers were done appropriately. The teacher leader did not question this practice for written products but did for the oral or social. Her actions did not indicate that she considered the goal of the teachers for students, the purpose of the participation, or the feasibility of her suggestions in a student-centered class. Her suggestions appear to be based on a personal view of what would be "fair."

Her suggestions were accepted by the teachers on one level and influenced what they wrote in the grading guidelines presented to the students on day 4. In practice, the teachers' own views mediated the distribution of points. The teachers can be seen as maintaining the culture of the class so as to support the student-centered orientation they and the students had begun to construct.

This example of the frame clash (a clash in perceptions or expectations; e.g., Mehan, 1979; Tannen, 1979) over credit/grading makes visible the intertextual links between life in the class and life outside the class. Our analysis was possible only because of the richness of the data set. Had we had to depend on what could be observed in the class alone, we would have been unable to "see" the intertextual links across contexts and the interactions that led to the frame clash. The class talk and actions of members would have indicated a problem, but we would have been unable to see the range of the personal and policy factors that were brought to bear on the final decision that was presented to the students on day 4. This analysis suggests that a dependence solely on observed action may mask or ignore factors that contribute to the opportunities students and teachers have to construct student-centered forms of literate action in classes.

What this analysis showed is that decisions are often made without consideration of what is occurring in the class. These decisions do not consider the individual members of the class or the nature of the opportunities provided.

TRANSFORMING LEARNING

In this final section, we will examine the implications of this work for defining literacy and literate actions, for professional development, and for research. While we see these three areas as interrelated and interactive, we will foreground each separately to highlight particular dimensions. Given that the examination of literacy reported in this chapter was part of the professional development processes and experiences of the two teachers, we begin with this element and then move to a discussion of literacy in classrooms. The chapter ends with a discussion of the implications of this study for research practice in similar settings.

Transforming Teacher Knowledge through Explorations of Literacy

In the description of literacy in the high school English class, we provided an overview of how two teachers went about constructing with students a student-centered model of literacy that they and the students defined as different. Another way to think about this class is that the participants were transforming knowledge, their own and that of other members. The transformations were part of the dynamics of the seminar model based on the work of Bartholomae and Petrosky (1986). Thus, both the teachers and students were exploring new patterns of literate action and new ways of teaching and being a student.

The teachers continued this transformation after the class ended as they sought ways of using the information gained in this summer class and the professional development project in their regular English (Susan) and German (Chris) classes. This process is captured in the excerpt below:

EXCERPT 7
CONTINUING THE TRANSFORMING PROCESS

Scene: The teacher is telling the in-service teacher group about her participation in the Carston Instructional Model program. In the first part of the excerpt she is discussing the first part of the program, a Spring program in which teachers explored ways of working together with other teachers and of engaging in action research.

Teacher Comments to other teachers:
We had staff development days [in Spring] and we had to come up with something we were interested in. We [four teachers] found that we had several different questions that we wanted to deal with and we found that there was something in common across curriculum [English, German, Science, Math]... One of them was my primary interest, questioning... I chose an area

that I thought was fairly specific. I chose questioning because I thought it was something I could cope with... Maybe I could ask better questions during the class. Maybe I'm not asking the right questions.... That sort of mushroomed out. I started thinking, maybe it's the students' questions. When they ask me things, what kinds of questions are they asking me? How am I responding? Am I asking them questions back...
I had myself taped by another team member which was a very nonthreatening situation. When I thought I was asking questions and thought half of the class was responding,... I had only five or seven out of a class of thirty. They were doing a lot of studenting[7] to me that I was not really aware of... as I was forced to be when I looked at the tape... I had this whole elaborate research plan that I laid out where I was going to chart the kind of question that they asked me. It was totally blown when I realized that I was only talking to five or seven kids in the class. I was really frustrated by this.

The teacher continues talking to the other teachers about what she found. She told them that these awarenesses led her and her team members to volunteer to teach in the summer institute. She summarizes her reasons for trying a new direction in the following statement:

We had expanded our ideas beyond just being limited to questioning and we started to look at the student-centered classroom. Maybe things would work better and I could make more contact with students, Chris [her co-teacher] and I could if we weren't limiting ourselves to a very traditional classroom. We had an option of using Bartholomae & Petrosky, *Facts, Artifacts, & Counterfacts*... So with that in mind we constructed a curriculum that was basically very learner-centered, which was very different for both Chris and myself.

As indicated in this excerpt the transforming process took place over an extended period of time and involved interactions and examinations with a variety of participants in the teachers' professional lives. Figure 5.2 represents the transformational sequence for one of the teachers, the English teacher. What is indicated in the time line is that the process continues today and the teacher continues to work with the ideas she began to explore almost four years ago. What was an exploration is now a reality in her daily life.

---

[7] Studenting refers to the idea that teaching and learning are not theoretically or semantically equivalent (see Fenstermacher, 1986, for a philosophical discussion). If teachers teach then students student and through studenting they may or may not learn the content the teacher desires. They may learn other aspects of social life, that is, how to be a participant in this group instead. This type of studenting builds particular ways of being in a class and may not reflect actual ability. See Bloome, Theodorou, and Puro (1990) for a discussion of mock participation and procedural display, two concepts related to studenting. For a discussion of the consequences of studenting see Green, Kantor, and Rogers (1990).

Figure 5.2. Phases in Transforming Learning in One Teacher's Classroom Past, Present and Future of the Experimental High School English Class

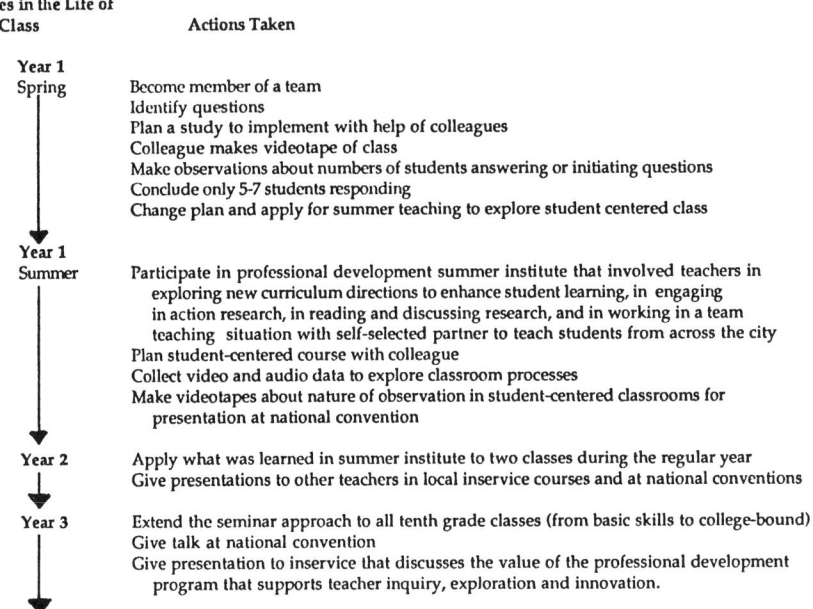

What is not visible in the time line or teacher's comments is that there have been two changes in superintendent, and that these changes in superintendent have had consequences for both this teacher and other teachers. The first change in superintendent brought an end to the professional development program that involved teachers in action research and supported exploration of student-centered curriculum. This change in superintendent shifted district resources to other ways of transforming teaching and learning as did the second change in superintendent (Bergamo, Green, & Ridgeway, 1989).

A recent interview with this teacher indicated that while she has been able to maintain the innovation in her own teaching, other teachers are unable to benefit from this type of program. She reports, however, that her students have had an influence on some of the other teachers because these teachers see that the students can take independent action and work in groups to construct and justify meanings. The success she has experienced makes one wonder what might have happened with others if this innovation had not been stopped.

The superintendent who initiated the innovative professional development program stated that it would take 10 years to transform the district and then only 90 percent of all teachers would take up the new direction. He left two years into this process (Bergamo, Green, & Ridgeway, 1989). We will return to this issue again throughout the sections that follow.

Defining Literacy in the Interactions of Teachers and Students

This study showed that literate action and literacy processes are socially constructed opportunities that students have in classrooms. These opportunities are accomplished through the everyday actions of teachers and students. This way of defining literacy challenges two commonly held views: one about literacy and one about learning in school settings. As we indicated at the outset of this chapter, the commonly held view of literacy in schools equates literacy with reading, writing, and literature. In a few instances, speaking and listening are considered part of the literacy process. Social context has also been considered more recently, but it is often viewed as the setting or a background variable. As indicated in this chapter, such a view of literacy is a compartmentalized view that ignores the fact that literacy is accomplished through interactions and communications of members of a group. In other words, as members of a group accomplish the events of everyday life, they construct a model or models of literate action that define the boundaries of what counts as literacy in their particular group. In turn, this model serves as a frame for future interactions, which in turn modify the model.

From this perspective, then, literacy is continually being defined, redefined, constructed, and reconstructed in the social life of a group. The outcome of this process is not a single definition of literacy, but an understanding of the multiplicity of literacies individuals face as they become members of ever-expanding groups and communities.

The second commonly held view that is challenged by the work presented in this study is the view that what we see in students' actions in classrooms is an indication of ability. What this study suggests is that what we see in student actions and statements is a patterned way of acting or communicating that students have learned from the opportunities afforded them in this and other classrooms. For instance, in the example about characters previously cited, if the teachers had not provided students with an opportunity to explain why they held the view that they held, half of the class might have been viewed as wrong, as not knowing, or as lacking ability. That is, if the teachers had relied on the answers alone without considering the rationales provided by students, they would have had limited information and might have arrived at an interpretation of student knowledge, ability, or actions that underrepresented or even misrepresented the actual case. The character discussion shows that the type of opportunity to display knowledge and understanding afforded students influences what is available to be observed.

The discussion of the socially constructed nature of learning and knowledge suggests the need to return to the issue of professional development discussed previously. On a parallel level, the same issues apply to teacher learning and knowledge. This study raises questions about whether what we see in teachers' actions is an unwillingness of teachers to engage in innovative practice (Cuban, 1984), or the lack of opportunity teachers have to construct new patterns of action. As indicated above, the instability of top-level administrators was consequential for both teachers and students. The actions of the superintendents established conditions that supported particular directions and simultaneously constrained the opportunities that the teachers had to examine other approaches (e.g., student-centered approaches to learning in classrooms). In addition, the changes in administration did not provide supportive conditions that helped the teachers expand their repertoires. Thus, like their students, the teachers were influenced by the opportunities they have to learn new ways of being teachers and engaging students in learning.

That one of the teachers was able to instantiate new patterns of action in all of her classes in the face of this instability is important to consider. This teacher had time before the change to: ask questions; establish her own need to know about alternative approaches; work with colleagues to examine research; engage in her own research; construct and experiment with alternatives in a special situation before implementing the approach in her regular classes; experiment with the new knowledge in particular classes; and only then, implement the program with all of her classes.

One way to interpret this sequence of actions is that the teacher had opportunities to engage in learning new ways of being a teacher in which she had control over the phases of implementation of knowledge. She applied the knowledge she felt comfortable with and engaged in new patterns of action when she saw benefits for her students. Recent interviews with her indicated that she implemented the new actions because they helped students learn to respond to literature and expanded their abilities to provide rationales for their own actions.

The issues of literacy and professional development, therefore, are intertwined for these teachers. Like Peterson's teacher (Peterson, Chapter 6, this volume) and the teachers with whom Weade worked (Weade, Chapter 4, this volume), as the teachers in this study explored ways their students learned to be literate, they extended, modified, and refined their own knowledge and views of literacy. This study suggests that exploration of subject-matter content is an important component in the study of learning in classroom settings, and that content and process are synergistic when brought together in a single study. This work also suggests that research on student learning needs to be paralleled by research on teacher learning and by consideration of prior opportunities teachers have had to examine ways of teaching and engaging students in learning. Teaching is not a unitary process, but rather one that is influenced by the repertoires that include patterned ways of acting and beliefs about what counts as appropriate action of students.

Researching Learning from a Social Perspective

In this final section, we consider the implications of this study for research practice. In this study, we illustrated that the actions of people outside of the classroom both support and constrain what can and will occur, who the learner is, what counts as knowing within a group, and what conditions are necessary to support the transformation of ways of being students and teachers. To interpret the patterns of observed life in the classroom, we had to draw on a wide variety of additional data sources. Observations of classroom life were not sufficient in and of themselves. As discussed previously, we had to draw on observations of interactions of teachers with others outside of the classroom, on documents not visible in the classroom, on district policies, and on interviews with teachers and members of the professional development program.

The need to consider multiple sources of information raises serious questions about sampling, about instrumentation, about documentation of observed phenomena, and about presentation of evidence. In the description of our data, we indicated that this data set was a *site* to examine particular aspects of classroom life. No claim was made that we had captured what actually occurred as perceived by members of the class. This study confirms work on multiple perspectives that indicates that the ways in which we as researchers go about the research process influences the understandings obtained from this process (see Green, Harker, & Golden, 1987; Green & Harker, 1988; Morine-Dershimer, 1988a, 1988b; Wallat & Piazza, 1988).

Finally, the study of both classroom life and the factors that support and/or constrain this life required overtime observations within and across a variety of settings. Life in the classroom was constructed over time, events often occurred across time, intertextual relationships were identified among elements of life, continuity of experiences as well as discontinuities were part of the analysis, and common knowledge as well as individual knowledge was visible in the actions of members. This study, therefore, joins a growing body of work over the last two decades that has raised questions about the representatives of events being studied, the boundaries of events, and the tied nature of human activity. In other words, this study raises questions about the claims one wishes to make and the ways in which we go about our research. One way to view the implications of this work for research practice is that, like teachers and students, the types of opportunities researchers construct influence what they come to know.

REFERENCES

Allington, R. (1984). Oral reading. In P.D. Pearson (Ed.), *Handbook of reading research* (pp. 829–864). New York: Longman.

Alvermann, D.E. (1989). Teacher-student mediation of content area texts. *Theory Into Practice, 18*(2), 142–147.

Applebee, A.N. (1961). *Writing in the secondary school: English and the content areas* (Report No. 21). Urbana, IL: National Council of Teachers of English.

Baker, C., & Luke, A. (Eds.). (1991). *Toward a critical sociology of reading pedagogy.* Philadelphia: John Benjamins.

Bartholomae, D., & Petrosky, A.R. (1986). *Facts, artifacts and counterfacts: Theory and method for a reading and writing course.* Portsmouth, NH: Boynton/Cook Publishers.

Bergamo, H., Green, J.L., & Ridgeway, D. (1988, October). *Reflection and beyond: Emerging strategies and issues in professional development, a case of the Columbus Instructional Model.* Unpublished paper presented at the Reflection Conference, Orlando, FL.

Bergamo, H., Green, J.L., & Ridgeway, D. (1989, July). *Making professional development last: Issues and research, policy and practice.* Unpublished paper presented at the Invitational Conference on Professional Development, University of New England, Northern Rivers, Lismore, Australia.

Bloome, D. (Ed.). (1986a). *Literacy and schooling.* Norwood, NJ: Ablex.

Bloome, D. (1986b). Building literacy and the classroom community. *Theory Into Practice, 15*(2), 71–76.

Bloome, D. (1986c). Reading as a social process in a middle school classroom. In D. Bloome (Ed.), *Literacy and schooling* (pp. 123–149). Norwood, NJ: Ablex.

Bloome, D. (1989). *The social construction of intertextuality on classroom literacy learning.* Unpublished paper presented at American Educational Research Association, San Francisco.

Bloome, D., & Theodorou, E. (1988). Analyzing teacher-student and student-student discourse. In J. Green & J. Harker (Eds.), *Multiple perspective analysis of classroom discourse* (pp. 217–248). Norwood, NJ: Ablex.

Bloome, D., Theodorou, E., & Puro, P. (1989). Procedural display and classroom lessons. *Curriculum Inquiry, 19*(3), 265–291.

Cazden, C. (1986). Classroom discourse. In M. Wittrock (Ed.), *The handbook of research on teaching,* (3rd. ed., pp. 432–463). New York: Macmillan.

Cazden, C., John, V., & Hymes, D. (1972). *Functions of language in the classroom.* New York: Teachers College Press.

Cochran-Smith, M. (1984). *The making of a reader.* Norwood, NJ: Ablex.

Collins, J. (1983). *A linguistic perspective on minority education: Discourse analysis and early literacy.* Unpublished doctoral dissertation, University of California, Berkeley.

Collins, J. (1986). Using cohesion analysis to understand access to knowledge. In D. Bloome (Ed.), *Literacy and schooling* (pp. 67–97). Norwood, NJ: Ablex.

Cook-Gumperz, J. (Ed.). (1986). *The social construction of literacy.* New York: Cambridge University Press.

Cuban, L. (1984). *How teachers taught*. New York: Longman.
Edwards, A., & Mercer, N. (1989). *Common knowledge: The development of understanding in the classroom*. New York: Falmer Press.
Erickson, F. (1986). Qualitative methods in research on teaching. In M. Wittrock (Ed.), *Handbook of research on teaching* (3rd ed., pp. 119–161). New York: Macmillan.
Fenstermacher, G. (1986). In M. Wittrock (Ed.), *Handbook of research on teaching* (3rd ed., pp. 37–49). New York: Macmillan.
Fernie, D., Kantor, R., Klein, E., Meyer, C., & Elgas, P. (1988). Becoming students and becoming ethnographers in a preschool. *Journal of Research in Childhood Education, 3*, 132–141.
Fernie, D., Kantor, R., Scott, J., Schwarz, P., Kesner, J., & Klein, E. (1990, April). *Honeymooners: Teachers and children co-construct the school culture of a preschool*. Paper presented at the annual meeting of the American Educational Research Association, Boston.
Fish, S. (1980). *Is there a text in this class? The authority of interpretive communities*. Cambridge, MA: Harvard University Press.
Golden, J. (1984). If a text exists without a reader, is there any meaning? In B.A. Hutson (Ed.), *Advances in reading/language research* (Vol. 2). Greenwood, CT: JAI Press.
Golden, J. (1986). An exploration of reader-text interaction in a small group discussion. In D. Bloome (Ed.), *Literacy and schooling* (pp. 169–192). Norwood, NJ: Ablex.
Golden, J. (1988). The construction of a literary text in a story reading lesson. In J. Green & J. Harker (Eds.), *Multiple perspective analysis of classroom discourse* (pp. 71–106). Norwood, NJ: Ablex.
Golden, J. (1989). The literary text event. *Theory Into Practice, 28*, 83–87.
Golden, J. (1990). *The narrative symbol in childhood literature*. New York: Mouton de Gruyter.
Green, J.L. (1977). *Pedagogical style differences as related to comprehension: Grades 1 through 3*. Unpublished dissertation, University of California, Berkeley, CA.
Green, J.L., & Harker, J.O. (1982). Gaining access to learning: Conversational, social, and cognitive demands of group participation. In L.C. Wilkinson (Ed.), *Communicating in the classroom* (pp. 183–221). New York: Academic Press.
Green, J.L., & Harker, J.O. (Eds.). (1988). *Multiple perspective analyses of classroom discourse*. Norwood, NJ: Ablex.
Green, J.L., Harker, J.O., & Golden, J.M. (1987). Lesson construction: Differing views. In G. Noblitt & W. Pink (Eds.), *Schooling in social context: Qualitative studies* (pp. 46–77). Norwood, NJ: Ablex.
Green, J.L., Kantor, R., & Rogers, T. (1990). Exploring the complexity of language and learning in the classroom. In B. Jones & L. Idol (Eds.), *Educational values and cognitive instruction: Implications for reform* (Vol. II, pp. 333–364). Hillsdale, NJ: Erlbaum.
Green, J.L., & Meyer, L.A. (1991). The embeddedness of reading in classroom life: Reading as a situated process. In C. Baker & A. Luke (Eds.), *Toward a critical sociology of reading pedagogy* (pp. 141–160). Philadelphia: John Benjamins.

Green, J.L., & Wallat, C. (1981). Mapping instructional conversations—A sociolinguistic ethnography. In J. Green & C. Wallat (Eds.), *Ethnography and languages in educational settings* (pp. 161–195). Norwood, NJ: Ablex.

Gumperz, J. (1986). Interactive sociolinguistics on the study of schooling. In J. Cook-Gumperz (Ed.), *The social construction of literacy* (pp. 45–68). New York: Cambridge University Press.

Gumperz, J., & Herasimchuk, E. (1973). The conversational analysis of social meaning: A study of classroom interaction. In R. Shuy (Ed.), *Sociolinguistics: Current trends and prospects* (Monograph Series on Language and Linguistics, 23rd Annual Round Table Vol. 25, pp. 99–134). Georgetown, VA: Georgetown University Press.

Heap, J.L. (1980). What counts as reading: Limits to certainty in assessment. *Curriculum Inquiry, 15*, 245–279.

Heap, J.L. (1991). A situated perspective on what counts as reading. In C. Baker & A. Luke (Eds.), *Toward a critical sociology of reading pedagogy* (pp. 103–139). The Netherlands: John Benjamins.

Mehan, H. (1979). *Learning lessons.* Cambridge, MA: Harvard University Press.

Morine-Dershimer, G. (1988a). Three approaches to sociolinguistic analysis: Introduction. In J. Green & J. Barker (Eds.), *Multiple perspective analyses of classroom discourse*, (pp. 107–112). Norwood, NJ: Ablex.

Morine-Dershimer, G. (1988b). Comparing systems: How do we know? In J. Green & J. Harker (Eds.), *Multiple perspective analyses of classroom discourse* (pp. 195–214). Norwood, NJ: Ablex.

Robinson, J. (1986). Literacy in society: Readers and writers in the world. In D. Bloome (Eds.), *Literacy and schooling* (pp. 327–353). Norwood, NJ: Ablex.

Salinger, J.D. (1951). *Catcher in the rye.* Boston: Little Brown.

Singer, H., & Ruddell, R. (1985). *Theoretical models and processes of reading.* Newark, DE: International Reading Association.

Spradley, J. (1980). *Participant observation.* New York: Holt, Rinehart & Winston.

Street, B. V. (1984). *Literacy in theory and practice.* New York: Cambridge University Press.

Tannen, D. (1979). What's in a frame? Surface evidence for underlying expectations. In R. Freedle (Ed.), *New directions in discourse processing* (pp. 137–182). Norwood, NJ: Ablex.

Wallat, C., & Piazza, C. (1988). The classroom and beyond: Issues in the analysis of multiple studies of communicative competence. In J. Green & J. Harker (Eds.), *Multiple perspective analyses of classroom discourse* (pp. 309–342). Norwood, NJ: Ablex.

Weade, G., & Green, J.L. (1989). Reading in the instructional context: An interactional sociolinguistic/ethnographic perspective. In C. Emihovich (Ed.), *Locating learning across the curriculum: Ethnographic perspectives on classroom research* (pp. 17–56). Norwood, NJ: Ablex.

Chapter 6
Revising Their Thinking: Keisha Coleman and Her Third-Grade Mathematics Class*

Penelope L. Peterson

Michigan State University
College of Education
Erickson Hall
Michigan State University

INTRODUCTION

Classrooms in our nation's schools reflect an "assembly-line model" of work reminiscent of the era of Henry Ford. Yet contemporary experts in

---

* The work reported in this article was conducted as part of the research of the Center for the Learning and Teaching of Elementary Subjects at Michigan State University. The Center for the Learning and Teaching of Elementary Subjects is funded primarily by the Office of Educational Research and Improvement, U.S. Department of Education. The opinions expressed in this chapter do not necessarily reflect the position, policy, or endorsement of the Office or the Department (Cooperative Agreement No. G0087C0226). An earlier version of this chapter was presented at the annual meeting of the American Educational Research Association, in Boston, in April 1990. Special thanks to four people who read and commented on earlier versions of this chapter—Sarah McCarthey, Jere Brophy, Deborah Ball, and Keisha Coleman. Ms. Coleman requested that I not use her real name, so I have honored her request. I also thank Nancy Knapp, Janine Remillard, and James Reineke, who interviewed children in Ms. Coleman's class. Finally, I wish to express my appreciation to Ms. Coleman and the students in her third-grade class who allowed me to come and visit their mathematics class for a year, and to look, listen, and learn along with them.

business and industry argue that the nature of work has changed even in manufacturing and that the quality of the educational "product"—students' performance and abilities learned in school—needs to be changed and improved to keep the United States competitive in a global economy (cf. Zuboff, 1984; National Academy of Engineering, 1985; Ross, 1988). Business and industry need workers who are literate and numerate, can think for themselves, work and learn collaboratively, solve problems, access and use knowledge as needed, and revise and transform the information given.

Contemporary educators too are critical of the old factory model as a way of conceptualizing what should be going on in classrooms. For example, in a recent article, Marshall (1988) pointed out the limitations of the "workplace metaphor" as a way of thinking about classrooms. In its place, she suggested the metaphor of "learning-oriented classrooms." She argued that, in contrast to the old factory model where the goal was to produce a product, in classrooms the goals should be to learn and to develop knowledge. Further, in contrast to these work settings where authority relationships were based on the status and expertise of the manager, in learning settings authority relationships should be "based on expertise and knowledge *to be shared or developed* rather than held by the authority and on the *desire to help individuals acquire or construct knowledge*" (Marshall, 1988, p. 14; emphasis in original).

Underlying much of the rhetoric of the current reform both in industry and in education is a new view of knowledge. According to this view, knowledge is seen not as fixed and static, but rather as continuously undergoing revision and transformation. Manufacturing is no longer seen as the application of fixed knowledge (for example, as instantiated in the assembly line) to produce a static, unchanging product (for example, your father's Oldsmobile). Rather, manufacturing is seen as "a process which transforms information into a product. The information includes design data, quantities required, and delivery dates. The transformation involves developing tools and processes, obtaining material, processing material, assembly, testing, and delivery" (Shea, 1985, p. 12). The information or knowledge itself is not viewed as static, but rather as in need of ongoing revision and transformation because "the companies that gain nearly unassailable positions in the world market" will be those who are able "to produce quality products tailored to special customer requirements on a very short lead time" (Shea, 1985, p. 12).

Similarly, education reformers are creating new visions of the knowledge base for teaching and are offering new views of what it means to "know" and understand academic subjects. Shulman (1987) proposed that "a knowledge base for teaching is not fixed and finite," and he argued for building teaching reform on a view of teaching that emphasizes comprehension, reasoning, transformation, and reflection. The Mathematical Sciences Education Board of the National Research Council [MSEB]; (1990) has asserted the need to change two popular and outdated assumptions—that mathematics is a fixed and unchanging body of facts and procedures, and that to do mathematics is to calculate answers to set problems using a specific catalogue of rehearsed techniques. The Board proposes instead that "mathematics is a creative, active process"; that in mathematics, "reasoning is the test of truth"; and that "mathematics is a language—the language through which nature speaks...and an apt language for business and commerce" (MSEB, 1990, pp. 10-12).

What do these revised views of teaching and what it means to know mathematics imply for how mathematics should be taught and learned in elementary classrooms? This question has generated and is generating substantial debate and discussion among mathematics education researchers and education reformers as well as among teachers as they struggle to enact these new visions of mathematical knowing and teaching in their classrooms. Two compelling portraits of such attempts are provided by Lampert (1990) and Ball (1990).

In her teaching of elementary mathematics to fifth-grade students, Lampert tries to "bring the practice of knowing mathematics closer to what it means to know mathematics within a discipline by deliberately altering the roles and responsibilities of teachers and students in classroom discourse" (Lampert, 1990, p. 29). To do so, she has developed new forms of classroom discourse and teacher–student interaction where content and discourse are intertwined and words take on new meanings. Some of the words that take on new meanings are *knowing, thinking, explaining,* and *revising.* Lampert begins by posing a problem to her students. As students volunteer solutions to the problem, she writes them on the board for consideration. These solutions are up for discussion and revision. If students want to disagree with a solution, they say that they want to "question so-and-so's hypothesis" and then give the reasons for disagreeing. The student who gave the solution is free to respond or not to respond with a "revision." When Johnny says that he wants to "revise his thinking," he is using words that Lampert has encouraged her students to use, and he means that he wants to change his mind about an assertion that he made earlier in their class discussion. Lampert views this as important, because "when a student is in charge of revising his own thinking, and expected to do so publicly, the authority for determining what is valid knowledge is shifted from the teacher to the student and the community in which the revision is asserted" (Lampert, 1990, p. 52).

Like Lampert with whom she collaborates in a National Science Foundation project to document their teaching, Deborah Ball aims to develop a "practice that respects both the integrity of mathematics as a discipline *and* of children as mathematical thinkers" (Ball, 1990, p. 3; emphasis in original). She strives to create a classroom environment in which the norms of discourse are informed by patterns of discourse in the mathematics community as well as by the culture of the classroom. Further, she strives to shift authority for mathematical knowledge from the teacher and the "text" to the community of knowers and learners of mathematics in her classroom. While Ball and her students engage in extensive discourse in the whole-class setting, they also work in small groups. She tries to select and create mathematics tasks that engage students in learning the content of mathematics as they learn the ways of knowing. Ball (1990) provides an example of discourse from her third-grade mathematics class in which students discuss the problem: $6 + (-6)$. Ball and her students spent over 30 minutes discussing solutions for that problem. At one point, a student gave the correct answer, but the student's explanation was problematic. Students gave two other solutions that received "equal air time." Ball states that at no time did she "tell or lead the students to conclude that $6 + (-6)$ equals zero—by pointing them at the commutativity of addition or at the need for the system of operations on integers to be sensibly consistent. At the end of class only half the students knew the right answer" (Ball, 1990, p. 26). Ball thinks that the time that students spend "unpacking ideas" is time well spent. Too often she has seen evidence of students who fail to understand even though they have been "taught" the mathematical procedure. Ball noted that, when they "moved on from negative numbers a week or so later almost every student was able to add and subtract integers accurately if the negative number was in the first position, for example, $-5 + 4$, or $-3 - 8$" (Ball, 1990, p. 25).

The portraits provided by Lambert (1990) and Ball (1990) provide two examples of how teachers might enact revised views of mathematics and what it means to know mathematics in their elementary classrooms. Such case analyses are important because they provide insights into the dilemmas that elementary teachers face as they attempt to enact reformers' visions of desired changes in mathematics instruction—less emphasis on practice of isolated computational skills, more emphasis on understanding, problem solving, and flexible mathematical reasoning (e.g., National Council of Teachers of Mathematics [NCTM], 1989; National Research Council, 1989). Such case analyses are needed both to advance researchers' understandings of what it means to learn and teach mathematics with understanding in light of calls for reform and also to inform teachers, teacher educators, and others as they attempt to effect fundamental changes in mathematics teaching and learning in our elementary schools (Hiebert & Carpenter, 1992). The purpose of the present study was to attempt to understand another teacher's attempt to enact these revised views in her classroom.

During the 1989–1990 school year, I studied an elementary teacher, Keisha Coleman, as she revised her teaching of third-grade mathematics. In this chapter I relate a bit of the story of Keisha Coleman's mathematics teaching—a story that is, of course, still unfolding. I focus on the changes in her thinking and her mathematics teaching during the fall of that year and how they came about. I conclude with some tentative ideas about what I have learned and some questions for further thought.

A BRIEF NOTE ON METHOD

In October 1989, I began spending at least one day a week in Keisha's third-grade classroom observing her teach mathematics. During my observations, I wrote narrative descriptions of what occurred, focusing particularly on the discourse and the mathematics that was taught. I recorded what was written on the board and any written work that the students did. The teacher and student discourse in each lesson was audiotaped and later transcribed. During the postobservation interview, my conversation with Keisha focused on what she was trying to teach, why she was trying to teach it, how she was trying to teach the mathematics, what Keisha hoped that the students would get out of the mathematics lesson, and what Keisha thought the students actually got out of the lesson. My post-observation interview questions and techniques were adapted from those we have used in the California Study of Elementary Mathematics (cf. Peterson, 1990), which were adapted from interviews developed by the National Center for Research in Teacher Education (1989). In conducting the interviews, I relied not so much on a structured interview format, but rather, on my own knowledge and experience gained from interviewing elementary teachers. Thus, I asked Keisha questions that would help me understand how she was thinking, how she construed the mathematics lesson, and how she thought about mathematics teaching and learning in her classroom.

In October, January, and June each student in the class was interviewed individually for 1 to 2 hours about their solutions for some mathematics problems and their thinking about these problems. The intent of the interview was to probe in depth the student's knowledge and understanding of key mathematical ideas, and the student's attitudes and beliefs about mathematics and about the learning and teaching of mathematics.

This chapter focuses on Keisha's mathematics teaching and her thinking about her mathematics teaching during Fall 1989. Peterson and Knapp (in preparation) provide further analyses of the teaching and learning of mathematics in Keisha's classroom during the winter and spring of the 1989–1990 school year.

THE "LEARNING" CONTEXT OF KEISHA COLEMAN'S CLASSROOM

Ms. Coleman teaches in a school that has a high percentage of ethnically and linguistically diverse children, some of whom are eligible for and receive free or reduced lunch. Most of the children's parents are undergraduate or graduate students who are attending Michigan State University. Children in the school speak 20 different languages. Although some children attend English as a Second Language (ESL) classes, all the regular classroom teachers teach their lessons in English. Ms. Coleman, the principal, and the teachers in the school themselves represent the ethnic diversity characteristic of the school, and Ms. Coleman often focuses on issues of ethnic identity and culture in her teaching. She grew up in nearby Detroit, and received her teaching degree from Michigan State University. She began teaching at her school 15 years ago, a year after her colleague Deborah Ball also began teaching there, and the current principal started at the school.

During the previous year, Keisha's school had become a "professional development school" affiliated with Michigan State University in efforts "to develop and put in place new forms of teaching for genuine conceptual understanding in core subject areas, for problem solving, and thinking skills, for higher order literacy, for the skills of learning to learn autonomously, for teamwork skills, and for other aspects of the education required for success in the emerging knowledge age society and economy" (College of Education, Michigan State University, 1989). A major focus is on facilitating teachers' learning (cf. Holmes Group, 1990).

At the beginning of the year, Keisha stated that one of her intentions for the year was to work on learning more and on changing and improving her mathematics teaching. This is how she defined her work for the year as an elementary teacher of mathematics. She agreed to be the focus of this study and to participate in the research project because she saw it as a way to reflect on, learn about, and work on improving her mathematics teaching. During the course of this case study year, Keisha engaged in several other influential learning activities including participating in long lunchtime meetings on Friday with the whole staff of the school and serving as a member of the East Lansing school district's mathematics committee. In addition, she observed two of her peers teach—Deborah Ball, a colleague in the same school; and Elaine Hugo. As the district's mathematics support teacher for the Comprehensive School Mathematics Program (CSMP) (Mid-continent Educational Research Laboratory [CEMREL], 1985), Elaine Hugo came into Keisha's classroom and taught during the 1989–1990 school year. (See Putnam & Reineke, 1991, for a case study of Elaine Hugo.) As Hugo sees it, "CSMP has helped a lot of teachers do more verbalizing in math whether it's just by asking more questions, or by getting the kids to talk more about mathematics" (Putnam & Reineke, 1991, p. 7). Based on their observations of Hugo's practice, Putnam and Reineke (1991) noted that, consistent with her beliefs about the importance of giving students opportunities to talk about mathematics, Hugo structures her lessons to allow students to express their thinking. However, they noted that, in her classroom, Hugo gives the most attention to students' *correct* understandings. She is "fairly convergent about where she is going; she wants the students to say a particular thing" (Putnam & Reineke, 1991, p. 14).

Consistent with Hugo's idea that CSMP has helped teachers change, Keisha Coleman sees her mathematics teaching as having evolved over the last four years as she has been influenced profoundly by using CSMP. CSMP is an innovative mathematics curriculum that focuses on mathematical problem solving and thinking and on providing students with distinctive mathematical tools (e.g., Venn diagrams or "string pictures," a kind of abacus called the "minicomputer," and "arrow roads" showing mathematical functions) for representing their mathematical ideas and thinking (cf. Remillard, 1991). She reported that, when she first started teaching, the district had an individualized mathematics program, and she hated it. "Everybody was just everywhere in the book," she said, and she felt that all her instruction "was just hit and miss." One of Keisha's colleagues in the school, a fifth-grade teacher, who had also taught at the school for 15 years, referred to teaching mathematics during those years as "a paper chase." Then the district adopted CSMP, and Keisha felt that teaching CSMP really changed her feelings about mathematics and about teaching mathematics. As Keisha put it:

> With CSMP, I felt like I was *teaching* because of the questions that you're constantly asking children, trying to get them to rethink or to think about their responses rather than just giving an answer. I'm not real sure I was comfortable with that in the beginning, but I think that is a thing that helped me. I actually felt like I was *teaching* math, and that was a feeling that I wanted. There was all sorts of information, workshops that you could go to. We always had a reading consultant here in our district—somebody who could always assist you with any kind of problems in reading. We didn't have that in math so we began to reevaluate what we were doing. I think Debbie [Ball] sort of felt a lot of that too—trying to look for ways the teachers could actually teach math and feel comfortable with it. Before I had always told her [Deborah Ball], "Don't bring anything math-like my way because I'm not good at it."

KEISHA'S CLASSROOM IN NOVEMBER 1988: FOLLOWING THE "TEXT"

When I first met Keisha in November 1988, she had been teaching mathematics using CSMP for 3 years, and she taught like a teacher who was committed to using CSMP to teach mathematics. She held the CSMP teacher's guide in her hand while she was teaching, and she seemed to be reading from the guide much of the time. The picture (an "arrow road") that Ms. Coleman drew to represent mathematical ideas seemed to come from the text rather than from her own head or from the thinking of the students. She taught the entire mathematics lesson using lecture-recitation in a teacher-led whole group format. The CSMP teacher's guide is scripted with the kinds of questions the teacher should ask, and the kinds of student responses the teacher should expect to get. Although Keisha's fourth-grade students verbalized some strategies that they used to solve mathematical problems that she posed, Ms. Coleman acknowledged or encouraged only students' contributions that seemed to fit with her "script." The classroom discourse was mostly convergent, focusing on coming up with a solution. For example, in one place in the mathematics lesson, Ms. Coleman asked the students to tell a story for the number sentence: $20 - 14 = 6$. One child told the story: "Garner has 20 houses. A giant stepped on 14. How many are left?" Ms. Coleman responded by asking the students, "What is my question? What would my question be?" Although several children gave plausible responses to her query, Ms. Coleman ignored them because they were not the one she was looking for. Finally, she wrote on her board the response she had been looking for—the question, "How many houses were left?"

The classroom dialogue was primarily teacher–student rather than student–student. Further, where Ms. Coleman had opportunities to explore student's thinking or "unpack" mathematical ideas, she often did not follow up on them. When Ms. Coleman asked her students to tell a story for the number sentence as described above, one fourth-grade child proposed, "There were 20 punks; 14 had mohawks. How many didn't have mohawks?" Another child suggested, "Steve has 20 cents. He bought gum with 14 cents. How many does he have left?" A third child pointed out that these two problems are different—one is comparing and one is subtracting—but he added, "We still had to minus it." Although Ms. Coleman acknowledged this student's thinking as good, she did not build on it or ask other students what they thought of this student's idea.

A final noteworthy aspect of Keisha's mathematical teaching on that day was the extensiveness, yet disconnectedness, of the mathematics content that she covered and the classroom discourse that occurred. In a 1-hour mathematics lesson Ms. Coleman covered four different mathematical topics, and she made no explicit connections between them. The first topic dealt with different ways to compute 6×7. The second topic involved asking the students to make up word problems for the number sentence, $20 - 14 = 6$. The third topic involved Ms. Coleman asking the students to make up a word problem like the one she gave: I have 5 envelopes. Each envelope has 6 picture postcards in it. How many picture postcards are there altogether? Finally, Ms. Coleman posed the following word problem from the CSMP teacher's guide:

> Andrew wants to buy a ticket good for one admission to Cedar Point. A ticket costs 9 dollars. Grandfather says he'll double whatever amount Andrew has. Grandma will give $1 more to Andrew. How much money does Andrew need

before visiting his grandparents? Which should Andrew go to first (Grandmother or Grandfather)?

This problem proved to be quite challenging for the fourth-grade students in her class so Ms. Coleman led the class through the solution by introducing a pictorial representation to help them solve it. Throughout the discussion of the problem solution, the talk was teacher–student–teacher–student, with no student–student discourse about the solution to the mathematics problem.

To what extent did Keisha's mathematics teaching on that day reflect important elements of teaching mathematics for understanding? Certainly, her lesson did focus on student's mathematical thinking and mathematical strategies in addition to correct mathematical solutions. Students verbalized solution strategies to mathematical problems, and some of students' thinking was made visible to others in the class—at least that part of students' thinking that fit with the script. Recent experimental research in elementary mathematics classrooms has shown that teachers who spend more time having students verbalize their different solution strategies for solving word problems have students who do better on tests of word problem solving and as well or better on computation problems as students of teachers who spend more time on computation and less time on having students verbalize their different solution strategies for solving word problems (Carpenter, Fennema, Peterson, Chiang, & Loef, 1989). Further, reformers and researchers alike argue that having students verbalize different solution strategies for solving word problems is key to learning mathematics with understanding (cf. California State Department of Education, 1985; NCTM, 1989, Fennema, Carpenter, & Peterson, 1989).

For this reason, and because Keisha's mathematics teaching and her focus on students' thinking and problem solving stands out in stark contrast to most other elementary mathematics teaching, where the focus is solely on mathematical computations and procedures, Keisha's mathematics lesson on this day was *exceptional*. Clearly, Keisha's purpose in teaching the CSMP lesson was for her students to think about and learn the mathematics she was teaching. Thus, if I had asked her last year and if I asked her again this year, Keisha probably would have agreed that, of course, the purpose of school and assignments should be *learning*. However, as we shall see, Keisha views herself as continuously learning how to teach mathematics, and she sees her mathematics teaching as undergoing substantial revision.

LEARNING FROM HER PEER AND COLLEAGUE

Another major revision in Keisha's thinking and her mathematics teaching occurred during Fall 1989, when Keisha began observing the teaching of her long-time colleague and peer, Deborah Ball. Deborah Ball and Magdalene

Lampert are Michigan State University professors and researchers, as well as experienced elementary teachers, who teach mathematics one period each day in the school in which Keisha teaches. During the 1989–1990 school year, Keisha taught third grade in a classroom next to the room where Ball daily taught third-grade mathematics and across the hall from the fifth-grade classroom where Lampert daily taught mathematics.

Keisha observed Deborah Ball's classroom for a week in November 1989. I also observed Deborah teach while Keisha was there. On November 17, I returned to observe Keisha's mathematics classroom, and I was amazed by the discourse about mathematics that took place. Keisha posed questions and orchestrated the classroom discourse in ways similar to those of Deborah. These changes in Keisha's classroom behavior were unexpected, and I speculate that Keisha's easy facility and ability to perform these new behaviors might be related to her expertise as an aerobic dance instructor—a role that required her to learn new steps and new verbal directions weekly and to perform these with smoothness, drama, precision, and enthusiasm. Before I give you a glimpse into what I saw and heard in Keisha's classroom that day, I want to tell you about my conversation with Keisha before I observed her teach on that day.

Our conversation revolved both around what Keisha was going to do in mathematics class that day and what she had learned from watching Deborah. These were interconnected because her plans were based on ideas that she had developed from watching Deborah and talking to Deborah about her mathematics teaching.

Thinking about Unpacking Mathematical Ideas

One thing that surprised Keisha was that Deborah and her students had spent an entire hour in thinking about and in discussion of only four mathematics problems. Keisha remarked that she was just amazed that the children were really involved in what they were doing, and that it "was not tedious or busy-work." In one particular part of the lesson, Keisha recalled that two girls, Betsy and Leann, came up to the overhead projector. They had beans and sticks, and they were trying to "prove" why the answers to two problems, 92 − 65 and 93 − 66, were the same. Keisha retold what she had witnessed in an amazed voice:

> And you could just see the wheels turning in Betsy's head, just turning as she was trying to explain. Then she became frustrated because she knew that her solution or what she was trying to say was not clear to everybody... Leann began to try to say what Betsy was trying to explain, but Betsy wasn't satisfied with that... But Deborah let those two girls go on, and even some of the other children became involved with that exchange... Never once did the kids turn to Debbie and say, "What is the answer? Why aren't you telling us?"

Keisha said that ordinarily she would never have let an exchange like that between Betsy and Leann go on like that in her class. However, now she is reconsidering that. She also was surprised that by the end of the class the students never came to any conclusion as to why those two numbers equal the same. That bothered her at first and it still bothers her a bit. But then she thought about it, and she said to Deborah, "You know, in my opinion, that might even stimulate interest in the other children—to try to go home and work that out. And they might come back and say, 'Well, you know, I finally figured out why those two numbers equal the same.'"

Thinking about New Mathematical Language

Keisha also noted that, not only in this episode but throughout Deborah's lessons, a lot of talk went on about proving. She thought that the children obviously understood what Deborah meant when she talked about "proving," because the children themselves were using the word *proving*. Keisha said that she planned to bring up the idea of "proving" with her children today by asking, "How do you think you might be able to prove an answer is right or correct?" She said that she was not sure that they would be able to give her very much but that she planned to write down what they said on the board and "just kind of go from there."

Keisha noted another important thing about Deborah's class:

> When a child comes up with a method for solving something, Debbie writes that down, and she posts it in the classroom. And the kids agree whether or not it works or it doesn't work. But then they are challenged to find out whether or not this method would work for other things or not or for other situations. And it may be 2 days or 2 weeks down the road where a child will come up and challenge the method and say that it needs to be revised period... Deborah also has these children write these methods down in their notebooks, and they are also still posted in the classroom, so they can challenge them at any point. What better way for an idea to stay with a child?

Then Keisha embellished upon why she thought it might be important to write down students' ideas about mathematical methods. She said that, last week, her children were working with a string picture (Venn diagram), and one circle in the string picture stood for even numbers and the other circle stood for multiples of five. She and the students began talking about what an even number was. She commented that, although this was very new to her, she listened to what the children had to say, and then she wrote down what someone said. But she didn't write it down on construction paper and post it in the room. The next Monday, when they came back to it and they talked about it, she asked the children, "Can you remember what we said about that?" Nobody could remember. She said that she could just "kick herself for that," because she knows it is going to come up again. She would like to be able to discuss with them the questions, "Is this true for all even numbers?" and "Can you find a situation where it doesn't apply to an even number?"

Thinking about Deborah's Knowledge of Her Students' Math Knowledge

A theme that Keisha brought up throughout the interview dealt with what she viewed as the impressive knowledge that Deborah had of the mathematical knowledge and thinking of her children. She reported that she had seen the report cards that Deborah had done on her students. Deborah had written narrative descriptions of each student's mathematical knowledge and thinking.

Keisha wondered, "How does Deborah get that kind of in-depth knowledge of her children's mathematical thinking and understanding?" Keisha commented that, all too often, she was frustrated, because although she had taught a mathematics lesson or given the children practice sheets, she was never able to sit down with the children individually and talk with them about how they figured something out. Thus, she felt like she never knew if the child had "grasped onto" what she had taught. Now she set a goal of being able to know more *in depth* what her children know and understand in mathematics.

Thinking about Tools to Assess Students' Understanding

Keisha talked about three tools that she noticed that Deborah uses to get this kind of in-depth knowledge and understanding of her children's knowledge and thinking. She speculated on how she might incorporate some of these techniques in her own teaching. One thing that she noted is that Deborah gains extensive knowledge and understanding of her children's mathematical thinking and knowledge from the kind of discourse that occurs during her mathematics class, in which the thinking and understanding of individual children become more visible because they are the focus of discussion. On the other hand, when she reflected on what Deborah had written in her narrative reports of children, Keisha thought, "Geez, how is she getting all this? She can't be getting it just from the discussion period."

Keisha speculated that another way Deborah learns about her students' mathematics thinking is by having the children write their mathematics work in a notebook. Not only do they have to solve the problems in their notebooks, but they also have to prove their answers, either by using manipulatives or writing out explanations. Further, Deborah has her students write in ink rather than pencil, so that, by not being allowed to erase, she can, "Just kind of see their thinking so that she can see the children's thinking, through their mistakes, or as they cross things out, or as they try to rework the problems." Keisha noted that Deborah also has the children use manipulatives such as popsicle sticks to prove their answers so that she and other members of the class can see how the students are thinking about the problem.

Keisha told me that she had set as a goal that she will be able to get information about how her children are thinking about things. She feels that she does that for reading, but she wants to be able to do the same thing for mathematics, and the same thing for social studies, and the same thing for science. Although she was not sure yet how she would use this information, she had a clear goal for what she thought she wanted the children to be able to do. What she wanted her class to be able to do was to say, "This is how I'm thinking about this," and then for students to say that "I think that your idea is good, but I think we need to look at this, too." Keisha emphasized that she wanted to be "able to see the wheels turn in terms of their own thinking, and I don't have that right now."

A third tool that Deborah uses that Keisha planned to incorporate in her own teaching is one that she had just tried. Keisha gave her students a homework sheet that she had gotten from Deborah. On the top of the homework sheet was a number line. Then there were some problems like "$\hat{1}0$ plus 10 equals..." and "0 minus 2 equals..." (In the CSMP textbook, a "$\wedge$" above a number represents a negative number.) Under each of these problems was the question, "How do you know?" Keisha thought that this is one way that Deborah is able to come to know and understand her students' mathematical thinking—by looking at her students' answers to such questions.

Keisha gave the worksheet to her children the night before, and she reported that, although the children wrote down answers to the problems, only one or two of the children actually gave reasons why their answers came out the way they did. She said that she made comments on each one of the children's papers in terms of how they responded. When I looked later at the kinds of comments that Keisha had written on the students' worksheets, they were open-ended queries that seemed to be intended to get the student to think about his or her answer and how set got it. For example, on Ali's paper, Keisha had written, "Are you sure about your answers?" On Chang's paper, she had written, "How do you know?" Tessa had written "0" for the answer to "$\hat{1}0 + 10$," and the reason that Tessa had given was, "Because we give tacks away things." On Tessa's paper, Keisha had written, "What does this mean?"

Keisha assessed her students' responses to the homework by saying, "You know, my kids have never had to do that before—write down a reason why their answer is correct or how they got the answer." She stressed that that was one of the things she intended to talk about today—proving your answer.

With that, we concluded our conversation, and Keisha moved to begin her mathematics teaching for the day. What did Keisha's mathematics lesson look like that day, and how did it reflect the thinking that she was doing about her teaching? Let us take a look.

Looking in Keisha's Classroom in November, 1989

The mathematics lesson in Keisha's third-grade classroom on this day revolved around one problem from the homework assignment that Keisha had given her students the night before. The homework sheet was the one that Keisha had gotten from her colleague, Deborah Ball. At the top of the worksheet was this number line:

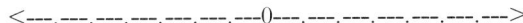

Under the number line was the direction: "Put the other numbers on this number line."

Below the number line were twelve different problems, some of which involved adding and subtracting positive and negative one-digit numbers. Ms. Coleman and the students spent the entire half-hour mathematics lesson "unpacking" students' mathematical ideas about the first problem on the page:

$$\hat{10} + 10 = ? \qquad \text{How do you know?}$$

Ms. Coleman began by asking if the students remembered the homework sheet that she had given them the night before. After she handed back the homework sheets, she told the students that she wanted to find out what they thought she meant by "proving" their answers. She said that everyone was able to fill in the number line, and that that was fine. She had the class look at the first problem on the page, "negative ten plus ten." Ms. Coleman reminded the students that they were supposed to give an answer and then tell why they knew their answer was the correct one. Ms. Coleman then asked for a volunteer who would like to share the answer she got. Marta volunteered and said, "Zero." Ms. Coleman wrote, "$\hat{10} + 10 = 0$" on the board and said, "Negative ten plus ten equals zero" aloud as she wrote. Ms. Coleman followed up by asking Marta if she could tell them *why* she knew that. Marta replied with an affirmative, and then the following whole-class dialogue ensued:

Ms. Coleman (C):   What did you say? *I would like for the rest of you to listen very carefully because I want you to be able to tell us, or tell Marta, if you agree with what she says or perhaps you disagree with what she says.* Marta?

Marta: You have to count ten numbers to the right....

[Here Ms. Coleman asked Marta to "say that again" and *Ms. Coleman wrote Marta's exact words on the board* as Marta said them.]

C: All right. Marta says that negative ten plus ten equals zero so you have to count ten numbers to the right. What do you people think about that? Harold?

Harold: I think it's easy, but I don't understand how she explained it.

C: O.K. Does anybody else have a comment or a response to that? Tessa?

Tessa: I think it's zero 'cause negative ten plus ten equals zero.

C: O.K. And? Right now, I'm asking about what Marta said. A comment? Agreements? Disagreements? Tessa.

Tessa: There's not... I don't agree.

C: You don't?

Tessa: I mean I do agree.

C: What do you agree with?

Tessa: That negative ten plus ten equals zero.

C: But that's not all Marta said.

Tessa: I disagree with that.

C: What do you disagree with?

Tessa: You have to count numbers to the right. If you count numbers to the right, then you couldn't get to zero. You'd have to count to the left.

C: Could you explain a little bit more about what you mean by that? I'm not quite sure I follow you. And the rest of *you need to listen very closely so you can make comments about what she's saying* or say whether or not you agree or disagree. Tessa?

Tessa: Because if you went that way [points to the right] then it would have to be a higher number.

In the above exchange the thinking of both Tessa and Marta became visible to Ms. Coleman and their peers. Tessa's responses led me to suspect that her understanding of negative numbers was not the same as Marta's. Indeed, my earlier interviews with these two girls in October also suggested that this was the case. In the interview, the interviewer showed Tessa two numbers, "$\hat{7}9$ and 2," and asked her which one was smaller. Tessa pointed to the 2 and said that it was smaller because it was 2 and the other was 79. When asked what the numbers would add up to, Tessa said, "81, because the next one [after 79] is 80 and then 81." In contrast, Marta showed greater understanding of negative numbers in her interview. In response to the same questions, Marta pointed to $\hat{7}9$ when the interviewer asked which number was smaller. Further, Marta explained correctly that it was because, "when they have the hats like that, they are smaller—they're not as much as zero."

In this first part of the classroom dialogue, Ms. Coleman set the scene for the students to construct a new orientation to mathematics learning in her classroom by indicating, first, that students would need to explain why they got the answer that they did, and second, that they would need to listen and think about their peers' explanations so that they could *decide whether or not they agreed or disagreed*. Further, they would need to know *with what* they agreed or disagreed, and then be prepared to explain *why* to their classmates. Thus far in the dialogue, Marta and Tessa had both gotten their thinking out on the table, and they indicated that they disagreed. However, up to this point, the discourse had still been teacher–student–teacher–student, and the conversation between Marta and Tessa had been mediated by Ms. Coleman. In the next part of the dialogue, Ms. Coleman helped change the pattern of discourse by suggesting that Chang, who disagreed with Tessa, talk directly to Tessa so that they could try to understand each other:

Ms. Coleman (C): Any comments about what Tessa's trying to say? Chang?
Chang: I disagree with what she's trying to say.
C: O.K. Your disagreement is?
Chang: Tessa says if you're counting right, then the number is—I don't really understand. She said, "If you count right, then the number has to go smaller." I don't know what she's talking about. Negative ten plus ten is zero.
C: You said that you don't understand what she's trying to say?
Chang: No.
C: Do you want to ask her?
Chang: [Turns to Tessa and asks]: What do you mean by counting to the right?
Tessa: If you count from ten up, you can't get zero. If you count from ten left, you can get zero.
Chang: [to Tessa]: Well, negative ten is a negative number—smaller than zero.
Tessa: I know.
Chang: Then why do you say you can't get to zero when you're adding to negative ten, which is smaller than zero?
Tessa: OHHHH! NOW I GET IT! This is positive.
C: Excuse me?
Tessa: You have to count right.
C: You're saying in order to get to zero, you have to count to the right? From where, Tessa?
Tessa: Negative 10.

From the October interview with Tessa, I knew that Tessa thought that "7̂9" was the same as "79." During the above interaction, I suspected that Tessa was thinking of "1̂0" as the same as "10," so she said that, when you count up from "1̂0" (actually negative 10, but what she thought was positive 10), then you couldn't get to zero. In response to Chang, Tessa said that she knew that a negative number was smaller than zero. And it dawned on Tessa that "10" is positive, and "1̂0" is a negative number.

The class went on to discuss what it means, "to count 10 numbers to the right"—the words in Marta's original explanation that Ms. Coleman had put on the board. However, at this point in the lesson, a concrete referent still had not been given for what was meant by counting 10 numbers to the right. Ms. Coleman asked the students if anyone would like to *revise* what Marta has said (here on the board) "so that it will say exactly what you feel in terms of *proving* your response."

Chang suggested revising Marta's explanation to say,"If you're on negative 10 and add 10, it equals zero." Chang was a student who, in the October interview, demonstrated some understanding of negative numbers by correctly identifying "79" as smaller than "2" because "negative 79 is smaller than zero. Zero is smaller than 2." However, Chang thought that adding negative 79 and 2 would give you "negative 97," even though he then correctly told the interviewer spontaneously that, "if you had 1 and you had negative 2, and you added them you would get negative 1."

Later in the classroom discourse, Ms. Coleman became more directive than she had been thus far. She gave Chang the pointer and asked him to "show us on the number line." The number line (e.g., $-10\ -9\ -8\ -7\ -6$ $-5\ -4\ -3\ -2\ -1\ 0\ 1\ 2\ 3\ 4\ 5\ 6\ 7\ 8\ 9\ 10$) was posted above the chalkboard. Chang said:

> Negative 10 (Chang pointed to negative 10 on the number line) is 10 times smaller than zero (Chang pointed to zero). And the regular 10 (Chang pointed to positive 10 on the number line) is 10 times bigger than zero, so if you add negative plus the regular 10, you're going upwards. You're going the adding way—if you plus negative 10 plus the regular 10, it would equal zero.

Then Ms. Coleman asked, "Is that clear to everybody what Chang is saying?" All the students chorused, "NO!" resoundingly.

In this part of the classroom discourse Chang's thinking became visible to others reflecting the fragility of his mathematical understanding, even though he had previously given the correct answer to the problem in question (negative 10 plus 10 equals zero). Not only was Chang unable to use the number line to explain or prove why his answer was correct, but he also introduced some misinformation into the discussion by suggesting that "regular 10 is 10 times bigger than zero" and "negative 10 is 10 times smaller than zero." What was striking was the way that Ms. Coleman then responded to Chang's explanation and introduction of what might be considered incorrect mathematics. Rather than correcting him, as she might have done previously, Ms. Coleman asked the class whether Chang's explanation was clear to them. The students responded with an overwhelming, "NO!" Then Ms. Coleman continued by requesting that the students ask Chang a question that might help make clearer what Chang was trying to say, but no one was able to do so.

Finally, Ms. Coleman asked again if anyone could "show us in some way that negative 10 plus 10 equals zero?" At that point, Tessa, who had been struggling to understand throughout the class, volunteered. She picked up the pointer, walked to the board and pointed to numbers on the number line as she said:

> You start at negative 10 (she correctly pointed to this number). Then you add, "1" (pointed to negative 9), "2" (pointed to negative 8), "3" (pointed to negative 7), "4" (pointed to negative 6), "5" (pointed to negative 5), "6" (pointed to negative 4), "7" (pointed to negative 3), "8" (pointed to negative 2), "9" (pointed to negative 1), "10" (pointed to zero). That equals zero.

Rather than affirming Tessa's explanation as correct, Ms. Coleman turned to the class and asked them to evaluate it by asking if there were any questions or comments about Tessa's method or what she did. Chang said that he didn't quite see it, so Tessa went to the board and explained again in the same way, using the number line and the pointer. At that point, Chang stated that he agreed with Tessa, and he described what he thought she was doing:

> I sort of know what she's doing because she's counting by 10 plus the other 10, she's counting by 10, but she started at negative 10 and counted up 10 times.

Ms. Coleman then asked for another volunteer to explain what Tessa was doing. The incomplete understandings of two other students, Harold and Josephia, were then revealed. Josephia suggested that Tessa "was going backwards." When Ms. Coleman asked what she meant, Josephia said, "going smaller." Harold then added that, "When you're using negative numbers, it goes the same way as the regular ones, but the numbers go lower—go over zero, not higher than it." Ms. Coleman wrote Harold's words on the board exactly as he said them. Then Ms. Coleman turned to the class and asked the students if it was clear to everyone what Harold had said. Chang and several other students said they didn't understand Harold's explanation; Ms. Coleman admitted that she didn't understand either.

Ms. Coleman then concluded the lesson by saying that, on their homework for tonight, they were going to have some more of the same kinds of things—thinking about ways that they could prove their answers. She finished by adding, *"What we need to start doing is thinking about how to formulate our words so they say exactly what we mean."*

As students began to get ready to go home, Ms. Coleman got her notebook and wrote down what was written on the board, including the words and ideas that each student had come up with and the name of the student. I noted in my fieldnotes that the class "did not converge on a solution or answer, although at one point it looked like Keisha might be trying to get some convergence."[1]

IN WHAT WAYS DID KEISHA REVISE HER MATHEMATICS TEACHING?

This lesson captures some of the important ways in which Keisha's mathematics teaching changed during Fall 1990. These changes began as tentative revisions and then became more stable elements of Keisha's mathematics teaching in the months that followed.

In her mathematics teaching, Ms. Coleman had definitively moved away from "teaching as telling," because she had found that she could "teach it 1 day, and 2 weeks down the road, the kids didn't even remember one iota of what we dealt with." As Keisha put it, you can't assume that the students "know" just because you, the teacher, told them.

Thus, Ms. Coleman no longer "told" students the answer or the mathematical procedure, nor did she indicate whether an answer was correct or incorrect because she had begun to believe that students learn mathematics better if they hear it from their peers. *With skillful guidance and questioning from the teacher, students had to figure out solutions to mathematical problems for themselves.* An important result was that Ms. Coleman was no longer the sole source of mathematical knowledge in the classroom.

Students did the explaining, talked about how they solved the problem, and clarified the meaning of their explanations. As a result, students' thinking became visible; and students learned from each other.

---

[1] During this mathematics lesson, 16 students were present. At the end of the year, 14 of these students were still in the class. Two students had returned to their foreign countries, because their parents had completed their education at Michigan State University. These 14 students were interviewed in a 1½-hour clinical interview at the end of the year by either Penelope Peterson or Nancy Knapp, a graduate assistant. Thirteen of the 14 students were able to identify $\hat{7}9$ as smaller than 2, to provide an explanation of why this was the case, and to correctly give a number that was smaller than $\hat{7}9$. These students included Chang, Marta, Harold, Calvin, Josephia, Yan, Ataia, Aurora, Bert, Ali, Selvaranee, Arnie, and Ron. The 14th student, Tessa, showed partial understanding. While she identified correctly $\hat{7}9$ as smaller than 2 and referred to it as "negative 79," she explained that it was because negatives are a lot smaller than twos." Although she seemed to understand that any negative number was smaller than zero, when asked to give a number smaller than negative 79, Tessa incorrectly gave "negative 1." We also interviewed two additional students, Melissa and Frankie, who joined the class during second semester. Although Melissa had not been present for the November discussion, she identified correctly $\hat{7}9$ as smaller than 2, gave a correct explanation, and said that "negative 100" was a number that was smaller than negative 79. Frankie incorrectly identified $\hat{7}9$ as bigger than 2 and was unable to articulate why he thought so.

Keisha began to think differently about how she assessed her students' mathematical knowledge. She planned to pay less attention to students' mathematics scores on the CTBS test as measures of students' knowledge and to rely instead on what students said during classroom discussion, what students wrote in their explanations for mathematical solutions on their written work, and what students said and did during small group clinical problem solving interviews that she began to conduct every couple of months.

Rather than focusing on "covering mathematical content," Ms. Coleman focused on solving mathematical problems and discussing students' solutions and explanations. Students worked on one or two mathematics problems for the whole period. The mathematics lesson focused on discourse about how to think about and solve the mathematics problem. In focusing her whole mathematics lesson on solving one or two mathematics problems, Keisha Coleman was able to focus on "unpacking" mathematical ideas in greater depth and in a more coherent way than she had previously (cf. Stigler & Perry, 1988; Lampert, 1990; Ball, 1990).

Keisha ceased following the CSMP script and finally ceased using a textbook altogether. Rather, she followed the chain of students' thinking about and sense making of the mathematics problem. Such an approach is characteristic of teachers who have come to take a constructivist view of children's learning (see, for example, Lampert, 1988; Wilson, in press; Peterson, Fennema, & Carpenter, 1991).

In all classrooms, part of the academic work for students is making sense of the task and what the teacher wants (see, for example, Doyle, 1983). *In Ms. Coleman's class, students had to work on making sense of the mathematics and how their peers were thinking about the mathematics.* Classroom work in Ms. Coleman's classroom focused on the construction of mathematical knowledge and the negotiation of shared mathematical meaning (Wood, Cobb, & Yackel, Chapter 7, this volume). However, Keisha did not use these words, and it was not clear that she saw or thought about the changes in her mathematics teaching in the same way as I saw them and thought about them. So, how did Keisha think about the changes she was making in her mathematics teaching?

IN WHAT WAYS DID KEISHA REVISE HER THINKING?

The major ways in which Keisha revised her thinking during Fall 1989 revolved around changes in her view of how students learn mathematics. In an interview in January, I asked Keisha how she thought she had changed. She replied:

> Basically building on what the children already know... Before everything was more or less programmed [or scripted in CSMP], and it's not that

programmed right now, if that makes sense. Because when I teach the lesson, I have an idea what I want them [the children] to understand. And however they arrive at that is okay. I don't know why it's different, but it is different. I'm just not getting the responses [from students] that I had in the CSMP book, because I'm not anticipating or saying to myself, "Well, this is what they should say." Rather, I'm taking what they're giving me and building upon that. I know a lot of times in CSMP, when you [the teacher] have the anticipated response there, if you don't get that, then you would somehow rephrase it and tell it to them. With this [the way I am teaching now] I don't do that; everything comes from them [the students]. And we can build upon what they bring to the lesson, and I think that's really exciting.

Why did Keisha believe that it was important to build on what children know and follow the chain of their thinking and ideas rather than the script in the textbook? A major reason was that Keisha was developing and trying out the idea that children learn mathematics better when they hear it from one of their classmates rather than from the teacher, even though what the children hear from their peers might be explanations of the same mathematical knowledge or procedures that she, as the "teacher" would have given. One might say that Keisha had this idea as a "working hypothesis." As she put it in the January interview:

> I think this [mathematical knowledge] will stick with more of the children than me trying to stand there and force feed them that [knowledge] which I think is really interesting. But I think it's good also because they [the children] hang on to what their classmates say a lot more than any information that I could give them. And I always think that I'm trying to explain it so that they understand it and then giving them examples to prove it. But rather than *me* doing that, give *them* that task.

By giving the students the task of learning, Keisha sees that students have begun to change their orientation toward the task so that they no longer view it as "just work to be done." Then Keisha gave the example of having taught concepts in CSMP last year and giving students a page from the CSMP textbook to work on. If they were asked to draw an arrow road, for example, the children would just *draw it*. Now Keisha sees the students as "thinking a little bit more" and asking themselves, How should I do this? What is the best way for me to do this? "Rather than just sitting down and going through it, students are thinking lots more." She then described an example of a problem students had worked on the day before: "See if you can figure out a way that you can show how you get from 7 to 135 on the minicomputer." The students had one, the problem with arrow roads, but now they had to do it with their paper abacus—the minicomputer. Keisha noted with amazement:

> Students were discussing it with one another. They were talking about it... And I mean, they were *really* working with it, rather than sitting there.

There's just a difference, I think. Because it's okay for them to come up with different strategies.

One reason Keisha believes that students are learning more is that they are more "involved." She sees students as more "involved" because, as the teacher, she uses "their input" and builds on what students say, and she believes that the more she, as the teacher, does that, the more that students are "going to retain it."

Thus, through her own mathematics teaching and observations of her students' mathematics learning as a result of the revisions she has made in her mathematics teaching, Keisha seems to have discovered the power of what Flanders (1970) referred to as "use of student ideas." In his Interaction Analysis Scheme, Flanders included in this category acknowledging a student's idea, modifying the idea, applying the idea, comparing the idea, or summarizing what was said by an individual student or group of students. As Rosenshine (1971) noted, using students' ideas seem to be related to two of the greatest tributes and motivators in the academic world—being published and being cited. Rosenshine also noted in his 1971 review that, in eight of nine studies where researchers observed teachers' use of student ideas, they found a positive relationship between the frequency with which teachers used students' ideas and student achievement. However, an important difference exists between what Rosenshine had in mind and what seems to be happening in Keisha's classroom. The discourse in Keisha's classroom revolves around not just the *teacher's* use of students' ideas, but also the *students'* use of other students' ideas. Not only are students using other students' ideas, but they are evaluating them, piggy-backing on them, and building on them to construct new understandings.

The research on teacher behavior conducted and reviewed by Flanders, Rosenshine, and others formed the research base for models of direct instruction and effective instruction that were promulgated in the late 1970s and early 1980s. Indeed, Keisha views herself as teaching within what she refers to as an "effective instruction" frame.

Keisha says that she teaches everything "as part of her effective instruction" that she learned in a district workshop the previous year. One of the important elements of effective instruction is the use of "sponge activities." The mathematics problem or problems that she gives students to work on as they come into mathematics class is a "sponge activity," according to Keisha. Keisha gives her students the mathematics sponge activity because she likes her students to be "on task" as soon as they come into the classroom, and she wants them to be "ready for learning." She says that her sponge activity is basically her "anticipatory set." When asked why it was called a *sponge,* Keisha speculated that it had to do with the "soaking in of information." When Madeline Hunter (1983) proposed the idea of a sponge, she presented it as a way of soaking up loose time that otherwise might be wasted.

CONCLUSION

In her thinking as of January 1990, Keisha Coleman had a developing view of children's mathematics learning and her own teaching that reflected some elements of constructivism and some elements of behaviorism. In this way Keisha is like others in mathematics education who are struggling to move from a behavioral view of mathematics learning and teaching that has dominated American classrooms toward a practice that takes seriously the question of what it means to know and do mathematics. It should come as no surprise that, even within the same elementary school, mathematics teachers such as Keisha Coleman, Deborah Ball, and Magdalene Lampert, like researchers within the mathematics education community, are not agreed upon this epistemological point. For example, in their summary of the research agenda-setting conferences held by the National Council of Teachers of Mathematics, Sowder (1989) and her colleagues distinguished five contemporary scholarly views of what mathematics is and how one comes to know mathematics:

According to the first view, mathematics is external to the knower, static, and bounded. Learning and teaching mathematics involve the acquisition of information. In the second view, mathematics is also external to the knower, but it is a growing unbounded discipline that changes over time. Learning and teaching mathematics focus on how students acquire meaning for what is to be learned. The other three views involve some variation on "constructivist" ideas that knowledge is personal or social. According to the third constructivist perspective, to know mathematics means to do mathematics by "abstracting, inventing, proving, and applying" (Sowder, 1989, p. 22). The fourth constructivist position assumes an epistemology of mathematical knowledge that is consistent with the contents of individual minds. Finally, the last constructivist perspective regards mathematical knowledge as the product of social and cultural processes. This latter perspective seems to best describe the views of Lampert (1990) and Ball (1990), while the view of Keisha Coleman in 1990 seems to reflect elements of the first two perspectives. Keisha regards the learning and teaching of mathematics as the acquisition of information, but she also endorses the importance of her students acquiring meaning for what is to be learned.

How will Keisha's thinking develop and what will emerge as revisions in her thinking and her mathematics teaching in the future? Although we cannot predict what changes will occur, we predict that changes will. At the point that we leave Keisha Coleman in January 1990, she remains committed to learning and to improving her own mathematics teaching. She continues to feel excited by the challenge of her movement away from following the CSMP text. She continues to define her work as a teacher to include her own learning and reflection on her mathematics teaching. She engages constantly in thinking about her mathematics teaching and also in evaluating what she is learning, for example, from her colleague, Deborah Ball. She views her principal and the colleagues in her school as having played important roles in her own learning and development as a mathematics teacher over the last 7 years, and she believes they will continue to do so. While the "professional development" context of the school is important to Keisha Coleman, she believes that the principal and the teachers had established such a context through their own efforts at supporting and learning from one another well before last year, when the school officially became a "professional development school" associated with Michigan State University.

Revisions are likely to continue to occur in Keisha's thinking and in her mathematics teaching. For Keisha, her knowledge of the teaching and learning of elementary mathematics is all at once unbounded, dynamic, and changing, and very much the result of personal and social processes occurring within her, within her classroom, and within the school context.

REFERENCES

Ball, D. L. (1990). *With an eye on the mathematical horizon: Dilemmas of teaching elementary school mathematics* (Craft Paper No. 90–3). East Lansing, MI: National Center for Research on Teacher Education.

California State Department of Education. (1985). *Mathematics framework for California public schools, kindergarten through grade twelve.* Sacramento, CA: Author.

Carpenter, T. P., Fennema, E., Peterson, P. L., Chiang, C., & Loef, M. (1989). Using children's mathematics thinking in classroom teaching: An experimental study. *American Educational Research Journal, 26,* 499–531.

College of Education, Michigan State University. (1989, October). *Educational extension service first year (1988–89) report and second year (1989–90) plan.* East Lansing, MI: College of Education, Michigan State University.

Doyle, W. (1983). Academic work. *Review of Educational Research, 53,* 159–199.

Fennema, E., Carpenter, T.P., & Peterson, P.L. (1989). Learning mathematics with understanding. In J. E. Brophy (Ed.), *Advances in research on teaching* (Vol. 1, pp. 193–220). Greenwich, CT: JAI Press.

Flanders, N.A. (1970). *Analyzing classroom behavior.* New York: Addison-Wesley.

Hiebert, J., & Carpenter, T. P. (1992). Learning and teaching with understanding. In D. A. Grouws (Ed.), *Handbook of research on mathematics teaching and learning* (pp. 65–97). New York: Macmillan.

Holmes Group. (1990). *Tomorrow's schools: Principles for the design of professional development schools.* East Lansing: MI: The Holmes Group.

Hunter, M. (1983). *Mastery teaching.* El Segundo, CA: TIP Publications.

Lampert, M. (1988). Connecting mathematical teaching and learning. In E. Fennema, T. Carpenter, & S. Lamon (Eds.), *Integrating research on the teaching and learning of mathematics* (pp. 132–165). Madison, WI: Wisconsin Center for Education Research.

Lampert, M. (1990). When the problem is not the question and the solution is not the answer: Mathematical knowing and teaching. *American Educational Research Journal, 27,* 29–64.

Marshall, H. (1988). Work or learning: Implications of classroom metaphors. *Educational Researcher, 17*(9), 9–16.

Mathematical Sciences Education Board, National Research Council. (1990). *Reshaping school mathematics: A philosophy and framework for curriculum.* Washington, DC: National Academy Press.

Mid-continent Educational Research Laboratory (CEMREL). (1985). *Comprehensive school mathematics program.* Kansas City, MO: CEMREL.

National Academy of Engineering. (1985). *Education for the manufacturing world of the future.* Washington, DC: National Academy Press.

National Center for Research on Teacher Education (NCRTE). (1989). *Study package: Tracking teachers' learning.* East Lansing, MI: Michigan State University, College of Education.

National Council of Teachers of Mathematics. (1989). *Curriculum and evaluation standards for school mathematics.* Reston, VA: Author.

National Research Council. (1989). *Everybody counts: A report to the nation on the future of mathematics education.* Washington, DC: National Academy Press.

Peterson, P. L. (1990). The California study of elementary mathematics. *Educational Evaluation and Policy Analysis, 12,* 257–262.

Peterson, P. L., Fennema, E., & Carpenter, T. (1991). Using children's mathematical knowledge. In B. Means, C. Chelemer, & M.S. Knapp (Eds.), *Teaching advanced skills to at-risk children* (pp. 68–101). San Francisco: Jossey-Bass.

Peterson, P. L., & Knapp, N. (in preparation). *Using students as sources of mathematical knowledge: The case of Keisha Coleman.* East Lansing, MI: Center for the Learning and Teaching of Elementary Subjects.

Putnam, R., & Reineke, J. (1991, April). *The case of Elaine Hugo: Subject matter is not enough.* Paper presented at the annual meeting of the American Educational Research Association, Chicago, IL.

Remillard, J. (1991). *Is there an alternative? An analysis of commonly used and distinctive mathematics curricula* (ESC Series No. 31). East Lansing, MI: Center for the Learning and Teaching of Elementary Subjects.

Rosenshine, B. (1971). *Teaching behaviours and student achievement.* London: National Foundation for Educational Research in England and Wales.

Ross, D. (1988, September). *Work and the economy in Michigan.* Invited address by the Secretary of Commerce of the State of Michigan to the faculty of the College of Education, Michigan State University, East Lansing: MI.

Shea, J. F. (1985). The changing face of U.S. manufacturing. In National Academy of Engineering (Ed.), *Education for the manufacturing world of the future* (pp. 9–20). Washington, DC: National Academy Press.

Shulman, L. S. (1987). Knowledge and teaching: Foundations of the new reform. *Harvard Educational Review, 57*(1), 1–22.

Sowder, J. (Ed.). (1989). *Setting a research agenda* (Vol. 5). Reston, VA: Erlbaum and the National Council of Teachers of Mathematics.

Stigler, J. W., & Perry, M. (1988). Cross-cultural studies of mathematics teaching and learning. In D.A. Grouws & T.J. Cooney (Eds.), *Perspectives on research on effective mathematics teaching* (Vol. 1, pp. 194–223). Reston, VA: Erlbaum and the National Council of Teachers of Mathematics.

Wilson, S. (in press). Mastodons, maps, and Michigan: Exploring uncharted territory while teaching elementary school social studies. *Elementary School Journal*.

Zuboff, S. (1984). *In the age of the smart machine*. New York: Basic Books.

Chapter 7
Change in Learning Mathematics: Change in Teaching Mathematics*

Terry Wood

Curriculum & Instruction
Purdue University

Paul Cobb

Curriculum & Instruction
Purdue University

Erna Yackel

Mathematical Sciences
Purdue University Calumet

The recent concern for reform in mathematics education in the elementary school has emphasized the necessity for changing the role of the student and the teacher in the classroom (National Council of Teachers of Mathematics, 1989, 1991; National Research Council, 1989). The traditional practice of elementary school mathematics consists of learning rules for solving problems and then using them to practice computing correct answers. From this perspective, doing mathematics involves calculating answers and mastering the procedures and rules to do so. Thus, in this tradition,

---

* The research reported in this chapter was supported by the National Science Foundation under grant numbers MDR 874-0400 and MDR 885-0560. All opinions expressed are those of the authors.

learning mathematics is thought to consist of absorbing pieces of knowledge with an emphasis on acquiring skills rather than on conceptual operations (Porter, 1989). The consequence of this view is a practice of teaching that is characterized by the procedures of presentation and repetition. The teachers' role in this exercise is to make mathematics understandable by breaking the procedures into small parts, leading students through each piece, and providing practice tasks that insure students a high rate of success (Rosenshine & Stevens, 1986). This form of practice acts to perpetuate the teachers' and students' beliefs that school mathematics is about finding ways for calculating correct answers rather than for developing numerical relationships through their own reasoning.

These recent calls for reform advocate a view of the nature of mathematics and learning mathematics that is highly contradictory to the current practice traditionally found in most elementary schools. This reform calls for a view of mathematics as a "science of pattern and order" that

> relies on logic rather than on observation as its standard of truth, yet employs observation, simulation, and even experimentation as a means of learning truth. (NRC, 1989, p. 31)

Mathematics, then, becomes a human activity in which individual meaning is constructed through sensorimotor and conceptual activity (Davis & Hersch, 1981; von Glasersfeld, 1987). These personal meanings are coordinated with those held by the wider community through the process of social interaction and communication. It is during this process that the individual mathematical meanings of the participants are constituted as taken-as-shared.[1] This perspective implies a view of learning mathematics in which problem solving, reasoning, and communication are essential aspects. These changes in the stance taken toward the nature of mathematics and the manner in which it is learned have definite implications for how mathematics is taught. Moreover, this view of mathematics requires decisive changes in the current form of practice found in most elementary schools.

The purpose of this chapter is to illustrate how establishing classrooms as settings in which mathematical learning is defined as constructing relationships, and in which communicating about mathematics is of central

---

[1] The term originated with Schutz (1962) as *taken-to-be-shared* and was later changed to *taken-as-shared* (Streeck, 1979). It refers to the meaning that is thought to be shared by others. While the meanings individuals hold are unique to them, the ability to communicate with others depends on the negotiation of meaning that is understood to be shared among the participants. In other words, "the mathematics we experience as objectively existing in the world is the product of an active construction on our part which we take as being shared with others" (Cobb in Wood, Cobb, & Yackel, in press).

CHANGE IN LEARNING AND TEACHING MATHEMATICS 179

importance, creates opportunities for learning not found in traditional classrooms for both students and teachers. In these settings, teachers have an opportunity to learn about the processes by which children construct their mathematical meanings and the ways in which they as teachers can act to guide children's learning. The ongoing context of their classrooms provides a setting for their learning. The form of practice that develops as students and teachers communicate consists of complex and sophisticated patterns of interaction that are distinct from traditional school patterns. In these interactions students participate as partners with the teacher in discourse that enables them to sincerely talk about their mathematical thinking. The essence of this discourse is uniquely different from ordinary conversation. In this setting, students partake in a form of argumentation in which the meaning for mathematics is expected to be logically consistent (Forman, in press; Krummheuer & Yackel, 1990). Students are obligated to explain and, when asked, justify their interpretations and solution methods to others. The others are expected to listen, make sense of the explanation, and ask for clarification. Participating in this form of dialogue creates opportunities to learn that occur because students are engaged in negotiating mathematical meaning (Cobb, Wood, Yackel, & McNeal, in press; Yackel, Cobb, & Wood, 1991). In this situation, children not only engage in talk in which they construct individual ideas about mathematical relationships, but they also participate in the communal activity of doing mathematics.

This chapter will first discuss the traditional practice of elementary school mathematics, which will be contrasted with a constructivist view of learning and the subsequent implications for teaching. Next, our research in a second-grade classroom will be described, followed by a case study of the changes the project teacher made as she developed a form of practice compatible with a constructivist view of learning. Finally, the implications of this change in other subject matter areas for our initial project teacher and other teachers who are now involved with the project will be discussed.

THE TRADITION OF ELEMENTARY SCHOOL MATHEMATICS

Teaching mathematics in elementary school is characterized by heavy reliance on the textbook by teachers both as a source of activities and for explanations of procedures to use in completing the tasks. Typically, these textbooks are arranged so that a significant amount of review occurs at the beginning of the year. Thereafter, new concepts are presented as distinct 1- or 2-week units. The focus is typically on mastering mathematical computational procedures and completing tasks for the purpose of practicing computation. The role of teacher and student in this context is one in which the teacher asks questions, not for the purpose of exchanging information, but for evaluating whether the students know the answer. This interaction pattern is characterized by dialogue in which the teacher makes an "initiating move" followed with a "response move" by the student, which is then followed by "feedback" or "follow-up" by the teacher (Sinclair & Coulthard, 1975; Mehan, 1979). While this dialogue pattern characterizes the nature of the interaction that occurs between teachers and students and creates the "smooth functioning" of the classroom (Mehan, 1979), several studies have provided analyses that indicate that these "hidden regularities" create a ritualized exchange in which learning mathematics is reduced to a linguistic exchange of which the litany of "put down the zero and carry the one" is familiar (Bauersfeld, 1980; Edwards & Mercer, 1987; Voigt, 1985; Walkerdine, 1988).

As a way to further illustrate the pattern of interaction and the nature of the communication, the following example[2] from a traditional mathematics class is presented. The scene is a lesson for which the teacher's intention is for the students to learn about tens and ones. In this episode, the teacher (following the directions given in her teacher's manual) has put 45 tally marks on the board and has just finished circling four groups of 10.

Teacher: How many groups of ten do we have there, boys and girls?
Children: 4. 44.
Teacher: We have 4 groups of ten, and how many left over?
Children: 5.
Teacher: We had 4 tens and how many left over?
Beth: 4 tens.
Sarah: 5.
Teacher: 5. Now, can anybody tell me what number that could be? We have 4 tens and 5 ones. What is that number, Ann?
Ann: (remains silent).
Teacher: If we have 4 tens and 5 ones, what is that number?
Ann: 9.
Teacher: Look at how many we have there (points to the 4 groups of ten) and 5 ones. If we have 4 tens and 5 ones, we have? (slight pause) 45.
Children: 45.
Teacher: Very good.

This typical pattern of interaction is characteristic of school mathematics in a majority of classrooms (Goodlad, 1983; Stodolsky, 1988). As given, this exchange illustrates a ritualized interaction in which opportunities for students to participate in the negotiation of mathematical meaning do not exist. The only requirement for students in this interaction is to provide single-word responses to the questions the teacher asks.

The manner in which the teacher and student interact and the oppor-

---

[2] From the work of Betsy McNeal.

tunities for children to participate in the discourse also serve to reveal the nature of the teacher's beliefs about her role, the student's role, and the nature of mathematical activity. These can be contrasted with classrooms in which the interaction patterns and discursive practices reflect another view of what it means to learn mathematics.

LEARNING AND TEACHING MATHEMATICS: A CONSTRUCTIVIST PERSPECTIVE

A constructivist theory of learning guides the theoretical orientation of our research in which we attempt to understand the learning process as a coordination of cognitive and sociological perspectives (Cobb, 1990). Our work has been influenced by the psychological theories of Piaget (1970, 1980) and von Glasersfeld (1984, 1987), in which the process of cognitive conflict, reflective abstraction, and conceptual reorganization play a major role in learning. From this perspective, learning is considered an individual process by which:

- Mathematical knowledge is actively constructed by the child.
- Children create new mathematical meaning by reflecting on their physical and mental activity.
- Children create their own individual interpretations of mathematics.

We have also been influenced by the sociological theories of Blumer (1969), Mead (1934), and Schutz (1962), in which opportunities for learning occur during social interaction. In these situations, mathematical meanings are negotiated through a process of communication which involves collaboration and argumentation (Barnes & Todd, 1977; Cobb, Wood, & Yackel, in press; Yackel, Cobb, Wood, Wheatley, & Merkel, 1990). Learning from this position is viewed as a social process in which:

- Children grow into the intellectual life of those around them.
- Mathematical ideas and truths, both in use and meaning, are cooperatively established by the members of community.
- Taken-as-shared meaning is established through participating in communicative discourse involving explanation, justification and negotiation of meaning.

Implications for Teaching

A constructivist perspective that mathematical learning involves both a personal construction of meaning and a negotiation of taken-as-shared meaning of the wider community has definite implications for teaching (Clements & Battista, 1990). These are:

- Teachers should provide instructional activities that will give rise to problematic situations for children.
- Children's actions are rational to them, and teachers should attempt to view students' solutions from their perspective.
- Teachers should recognize that what seem like errors and confusions from an adult point of view are children's expressions of their current understanding.
- Teachers should realize that substantive learning occurs in periods of conflict, confusion, surprise, over long periods of time, and during social interaction in which negotiation of taken-as-shared-meaning is essential.

From this perspective, teaching is viewed as a process of encouraging children's individual constructions of mathematical ideas on the one hand, and, on the other, acculturating them to the taken-as-shared mathematical practices of the community through participation in communicative discourse. Similarly, opportunities are created for teachers to learn about children's mathematical conceptualizations as they interpret students' explanations, which can then inform their subsequent teaching practice and enhance their own understanding. These new understandings influence the manner in which teachers are able to initiate and guide the development of the mathematical meanings of their students. The knowledge of their students' current mathematical understanding, and the manner in which it develops, provide them with a framework for guiding students' participation in communicative discourse. Thus teaching and learning are viewed as a dialectical process, each informing the other.

CLASSROOM TEACHING EXPERIMENT

We began our work by attempting to extend the methodology of the constructivist teaching experiment, as described by Steffe (1983), to the setting of the school classroom. The teaching experiment, as used by Steffe, is an extension of Piaget's clinical interview methodology and is conducted in a one-to-one situation with the researcher as teacher. Initial interviews are conducted with the child, which are then followed by teaching episodes that enable the researcher to investigate the processes by which an individual child constructs mathematical meaning (Cobb & Steffe, 1983). During these longitudinal investigations, the researcher as teacher attempts to interpret the child's mathematical activity in order to create a tentative model of the child's constructions and to use this model to create new situations and tasks to encourage further learning.

Our attempt to extend this methodology to a classroom with one teacher and 20 children formed the basis of our second-grade teaching experiment. In conducting this classroom teaching experiment, the classroom teacher, not the researchers, provided the instruction for the students. In this situation, the emphasis was on students solving a few challenging problems rather than completing the traditional large number of tasks as practice in facilitating efficient paper-and-pencil computation. Because of the emphasis placed on children's construction of meaning in problem solving situations, opportunities for children to interact with each other and with the teacher were essential. These interactions provided the teacher with the crucial opportunity to listen to children's explanations and attempt to infer their current understanding. These interpretations formed the basis from which the teacher could create suggestions and questions that might encourage children's further constructions. This view of the classroom, in which creating opportunities for children to learn mathematics with meaning is of central concern, creates a different atmosphere then that found in the traditional classroom, which is seen as a place to do work and complete tasks (Marshall, 1988).

As researchers, our intention was to investigate children's learning of mathematics in this setting and to let the teacher provide the instruction. Further, because our goal was to have the teacher focus her energy and time on interacting with her students in order to interpret and understand their thinking, we took the responsibility for developing the problem-centered activities for students to use. As these activities were likely to be challenging for most children, we used the instructional strategies of pair collaboration followed by whole class discussion of children's solutions.

Problem-Centered Instructional Activities

The development of these activities was influenced by the cognitive models developed by Steffe, Cobb, and von Glasersfeld (1988) and Steffe, von Glasersfeld, Richards, and Cobb (1983). These cognitive models provided information about the possible constructions second graders might make over the course of the year. In addition, the development of these activities was informed by interviews that were conducted by the researchers at the beginning and middle of the year with each child. The information provided from these sources, along with daily observations in the classroom, formed the basis from which the instructional activities were created. Each of the activities was developed to consider the range of abilities that existed within the class. The activities were designed to be tasks in which a wide variety of solution methods were possible, allowing students to

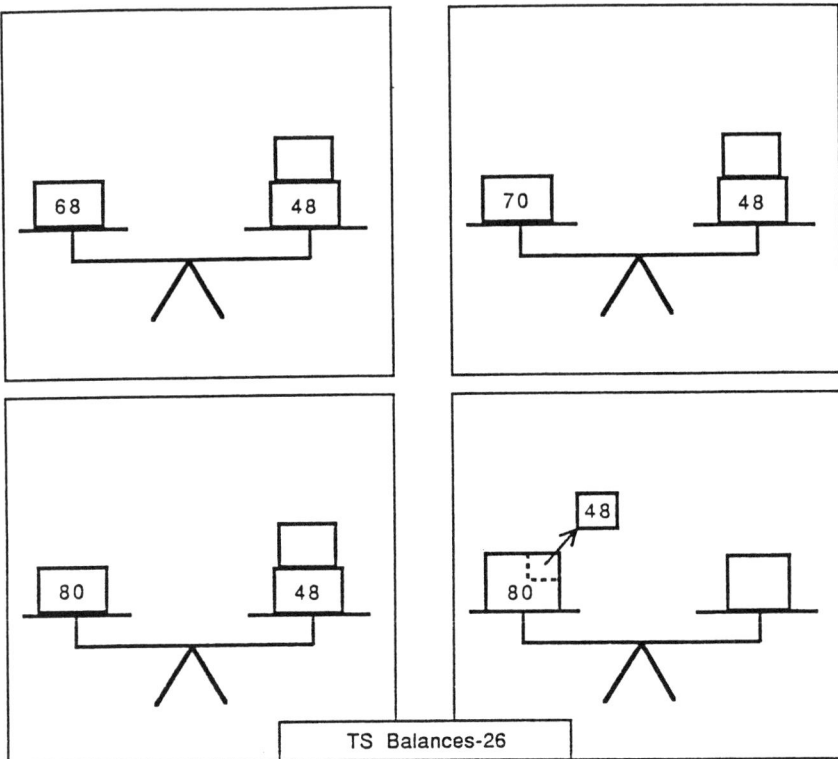

Figure 7.1. Balance Activity for Concept Ten

develop more complex concepts through reflection on their own or others activity. These activities were created to be problem centered to encourage learning through resolution of conflict and confusion. Conceptual development was the intent in all of the activities, while the procedural aspects were intertwined to be part of the problem solving activity. As an example, the balance format (Figure 7.1) was used continuously throughout the year for a variety of arithmetical activities including basic facts, addition/subtraction, and multiplication/division. The example (shown in Figure 7.1) was used at mid-year to encourage children to develop a conceptual basis for ten as part of a series of activities that extended throughout the school year.

In this activity, children can solve problems with a variety of solutions ranging from modeling with manipulatives and counting by tens and ones to using nonstandard algorithms. In addition to whole-number activities, other aspects ranged from spatial imaging to clock face reading. All of the activities were presented in a problem-centered manner. Examples of some of the spatial activities can be found in Yackel and Wheatley (1990).

Pair Collaboration

Although the problem-centered activities were essential for providing the teacher a starting point for conducting the mathematics lesson, they were in themselves not sufficient. These activities were challenging for the children and thus appropriate in settings which would allow children to discuss possible ways the problems could be solved. As they worked together, the children engaged in discourse about their mathematical activity. As they exchanged their ideas with one another, opportunities arose for them to explain and justify their thinking, to resolve conflicting points of view, and to negotiate meaning (Barnes & Todd, 1977; Yackel, Cobb, & Wood, 1991). As the children worked together, opportunities were created for learning mathematics that did not occur in traditional classrooms (Yackel, Cobb, Wood, Merkel, & Wheatley, 1990). From the point of view of the teacher, collaborative learning provided opportunities for children to complete the activities themselves without her help. This gave her opportunities to listen and observe these students as they engaged in mathematical thinking and to make interventions to offer suggestions or make probes to help children engage in collaborative dialogue (Wood & Yackel, 1990) and to build new ideas. Listening to children in small groups also provided the teacher with an opportunity to learn more about the quality and flexibility of children's mathematical thinking.

Whole-Class Discussions

In general, it was beneficial for both the children and the teacher to follow the small group work with a whole-class discussion of the activities. Listening to others' solutions in the whole class provided the students an opportunity to hear other ways to solve the problems they might not have thought of by themselves. The discussion also provided opportunities for the children and teacher to engage in discourse in which their mathematical thinking was valued. In this way, children could explain and justify their ideas and also challenge the thinking of others as they tried to make sense of each other's solutions. This also created an opportunity for the teacher to highlight and validate mathematical ideas to constitute the taken-as-shared meaning of the culture.

The problem-centered activities, pair collaboration, and class discussion were highly interrelated aspects necessary to establish a classroom atmosphere in which children were learning mathematics in a relational manner (Skemp, 1976). In so doing, the children were gaining inner satisfaction from solving challenging problems and were becoming more responsible for their learning (Cobb, Yackel, & Wood, 1989; Kamii, 1982).

DEVELOPING A FORM OF TEACHING COMPATIBLE WITH A CONSTRUCTIVIST PERSPECTIVE OF LEARNING

As the teacher and students mutually established an atmosphere that encouraged and supported learning mathematics meaningfully, situations arose which were learning opportunities for the teacher as well as the children. The teacher encountered situations which, unlike her previous experiences in teaching mathematics, created conflicts and contradictions with her previous beliefs about children's learning, teaching, and the nature of mathematics. In resolving the conflicts that occurred between her former textbook-dominated ways of teaching, she developed a form of practice that respected, encouraged, and supported children as they created their own understanding of mathematics and yet acculturated them into the mathematical practice of the community (Wood, Cobb, & Yackel, 1991).

Mutually Establishing Social and Mathematical Norms in the Classroom

The extent to which children did in fact talk about their understanding of mathematics can largely be attributed to the social setting of the classroom (Cobb, Wood, & Yackel, in press; Cobb, Yackel, & Wood, 1989; Cobb, Yackel, Wood, Wheatley, & Merkel, 1988). The nature of the teacher and student interactions that occurred within the whole-class discussions were crucial to establishing the social norms essential for developing a setting in which the children would feel psychologically safe to express their mathematical thinking and to question other students' ideas. The mutual obligations and expectations were negotiated at the beginning of the year by the teacher and the students. These social norms were then subject to renegotiation throughout the school year as they worked to establish routines that would form the basis of the interaction patterns in which understanding mathematics was the goal (Cobb, Wood, & Yackel, in press; Collins & Green, this volume; Weade, this volume).

At the beginning of the school year, the intention during class discussion was that students would explain their methods for solving the mathematical problems, and that the others would listen and determine if the explanation made sense or not. These expectations for children's actions were quite different from those of the children's previous experiences in school (Wood, Cobb, & Yackel, 1990). In traditional mathematics lessons, unlike other subject areas, discussions rarely occur. In general, mathematics lessons consist of students calculating answers to problems as independent seatwork. When discussion does occur, it is during the introduction to the lesson and serves the purpose of allowing the teacher to evaluate students' responses and indicate whether they were correct or not. The children, for their part, are expected to say what the teacher wants them to say rather than express their own thinking (Voigt, 1985; Weber, 1986). In contrast, in this mathematics class, the teacher's expectation is for students to express their thinking during class discussions.

The nature of the discourse that evolved over the course of the school year reflects the social norms that were mutually constituted for the purpose of establishing what counts as doing mathematics in this classroom. These expectations which the teacher initiated for doing mathematics were not without reciprocal obligations for her as well. It was her intention that students would think about and make sense of the problems and then would talk about their ideas in the public arena of the class discussion. Consequently, her expectation placed the children under the obligation to reconstruct their solutions and explain them to others. From the children's perspective, a certain amount of risk was involved in fulfilling the teacher's expectations. To them, expressing their thinking to the rest of the class created a situation in which the possibility of embarrassment and feelings of incompetence could arise as their thinking was questioned and challenged by their peers. Thus, the children expected the teacher to accept certain obligations for her actions as well. If they were to accept the obligation to express their thoughts, then they expected the teacher to accept and respect their thinking as well (Cobb, Yackel, Wood, Wheatley, & Merkel, 1988; Wood, 1989).

The establishment of norms for class discussion was also crucial to the development of the norms for pair collaboration in which children engaged in mathematical activity as they solved their problems. In this setting, children were also expected to express their ideas for solving the problems to one another, to agree or disagree, and to arrive at a solution method. The children were expected not only to cooperate but to collaborate as they worked together to negotiate mathematical meaning. Subsequently, during the whole-class discussions, each member of the pair was expected to be able to express his or her thinking to the rest of the students (Yackel, Cobb, & Wood, 1991).

Teaching as a Process of Negotiation

As these social norms became established, the patterns of interaction that formed the basis for the smooth functioning of the class began to emerge. The teacher became confident that children would work collaboratively without her continued monitoring and that they would offer their ideas during class discussion. As she listened to them during discussion, she was surprised at what the children already knew about mathematics. She began to realize that children were capable of very powerful and complex thinking that she had not anticipated. Reciprocally, the children were learning that doing mathematics in this class meant that they were expected to make sense of it for themselves and to discuss their solution methods with others. The teacher realized that the children's way of solving problems did not always make sense to her. She also realized that they often gave incorrect answers. However, she had learned that children's methods were meaningful to them, and she tried to understand their explanations by paraphrasing students' solutions or asking clarifying questions. In doing this, she conveyed to the children that their solution methods, not their answers, were most important. Nevertheless, accepting her students' incorrect answers unconditionally created a contradiction with her prior beliefs about mathematics and teaching. She still believed that it was her responsibility to correct and eliminate children's errors by intervening and providing the student with the right answer (Labinowicz, 1987). Her initial attempts to resolve this conflict were characterized by participating in an interaction pattern referred to as the "funnel pattern" (Bauersfeld, 1988; Voigt, 1985). This pattern frequently is initiated when the student has made a mistake that the teacher then uses as a starting point for leading the student through a series of explicit questions until he or she gives the answer the teacher wanted.

The following episode illustrates the pattern of interaction and the nature of the discourse that occurred during a whole-class discussion, in which the instructional activity being discussed consisted of a series of number sentences created to encourage students to develop numerical relationships. These thinking strategies have been shown to be an effective method that children use to remember basic facts (Rathmell, 1978; Thornton, 1978) and to develop nonstandard addition/subtraction algorithms (Cobb & Merkel, 1989; Labinowicz, 1985). As the episode begins, the problem being discussed is $9 + 7 = $ ____. The teacher calls on Jim to give the answer.

Jim: 14.
Teacher: Okay. 7 plus 7 equals 14. 8 plus 7 is just adding one more to 14 which makes ____? (voice slightly rising).
Jim: 15.
Teacher: And 9 is one more than 8. So 15 plus one more is ____?
Jim: 16.
Teacher: So 9 plus 7 is ____? 16.

As can be seen, the student's role in participating in this dialogue is to simply add "one more" to whatever sum the teacher provides. The teacher, on the other hand, is the one who is engaged in the process involved in using thinking strategies as she created a series of related number sentences for basic facts.

As the teacher later reflected on situations like these, she realized that her attempts to guide the discourse in this manner were just another way of ensuring that students "get the right answer," whether they understood or not. She referred to this as "telling not teaching." However, as teacher, she was still responsible for guiding children's experiences. Instead of imposing her view or directing students to her way of thinking, she learned to negotiate with the students other solutions to the problems. She began to expect children to provide explanations for their solutions that could be understood for the most part by the rest of the class. She asked the other children if they agreed or understood the solution given. The children accepted their obligation and began offering alternative ways to solve the problems. Reciprocally, they expected that, as the teacher, she would allow them to exchange points of view and offer their justifications for their thinking. In so doing, she learned that teaching mathematics involved a process of negotiation rather than imposition (Bishop, 1985). The students, for their part, realized that doing math in this class also involved providing reasons for their thinking and being prepared to justify them if challenged.

Negotiating Mathematical Meaning

In providing their explanations, however, the students often presented ideas that were incompatible with respect to the institutionalized mathematical practices of the wider community. Consequently, the teacher encountered a conflict between encouraging children to make personal constructions or teaching the conventions of the wider culture. On the one hand, she wanted to facilitate children's construction of their mathematical meanings. On the other hand, she wanted to guide the development of taken-as-shared interpretations that fit with those of the wider society (Cobb, Wood, & Yackel, 1990; Wood, Cobb, & Yackel, in press). The development of a fit between personal constructions and those held by the wider society makes possible the subjective experience of shared objective mathematical reality and mathematical communication (Pierce, 1935).

In the discussions with her students, she had learned that they were capable of constructing concepts for themselves as they engaged in mathematical activity, and that children at different conceptual levels used different solution methods. She also realized that imposing methods on children served to interfere with their ways of thinking productively about mathematics. Yet she realized that it was necessary for students to be acculturated to the practices of society and for their personal constructions to fit with those conventions of society. She was, in a sense, "walking a tightrope." On the one hand, she wanted to be sensitive to guiding children in their constructions and not make interventions that would inhibit their thinking. On the other hand, she wanted them to develop taken-as-shared meanings that form the basis for mathematical communication within the society.

A highly sophisticated form of practice developed over the course of the year, as the teacher became skillful in facilitating discussions in which mathematical meanings were negotiated while avoiding the precariousness of overdirection and intervention. The following episode was selected to illustrate a process of negotiating meaning that occurred during class discussion and the complexity of the teacher's role in the process. On this day, the teacher and students had been discussing the following problem: *Daisy Duck invited 50 children to her birthday party. Nineteen of them were girls. How many were boys?* This problem was part of an activity sheet the students had done earlier with their partners which consisted of a series of word problems. The children had been offering solutions which involved subtracting 19 from 50, but which had resulted in different answers. The incident began as the teacher asked Alex for his solution.

Teacher: Okay, Alex what do you say?
Alex: It's 31.
Teacher: You think it's 31.
Alex: Because 30 plus 20 is 50.

Alex's explanation, *"30 plus 20,"* indicated that he was explaining his solution to the problem as addition. For the teacher, Alex's explanation was unanticipated in the context because the discussion had been about solving the problem as a subtraction problem. As a consequence, his response did not immediately make sense to her. She attempted to understand his method by asking for further clarification which Alex provided the following justification.

Alex: [It] equals 50, and that takes up the 50 children that were at the party.
Teacher: But this is 19, right? (pointing to the number).
Alex: I know. And so, 50 minus 20 would be 30.
Teacher: Okay. What he is saying instead of taking 19, I [Alex] made it 20.

Alex's initial response to the teacher's question further exemplified that he interpreted the problem as one of addition. The teacher responded by asking, *"But this is 19, right?"* to which she expected him to provide a rationale for using the number 20. Alex in trying to understand the teacher's question interpreted it as asking for a reason why he solved the problem using addition rather than subtraction as the other students had done. He then offers an explanation that presented the problem as subtraction, *"50 minus 20,"* to accommodate his explanation to the teacher's interpretation of the problem. The teacher, however, was asking a different question, which had to do with the number 19 given in the problem. In attempting to make sense of Alex's explanation, she provided a justification for his solution and inferred that he had added one to 19 to get 20 to which Alex responded,

Alex: No.
Teacher: No, you didn't?
Alex: 50 minus 30 is 20.
Teacher: 50 minus 30.
Alex: 50... (pause). Well, I don't know what I did. 50 minus 20 is 30... (pause).
Teacher: Right.

The teacher accepted her obligation that in this class the children were allowed to express their disagreement even with the teacher. However, she also expected that if they disagreed, they would then provide a reason. As Alex reflected on his thinking, he realized that attempting to change his explanation from addition to subtraction to accommodate the teacher's meaning, he was unable to provide a justification for his initial answer of 31. Thus he continued.

Alex: But its a 19 instead of 20, so it has to be one higher than it, because that number is one less than 20. So it's 31.
Teacher: All right.

In this example, Alex and the teacher have engaged in a discussion in which their initial interpretations of the problem were quite different. As the discussion evolved, they each adjusted their personal interpretations of the situation to negotiate a taken-as-shared meaning. It is this evolving process of continual shifting of meanings that occurred between students and teacher that created opportunities to learn not found in traditional elementary school mathematics classes. Notably, Alex's *"So it has to be one higher than it because,* as a justification for his thinking, has the logical inferencing and impersonal third-person similar to a mathematician providing a proof. In this example, Alex's final explanation provided a rationale and justification for his solution that involved understanding of numerical relationships that, together with his initial explanation, were more complex than his first solution. His initial explanation of *"30 plus 20 is 50"* and *"50 minus 20 is 30"* suggested that, conceptually, Alex was able to view addition and subtraction as inverse relationships and thus adjust his meaning. In this setting, the teacher was also shifting her only interpretation of the problem to fit Alex's meaning. His final explanation, and in which he decreased the amount of one addend and increased the other by the same amount (Cobb & Merkel, 1989), indicated, in this situation, he had developed another powerful concept in the process of negotiation of meaning with the teacher. The teacher's response of *"all right"* indicated her agreement, and the completion of the process.

CREATING OPPORTUNITIES TO LEARN DURING SOCIAL INTERACTION

Teaching in classrooms in which children are encouraged to express their thinking during class discussions creates situations in which it is impossible for teachers to fully anticipate the nature of the student's responses. Teaching in this manner is fraught with uncertainty and unpredictability in a setting in which teachers have usually been the authority with control of the information. The manner in which teachers guide and facilitate a discussion in which the students have opportunities to do the thinking requires a great deal of thought on the part of the teacher, which must occur during the course of the discussion (Lampert, 1988). In many respects, the pattern of interaction that occurs, and the opportunities created for children to learn, could be viewed as similar to those reported in studies of emergent literacy (Morrow, 1988; Nino & Bruner, 1978; Wells, 1985) in which the theory of Vygotsky (1978) underlies the interpretation. However, two major theoretical distinctions differentiate our theoretical perspective from the Vygotsky-inspired position. One fundamental contention is that students do not learn through a process of internalizing mathematics directly from objects or pictures. Instead learning occurs through their experiences which involve sensorimotor and conceptual activity as the origins of their personal constructions of mathematical knowledge. A second contention is that mathematics is a communal practice in which normative activity is taken-as-shared and learning mathematics is seen as becoming a participant in that practice. As a unifying thread, the process of teaching and learning can be viewed as "interactive communication in which both the teacher and students reflexively influence each others' interpretations and actions" (Cobb, 1991, p. 8). In this case mathematical meaning is interactively constituted during social interaction in which the child's interpretation, as well as the adult's, contribute to his or her development.

The interlocking network of mutual obligations and expectations that are developed at the beginning of the year and renegotiated throughout the year is crucial to the development of the routines and patterns of interaction that create the atmosphere in which participation in the discourse is characterized by a process of meaning negotiation wherein children explain and justify their mathematical thinking. In these mathematics classrooms, children are expected to talk about their ideas and to listen to the ideas of others. As they listen, they are expected to try to understand and to ask for clarification if they do not. They are also expected to provide reasons if they disagree with others ideas. The teachers in this setting must also accept certain obligations

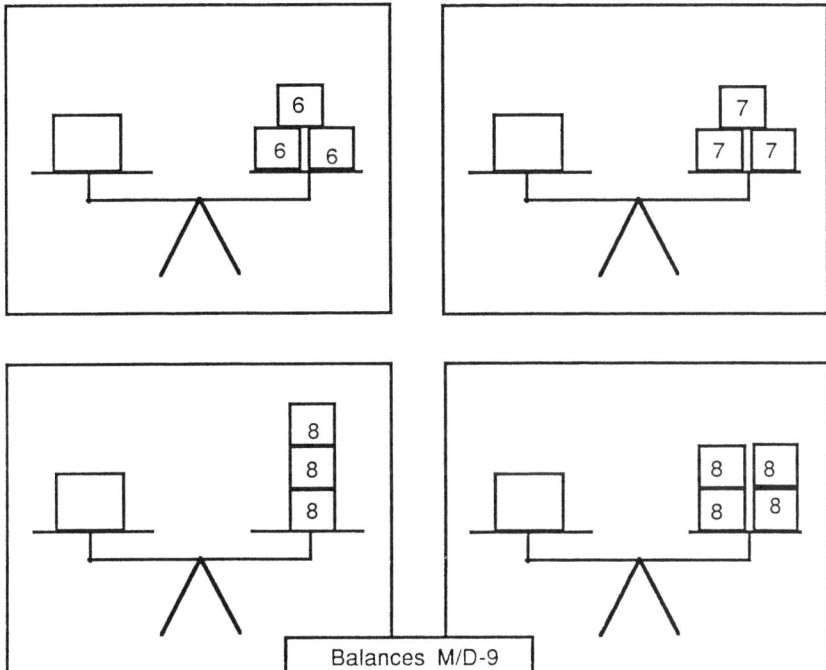

Figure 7.2. Multiplication Balance Activity

for themselves. In their role, they are expected to respect students' ideas and to understand that students' explanations reflect their current level of conceptual understanding. Additionally, the teachers' role is to guide the constitution of the taken-as-shared meanings that form the basis for mathematical communication within the wider society.

The process by which the children and teacher have become acculturated to a practice of mathematics is illustrated in the following episode that occurred recently in a project classroom in another school. The teacher has been teaching in this manner for the past 4 years. The characteristics of the interaction pattern and the meaning that is constituted between this teacher and her students is presented to give a flavor for the way in which this mathematical practice differs from the conventions of traditional school mathematics (McNeal, 1991). This example occurred after students had completed activities which were developed to encourage the construction of conceptual operations for multiplication using the balance format (see Figure 7.2). Children's initial construction of these operations developed from their conceptualization of multiplication as repeated addition (Steffe, 1989). The intent of the activity is to encourage the development of relationships among the basic facts and to stimulate the curtailment of counting by ones. The teacher, for her part, is anticipating that the students are going to give an addition or multiplication number sentence as they express their methods for solving the problems.

Teacher: The first balance that we have shows nothing on one side, an empty box, and three boxes of 6 on the other side. What did you and your partner decide to do there, Clint?
Clint: 18.
Children: Agree.
Teacher: Clint, did you have a number sentence?
Clint: Well, 12 plus 6 equals 18.
Teacher: We have some different ones it looks like (as other children are waving their hands).

She writes the number sentence above the problem and continues to solicit and write the students' number sentences. This interaction pattern is characteristic of the whole-class discussions which follow pair collaboration in this classroom. The number sentences given in order in this case are: $12 + 6 = 18$; $3 \times 6 = 18$; $16 + 2 = 18$ and $6 \times 3 = 18$. The teacher then calls on Clint and his partner to tell how they solved the problem.

Clint: We knew these two 6's were 12, and we just added on 6 so 13, 14, 15, 16, 17, 18.
Teacher: Does that make sense? (asking the others who nod in agreement) That's one way to do it. Who gave us 3 times 6 equals 18? Justin.
Justin: We had that one (points to $3 \times 6 = 18$) and I knew that these two equal 12 (points to the two 6's). I took off that [4 from the remaining 6] and that made 16 and then add that 2 back on made that 6 [in 16] an 8.
Teacher: What was your number sentence?
Justin: The 3 times 6. But we had...
Teacher: (interrupts) How did you decide that?
Justin: Because here's three 6's (points to the boxes of 6) and three. And you're just adding three times.

Listening to Justin's explanation, the teacher notices that the number sentence he used (3×6), did not fit with his explanation, yet $16 + 2$ did. In asking, *"How did you decide that?"* she is asking Justin to give a rationale for notating the problem with a multiplication sentence, and yet solving it as addition. At this point, Mandy is frantically waving her hand.

Teacher: Do you have a question, Mandy?
Mandy: Yeah, but you're adding 6's (she goes to the front).
Justin: I know! That's what I meant.
Mandy: Yeah, but you should change it around [6×3].
Justin: You don't have to!
Jim: They say the same thing.

Mandy, interpreting the discussion to be about writing the number sentence for the problem pictured, challenges Justin's explanation. Justin, in giving his response, does not provide a complete justification for his solution, so another student, Jim, tries to extend Justin's comment by offering a rationale.

Teacher: They say the same thing, you say?
Jim: Because they're the same number, but they're just switched around.
Teacher: Some people seem to think 6 times 3 and 3 times 6 mean the same thing. (She points to the two number sentences.)
Children: They do! They do!

Within the context of the discussion, Jim's explanation of commutativity is unexpected by the teacher. She recognizes that he is trying to convey an idea that expresses a more powerful conceptualization about multiplication, which she would like to have explained further. She decides to capitalize on the situation and, as the teacher, exert her authority to provide a challenge to Jim's comment, "*They say the same thing, you say?*" As a consequence, he is obligated to respond to her challenge and justify his statement. The teacher then uses Jim's explanation to further extend his meaning by relating it to conventional symbol notation and to suggest that others ("*some people*") also think this. At this point, Mandy again asserts that the appropriate number sentence for the balance shown is $6 \times 3 = 18$. This discussion continues briefly among the children without resolution. The teacher decides to intervene with a different question to help clarify the situation and asks, "*So what are you saying his number sentence is really showing? Boxes or what?* On the overhead, she draws a balance of six boxes with the numeral 3 in each of them and writes a corresponding number sentence. After procuring agreement from the class, she then asks Jim, "*But what are you trying to say though?*" directing the topic of the discussion back to the point Jim has made about commutativity.

Jim: They both say the same thing! Six 3's equals 18 and three 6's equals 18!
Teacher: (To whole class). Do you agree with that?
Children: Yes. No. No. Yes. No.
Teacher: What if we forget the picture part for a minute. Do we all agree that 3 times 6 is 18?
Children: Yes. No. No.
Teacher: What is 6 times 3?
Tom: 3 times 6 is (pause) 3 and 3... (pauses) and 3. It's 18!
Teacher: Oh, so you agree with that? So only the number sentence is false?

The teacher, in attempting to guide the constitution of a taken-as-shared meaning for $3 \times 6 = 6 \times 3$, recognizes that some children are still interpreting the situation to be about writing a number sentence that matches the balance pictured. She attempts to facilitate the discussion by eliminating the concern for *"the picture part"* and focuses on 3 times 6, to which Tom volunteers to prove is *"18"*. At this point Dale interjects, *"I have a question."* His question is again about the most appropriate number sentence for the balance pictured. At his level of conceptual understanding 6 × 3 and 3 × 6 *"...are different sentences. You're adding more on that one (6 × 3). That's 18 (3 × 6) and that's (6 × 3) way past 18."* The teacher decides at this point to again intervene in the discussion. She begins by restating the ideas that have been agreed upon by the class.

Teacher: Okay. Can we stop a minute boys. I think we have all agreed on something that I kind of want to get clear. We all agree that 3 times 6 is 18?
Children: Yes.
Teacher: And we all agree 6 times 3 is 18?
Children: No. No. Yes. (Children all begin to talk).
Matt: But I'll count on my fingers. (He goes to the front). Watch. 6 plus 6 is 12.
Teacher: Let's listen.
Matt: So that's two (holds up two fingers for the two 6's) and then add 6 more on. 6 (putting his thumb up then pausing to think), 12, 13, 14, 15, 16, 17, 18 (counts on using his other hand).
Teacher: Okay. We have agreed on that haven't we?
Children: Yeah.
Teacher: We've agreed that 3 times 6 is 18 and that 6 times 3 is 18, so is it possible to switch them around and still come up with the same answer?
Children: Yes.
Teacher: I think we have pretty much agreed on that haven't we?
Children: Yes.
Teacher: So the part that is confusing us a little was how we should write the number sentence to match the picture.

The tension that existed for the teacher between encouraging children's individual constructions and the negotiation of taken-as-shared meanings was well illustrated in this episode. The manner in which she skillfully orchestrated the discussion exemplified that one of the goals of her instruction was to encourage her students to construct mathematical meaning for themselves. She did this by providing the children with opportunities to engage in mathematical activity and to make sense of the mathematical relationships for themselves. Rather than providing the explanations and justifications herself, she encouraged her students to do this instead. Thus, her emphasis in teaching was on the development of their mathematical thinking and underlying conceptual operations. By allowing children the opportunity to individually construct their own mathematical meanings in a setting in which their ideas were validated through communication which consisted of explanation and justification encouraged students to rely on their own ways of thinking to make sense of the world rather than on the authority of the teacher (Kamii, 1985; Nicholls, 1989).

However, she realized that, while learners were active constructors of their own knowledge, they must also grow into the intellectual life of those around them (Bruner, 1986, 1990). As a teacher, she recognized she had an obligation to acculturate her students to the mathematical practices of the culture in which meaning had been interactively constituted by the members. In this episode, the teacher acted to guide the students in the constitution of a meaning for the commutativity of multiplication that was compatible with that held by the wider society. The skillful manner in which she engaged students in a process of reasoning through explanation and proof to arrive at a consensus exemplified her goal of helping children become members of a community. Therefore, her role as teacher was to encourage students to be participants in a discourse in which mathematical meaning was being established through a process of communication involving negotiation of meaning.

ASSESSMENT OF MATHEMATICAL BELIEFS, MOTIVATION, AND ACHIEVEMENT

Although our personal research interests are concerned with the processes by which children learn mathematics in a meaningful manner, the measurement dominated practices of public schooling require that we administer standardized achievement tests. We had initially anticipated that our goal of students' appropriation of mathematics would be at the expense of their efficiency. Thus we anticipated that our students would do well on the portion of standardized achievement test that involved concepts and applications, but might not do as well on the computation section as those students familiar with conventions found in traditional textbooks. At the end of the second year of the project in which 18 additional teachers used the project in their classrooms, a statewide accountability test was administered to all second-grade classrooms within the school system. Three of the schools involved with the project also had classes in which traditional textbook instruction occurred. We selected these schools (10 project classes and 8 nonproject classes) to assess students' achievement on traditional measures. The particular test contained the items from the California Achievement Test and was composed of two subtests, (a) Computation and (b) Concepts and Applications. The Computation subtest evaluated addition and subtraction skills using the vertical format that is predominant in the textbooks. The Concepts and Applications subtest included items using specific representations emphasized in textbooks and items that required students to associate number words and numerals (e.g., 62 identified as 6 tens and 2 ones). The results of the analysis indicated that on the Computation subtest, achievement between the two groups was equal. On the Concepts and Applications subtest, a significant difference in the means was found in favor of the project classrooms (further details about these studies can be found in Cobb, Wood, Yackel, Nicholls, Wheatley, Trigatti, & Perlwitz, 1991; Nicholls, Cobb, Wood, Yackel, & Patashnick, 1990).

In addition to the instruments designed to measure mathematical achievement, we also attempted to evaluate children's beliefs and motivations about mathematics. It was our belief that children in project classrooms would have different perceptions about mathematics and doing mathematics from students in traditional classrooms. The theoretical background that formed the basis for the Beliefs Scale we used was derived from Kamii's (1985) theory of autonomy and Nicholls's (1983) research on achievement motivation. Two goal dimensions, task orientation and ego-orientation, have previously been shown to be relevant to learning in school (Nicholls et al., 1990). Ego-orientation, in this regard, refers to the notion that, while one might seek to learn or perform to the best of one's ability, these actions would only be the means for establishing oneself as having superior ability to others. Task orientation refers to the notion that one's goal is to gain understanding.

Nicholls and colleagues have developed motivational and beliefs scales to assess these two dimensions with adults and junior and senior high school students. These scales were adapted to make them appropriate for second-grade students, and the items were related specifically to their beliefs and motivation about mathematics. The Beliefs Scale was also given to students in the 10 project classes and 8 nonproject classes from three schools in the school system. The results indicated that students from project classes had personal goals in mathematics in which they were less motivated to be superior to their peers. They also held beliefs that trying to understand and collaborate leads to success in mathematics. Students from traditionally instructed classes were likely to believe success depended on the importance of conforming to the solution procedures of others and in being lucky, neat, or quiet in class (cf. Cobb et al., 1991; Nicholls et al., 1990).

CHANGE IN TEACHING IN OTHER SUBJECT-MATTER AREAS

During the initial teaching experiment, the project teacher learned to accommodate her prior ways of teaching to be compatible with a constructivist approach to learning mathematics. In essence, she was acculturated to a form of practice in which the goal and purpose of teaching was for students to learn that doing mathematics is a meaningful activity involving reasoning. This change in the process of teaching was uniquely distinct from her former practice of teaching mathematics.

As the teacher began to reorganize her beliefs about teaching mathematics at the beginning of the school year, we, as researchers, wondered whether this change would be reflected in her other teaching specifically in reading (see Wood, Cobb, & Yackel, 1990, for further explanation). Our general conclusion was that, after 1 year as project teacher, change in her beliefs were generally confined solely to the teaching of mathematics. Whereas this seemed like a contradiction to us, nonetheless, it was not a contradiction for the teacher. We realized that the teacher's activity was rational and reasonable to her, and we tried to view the situation from her perspective. In doing so, we speculated three possible explanations for her activity. First, she did not consider herself to be a strong teacher of mathematics, and the manner in which she interacted with her students created contradictions with her former ways of teaching mathematics. In reading, the same contrast did not occur. She viewed herself as being capable of teaching language arts and therefore did not question her practice. Second, the problem-centered instructional activities that were created to encourage children's individual interpretations also provided opportunities for the teacher to learn about children's thinking. The reading activities, on the other hand, emphasized specific skills to be learned and as such had not created opportunities for students to express their ways of thinking. The third explanation relates to the goals of instruction for mathematics and reading. In mathematics, the goal established by the researchers was for students to understand mathematical relationships. The goals in reading were set by the institution of the school and emphasized achievement on standardized tests (McNeil, 1986; Shannon, 1983). It has been well established that high performance on these tests is most easily accomplished by emphasizing learning of isolated facts and skills rather than for understanding. Similar goals of the school for mathematics were held by the school but were deflected to the researchers, because school administrators viewed the project as a "pilot program" and the researchers as accountable for students' learning.

As we have continued to be involved with all of the teachers who participate in the project, we have had the opportunity to observe in their classrooms and talk with them about the changes they have made. It appears that, as teachers gain more expertise in teaching mathematics, they do reconsider the manner in which they conduct what they refer to as their "questioning" of students. In this respect, they have changed in that the intent of their questioning is to encourage children to express their own ways of thinking rather than as an opportunity to evaluate the correctness of their children's answers. In addition, the current interest in whole language reading that has been incorporated into many basal reading series (Barr & Sadow, 1989) reflects a developmental view of literacy that is highly compatible with our perspective of learning mathematics. The basal reading series recently adopted by the school corporation contains many aspects of this approach to teaching reading along with the traditional skill approach. However, the manner in which the whole-language approach is currently being implemented provides little support and leaves teachers with the responsibility to accommodate their teaching to this approach simply through the use of the materials contained in the reading series. Many of our teachers were aware of the commonalities between the two approaches and tried to use their understanding of teaching mathematics to make the transition. However, as one teacher commented, *"I don't' know what the problem is, but I have tried to use those readers in the same way I do math. But it doesn't work. The discussions are just not the same as they are in math."*

One possible explanation for the difference between reading and mathematics may relate to the way in which teachers were expected to change their practice and the nature of the activities available. In the case of this particular reading program, the teachers were expected to rely on their teacher's manuals as the major source of support. The manuals, while advocating teaching from one perspective, provide directions for teachers' to follow that represents a contradictory perspective. The instruction given still directs the teachers through the specific steps they should follow to implement the materials successfully. Any specific difficulties or questions that arise for an individual teacher in the course of their daily instruction can not possibly be addressed in this format. Thus, the teachers are left to their own devices in their attempt to make sense of the approach. As researchers, we feel that the learning that occurs while the teachers are teaching mathematics in the setting of their classroom is crucial to the success of our project. From our view, in order for teachers to make major accommodations in their practice, sufficient support and guidance is needed in this process.

Our approach follows Richardson's (1990) view of "teaching embedded in theory." In our case, a constructivist theory of children's mathematical learning provides an alternative way for teachers' to view their teaching. In the summer we provide an initial 1-week working session, which is followed by weekly visits to the teachers in their classrooms in which the emphasis is on continuing to make them aware of the ways children learn (Cobb, Wood, & Yackel, 1990; Simon, 1989). Our intent is to develop a relationship with the teachers in which our role is to make their current ways of teaching problematic. As such, we offer suggestions either to their own questions about their practice or by building from concrete incidents that occur in the classroom with their students. We in no way act in an evaluative manner. Instead, our intent is to create settings that allow teachers to reflect on their immediate activity with their students. In this way, suggestions and questions from the researchers can be related to the individual teacher's intuitions and to what is useful to know from his or her perspective. These suggestions and questions, which arise from concrete situations that occur in the teachers' classroom, provide opportunities for us to discuss the principles that underlie our theoretical perspective in a manner directly related to their practice. Our intention is to provide assistance as necessary to help teachers as they resolve what they find problematic and become acculturated to a new form of practice.

CONCLUSION

In these second-grade classrooms, students' learning of mathematics with understanding is the central focus and goal of the children's and teacher's activity. As students participate in discussion, they contribute their ideas and interpretations and give explanations and justifications of their solutions to others. In these settings, opportunities for learning exist for students to solve challenging problems and participate in collaboration with others. The experience of communicating about their mathematical ideas acts to expand and enrich their concepts of number and the operations (e.g., addition) so that students develop mathematical potential and confidence in their ability to investigate new ideas and solve nonroutine problems. The teachers' role in these classrooms is decidedly different from their previous way of teaching mathematics. In this setting, they act to guide, question, and challenge students' thinking and to negotiate their acculturation into the mathematical practice of society. The complexity of the teachers' activity in these situations requires an understanding of the process of teaching and learning that involves more than merely "knowing the subject" and "managing the classroom" (Shulman, 1990). Teaching in this manner requires an understanding of the possible ways children develop mathematical meaning, as well as being well grounded in the knowledge of the mathematics they are teaching. In addition, teaching involves more than controlling students' behavior. The teacher must maintain the delicate balance between creating the challenges and probes that encourages students' learning and preserving those interlocking expectations and obligations that constitute the social norms that underlie the success of the social interaction.

It has been our experience in working with teachers that the classroom creates opportunities for their learning that do not occur in other situations. These learning experiences, which are essential to teachers' success in developing a new form of practice, necessarily require support and guidance during the process. Initially, this support can be provided by researchers, and later by the teachers themselves. In this way, it may be possible for the reform in mathematics education currently being advocated to achieve success.

REFERENCES

Barnes, D., & Todd F. (1977). *Communication and learning in small groups.* London: Routledge & Kegan Paul.

Barr, R., & Sadow, M. (1989). Influence of basal programs on fourth-grade reading instruction. *Reading Research Quarterly, 24*(1), 44–71.

Bauersfeld, H. (1980). Hidden dimensions in the so-called reality of a mathematics classroom. *Educational Studies in Mathematics, 11,* 23–41.

Bauersfeld, H. (1988). Interaction, construction, and knowledge: Alternative perspectives for mathematics education. In T. Cooney & D. Grouws (Eds.), *Effective mathematics teaching* (pp. 27–46). Reston, VA: National Council of Teachers of Mathematics and Lawrence Erlbaum Associates.

Bishop, A. (1985). The social construction of meaning—a significant development for mathematics education? *For the Learning of Mathematics, 5*(1), 24–28.

Blumer, H. (1969). *Symbolic interactionism: Perspectives and method.* Englewood Cliffs, NJ: Prentice-Hall.

Bruner, J. (1986). *Actual minds, possible worlds.* Cambridge, MA: Harvard University Press.

Bruner, J. (1990). *Acts of meaning.* Cambridge, MA: Harvard University Press.

Clements, D., & Battista, M. (1990). Constructivist learning and teaching. *Arithmetic Teacher, 38*(1), 34–35.

Cobb, P. (1990). Multiple perspectives. In L. P. Steffe & Wood T. (Eds.), *Transforming children's mathematics education. International perspectives* (pp. 200–215). Hillsdale, NJ: Erlbaum.

Cobb, P. (1991). Reconstructing elementary school mathematics. *Focus on Learning Problems in Mathematics, 13*(2), 3–32.

Cobb, P., & Merkel, G. (1989). Thinking strategies as an example of teaching arithmetic through problem solving. In P. Trafton (Ed.), *1989 Yearbook of the National Council of Teachers of Mathematics* (pp. 70–81). Reston, VA: National Council of Teachers of Mathematics.

Cobb, P., & Steffe, L. P. (1983). The constructivist researcher as teacher and model builder. *Journal for Research in Mathematics Education, 14,* 83–94.

Cobb, P., Wood, T., & Yackel, E. (1990). Classrooms as learning environments for teachers and researcher. In R.B. Davis, C. A. Maher, & N. Noddings (Eds.), *Constructivist views on teaching and learning mathematics* (pp. 125–145). Reston, VA: National Council of Teachers of Mathematics.

Cobb, P., Wood, T., & Yackel, E. (1991). A constructivist approach to second grade mathematics. In E. von Glasersfeld (Ed.), *Radical constructivism in mathematics education* (pp. 157–176). Dordrecht: Kluwer.

Cobb, P., Wood, T., & Yackel, E. (in press). Discourse, mathematical thinking, and classroom practice. In N. Minick, E. Forman, & A. Stone (Eds.), *Education and mind: Institutional, social, and developmental processes.* Oxford: Oxford University Press.

Cobb, P., Wood, T., Yackel, E., & McNeal, B. (in press). Characteristics of classroom mathematics traditions: An interactional analysis. *American Educational Research Journal.*

Cobb, P., Wood, T., Yackel, E., Nicholls, J., Wheatley, G., Trigatti, B., & Perlwitz,

M. (1991). Assessment of a problem-centered second grade mathematics project. *Journal for Research in Mathematics Education, 22,* 3–29.

Cobb, P., Yackel, E. & Wood, T. (1989). Young children's emotional acts while doing mathematical problem solving. In D. B. McLeod & V. M. Adams (Ed.), *Affect and mathematical problem solving: A new perspective* (pp. 117–148). New York: Springer-Verlag.

Cobb, P., Yackel, E., Wood, T., Wheatley, G., & Merkel, G. (1988). Research into practice: Creating a problem solving atmosphere. *Arithmetic Teacher, 36*(1), 46–47.

Davis, P.J., & Hersh, R. (1981). *The mathematical experience.* Boston: Houghton Mifflin.

Edwards, D., & Mercer, N. (1987). *Common knowledge.* London: Methuen.

Forman, E. (in press). Discourse, intersubjectivity and the development of peer collaboration: A Vygotskian approach. In L. T. Winegar & T. Valsiner (Eds.), *Children's development within social contexts: Meta theoretical, theoretical and methodological issues.* Hillsdale, NJ: Erlbaum.

Goodlad, J.I. (1983). *A place called school.* New York: McGraw-Hill.

Kamii, C. (1982). *Number in preschool and kindergarten* (pp. 73–88). Washington, DC: National Association for the Education of Young Children.

Kamii, C. (1985). *Young children reinvent arithmetic: Implications of Piaget's theory.* New York: Teachers College Press.

Krummheuer, G., & Yackel, E. (1990). The emergence of mathematical argumentation in the small group interaction of second-graders. In G. Booker, P. Cobb, & T. de Mendicuti (Eds.), *Proceedings of the Fourteenth International Conference on the Psychology of Mathematics Education* (pp. 109–122). Oxtapec, Mexico: PME.

Labinowicz, E. (1985). *Learning from children: New beginnings for teaching numerical thinking.* Menlo Park, CA: Addison-Wesley.

Labinowicz, E. (1987). Children's right to be wrong. *Arithmetic Teacher, 35*(2), 9.

Lampert, M. (1988). The teacher's role in reinventing the meaning of mathematical knowing in the classroom. In M. Behr, C. LaCampagne, & M.M. Wheeler (Eds.), *Proceedings of the Tenth Annual Meeting of the Psychology of Mathematics Education - North America* (pp. 433–480). DeKalb, IL: Northern Illinois University.

Marshall, H. (1988). Work or learning, Implications of classroom metaphors, *Educational Researcher, 17,* 9–16.

McNeal, M. (1991). *The social context of mathematical development.* Unpublished doctoral dissertation, Purdue University, West Lafayette.

McNeil, L. (1986). *Contradictions of control: School structure and school knowledge.* New York: Methuen/Routledge & Kegan Paul.

Mead, G. H. (1934). *Mind, self and society.* Chicago: University of Chicago Press.

Mehan, H. (1979). *Learning lessons.* Cambridge, MA: Harvard University Press.

Morrow, L. M. (1988). Young children's responses to one-to-one story reading sessions in school settings. *Reading Research Quarterly, 23,* 89–107.

National Council of Teachers of Mathematics. (1989). *Curriculum and evaluation standards for school mathematics.* Reston, VA: Author.

National Council of Teachers of Mathematics. (1991). *Professional standards for teaching mathematics.* Reston, VA: Author.

National Research Council. (1989). *Everybody counts*. Washington, DC: National Academy Press.

Nicholls, J. G. (1983). Conceptions of ability and achievement motivations: A theory and its implications for education. In S. G. Paris, G. M. Olson, & W. H. Stevenson (Eds.), *Learning and motivation in the classroom*. Hillsdale, NJ: Erlbaum.

Nicholls, J. G. (1989). *The competitive ethos and democratic education*. Cambridge, MA: Harvard University Press.

Nicholls, J., Cobb, P., Wood, T., Yackel, E., & Patashnick, M. (1990). Dimensions of success in mathematics: Individual and classroom differences. *Journal for Research in Mathematics Education, 21*(2), 109–122.

Nino, A., & Bruner, J. (1978). The achievement and antecedents of labeling. *Journal of Child Language, 5*, 1–15.

Pierce, C.S. (1935). *Collected papers of Charles Sanders Peirce* (Vol. 5, C. Hartshorne & P. Weiss, Eds.). Cambridge, MA: Harvard University Press.

Piaget, J. (1970). *Genetic epistemology*. New York: Columbia University Press.

Piaget, J. (1980). *Adaptation and intelligence: Organic selection and phenocopy*. Chicago: University of Chicago Press.

Porter, A. (1989). A curriculum out of balance. The case of elementary school mathematics. *Educational Researcher, 18*(5), 9–15.

Rathmell, E. C. (1978). Using thinking strategies to teach the basic facts. In M. Suydam & R. Reys (Eds.), *Developing computational skills* (pp. 13–38). Reston, VA: National Council of Teachers of Mathematics.

Richardson, V. (1990). Significant and worthwhile change in teaching practice. *Educational Researcher, 19*, 10–18.

Rosenshine, B., & Stevens, R. (1986). Teaching functions. In M. G. Wittrock (Ed.), *The handbook of research on teaching* (3rd ed., pp. 376–391). New York: Macmillan.

Schutz, A. (1962). *The problem of social reality*. The Hague: Martinus Nijhoff.

Shannon, P. (1983). The use of commercial materials in American elementary schools. *Reading Research Quarterly, 19*, 68–85.

Shulman, L. (1990). *Aristotle had it right: On knowledge and pedagogy* (Occasional Paper #4). East Lansing, MI: The Holmes Group.

Simon, M., (1989, April). *The impact of intensive classroom followups in a constructivist mathematics teacher education program*. Paper presented at the annual meeting of the American Educational Research Association, San Francisco, CA.

Sinclair, J., & Coulthard, R. (1975). *Towards an analysis of discourse: The English used by teachers and pupils*. London: Oxford University Press.

Skemp, R. (1976). Relational understanding and instrumental understanding. *Mathematics Teacher, 77*, 20–26.

Steffe, L. (1983). The teaching experiment methodology in a constructivist research program. In M. Zweng, T. Green, J. Kilpatrick, H. Pollak, & M. Suydan (Eds.), *Proceedings of the Fourth International Congress on Mathematical Education* (pp. 469–171). Boston: Birkhauser.

Steffe, L. (1989). *Children's multiplying and dividing schemes: An overview*, Athens, GA: University of Georgia.

Steffe, L. P., Cobb, P., & von Glasersfeld, E. (1988). *Construction of arithmetical meanings and strategies*. New York: Springer-Verlag.

Steffe, L. P., von Glasersfeld, E., Richards, J., & Cobb, P. (1983). *Children's counting types: Philosophy, theory, and application*. New York: Praeger Scientific.
Stodolsky, S.S. (1988). *The subject matters: Classroom activity in math and social studies*. Chicago: University of Chicago Press.
Streeck, J. (1979). Sandwich. Good for you. In J. Dittman (Ed.), *Arbeiten Zur Konversations analyse* (pp. 235–257). Tubingen: Neimeyer.
Thornton, C. (1978). Emphasizing thinking strategies in basic fact instruction. *Journal for Research in Mathematics Education, 9*, 214–227.
Voigt, J. (1985). Patterns and routines in classroom interaction. *Recherches en Didactique des Mathematiques, 6*, 69–118.
von Glasersfeld, E. (1984). An introduction to radical constructivism. In P. Watzlawick (Ed.), *The invented reality* (pp. 17–40). New York: Norton.
von Glasersfeld, E. (1987). Learning as a constructive activity. In C. Janvier (Ed.), *Problems of representation in the teaching and learning of mathematics* (pp. 3–17). Hillsdale, NJ: Erlbaum.
Vygotsky, L.S. (1978). *Mind in society*. Cambridge, MA: Harvard University.
Walkerdine, V. (1988). *The mastery of reason*. London: Routledge.
Weber, R. (1986, April). *The constraints of questioning routines in reading instruction*. Paper presented at the annual meeting of the American Educational Research Association, San Francisco, CA.
Wells, G. (1985). Pre school literacy related activities and success in school. In D. Olson, N. Torrance, & A. Hilyard (Eds.), *Literacy, language and learning* (pp. 229–265). Cambridge, MA: Harvard University Press.
Wood, T. (1989). Whole class interaction as the negotiation of social contexts within which to construct mathematical knowledge. In C. Keitel, A. Bishop, P. Damerow, & P. Gerdes (Eds.), *Mathematics, education and society* (pp. 34–35). Paris: UNESCO.
Wood, T., Cobb, P., & Yackel, E. (1990). The contextual nature of teaching: Mathematics and reading instruction in one second-grade classroom. *Elementary School Journal, 90*(5), 497–513.
Wood, T., Cobb, P., & Yackel, E. (1991). Change in teaching mathematics: A case study. *American Educational Research Journal, 28*(3), 587–616.
Wood, T., Cobb, P., & Yackel, E. (in press). Reflections on learning and teaching mathematics in elementary school. In L.P. Steffe (Ed.), *Constructivism in teacher education*. Hillsdale, NJ: Erlbaum.
Wood, T., & Yackel, E. (1990). The development of collaborative dialogue within small group interactions. In L.P. Steffe & T. Wood (Eds.), *Transforming children's mathematics education. International Perspectives* (pp. 244–252). Hillsdale, NJ: Erlbaum.
Yackel, E., Cobb, P., & Wood, T. (1991). Small group interactions as a source of learning opportunities in second grade mathematics. *Journal for Research in Mathematics Education, 22*,(5), 390–408.
Yackel, E., Cobb, P., Wood, T., Wheatley, G., & Merkel, G. (1990). The importance of social interaction in children's construction of mathematical knowledge. In T. Cooney (Ed.), *1990 Yearbook of the National Council of Teachers of Mathematics* (pp. 12–121). Reston, VA: National Council of Teachers of Mathematics.
Yackel, E., & Wheatley, G. (1990). Promoting spatial imagery in young children. *Arithmetic Teacher, 37*(6), 52–58.

Chapter 8
Translating Motivation into Thoughtfulness*

Phyllis C. Blumenfeld
Pamela Puro

University of Michigan
School of Education
Ann Arbor, MI

John R. Mergendoller

Beryl Buck Institute for Education
Novato, CA

How can I motivate children to think about what they are doing, and not just focus on getting it done? Teachers struggle with this question, because their experience has convinced them that students who are motivated to learn and who think carefully about what they are learning develop deeper understanding of the material being covered and attain higher achievement scores. These perceptions are supported by a number of studies focusing on the relationships between individual differences in students' motivational goals and their cognitive engagement in schoolwork (Meece, Blumenfeld, & Hoyle, 1988; Nolen, 1988). Cognitively engaged students use thinking, metacognitive, and self-regulatory strategies to approach learning thoughtfully. Research also demonstrates that teacher practices can influ-

---
* This study was supported by the National Science Foundation under Award MDR8550437 to Phyllis Blumenfeld and Judith Meece. The opinions expressed in this chapter do not represent those of the National Science Foundation, the University of Michigan, or the Beryl Buck Institute for Education, and no endorsement should be inferred.

ence the type of learning goals students adopt (Ames & Archer, 1988). Students who perceive their classrooms as places that stress learning versus performance goals report more positive attitudes toward the subject, more intrinsic motivation, and more cognitive engagement, that is, thoughtfulness.

These studies, however, rely on student perceptions of the classroom and rarely include actual classroom observation. We need to know a great deal more about how teachers create and sustain environments that emphasize learning for understanding rather than performing well on tests (see also Marshall, 1988). Moreover, most of the research has concentrated either on individual differences in students' learning goals or on their cognitive engagement during learning. It does not consider how classroom context affects the relationship between students' motivational orientation and their thoughtfulness. In other words, we know little about how teacher practices help translate students' learning goals into self-regulatory behavior. This chapter reports results of a study designed to answer this question. We conducted extensive observations of lessons in 10 fifth- and sixth-grade science classes taught by five experienced teachers and administered questionnaires to students about use of learning strategies. There were significant classroom differences in students' levels of motivation to learn and in levels of cognitive engagement.

Teacher practices that promote a learning motivational orientation and that promote cognitive engagement have been described elsewhere (Blumenfeld, in press; Meece, in press; Meece, Blumenfeld, & Puro, 1989) and will be referred to only briefly in the current chapter. Here, our focus will be on case studies that contrast the practices of two science teachers: Teacher A, whose students reported high levels of motivation and cognitive engagement, and Teacher B, whose students reported high levels of motivation but lower levels of cognitive engagement. Our intention is to compare practices of a teacher who successfully translated student motivation to learn into thoughtfulness with those of a teacher who failed to do so.

The chapter is divided into five sections. First, we briefly review the literature on enhancing motivation and cognitive engagement. We then describe the research on which this chapter is based. Finally, we present case studies of two teachers, discuss their similarities and differences, and conclude by considering how teachers can encourage students to be both motivated to learn and thoughtful about what they are learning.

REVIEW OF THE LITERATURE

How Teachers Enhance Motivation

Research indicates that students' engagement in achievement activities is motivated by a complex set of goals. Several sets of goal orientations have been proposed by different researchers: mastery versus ability (Dweck & Elliot, 1983), learning versus performance (Ames & Archer, 1988), and task-involved versus ego-involved (Nicholls, Patashnick, & Nolen, 1985). Each set of goals differs primarily in terms of whether learning is perceived and valued as an end in itself or as a means to external ends such as grades, gaining approval or avoiding negative evaluation of others. Findings consistently demonstrate that individual differences in self-concept of ability, perceived control, expectancies, and values are related to the goal orientations students adopt (Harter, 1983; Marshall, Chapter 1, this volume; Meece, Blumenfeld, & Hoyle, 1988; Nolen, 1988, Pintrich & deGroot, 1990; Pokay & Blumenfeld, 1990). These orientations in turn are related to the types of thinking in which students engage during lessons.

Recent research in motivation has moved from a focus on individual differences to a focus on situational factors that affect the goal orientations students adopt (Ames & Archer, 1988; Marshall, 1988). These factors can be grouped in three areas: (a) those affecting student perceptions of ability and expectancies for success, (b) those affecting student perceptions of the value or interest of the material, and (c) those that help sustain a task focus rather than performance focus. A number of articles have described ways teachers can enhance students' perceived ability and expectancies for success (see Brophy, 1987; Eccles & Midgley, 1989; Marshall & Weinstein, 1984; Rosen-holtz & Simpson, 1984). These factors include creating opportunities and support for student learning, grouping strategies, and grading practices. More specifically, teachers can communicate high expectations by choosing varied tasks that are at appropriate levels of difficulty, by scaffolding student learning, and by teaching learning strategies to enable students to accomplish tasks. Teachers who do not group their students by ability, do not treat higher and lower achieving students differently, and do not use reporting practices that highlight ability-related information will also enhance students' beliefs in their ability to learn.

Student interest in and the perceived value of the material being presented are enhanced when teachers: (a) emphasize intrinsic reasons for learning rather than stressing grades or other rewards; (b) relate material to students' lives and experiences or to current events; (c) offer choices about what, where, with whom or how work is done; (d) assign tasks that are varied and that include novel, humorous, fantasy, or gamelike elements; (e) assign problems for students to solve that are realistic and challenging; and (f) assign work that involves creating a product or provides some form of closure (see Brophy, 1987; Lepper, 1988).

Teachers' feedback, accountability, and evaluation practices also influence whether students adopt a motivational orientation that stresses learning rather than performance. Students' expectancies for success are increased when teachers: (a) hold students accountable for learning and understanding—not just for getting right answers, (b) give students the freedom to take risks and be wrong, (c) stress improvement over time, (d) minimize comparison with others, (e) minimize competition, and (f) use private rather than public evaluation (Ames & Archer, 1988; Eccles & Midgely, 1989).

A rich body of research has produced these findings. Nevertheless, with few exceptions (see Eccles & Midgely, 1989; Marshall & Weinstein, 1986), most studies of how classrooms influence student motivation have focused on a single element of the classroom, such as how grouping practices or evaluation practices influence ability perceptions. Moreover, many have used teacher reports or student reports of classroom practices rather than actual observation. The case studies in this chapter are based on extensive classroom observation and illustrate the influence of several elements simultaneously.

How Teachers Enhance Cognitive Engagement

Prior research points to problems teachers face in engendering and sustaining student thoughtfulness. Among others, Doyle (1983) reports that high-level cognitive tasks are ambiguous and risky. Students need considerable help with these tasks and often resist completing such assignments because they are worried about bad grades. Not only are cognitively complex tasks left uncompleted by students, those who do complete them are likely to make mistakes along the way. Consequently, cognitively difficult tasks slow the momentum of lessons. To avoid student failure and to ensure student cooperation and participation, teachers invent ways to modify difficult assignments and decrease cognitive requirements. The result is that lessons and tasks that initially require students to practice complex problem solving are often transformed into ones that merely require guessing the correct answer.

However, there are a number of ways teachers can enhance students' cognitive engagement in assigned tasks (see collection edited by Brophy, 1989). These include actively structuring information, guiding student efforts by teaching strategies for learning and by scaffolding instruction, and providing multiple opportunities for students to grapple with the information and represent their understanding in a variety of different ways. Nevertheless, it is important to note that most of the research on enhancing thoughtfulness has either described good practice (e.g., Lampert, 1989) or examined changes in student achievement after an intervention that involves teacher training, strategy training, or curriculum change (e.g., Anderson & Smith, 1987; Fennema, Carpenter, & Peterson, 1989) rather than actually using measures of student cognitive engagement. The work reported here differs from prior studies in that teacher behavior was observed and student self-reports of cognitive engagement were collected after several lessons on different topics.

Enhancing Motivation and Thoughtfulness

Studies of motivation and studies of cognitive engagement in classrooms have, for the most part, developed in isolation from each other. As a result, findings regarding learning, motivation, and instruction have not been well integrated conceptually or described in a way that is useful and accessible to teachers. (For an exception, see: Corno & Rohrkemper, 1985; Lepper, 1988.) Suggestions about improving student motivation are typically made without considering the nature of subject matter content, how teachers should go about instruction, or the difficulty of implementation. Another problem is that these suggestions are often not specified sufficiently for teachers to put them into practice. And, even if specific enough, they may appear contradictory, because they have not been integrated. Thus, the purpose of this chapter is to illustrate how teachers can integrate practices that promote student motivation and thoughtfulness and to provide specific examples of such practice.

DESCRIPTION OF THE RESEARCH

The Participants

To study how teacher practices influence student motivation and cognitive engagement we observed 10 fifth- and sixth-grade science classes taught by five teachers (three female and two male) and surveyed the 275 students in these classes. The teachers had taught an average of 14.5 years, with a range of 8 through 20 years. All had master's degrees and were members of both the science curriculum committees in their districts and the statewide science teachers' association. Four had degrees in science and one, trained in math, had taught science for 8 years. To find these teachers, we asked district science coordinators, university faculty, and school principals to nominate teachers who did "hands-on" science, who were experienced, and whom they considered to be superior. The classrooms were located in four different schools in middle- to lower middle-class neighborhoods.

We chose teachers from schools that used a platoon system, where students rotated as a class to different teachers for different subjects. This selection allowed us to separate the influence of class and teacher, since teachers were observed delivering the same lesson to two groups of students.

The Lessons and Tasks

Using several criteria, and in collaboration with each teacher, we selected three units and five lessons per unit to observe in each class taught by each teacher. Since each teacher taught two classes, we observed a total of 15 lessons per class, and 30 lessons per teacher. The units focused on different topics, including the human body, physical and chemical changes, space travel, and forms of energy. The lessons selected varied so that whole group, small group, and individual forms of instructional organization were represented. Some lessons occurred at the beginning, some at the middle, and some at the end of the unit. Each lesson we observed required students to complete some sort of a written product such as a worksheet, a chart, or a report.

Procedures

Assessing students' motivation and cognitive engagement. After each of six lessons in each class, questionnaires designed to tap student motivation to learn and cognitive engagement were administered. The motivation questions were designed to distinguish learning goals from performance goals. Sample items included: I wanted to learn something new, I wanted to do better than others. Examples of items intended to tap students' use of cognitive and metacognitive strategies included: I asked myself questions as I went along to be sure that the work made sense to me; I tried to figure out how today's work fit with what I had learned before in science. These measures are described more fully in Meece, Blumenfeld, and Hoyle (1988).

Classroom observations. Each of the 150 lessons (30 per teacher) was tape recorded. Observers also completed narrative records of the lessons. Both were combined in preparing transcripts that described: (a) lesson content, including number of facts and concepts or ideas presented in the lesson; (b) instruction, including directions, explanations of concepts, and modeling of cognitive strategies; (c) question and feedback patterns; (d) motivational techniques, including practices designed to enhance the value or interest of the task; (e) management, how teachers monitored tasks, and how they elicited and insured participation; and (f) accountability or how teachers evaluated task completion.

Results.

To test for teacher differences, data were collapsed across classes taught by the same teacher. This procedure was followed because, except in one instance, there were no significant differences in student reports of motivation or cognitive engagement in sections taught by the same teacher. A one-way analysis of variance was performed on learning goal scales and on cognitive engagement scales. Significant teacher differences appeared on both scales. Results of quantitative and qualitative analysis of teacher behavior based on the transcripts can be found in Blumenfeld (in press), Meece (in press), and Meece, Blumenfeld, and Puro (1988).

We analyzed the narratives using a series of questions that focused on patterns and sequences of behavior that could not be determined by examining the frequencies alone. Questions were generated based on the research reviewed above describing how teachers can promote motivation and cognitive engagement. We examined teacher practices during different types of lesson structures. We focused on how teachers introduced and developed content, how they managed and helped students accomplish tasks, how they questioned and gave feedback, how they summarized or reviewed, and how they evaluated student performance.

Analysis of the narratives revealed differences between teachers whose classes reported different levels of motivation and cognitive engagement. It should be recalled that the teachers were all experienced and would be considered "effective" by traditional standards—they were good managers and well organized, disruptions were minimal, and most class time was spent on work. Therefore, it is not surprising that most of the teachers were likely to use many recommended practices. What differentiated the teachers was the consistency and success with which they executed these practices.

Briefly, in classrooms where students reported higher levels of motivation to learn, teachers stressed ideas rather than facts, highlighted the value of science through stories about scientists or about how science was related to everyday events, and related their own excitement by telling personal stories of their scientific experiences. These teachers also made conceptual material more concrete and interesting by providing examples and by relating it to their own students and their experience or to current events. They also assigned tasks that were more varied and that encouraged student cooperation in small groups. In contrast, in the classrooms where students reported lower motivation, teachers more frequently focused on quizzes, grades and right answers.

Four factors characterized teacher practices in classrooms where students reported high levels of cognitive engagement.

- *Opportunities to learn.* Teachers created opportunities for students to learn in a variety of ways. They (a) focused lessons around mid-level concepts that were substantive but not overwhelming; (b) built lessons tightly so that the main idea was evident in presentations, demonstrations, discussions, and in the assigned tasks; (c) developed concepts by presenting concrete illustrations of scientific principles and relating unfamiliar information to the students' personal knowledge; (d) made explicit connections between new information and things students had learned previously and pointed out relationships among new ideas by stressing similarities and differences; (e) elaborated extensively on textbook readings rather than allow the book "carry the lesson"; (f) guided students' thinking when posing high level questions; and (g) asked students to summarize, make comparisons between related concepts, and apply the information they had learned.

- *Press.* Teachers pressed for thinking via their feedback and participation techniques. They (a) required students to explain and justify their answers; (b) prompted, reframed the question, or broke it into smaller parts when students were unsure, and probed students when their understanding was unclear; (c) monitored for comprehension rather than procedural correctness during activities; (d) encouraged answers from all students, by using techniques like asking for votes or asking students to compare their responses and debate the merits of different answers rather than allowing a target group to dominate recitation sessions, and (e) added questions requiring written explanations of results or alternative representations of the information in the form of diagrams or charts to "short answer" commercial workbook assignments.
- *Support.* Teachers supported students' attempts to understand via scaffolding. They (a) modeled thinking, suggested strategies, and problem solved with students when students had difficulty instead of providing the correct answer; (b) reduced procedural complexity of manipulative tasks by demonstrating procedures, highlighting problems, providing examples, allowing for planning time; and (c) encouraged collaborative efforts by requiring each student to make contributions to the group.
- *Evaluation.* Teachers' evaluation and accountability systems emphasized understanding and learning rather than work completion, performance, comparison, or right answers. Teachers used mistakes as ways to help students check their thinking and explicitly encouraged students to take risks. Moreover, they allowed students who had done poorly to redo assignments or quizzes.

MOTIVATION AND COGNITIVE ENGAGEMENT IN TWO TEACHERS' CLASSROOMS

To illustrate the practices described above, we will describe below the classroom behavior and the nature of teacher-student dialogue from two teachers in the study. These teachers had different effects on the motivation and cognitive engagement of their students. Students taught by the first teacher, "Teacher A," reported high levels of motivation and cognitive engagement in the lessons we observed. In contrast, students in the class of the second teacher, "Teacher B," reported high levels of motivation, but significantly lower levels of cognitive engagement.

We will first examine the manner in which each teacher conducted whole class recitation lessons, focusing attention on the way each teacher begins the lessons, develops the concepts being taught, questions students about their understandings, provides feedback to correct misunderstandings, and concludes the lesson. Next, we examine the way each teacher supervised small group, "hands-on" activities, emphasizing the nature of the activities, the way in which each teacher introduced them to the students, the way in which each teacher monitored the activities, and the way in which each teacher concluded the lesson.

Teacher A's Whole Group Lessons

Teacher A

Beginning the lesson. Teacher A created learning opportunities and press in a variety of ways. She began lessons by reviewing what was covered the previous day. Rather than just reminding students of the key points, she pressed for understanding by using review questions and demanded widespread participation in answering. For instance, the teacher began one lesson by asking:

> All week we have worked on rockets. Why do you think we spent so much time working on your rockets and racing them? When you revised your rockets, what did you learn?

Another time students had made class lists of problems that could be expected in planning a trip to the moon. At the beginning of the following lesson, the teacher and students examined lists produced by different classes and noted how similar each class's problems were. On another occasion, following a lesson about the movement of the moon, she began by asking several pairs of students to physically demonstrate what they had learned the previous day and explain its importance.

Concept development. Teacher A made extensive use of questions and discussion to develop lesson concepts. She often piqued student interest and created an opportunity for understanding content by relating material to what students already knew or had experienced. Then she proceeded to build concepts in small steps, asking students about each part of the concept and relating the questions to students' own experiences. She also used questions to check whether students understood each step in the concept being developed before adding new information.

For instance, in the selection below from a lesson on interdependence of living things, Teacher A first asked students to define dependence, then explained how the students depended on their parents, and subsequently pointed out that their parents and other people also depended on them. She checked students' understanding of this idea by asking several questions about who depends on them and for what. Note the widespread participation of the class in the excerpt below.

T: Who has an idea of what it means to depend on somebody? What does depend mean? (pause) Amy?
S: To count on.
T: To count on, okay, good. To count on somebody when you need help. Doug?

S: To rely on someone.
T: To rely on a person, good. Okay, when you trust somebody. Chris, what does depend mean to you? What do you think it means?
S: When you trust them.
T: When you trust, Phil, when you depend on somebody, what does that mean to you?
S: You trust them to do what they say.
T: Okay, you trust someone to do something, sometimes without checking up on them, too.

Teacher A asks students to give examples as a way to check their understanding of the concept.

T: Now I want you to think for a minute of somebody you depend on. Somebody you depend on, Chris?
S: My mother.
T: For what? What do you depend on her for?
S: Everything.
T: All right, can you think of something in particular?
S: She helps me.
T: Okay, does she help you out with some problems sometimes, okay. Michelle?
S: Becky.
T: Okay, why do you depend on Becky?
S: To be my friend.
T: Okay, ... okay. Becky?
S: Michelle.
T: (laughs) Okay, for the same reason maybe. Dan?
S: Mother.
T: For what?
S: Cooking.
T: For making sure you have something to eat, okay.... Now you have probably heard the word dependent. If your parents have filled out their income tax a while back you are a dependent of theirs. You depend on them and they can deduct you on their income tax because of that. But you are dependent on a lot of people, but there's also a lot of people dependent on you. Sometimes it's the same person you depend on who is also dependent on you and it is interdependent. Inter means between or among.
T: Some of you said that you depended on your parents for food, or for shelter or because they are nice and they'll listen to you. How do they depend on you? Beth?
S: To keep the house clean.
T: Okay, when they clean it up they want it to stay that way. What's another way your parents depend on you?
S: To do my homework.
T: Okay.
S: To clean my room.
T: Okay.

After it was clear that students understood the idea, Teacher A introduced the lesson topic "all living things depend on something or somebody else." She then extended the idea, asking students to indicate how they depended on their pets and how their pets depended on them. As she developed the idea, she repeatedly highlighted main points with examples, and when necessary, brief demonstrations.

When the teacher used the textbook, she explained the important concepts rather than relying on students to cull important points from the reading by themselves. She rarely had students read silently; when she did, she structured the task by posing questions to be answered. For instance, when students read a passage describing America's attempts to reach the moon, she told them to concentrate on finding three things scientists have discovered to make it easier for rockets to reach the moon.

The following excerpt from the same lesson illustrates how, when using the text, Teacher A made sure that students understood the reading. She restated the definition and asked students to explain how pictures in the book illustrated interdependence. Again, note also the widespread participation and the use of questions to highlight the idea.

T: Okay, so interdependence means that you depend on something and things depend on you also.
T: In the picture on page 282 that all of you opened your books to when you first came in, I want you to look at what you see there. There are some cows there. What do they depend on to survive?
S: Grass.
T: Okay, they depend on the grass that's there.
S: People depend on cows.
T: Who depends on cows? Amy?
S: People.
T: People do, why?
S: For milk.
T: For milk, any other reasons?
S: For meat.
T: For meat.
S: For leather.
T: Leather.
S: Steak dinners.
T: Steak dinners. Okay, so we depend on cows, cows depend on the... (pause for students to answer with teacher)... grass.
T: We've said before that people depend on cows for milk, for beef, for leather and so on and cows depend on the grass. Do cows depend on people?
SS: (various comments)
T: Raise your hand if you can think of one way that cows depend on people. Dan? Did you forget what you were going to say? Why don't you call on someone to help you out this time?
S: To keep them clean.

T: Okay, to keep them clean. Becky?
S: To plant grass.
T: To plant the grass, sure, there wouldn't be grass if people didn't take care of planting it. Phil?

In the next segment note that as the examples become more removed from student experience, Teacher A does more explaining and tries in other ways to make the content familiar. In this case, she asks students where to find lichen and connects the example to one students had just finished discussing:

T: Now, there's different kinds of interdependence and they can be very simple. There's one kind of interdependence I'd like to tell you about. Do you see the picture on page 285? How many have seen that stuff growing on trees? Have you noticed that in places? Does anyone think they could bring us in some sometimes, if they go up north or someplace where they might see some.
   There is a lichen and what's interesting about that is not just that is has one name but it is made up of two different things. It is made up of algae and algae is a green plant so it can make its own food but it doesn't have a place to live, it doesn't have any place in can survive so it depends on fungus. And fungus provides protection and moisture because it likes to live in moist places and where the fungus couldn't live, what does the fungus need? Remember we studied nongreen plants, we studied fungus, what does fungus need?
S: Food.
T: Food, yes, the fungus can't make its own food so where does the fungus get its food?
S: The algae.
T: The algae. What does the algae get out of the deal?
S: A place to live.
T: Yes, the algae gets a place to live, all right. And it gets moisture, and the fungus gets out of the deal, it gets food. If we go back to the idea of the cows again for a minute, there's a different kind of interdependence there that we didn't talk about yet. Cows eat what?
S: Grass.
T: Grass. Do you know that cows can't digest grass all by themselves? So cows have a bacteria that lives in their stomachs and, now the cows need this bacteria because the cows couldn't survive without the bacteria because the bacteria digests the grass, right? Okay, so the bacteria digests the grass, it helps the cows survive. What does the bacteria get out of this? The bacteria gets a nice warm moist place to live, so both things benefit from it. One gets a nice warm place to live and it helps the cows digest the food. So that's another kind of interdependence. That's called a complex interdependence.

Questions and feedback. Teacher A highlighted important points and pressed for students to organize information and make connections among concepts by asking them to explain their answers or by elaborating on them herself. When responding to student answers, Teacher A often reworded what students said into more precise or scientific terms. In addition, she communicated expectations that all students would formulate answers to the questions she was posing. During the lesson on food chains she asked a question relating to a textbook passage students had just finished reading silently. When only a few hands were raised, she said: "Only one person at each table with a hand up? It should be more than that." Occasionally, she waited for all students to raise their hands to indicate they had an answer before calling on anyone. Teacher A also monitored comprehension by having students think of an answer and then discuss it with a partner, or by asking students to indicate whether they agreed with a response offered by one of their classmates. She also asked all students to vote on what they had just heard, and was likely to say to those who did not raise their hand to vote, "We are waiting for you to make up your mind."

Once she called on someone, Teacher A encouraged thinking by waiting for that student to reply. She did not give the answer herself or call on someone else to do so. If a student did not respond, the teacher usually gave a hint or reworded the question. Teacher A never accepted incorrect answers. Instead, she helped students to come to the correct one. A student who could not answer could call on someone to "help." This practice contributed to the freedom to be wrong during the learning phase of the lesson. She also praised students for thoughtful answers.

The following excerpt from a lesson on the moon shows Teacher A's use of questions to check for understanding. Note how the teacher elaborates, asks for justification, and guides students during the exchange.

T: If a rocket leaves Earth for the moon would it want to land on the side closest to Earth or the opposite side?
S: Closest to Earth.
T: Why?
S: Signals travel in a straight line. If they would go to the opposite side, signals would slow down if it had to go all the way around.
T: Radio signals follow a straight path, not around or through something. Remember from our lesson on using radio waves that it takes $2^{3/4}$ seconds for the waves to bounce back. If we want to send pictures back, they have to go in a straight line.
T: Can you think of another reason?
S: Messages and pictures.
T: Okay, to send messages and pictures back.
T: When the light side is closest to the Earth, like it will be tonight, we have a full moon. What is the moon like at other times?
S: (called out) One-half, one-quarter.
T: Why would we land on the light side—why would we care? Audrey?
S: So you can see.
T: Yes, you could take good pictures.
T: What's another reason to land on the light side?
S: To know where they landed, they have better directions.

T: Yes, they would have better landings.
S: It would be warmer also.
T: Yes.

Ending the lesson. At the end of a lesson Teacher A made frequent use of questions requiring choral response as a way to reinforce student knowledge. She often supported and guided students by spending a few minutes summarizing the key concepts before asking high-level questions about connections among ideas. This scaffolding made key information available for students to draw on when answering high-level questions. Teacher A also pressed for thinking by having students write or draw in their journal notes. She thus made sure that all students could do the work regardless of writing ability. For example, she gave students pictures of plants and animals to use to illustrate food chains. Students also drew pictures showing the forces of gravity between the moon and the Earth and to represent the four eras of flight.

Before concluding, Teacher A often previewed the next day's material. For example, she finished the interdependence lesson by saying: "Tomorrow we are going to be continuing, we are going to be talking about a pond where there's a different kind of interdependence because of all the things in a pond, and if you take out one of them, how it's going to affect everything else."

Teacher B

Beginning the lesson. Teacher B typically spent several minutes at the start of a lesson piquing student interest. He used many different techniques including humor, relating the topic to student experience, and expressing his own enthusiasm. Teacher B's extensive use of humor included science riddles, amusing pictures, and jokes. In a lesson about the moon, he reminded students of the riddle: "What was the earliest satellite? The moon." In teaching about the phases of the moon, he asked this riddle: "How much is the moon worth? A dollar, because it has four quarters." A week before the moon lesson, he put up a bulletin board displaying a funny picture of the man in the moon, surrounded by statements of fact as if the moon said them, such as "I am your nearest neighbor in space." To introduce a lesson on the origin of the moon, Teacher B wrote on the board: "Hey, Mr. Moon, where did you come from?" He also used dramatic visual aids. Once he held up a raw chicken leg and a vial of red liquid, which he said was blood, to dramatize the change that food must undergo to be useful to the cells of the body. He then joked with students, asking if they thought the liquid really was blood.

Teacher B also related the topic to students' interests, experience or current events. For example, three days before a lesson on the moon, he asked students to interview their parents about the Apollo moon landing using a prepared interview sheet. He had students observe the moon nightly and each day talked about what they had seen. To start a lesson on nutrition, he had students bring in boxes of their favorite breakfast cereal and read the ingredients from the labels.

Teacher B frequently expressed his own interest and enthusiasm. Before the lesson on the moon he described viewing the places of the moon with his neighbors and also arranged to meet his students one night at the school with telescopes so they could observe the moon and planets. He recalled the thrill of the first moon landing and the relevance of new discoveries in science.

It is important to note that this "motivational" phase of the lesson often took quite a bit of time, typically at least 10 minutes. In addition, during the introduction Teacher B would sometimes interrupt to take care of housekeeping or administrative tasks before moving on to the rest of the lesson. He passed out papers, discussed deadlines, gave instructions for homework, arranged materials for activities, or waited for students to clean out their folders or find papers or materials. This practice made the lesson choppy.

Teacher B almost always made a statement about the lesson's purpose. These were primarily brief remarks which did not specify what students would be able to do with the information: "Today we will find out one way to calculate the distance to the moon and tomorrow we will find out another"; "today we're going to go a little further with Newton's Laws"; "let's talk about aiming for the moon." When introducing a new unit, however, Teacher B spent more time stating learning goals. For example, as he told about his own observation of the moon he said:

> We were looking at the moon and talking about it, whether it was waxing or waning. Those are some terms you are going to become familiar with in this next chapter, what phase it was in, what phase it will be in a couple of days, you'll be able to predict that after we are done with this unit.

Teacher B also reviewed previous lessons by briefly reminding students of the topic. "Yesterday we figured out how far away the moon was, so we solved that problem." His questions about the topic were low level and generally required only recall. He rarely checked whether the students understood the main idea of the previous lesson before proceeding. Thus, Teacher B created considerable interest in the topic, but he did not help students to make connections. In the following excerpt, the teacher does review information from the previous lesson, but note that there is little press for student thought. He does not call on many individuals to respond and tends to provide elaboration himself rather than asking students for further information.

The teacher reminds students that the demonstration of the previous day illustrated Newton's Law.

T: Who can tell us what Newton's Law is?
S: For every action there is an equal reaction.
T: Equal and opposite reaction. That's what the balloon-a-tic-showed.

Teacher holds up a model of the "balloon-a-tic" the students had made. He asks:

T: What's the action?
S: Spinning of the balloon.
T: In spinning of a balloon an action or reaction?
S: Reaction.
T: What's the action that causes the reaction?
S: When you blow it up.
T: Not only that, what else?
S: Air coming out.

The teacher elaborates rather than asking students to do so.

T: When air comes out of nozzle, when it shoots out, that's action. Which way will the balloon go? This way?

The teacher is trying to get students to demonstrate their understanding of equal and opposite reactions. Note however that he does not ask students to justify their predictions. Students point in different directions. The teacher then demonstrates which way the balloon moves; he does not ask those whose predictions were incorrect to indicate why their predictions were faulty. He asks:

T: Can I change that direction? Watch. He turns the straw so air goes the other way. Do you understand?

Developing the concept. Teacher B spent time asking what students knew about the topic to develop the main idea. While this practice probably continued to heighten interest, he did not help students successfully relate their knowledge to the point under discussion. In the following example, when he asked students what they knew about the moon, as they offered answers, Teacher B did not use their replies to teach the concept which appears later in this unit. Instead, Teacher B brought up many examples and repeated the concept, and asked about new examples. Also, he asked students to define and use the concept before they had the background to do so.

T: What else do you know about the moon before we start to learn about it? Facts and theories. Kim?
S: It can give off light.
T: Okay, it can give off light. Does it make the light?
S: No.
T: What makes that light, Dave.
S: Sun.
T: The sun. But how does the light come from the moon then if it's not making it? How does the light come from the moon if the sun makes it, Chuck?
S: It reflects.
T: It reflects. What does reflect mean, Lisa? What does reflect mean? If I say the word reflect, what does that mean? Lisa? Lisa B.? The light reflects off the moon, what does that mean? Did you ever see the light reflect off the moon before? Did you ever see the moon?
S: Yes.
T: In order to see the moon you need to have the light bounce off it, we are going to find that out. Anne?
S: Light bounces off the moon.
T: Does that sound like a good word, Lisa? Bounces off, to reflect off, to bounce off. If I reflect a softball off that wall right there, or a rubber ball, it will bounce off that wall. Okay, so light has to reflect off this in order to see it. Does light have to reflect off of Angie for us to see her?
SS: No.
T: Yes it does. Does light have to reflect off of Dallas for us to see him? Does light have to reflect off of anybody in this room for us to see them? Does light have to reflect off the ceiling for us to see it?
SS: No. Yes. (Mixed call outs).
T: Yes it does. 'Cause without light would you see anything. No. So without light we would have a hard time seeing this (points to picture of moon). There are some things in the sky that give us light, stars...
S: Planets. (call out)
T: Planets. Do planets make their own light?
S: No.
T: How do they get their light then?
S: From the Sun.
T: From the sun, it bounces off this planet and now we can see Mars because the sun light is bouncing way out to Mars and then it's bouncing back to our eyes. You can't see without light. Planets can't make their own light. This doesn't make its own light but look at it; Whee! Have you ever been able to be outside on a summer night and be able to actually participate in activities like playing catch because of moon light? Or maybe frisbee? Or maybe tag? Or anything where you are outside, where if it's a cloudy night you can't do it. All right, it depends on if the moon is full, like this, or not full.

Teacher B relied heavily on external media such as textbooks, handouts, charts, or bulletin board displays to convey information. He usually did not expand on what was written in these sources. Most frequently he used the textbook, reading from it himself or calling on students to read sections aloud. He kept student attention on the reading by posing questions about the topic of upcoming paragraphs. After a paragraph about chewing, Teacher B previewed the next paragraph by asking: "While chewing is going on, what else is happening? Lisa, read and let's find out." He often asked students to reiterate what had been read. After a selection about the digestive, respiratory, and circulatory systems, he asked:

> Of those three, which is concerned with getting food digested? Which is concerned with getting oxygen to the body? What does the circulatory system do?

It is important to note that the lesson stayed at the level of facts and information. The questions Teacher B asked required simple paraphrasing of the reading. Teacher B did not make the lesson more accessible for students by organizing concepts. Instead, he expected students to understand the ideas they were reading. He did not go beyond the written material to explain or elaborate on points raised. Students also were not asked to use the information or to relate it to other things.

The following excerpt is taken from a lesson introducing a unit on the moon. The concepts of rotation and revolution were important for this unit. He read the definitions aloud from the text, then moved around the room holding a poster of the moon to model rotation and revolution. He did not ask many questions, and failed to check for student understanding.

T: Next thing. Next paragraph down, please. You know those facts I just gave you? Don't memorize them but learn them. There's a difference between the two. "Rotation of the moon is equal to it's revolutional period so its same side always faces the Earth." Underline that please, the first sentence there: "The rotation of the moon is equal to its rotation period..."

And first of all you have to find out what rotation means and revolution. We're going to find that out. So, the same side of the moon always faces the Earth. That's the first sentence in the paragraph that is titled "rotation." Again, underline that, please. "The rotation of the moon is equal to its revolution period so its same side always faces the Earth." We always see this side, we never see the other side of the moon. Unless we send a satellite up there and it goes around. We have seen it, we have taken pictures of the other side of the moon. This is the only side we get to see from Earth. This is the only side we ever get to see from Earth.

Because as it rotates, class, watch what rotation is. Want to see the other side of the moon? In order to see the other side of the moon I have to turn this picture around. As it rotates, rotates means it spins on its axis. We'll never see

the other side of the moon anyway. As it rotates, it is also going around the Earth. This is a very tough concept, we're going to spend a couple days on this. It also goes around the Earth and it is rotating. But can you see it rotating?
SS: No.
T: Now if you're the Earth, in the center where Dan and Dave are seated, you still see the same side don't you?
S: Yeah.
T: And I'm revolving around you; you are the Earth. Revolve means to go around something. Rotate means to spin on your own, on your axis. Is it rotating?
SS: (sounds of students talking among themselves)
T: That's staying still, I'm revolving. Rotation of something means as it spins on its own. Okay?

Throughout the development phase of the lesson, Teacher B continued to place heavy emphasis on sustaining student interest. In expressing his own excitement, he sometimes introduced information tangential to the topic. For example, during a lesson on the space travel he spoke at some length about his own reaction to the moon landing.

Teacher B used brief demonstrations that were surprising or dramatic in order to develop ideas. For example, to illustrate the idea that objects remain in their same state of motion until a force acts upon them, he asked a student to walk in a straight line to the front of the classroom. When the student was across from him, he pushed the student to make him veer from his original path. To illustrate the differential perception of speed at various distances, he asked one student to go outside and run past the window while another boy ran inside in front of the windows. These demonstrations were interesting, but Teacher B did not make clear how they illustrated differential perception of velocity. Often he did not define relevant terms until after the demonstration, nor did he elaborate or explain sufficiently so student could understand the point being made. When there were indications of student confusion, Teacher B sometimes did not stop the lesson to elaborate or teach necessary background concepts. For example, as he worked through some mathematical problems illustrating the use of radio waves to calculate the distance to the moon, students told him they had not learned to do calculations with such large numbers. Instead of simplifying the numbers so the concept would be clear, Teacher B continued with the presentation and told students they would learn the math later.

Questions and feedback. During the development phase of the lesson, Teacher B used questions for motivational purposes. His many rhetorical questions were meant to create interest: "How many of you have ever played catch in the moonlight?" "How many of you have ever eaten chicken?" "Right now you are digesting what? Your breakfast." He also used questions to increase class participation by calling on different students to read answers from the bulletin board, the textbook, or worksheets. As the excerpts above illustrate, his questions were not designed to check student understanding or to help students apply or extend their knowledge.

He frequently encouraged students and praised responses as "perfect answers." At the same time, however, he often accepted or agreed with incorrect answers to encourage student participation. He also accepted called-out answers from a small group of "target" students who carried the lesson and responded to many of the hard questions. Before calling on other students, Teacher B sometimes heightened the target group's visibility by saying things like, "I know you know it, Mark, but let's let someone else try."

In the following section, Teacher B reviews what was read by repeating important information. Note that he does not ask students questions to check their comprehension, but does all the talking. Also, he adds interesting tidbits about the moon, which serve to enhance motivation but not to encourage thoughtfulness.

T: Okay, six times man has gone and landed on the moon and brought back rocks. Why didn't he bring back trees?
SS: (call out comments)
T: Dave?
S: No trees.
T: That's right. Why didn't he bring back some animals?
SS: No animals. (call out)
T: There are no animals on the moon. So all he could bring back, as exciting as it may not sound to you, were rocks. But they told us an awful lot about the moon. Sixteen-ten, Galileo had a telescope and he looked through his telescope and he saw the moon and he did an awful lot of discovering on the moon, just from his little tiny room, with his telescope.

Over three hundred years later three men set foot on the moon. That's not too slow really in three hundred years we went from looking at it through a little tiny piece of telescope to actually walking on the moon, that's moving pretty fast. And by the time you people are old enough to have kids and stuff maybe you will go to the moon and maybe your children will actually live on the moon. That's our intent to go to the moon, we want to find out, as man we are very curious about things and we want to find out about things.

Just like Cadillac came here in 1701, right, to Detroit, we are not going to stop exploring. That's part of our human nature.

Ending the lesson. Teacher B often made a one-sentence review of the day's lesson as students prepared to leave. He typically did not go over the main points or ask students to summarize what they had learned.

Small Group "Hand-On" Activities

Teacher A

Characteristics of the activities. The activities students completed in Teacher A's class were carefully chosen to illustrate the concepts being studied. Activities were presented as integral parts of coherent lessons. At the same time, by completing the activities, students were explicitly taught about the scientific process of inquiry. For example, during the habitat activity, students selected a variable for exploration, decided how to test it, built the necessary apparatus, tested their hypotheses, and reported their findings to others. Activities often extended over several days as students planned, carried out, and summarized what they had done. The teacher incorporated each step of the activity in the day's lesson and concluded the series of lessons by reviewing and summarizing what had been learned throughout the activity.

Science activities were structured to allow for choice and required both individual input and group discussion. At the beginning of an activity, students often were required to write down their ideas about what should be done, share them with their group, make a decision about how the group would proceed, and then write down the group decision, as well as what they had contributed to this decision. Sometimes, Teacher A would describe more than one way to do an assignment, giving students some choice in how to proceed. When students were creating a timeline about the history of flight, for example, she told students they either could read each event and then look at the information sheet to find the year, or they could read an informative article and then go back to find when the events occurred. Students also had considerable control over how to proceed during activities as they designed model rockets and experiments to determine insect habitat preference.

Introducing the activity. Teacher A reviewed concepts from previous lessons before starting an activity to ensure that all students understood and could draw on the same information. Before introducing the insect habitat experiment, for example, she reviewed the definition of habitat and asked every student a question about the habitats of different plants and animals.

Teacher A made sure students knew what they were to do by giving clear directions. She used simple, short sentences to explain what was to be done, highlighted potential problems, and followed her verbal explanations by passing out written directions, demonstrating procedures, presenting models of other work, and guiding students through a practice exercise, if necessary. These strategies helped to clarify directions and provided concrete models of correctly completed activities.

Teacher A always scheduled adequate time during activities for planning. She told students that planning was an important part of science, and when the activity included a planning phase, she did not allow students to start until they had completed their plans. For the rocket activity, planning took half a class period. In the insect habitat experiment, an entire class period was scheduled for planning. This emphasis on planning before working encouraged students to think about the purpose of the activity and to develop hypotheses on their own. She also held students accountable for planning by requiring them to complete and show her their planning sheets before passing out material necessary to proceed with the experiment. The following excerpt, taken from a lesson in which students designed experiments to determine insect preference for different habitats, illustrates these points. Two key ideas were (a) explicitly controlling variables, and (b) distinguishing observation from inference.

T: Today we are going to do some experiments to decide what [insect's] preference for habitat is. You will get a habitat worksheet and supplies, including grass, rocks, gravel, soil, sand, ice, bugs and boxes.

Work as a group and come up with preferences for habitats.

These are the rules: The group will come up with four ideas. You could test for wet versus dry, or light versus dark.

Think about how you could test this. There can be different ways to test. The a.m. class did different experiments with food, heat or coolness.

After you have four ideas, come up with one idea and star it.

Next, draw a picture and label the supplies you need either from the class or from home.

Next tell in your own words what you will be doing.

Next, what do you think will happen. What do you expect the results will be, will the bugs go to the wet or dry side, for example?
At the bottom draw your experiment, label the parts. (At this point the teacher held up some examples of student worksheets from the morning class.)

You will not be allowed to start before you have your worksheet filled in. Scientists must plan before they do experiments. A few of you might be able to start today. You must have two identical environments and only one variable. (At this point the teacher showed two experimental setups from the morning class, one a box with rocks, sand, and grass, half exposed to the light and half covered to be in the shade, and another one to test preference for wet and dry habitats.)

She then passed out a habitat experiment worksheet, saying, "This is where you write your ideas down." The worksheet provided spaces for students to write down the elements mentioned above: the variables they will test, the supplies they will need, the procedures they will use to actually carry out the experiment, and their prediction about what will happen. There is also room to draw what their experiment will look like.

During another lesson, Teacher A helped students prepare for a demonstration of the moon's movement and the difficulty rockets have in aiming for it. Although there were directions in the book for this activity, Teacher A demonstrated it with the whole class several times before allowing students to try it in pairs. During the demonstration, she broke the activity down into small steps and described each one. She also used choral response questions to highlight important points.

Monitoring. As Teacher A monitored student performance, she focused on comprehension rather than on procedures. She asked students questions intended to extend their ideas as they completed the activities. For example, during the balloon rocket activity, she asked each group to think of what they could do to make the design better or to make the rocket go faster. During the survival on the moon activity, she told students: "It would be a good idea to write down why something is important or not important to take [to the mother ship]." During the habitat experiment, Teacher A had several extended conversations with groups of students about the merits of placing different material such as mirrors or food in the habitats they were constructing. During these discussions, she also asked students to predict what would happen if they placed those materials in the habitats and to explain the reasoning behind their predictions.

Review. Teacher A always reviewed activities, usually by asking questions of the whole class. In the process she gave or asked students for explanations of correct answers. She encouraged participation by calling on many students and by asking students to vote on or evaluate answers. For example, after students had placed a series of pictures taken on the moon in temporal order, she pointed to the picture taken first and asked how many students had correctly identified that picture. She then called on students to give the letters of the rest of the pictures in order. After each answer she asked the class whether they agreed. If there was any disagreement, she called on someone to offer a different answer, and she asked for justification for both answers. Even with unanimous agreement, she asked students to justify the selection of the picture. After the model rocket activity, she spent one class period discussing variables which could have affected the distances the rockets traveled and had students make a graph showing the distance traveled by each group's rocket.

Teacher A also checked students' understanding by requiring them to write or draw the concepts illustrated by the activity. After the demonstration of the difficulties in firing a rocket from the earth toward the moon, she told students:

> Turn to a new page in your notebook. You have five minutes to write, "What I learned today" or draw stick figures—be sure you use the words rotate and revolve in your sentences or drawings. (She points to the words on the board.) Do this all by yourself. Before you leave I want to see the words revolving and rotation either in your sentences or pictures so I can be sure you understand."

The excerpt below is taken from the conclusion of the habitat experiment described above. Note how the teacher reviewed key issues of variables and inference, provided several opportunities for students to demonstrate their understanding via questions and written summaries, and used group collaboration and individual work to insure that students comprehended the material.

T: We did an experiment where we tried to test for the habitat of a sow bug. Who would like to tell about the habitat the insect preferred from your group's experiment?

The teacher called on one person from each group, probing, clarifying, or expanding student answers to press for thinking and clear explanations.

S: We had a wet and rocky habitat.
T: What were you testing?
S: Which side they went to.
T: Side of what?
S: The side of the box. One was rocky and wet, one was rocky and shaded. They liked the shade.

The teacher asked about the student's choice of words as a lead in to a discussion about observations and inferences.

T: When S said, "They liked the shade," is that an observation or an inference?"

There were no responses. The teacher recalled the students' statement and reframed the question:

T: Can't tell if they "like" the shade. He can't know that. What could he have said to make an observation?
S: The bug went and stayed under the rock.
T: (Asks another student for his group's conclusion.)
S: The bug liked wet, shaded rock over shady, dry rock.

Five additional students reported on their experiment and conclusions. During some of the reports, the teacher again emphasized the difference between an observation and an inference. In doing so, she pressed for thinking, asking students to make connections both to what they had learned previously and among the ideas under discussion.

T: Think about the beginning of the year when we talked about observations and inferences. Give me an example of an observation you saw about the insect in your experiment.
S: The grass was green.
S: The bugs walked all over.
S: The bug liked the rocks.
T: (probes) Why is that an inference?

When students did not respond the teacher reframed the question.

T: What about the word like? Do we know they like it?

Several students responded:

SS: No, it's an inference.
T: Right, you can't observe *like*. What about an inference about the sow bug?
S: There may not be anything they prefer. It might be they would go to the closest thing.
T: Very good. We don't know why they like something, we can just observe where they go. What's another inference?
S: The bug likes me!
SS: The bug is ugly!
T: Yes, those are inferences.

The teacher now held individuals accountable for understanding the group effort of the previous day by having each student summarize and draw conclusions from her experiment. She explained what to write:

T: What were you testing? Write in complete sentences. How did you set up your experiment? What did you observe? Write only the observation, not what the bug liked or that the bug was ugly or any of those words. They are inferences. You may have observed the speed, its color, direction, time it took to get from one part to another, or how long it stayed. Don't use the word like; use what you saw.

Finally, after a discussion about student observations, she encouraged students to extend their knowledge about setting up and controlling variables by critiquing the design of an experiment done by another class.

Teacher B

Characteristics of the activities. Teacher B conducted many activities offering opportunities for problem solving and for learning scientific skills. Students were asked to design rockets and control variables to determine which factors contributed to the distance the rockets travelled. They also constructed "balloon-a-tics" to test Newton's theory of action and reaction. Nevertheless, as described below, Teacher B was unable to help students capitalize on these opportunities for thoughtfulness.

There were several general problems with the way he selected and managed small group activities. First, some activities did not clearly illustrate the concept being studied. Second, he sometimes did not select materials carefully. For example, Teacher B included a small paper cup as part of the materials for building model rockets. When he realized that the cups added too much weight to the rockets and impaired their functioning, he attempted to discourage use of the cups but never simply told the students not to use them. Third, some activities required extensive supervision so that students had to wait for the teacher before they could proceed. For example, during an activity in which students were to observe blood circulating in a fish tail, students had difficulty focusing the misroscopes, and Teacher B had to adjust the focus for each group. Finally, the worksheets accompanying the activities did not ask students to explain their results or apply them to a new situation; they merely had to write down what they had found. Unlike Teacher A, Teacher B did not add questions that pressed for understanding.

Introduction to activities. Teacher B interested students in activities by using humor, fantasy, or student experience. In introducing an activity about being lost on the moon, he asked:

> Are you ready to go to the moon? No, you're not, because you don't have your spacesuits, and I don't have time to wait for you to go to the NASA surplus store and get them. We'll have to use our imaginations.

He described students as "little Robert Goddards" in the lesson on building balloon rockets. During an activity on heart rate, Teacher B had the students run in place for two minutes; while they were doing this, he conducted an imaginary trip around the neighborhood.

Teacher B always provided written directions which he often read aloud. However, he rarely expanded further or modeled how to do the activity. When students asked questions, he repeated the directions he had already read. Unless students asked, he generally did not define scientific terms. If Teacher B did not read the direction aloud, students were not given time to read them silently before starting the activity. Instead, they were expected to read them as they worked.

Planning was not an integral part of activities, and they did not require input from each student or cooperation among group members. For example, as Teacher B handed out the worksheets for the model rocket activity, he said: "I want you to think about a design you can present to your group." He did not, however, allow time for this planning or for discussion of potential designs, apparently assuming students would do this as he handed out the directions for the activity. After groups had started work, he said: "On the back of your papers write out the design for your rocket." This appeared to be an afterthought; no space was provided on the worksheet for that purpose, and Teacher B only made the announcement after students had begun working.

Monitoring. Teacher B generally monitored student participation to check that everyone was involved and following the correct procedures. If he noticed that many students did not understand the directions, he often stopped the class to clarify. As Teacher B moved among groups engaged in the activity, he asked questions about the procedures the group was following and offered specific suggestions. For example, as he watched the students make their balloon rockets, he gave advice about placement of paper cups and balloons. Not surprisingly, most student questions during activities were about procedures. He did not use questions to determine whether everyone understood the concepts demonstrated by the activity, but seemed to assume students understood the ideas illustrated by the activity, if they could complete it.

Teacher B did offer considerable encouragement and expressed enthusiasm for student efforts as he walked around the room. For example, during an activity in which students used balloons to make a rocket, he told a group of boys:

> So you're going to have a balloon on each side. I like that. Let's get it together and see if it works. Aren't you excited to try it? I am.

He tried to foster creativity and risk taking. Whenever Teacher B saw a student do something innovative during an activity, he congratulated him or her and often announced the innovation to the class.

Review. The class period often ended before Teacher B had a chance to review the period's activity. When this happened, he quickly told the students the point of the activity. The next day he did not begin with a review of the activity just completed, but launched immediately into a new one. When Teacher B did have time to review key ideas, he did not stress student understanding of these ideas. Few students participated in these discussions, because Teacher B relied exclusively on volunteers or on students who called out answers without being recognized first. For instance, when Teacher B asked what an activity about action and reaction illustrated, a student answered that the activity showed Newton's law. Teacher B did not ask how, but instead explained the air was the action and the twirling propellers the reaction. Thus, he did not check students' understanding of the concept, review it, or reinforce the main ideas. When he asked students about what the activity illustrated again the next day, they could not name the action or the reaction.

On the second day of the rocket experiment, students finished constructing and testing their rockets, and were very excited to see how far the rockets would travel. Teacher B watched each trial run and offered encouragement. He did not, however, discuss the key ideas of action and reaction demonstrated by the activity. Nor did he ask groups how it would be possible to control variables to determine which factors influence the distance rockets travel. Moreover, he did not review the rocket designs that worked well the previous day to help students figure out critical variables, and use these to redesign their own rockets. At the end of the period, after all groups had tested their designs, the teacher stressed differences in the distance travelled by the rockets rather than emphasizing the concepts the activity was to illustrate. He did not ask students to explain what happened, but simply expressed the hope that they learned something.

DISCUSSION

Teachers want their students to be motivated to learn and to think carefully about what they are learning. Teacher A and Teacher B differed in their success in meeting these goals. This difference can be summarized using two general constructs: (a) bringing the lesson to students, and (b) bringing students to the lesson. *Bringing the lesson to students* entails providing opportunities to learn and enhancing interest and value. *Bringing students to the lesson* entails requiring students to think about the material and supporting their efforts to accomplish this. Teacher A's instructional practices both brought the lesson to students and students to the lesson. Teacher B accomplished the former, especially enhancing interest and value, but was less successful at the latter.

Teacher A made assigned work meaningful by relating it to student experience, by asking for opinions, and by using what students already knew about the topic. She encouraged students to bring items from home and to communicate personal stories, both of which often were incorporated into the lesson. Her lessons stressed ideas and contained clear explanations, demonstrations and examples related to students' prior experience and knowledge. Her lessons were coherent and proceeded slowly and deliberately. She built ideas in small steps and actively elaborated on readings, helping students see connections among ideas. Activities highlighted key ideas and were not overly complicated. She conducted extensive reviews where students were asked to summarize what they learned. She added questions to workbook assignments that required students to synthesize and use what they had learned. These practices created interest and facilitated students' willingness to learn. At the same time, they also helped structure the lesson content so that it was cognitively accessible to students.

Teacher A required students to think about the material being covered—to actively construct knowledge by linking what they were learning to what they already knew and to make connections among new ideas themselves. She pressed for thinking by requiring all students to have answers and to justify their responses. She elaborated, rephrased questions to help guide students, and provided a "safe" retreat from incipient failure by letting them choose someone else to help them think through answers during class discussions. Teacher A asked many comprehension questions before requiring students to synthesize or apply what they were learning. When textbook assignments contained only lower level questions, she added synthesis and analysis items. She required students to demonstrate knowledge in numerous ways; they voted, wrote, debated, and diagramed. They also kept daily journals in which they answered the question: "What I learned today in science."

Teacher A supported student efforts to grapple with the material in a variety of ways. First, she proceeded in small steps so that students could follow the point and were prepared to answer high-level questions. Second, she broke complex activities into smaller segments, modeled procedures, provided time for planning, and checked progress at critical points so that students did not get too far off track. She supported effective small group collaboration by requiring individuals to write their ideas, to share them with the group, and to justify the group decision. In addition, she composed the groups so that poor readers were paired with those who could understand the written directions. To help less able students, she read directions aloud and let them draw rather than write answers. Students could retake tests and quizzes or redo assignments.

In contrast, Teacher B primarily focused on bringing the lesson to the students. His emphasis was on enhancing interest, not in actively structuring information so as to make it more cognitively accessible. He used novelty, humor, fantasy, and dramatic visual aids to introduce topics and gain student interest. He was enthusiastic and frequently told personal stories that communicated his own excitement about science. He also involved parents and stressed the value of science through discussions of current events, health, personal experience, and everyday phenomena. Performance and grades were not a salient aspect of the classroom. However, his strong emphasis on motivation was sometimes at the expense of promoting students' cognitive engagement.

Although he provided opportunities for students to think during his lessons, and his activities contained central ideas and problems, he was less active in organizing the information so as to make it understandable for students. He tended to let the text carry the lesson. He expected students to learn the material from reading and did little to elaborate further. If students expressed confusion, he did not stop the lesson but told them they would learn the material later. Frequent stories, interesting comments, or attention-grabbing stunts sometimes detracted from a focus on the main point of the lesson.

In conducting class recitation sessions, he did not press for thinking but did much of the mental work himself. He summarized main points briefly, connected ideas, explained the significance of experimental results, and gave answers when students had difficulty rather than helping students think through their own confusion and build upon what they did know. He encouraged widespread participation in the introductory phase of the lesson as students shared their ideas and experience, but did not do so during the development and review phases. He did not use questions as a way to check for comprehension as the concept was being developed or to press for synthesis or application during activities and review. Moreover, he usually did not ask students to justify answers; instead he elaborated on their answers himself. During activities he checked to see that students were following procedures rather than understanding key ideas. At the conclusion of activities, students were not asked to explain or apply their findings.

During activities, Teacher B supported students by encouraging their efforts and applauding their innovative attempts. He did not, however, break down the task to make it simpler, model procedures for complex activities, or allow time for group planning. Consequently, although students were enthusiastic and involved, they often needed his assistance to carry out the activities. Because he did not insure that assignments contained questions that forced students to summarize or use what they had learned, the focus on understanding was much less evident than in Teacher A's class.

CONCLUSION

The literature on motivation points to the importance of teachers practices that positively influence perceived competence, perceived interest and value, and encourage students to focus on the task they are completing rather than the grade they will receive. The literature on teaching for understanding points to the importance of stressing key ideas, scaffolding instruction, providing opportunities for students to actively construct their own understandings, modelling problem solving and teaching students how to be strategic in their learning. These literatures have developed largely in isolation from each other. The literature on motivation assumes that, when teachers enhance motivation, students will become more cognitively engaged. The literature on teaching for understanding assumes that, when teachers structure opportunities for meaningful learning and press for student understanding, students will be motivated to learn. The research presented here demonstrates that teachers can foster adoption of learning goals by using practices recommended by motivational researchers. Yet, unless teachers act in ways that promote cognitive engagement, student motivation to learn will not necessarily translate into thoughtfulness or greater understanding of subject matter.

The cases described above illustrate several practices that contribute both to motivation and to cognitive engagement. These include providing opportunities to learn, enhancing students' interest in and the perceived value of the content being covered, supporting students' cognitive efforts to learn and understand, and maintaining a task focus by holding students accountable for participation and careful thought. Teachers can maximize students' opportunities to learn by presenting material organized around concepts, and actively structuring material in ways that make these concepts clear and understandable for students. Students are able to understand material better when its relationship to their own experiences and to prior knowledge is apparent, and new ideas are presented in an organized manner using examples, explanations, summaries, and activities. When teachers use such instructional practices, they "bring the lesson to the students."

At the same time, however, students must "be brought to the lesson." Practices that promote cognitive engagement include pressing for widespread participation and for understanding through questions and feedback, activities, and assignments. Questions designed to check for comprehension of the concept under discussion and to determine whether students can apply the concept to new situations and identify links with other ideas encourage students to become cognitively engaged in the lesson. Feedback that requires justification and explanation provides opportunities for students and teachers to examine and diagnose students' thinking.

Activities can promote motivation by posing a problem, being novel, and allowing for students to exercise some choice and control. To promote cognitive engagement, activities must also require students to synthesize, represent, demonstrate, and apply their knowledge in a variety of ways, not merely arrive at the right answer. At the same time, while the evaluation system can create expectations that students will be held accountable for understanding, it should also minimize the salience of grades and the comparative performance of students.

The support system plays a critical role in sustaining students' motivation, especially their perceived competence and cognitive engagement. To insure that students can meet high-level intellectual demands without being overwhelmed by frustration and confusion, teachers need to employ practices that support and guide student efforts. Facilitative support practices include scaffolding material and questions so that students have information relevant to answer high-level questions, making tasks manageable by breaking them down into smaller parts, providing models, and reducing the complexity of procedures necessary to complete tasks. Small group collaboration and productivity can also be maximized by allowing times for groups to plan, share, and reflect upon what they have done. These practices reduce confusion, and make students feel capable of completing the assigned task, and solving problems they encounter. In so doing, they enhance students' abilities to be successful.

The cases of Teacher A and Teacher B shed light on the delicate balance of practices needed to foster motivation and cognitive engagement. They show (a) how teachers' attempt to enhance students' perceptions of competence and the interest and value of the material must be balanced and integrated with attempts to structure the material and insure thoughtfulness; (b) how providing opportunities to learn must be balanced with providing support, so that students are challenged but not frustrated in their efforts to understand the material; and (c) how maintaining a task rather than performance focus must be balanced with pressing for understanding and holding students accountable for learning.

REFERENCES

Ames, C., & Archer, J. (1988). Achievement goals in the classroom: Students' learning strategies and motivation processes. *Journal of Educational Psychology, 80,* 260–267.

Anderson, C.W., & Smith, E. (1987). Teaching science. In V. Koehler (Ed.), *Educator's handbook: A research perspective* (pp. 84–111). New York: Longman.

Blumenfeld, P.C. (in press). The task and the teacher: Enhancing student thoughtfulness in science. In J. Brophy (Ed.), *Advances in research on teaching: Planning and managing learning tasks and activities* (Vol. 3). Greenwich, CT: JAI Press.

Brophy, J. (1987). Synthesis of research on strategies for motivating students to learn. *Educational Leadership, 45,* 40–48.

Brophy, J. (1989). *Advances in research on teaching: Teaching for understanding* (Vol. 1). Greenwich, CT: JAI Press.

Corno, L., & Rohrkemper, M. (1985). The intrinsic motivation to learn in classrooms. In C. Ames & R. Ames (Eds.), *Research on motivation in education: The classroom milieu* (Vol. 2, pp. 53–84). New York: Academic Press.

Doyle, W. (1983). Academic work. *Review of Educational Research, 53,* 159–200.

Dweck, C.S., & Elliot, E.S. (1983). Achievement motivation. In P. Mussen (Ed.), *Handbook of child psychology* (pp. 643–691). New York: Wiley.

Eccles, J., & Midgley, C. (1989). Stage/environment fit: Developmentally appropriate classrooms for early adolescents. In R. Ames & C. Ames (Eds.), *Research on motivation in education: Goals and cognitions* (Vol. 3, pp. 283–331). New York: Academic Press.

Fennema, L., Carpenter, T., & Peterson, P. (1989). Learning mathematics with understanding. In J. Brophy (Ed.), *Advances in research on teaching* (Vol. 1, pp. 195–221). Greenwich, CT: JAI Press.

Harter, S. (1983). Developmental perspectives on the self system. In P. Mussen (Ed.), *Handbook of child psychology* (Vol. 4). New York: Wiley.

Lampert, M. (1989). Choosing and using mathematical tools in classroom discussion. In J. Brophy (Ed.), *Advances in research on teaching* (Vol. 1, pp. 223–264). Greenwich, CT: JAI Press.

Lepper, M.R. (1988). Motivational considerations in the study of instruction. *Cognition and Instruction, 5*, 289–309.

Marshall, H.H. (1988). Work on learning: Implications of classroom metaphors. *Educational Researcher, 17*, 9–16.

Marshall, H.H., & Weinstein, R.S. (1984). Classroom factors affecting students' self-evaluations: An interactional model. *Review of Educational Research, 54*, 301–325.

Marshall, H.H., & Weinstein, R.S. (1986). Classroom context of student perceived differential teacher treatment. *Journal of Educational Psychology, 78*, 441–453.

Meece, J.L., Blumenfeld, P.C., & Hoyle, R.H. (1988). Students' goal orientation and cognitive engagement in classroom activities. *Journal of Educational Psychology, 80*, 514–523.

Meece, J.L., Blumenfeld, P.C., & Puro, P. (1989). A motivational analysis of elementary science learning environments. In M. Matyas, K. Tobin, & B. Fraser (Eds.), *Looking into windows: Qualitative research in science education*. Washington, DC: American Association for the Advancement of Science.

Meece, J. (in press). The classroom context and students' motivational goals. In M. Maehr & P. Pintrich (Eds.), *Advances in motivation and achievement: Goals and self-regulatory processes* (Vol. 7, pp. 261–286). Greenwich, CT: JAI Press.

Nolen, S. (1988). Reasons for studying: Motivational orientations and study strategies. *Cognition and Instruction, 5*, 269–287.

Nicholls, J.G., Patashnick, M., & Nolen, S. (1985). Adolescents' theories of education. *Journal of Educational Psychology, 77*, 683–692.

Pintrich, P.R., & De Groot, E.W. (1990). Motivational and self-regulated learning components of classroom academic performance. *Journal of Educational Psychology, 82*, 33–40.

Pokay, P., & Blumenfeld, P.C. (1990). Predicting achievement early and late in the semester: The role of motivation and use of learning strategies. *Journal of Educational Psychology, 82*, 41–50.

Rosenholtz, S., & Simpson, C. (1984). The formation of ability conceptions: Developmental trends or social construction. *Review of Educational Research, 54*, 31–63.

Chapter 9
Assessment in the Context of Schools and School Change*

Roberta Camp

Educational Testing Service
Princeton, NJ

INTRODUCTION

Among the unwritten agreements frequently operating in schools is one that effects a separation between the design of assessment and the day-to-day life of the classroom. The bargain that has often been struck is that teachers are responsible for instruction in the classroom, and that someone else—the district, the supervisor of curriculum—is responsible for assessment, which is shaped outside the classroom. On the occasions when assessment crosses the threshold of the classroom, it is seen as an intrusion, an interruption to instruction.

In this situation, teachers often feel that the information derived from the

---

* Portions of this chapter have been adapted from "The place of portfolios in our changing views of writing assessment," to be included in *Construction Versus Choice in Cognitive Measurement* edited by R. Bennett and W. Ward and published by Erlbaum.

The Arts PROPEL work described in this chapter was supported by the Rockefeller Foundation and by Educational Testing Service. The views expressed are the author's own, although they are based on collaborative work with teachers and supervisors in the Pittsburgh Public Schools and researchers from Harvard Project Zero; some of the information about this work is adapted from the *Arts PROPEL Handbook for Imaginative Writing*.

assessment is not relevant to instruction, trusting rather to their own observations to discover whether and how much students are learning. At worst teachers perceive the assessment as the means by which agents outside the classroom hold them accountable for their students' performance on tasks bearing little resemblance to classroom activity. In such instances teachers are faced with a choice between resistance and acquiescence; either they risk looking bad in the test results or they teach to the test.

This tacit assumption about the separation of instruction and assessment is especially unfortunate when teachers and schools are engaged in change. Teachers taking the risks involved in change—exploring new approaches to teaching and new views of learning, trying out new roles in the classroom—are likely to be inhibited if they know their success with students will be judged on the basis of assessments that do not reflect their goals for learning or their students' experiences in the classroom (cf. Evertson & Murphy, Chapter 11, this volume). In these circumstances assessment becomes an obstacle to change.

If, however, the assessment brings teachers together with other teachers and members of the school community to evaluate examples of student work and to examine explicitly the relationship of assessment to instruction, if eventually teachers have a role in the design and implementation of assessment, then assessment itself can become a powerful instrument for institutional change. Thoroughgoing discussion grounded in evaluation of student work leads to examination of goals and standards for learning, of teaching strategies, and of classroom activities. In time, the assessment becomes the catalyst for development of a shared vision for the educational institution.

The point is that neither instruction nor assessment can be understood in isolation. Neither is independent of the other; nor is either a fixed, invariable phenomenon. To understand either requires seeing it as part of the entire educational institution; in times of change this means seeing both as parts of a dynamic system whose ultimate purpose is to promote student learning. To make decisions about either instruction or assessment without reference to the other is very likely to miss opportunities for realizing that purpose.

It is not surprising that educators calling for instruction based on richer and more complex views of learning should also call for assessment capable of accommodating such learning (Archbald & Newman, 1988; Snow, 1989; Wiggins, 1989; Wolf, Bixby, Glenn, & Gardner, 1991). The pages that follow here describe this new perspective on assessment, indicating its relationship to new views of learning and new roles for students, teachers, and others involved in the educational process. The reasons for seeing assessment in the context of schools will be delineated, and the characteristics desirable in such assessment will be described. The potential for conflict between traditional measurement perspectives and the new approaches to assessment will be sketched out as well. A major portion of the chapter will focus on the example of an evolving approach to writing assessment in the Pittsburgh public schools; this example will be used to illustrate the implications for teaching and learning of assessment integrated into the educational institution. Finally the chapter will close with a set of questions to be asked in creating assessment integrated into the school environment.

NEW VIEWS OF ASSESSMENT AND THEIR IMPLICATIONS FOR SCHOOLS

The current dissatisfaction with traditional forms of assessment, and the impetus for creating new ones, is based in large part on the conviction that traditional assessments do not yield information critical to learning. The familiar assessment formats and procedures, this argument suggests, give only a single-dimensional indication of what a student can do at the endpoint of a learning experience. At best, they allow opportunity only for highly constrained simulations of the actual performances in which we want students to engage, either in the classroom or in the world beyond (Archbald & Newman, 1988; Frederiksen, 1984, 1986; Mitchell, 1989; Wiggins, 1989). As a result, they do not elicit evidence of students' ability to engage in complex performances, of the processes and strategies used by students engaged in such performances, or of the mental representations that students bring to bear in solving complex problems (Shepard, 1991; Snow & Lohman, 1988). Further, they assume a theory of learning incompatible with current understanding—one that is componential, hierarchical, and unidimensional (Mislevy, in press; Shepard, 1991; Wolf et al., 1991).

A second set of concerns focuses on the effects of traditional forms of assessment on educational institutions. When high-stakes decisions are attached to test scores, as has been the case in recent decades, tests often determine educational goals. The indicators of achievement—tests—then become confused with goals; as a result, they lose their value as indicators, while distorting movement toward more fundamental goals (Gitomer, in press; Linn & Dunbar, 1990). The effect is most damaging if performance on the test is unlike the performances seen as essential to education. Thus, educators who believe that learning involves complex performances in which students integrate a variety of skills and call on different kinds of knowledge and mental representations are likely to see an emphasis on multiple-choice tests, with their small-scale, discrete tasks, as particularly detrimental to genuine learning.

The proponents of new approaches argue that assessment should be closely related to the educational context both in the performance called for and in the circumstances in which the performance is carried out. Assessment performances, they suggest, should themselves exhibit the characteristics of worthwhile educational experiences (Archbald & Newman, 1988; Mitchell, 1989; Snow, 1989; Wiggins, 1989). Assessment should be based in meaningful tasks—tasks that are complex and challenging, that are consistent with goals for learning and inherently valuable to learning, that are closely related to real-world skills and challenges, that allow students to use the processes and strategies relevant to genuine performance. In these performance assessments, knowledge and skills should be integrated rather than presented as discrete entities. Performances should occur in extended and flexible time frames, using such formats as open-ended problems, essays, hands-on activities, computer simulations, portfolios, and exhibitions. Opportunity should be provided in at least some of the performances for collaboration with peers, and support should be provided as needed in the performance environment.

These desirable characteristics are more feasibly incorporated in the performance if assessment occurs within the immediate educational context—the classroom or school. In addition, when assessment becomes part of the educational institution, the procedures associated with it can inform, and be informed by, the educational community likely to feel its effects most acutely. Assessment within the school or district requires that performance be evaluated in context by the knowledgeable parties closest at hand, usually classroom teachers. The need for informed professional judgment by teachers within the school or district in turn requires teacher discussion of criteria and standards for performance. In these discussions, as in the actual judgment of performance, attention is directed toward the essentials of performance and toward the processes and strategies involved as well as to outcomes. In this way, assessment-related discussion and experience with the assessment itself help to refine teachers' perceptions of students' skills and abilities.

Assessment developed in and related to the school context also provides opportunities for communicating results in ways that are immediately useful and interpretable to a number of parties interested in students' learning. Exemplars of performance can be made public, and the criteria for evaluation made explicit. The criteria are internalized first by the teachers who use them to evaluate performance, and eventually by students preparing for similar performances. They can also become part of the public discourse about student achievement. The evaluation itself is directed toward revealing what the learner can do and toward focusing attention on possibilities for future learning; thus it provides information immediately relevant to the classroom. Finally, the evaluation can be based on multiple indicators or facets of achievement directly relevant to performance; these are then reflected in reports of assessment results, thereby indicating to teachers, administrators, parents, and students themselves how performance can be improved.

When assessment becomes part of the ongoing life of the educational institution in this way, it becomes a force for moving everyone involved toward the goals set for instruction and learning. The benefits experienced by teachers and students are most direct. Teachers are familiar in advance with the criteria and standards for the assessment, having learned from published examples of performances and criteria, possibly from their own experience in evaluating performances or the products resulting from them. Teachers know that the performances required of students for assessment will resemble those of the classroom, and that the results of the assessment will provide meaningful indications of what students can do. Teachers can help prepare students for the assessment without distorting their program of instruction. Students know in advance what kind of performance will be required of them, though they may not know the details, and they know what criteria and standards will be applied. Students may have some practice in advance with performances similar to those called for by the assessment and with application of the criteria to their own and other students' performances.

Because the performances integrate knowledge and skills in ways that resemble real-world challenges, the evidence of learning in them and in the products resulting from them can be communicated directly. Appreciation of a student's achievement need not require technical training on the part of parents or other interested members of the community. Parents and community members might benefit from a discussion of criteria that helps them know what to look for in student work, but such discussion does not require the kind of technical expertise needed to understand the full meaning of percentile ranks or stanines. Parents and community can therefore enter directly into discussion of the goals and standards for learning for their own children or for the school or district. As a result, the assessment affords both teachers and school administrators the opportunity to present evidence of student learning to those in the community most immediately interested in it.

What all this means is that the costs and value of assessments need to be estimated, not only in terms of numbers of students tested and cost per test administration, and not only in terms of the match between stated instructional objectives and test items, but in terms of impact on the entire educational system. This contextual perspective suggests new questions to be raised in evaluating assessment: Does the assessment create distortions in curriculum, either in what is taught or how it is taught, or does it support and enlighten curriculum? How much time do students invest in preparing for the assessment? Does the time so spent contribute to their learning? Does it contribute to students' development of standards and criteria for their own work? How much of teachers' time is directed toward the assessment? What do teachers learn during this time that contributes to better teaching and learning? How do teachers see themselves in relation to their students and the school as a result of the assessment? How do students see themselves as learners and as participants in the educational community?

DESIRABLE CHARACTERISTICS OF ASSESSMENT INTEGRATED WITH SCHOOL CONTEXT

Evaluation of assessment in the context of the educational system as a whole requires taking into account a number of considerations not traditionally thought relevant to the worth of assessments, as well as some that are more familiar. To identify the characteristics desirable in contextualized assessment therefore requires examination of measurement issues and issues of accountability as they are currently understood.

Measurement Issues

Recent developments in measurement theory, particularly discussions of validity, suggest that investigations of the value of assessment should extend well beyond the properties of test instruments themselves. The unified and expanded notions of validity developed by Cronbach (1988), Cole and Moss (1989), and Messick (1989a, b) indicate that validity must be considered in relation to the construct—the theoretical understanding of what is measured by the test—and that they must take into account the social consequences of inferences based on test scores. What this view of validity suggests in the current situation is that valid assessments must accommodate and address the complex and interrelated nature of knowledge and skills now believed to be central to learning. Assessments that do not fully represent the current understanding of knowledge and skills, especially as that understanding becomes increasingly the basis for curriculum and instruction, will not provide information adequate to educational decision making. For some groups of students, in fact, particularly those who have traditionally done least well on assessments and in academic settings, the information derived from assessments based on narrow views of learning may be especially inadequate.

The emphasis on the social consequences of assessment has been further extended to focus attention on the effect of assessment on the whole of the educational system it is intended to serve. Frederiksen and Collins (1989) argue that assessments should demonstrate "systemic validity," that is, that they should support instruction and learning that foster the development of the complex and interrelated knowledge and skills the assessment is intended to measure. Examples of practices demonstrating systemic validity are to be found in writing assessment, where writing samples have long been used to discover whether students are capable of orchestrating the knowledge and skills required to generate text. Because assessment based on writing samples requires judgment by individuals familiar with student writing, they involve scoring sessions in which teachers of writing develop, apply, and eventually internalize standards and criteria for writing. Exemplars of writing performance, and analysis of the exemplars in terms of the criteria applied, are then published as models that teachers can use with students to inform their sense of worthwhile writing tasks and exemplary performance. The experiences and procedures associated with the assessment thus promote an emphasis in writing classrooms on the knowledge and skills addressed by the assessment.

The recent thinking about validity provides a possible theoretical basis for expanding the range of criteria to be applied in evaluating the worth of assessments (Linn & Dunbar, 1990). In fact, a number of researchers have begun to identify criteria and issues to be considered in evaluating the worth of new forms of assessment: Archbald and Newman (1988), Frederiksen and Collins (1989), Linn and Dunbar (1990), Snow (1989), and Wiggins (1989). None of the sets of criteria or issues claims to be exhaustive or conclusive, but they are part of a common effort to lay the groundwork for a theory of measurement that is "more suited to the new constructs" (Snow, 1989, p. 8), that can "provide a theoretical basis for developing new assessment methods" (Frederiksen, 1990, p. ix) and can "link testing with the cognitive process of learning" (Mislevy, in press). Together, they suggest the beginnings of a theory of measurement in which the criteria for judging the value of an assessment extend beyond narrow concerns with efficiency, reliability, and comparability.

In many cases, however, measurement practice lags far behind measurement theory—and so behind current views of teaching and learning. In practice, "validity is usually viewed too narrowly and given short shrift (Linn & Dunbar, 1990, p. 23), while reliability is "too often overemphasized at the expense of validity" (p. 11). What is more, the problem is compounded by a lack of methodology for new forms of assessment. This deficit will not be soon or easily filled, since the assumptions about learning on which traditional psychometrics are based are incompatible with current views of learning (Mislevy, in press; Shepard, 1991; Wolf et al., 1991). For the next several years, therefore, it may be necessary to create assessments compatible with emerging concepts and goals for learning, designing them to be responsible to the principles of good measurement, even though they cannot be demonstrated to be responsible by means of the methodology available from conventional measurement.

In the present situation, lacking established methodology to support measurement consistent with the new views of learning, the most prudent policy may be to adapt practices developed in existing assessments in which students engage in complex performances integrating knowledge and skill. With adaptation, the procedures associated with such assessments can provide interim methodology for assessment accommodating more complex performances than those associated with them in the past.

Issues of Accountability

A recent theoretical development related to measurement issues is the redefinition of accountability by Darling-Hammond and her colleagues (Darling-Hammond & Ascher, 1991) at the National Center for Restructuring Education, Schools and Teaching. In their work, accountability is defined systemically, as "a set of commitments, policies, and practices" (p. 2) that encourage and support good teaching and valuable learning within an educational system while providing correctives to potentially harmful or ineffective practices. Accountability is a matter of shared responsibility for all parties whose decisions and actions affect student learning, rather than one in which administrators hold teachers accountable for the performance of students:

> Massive testing or any other data collection effort does not create an accountability system, nor does it guarantee improvement in urban or nonurban schools. A school or school district creates various policies and practices that make it more accountable by using many different tools, including methods for teacher and parent participation in decisionmaking, bureaucratic regulations, legal recourse, safeguards and support for the competence of staff, and options for choice. Data about student and school progress should inform the system so that responsible decisions are made and problems are corrected when they arise.
> Since each accountability tool has different strengths and weaknesses and provides different incentives, a careful blend of methods is needed to improve schools for all students. Although simple answers are appealing, it is only by struggling with tough questions of who is responsible, for what, and to whom that education, particularly in large urban schools, becomes truly responsive to students, parents, educators, politicians, and the general public. (pp. 11-12)

Assessment-derived evidence of student achievement and progress is seen as only one piece of information gathered to guide decisions in the system, and it is regarded as useful only when it reflects curriculum and instruction and when it is interpreted in relation to the context and practices of the school. In this view an equally important responsibility of the educational system, for example, is to create stimulus and opportunity for teachers' ongoing professional development. The implication is that assessment should take its place alongside other sources of information about the functioning of the educational system; it should be judged for its usefulness in informing the various parties involved in students' education and for its effect on the system as a whole. Clearly, assessment that is incorporated into the immediate context of the educational institution is more likely to serve accountability seen in this systemic way than is assessment that stands largely outside the educational context.

Summary: Implications for Assessment

As yet, no single set of criteria for the new approaches to assessment is seen as definitive. Nevertheless, some common points of emphasis relevant to assessment in a school or district context can be identified from the various discussions of assessment and accountability, at least for the present:

1. The content, formats, and procedures of assessment should be consistent with and supportive of the school's or district's view of learning; where possible, the assessment should actively further the goals set for learning.
2. Student performance on the assessment should be evaluated by teachers from the school or district in terms of criteria and standards that are made explicit and shared throughout the school community; teachers should have the opportunity to participate in the development of shared criteria and standards and to discuss student performance on the assessment in relation to goals for instruction and curriculum.
3. The design of the assessment should be based on sound measurement principles, although methodology to indicate adherence to these principles may not yet be established; these principles include fairness to all students, adequate representation of the scope and range of learning, and trustworthiness of information derived from the assessment.
4. The information provided by the assessment should be meaningful to all parties interested in students' learning and should be interpretable by them; this may mean that the information will need to be presented in different terms to different audiences, but as far as possible all information relevant to improving student learning should be available to all parties.
5. The information provided to the various parties should be relevant to the decisions each needs to make and the actions each needs to take in order to improve student learning; thus, for example, students and their teachers should receive feedback on performance in a format that encourages them to apply the assessment criteria and standards to the students' assessment performance and to subsequent performances, thereby improving performance over the long term.

ASSESSMENT IN CONTEXT: EXAMINATION OF ONE EXAMPLE

To understand how the issues of measurement and accountability are actually experienced in classrooms, schools, and districts, and to understand as well the implications of contextualized assessment exhibiting the characteristics identifiable from current discussions of assessment and accountability, an illustration is presented here. It is taken from one urban public school district, Pittsburgh, and one area of the curriculum, language arts. However, the issues and principles involved apply in major respects to any district and any area of the curriculum experiencing a shift toward views of learning that emphasize complex performances integrating knowledge and skills, the processes that students use in such performances, and the development of student autonomy in learning.

Examination of the Pittsburgh experience and of other schools and districts in the process of change suggests that new views of learning bring new roles for all participants in the educational process—students, teachers, parents, principals, supervisors, superintendents, even school board members. If learning is understood as inquiry and construction of meaning, and if knowledge and skills are seen as resources to be used in investigating and constructing meaning, for example, then it follows that students need to take an active role in their own learning. With the change in students' roles will come a change in teachers' roles. Teachers become designers of classroom activities in which students can inquire, discover, and learn; they are also advisors to students engaged in activities, and observers capable of valuing and guiding students' efforts in relation to larger curriculum and developmental contexts.

Simultaneous with the changes in students' and teachers' roles, changes are needed in the roles of school and district administrators. Some of the traditional administrative functions, including those related to assessment, are likely to take on new focus or purpose. Principals and superintendents, for example, will probably continue to function as negotiators between school personnel and the public, but the issues to be addressed are likely to change. Administrators may continue to monitor the functioning of the overall educational system, but the purpose of monitoring may have less to do with checking up on the performance of individuals at various levels in the system and more to do with facilitating desired changes, enhancing communication, and providing support to school personnel where it is needed. In addition, effective administration of schools and districts will require substantive intellectual leadership as educational systems are reshaped to meet new goals for student learning.

A comprehensive study of schools and districts moving toward new views of student learning would no doubt provide numerous examples of changing roles among students, teachers, administration, and community members—and of the ways in which the role of each group affects and is affected by assessment. For the purposes of this chapter, however, the experience of the Pittsburgh Public School District, particularly its evolving program of writing assessment, may provide sufficient illustration of the issues involved and of possible ways to address them.

Illustrations from Pittsburgh Writing Assessment

Assessment is clearly seen as part of a process of educational change in Pittsburgh, indeed as an instrument of change, both by the superintendent's office and at the supervisory level. In addition, the relationship between measurement issues and the realities of school and classroom life are carefully examined (see LeMahieu & Wallace, 1986), and assessment is seen as closely related to curriculum and professional development.

This vision of assessment extends beyond the superintendent's office. Thus, the Director of Speaking and Writing, who is responsible for the development of curriculum and assessment in language arts K-12, describes the evolution of writing assessment in the district in terms of balances and counterweights among four interdependent elements: paradigms of writing, the roles of teachers, modes of assessment, and district administration (Eresh, 1990). In this perspective assessment is seen as evolving through successive generations, stimulating and stimulated by changes in the three other elements; change in any one of the elements creates the need for change in each of the others to arrive at a new balance. Thus, the existing curriculum and assessment are examined by committees of teachers under the leadership of administration and are revised to reflect improved views of learning; involvement with the development of new curriculum and assessment leads teachers to think of themselves in new roles; the revised curriculum and assessment then stimulate better instruction by all teachers; professional development supported by the district and associated with the changes in curriculum and assessment stimulate significant numbers of teachers to yet richer views of learning; and again curriculum and assessment are reviewed and revised to reflect the new views.

Writing assessment in Pittsburgh has moved through two distinguishable phases in this evolutionary cycle and is now entering into a third (Eresh, 1990). In the first phase, the mode of assessment was a standardized multiple-choice test of grammar and usage; in the second, it was a writing sample. In the current generation of assessment, teachers are engaged in developing curriculum units that combine instruction and assessment over a 4- to 6-week period and culminate with an extended assessment activity in which students reflect on their work and write about what they value and what they would change in it. At the same time, a relatively small group of teachers has been developing a portfolio approach to assessment.

Portfolio assessment is a natural extension of the practice long established in Pittsburgh language arts classrooms of keeping folders of student writing. The folders, which are unstructured collections of all of a student's writing, are transformed into portfolios, which consist of a smaller subset of selected works. The procedures for selecting works and shaping the portfolios have been developed by a group of Pittsburgh teachers and supervisors working collaboratively with researchers from Harvard Project Zero and Educational Testing Service. The experience with portfolio development in Pittsburgh is cited here because it illustrates the issues involved in creating assessment integrated into the school context. In addition, the design of the portfolio as it eventually developed suggests that attention to school context can result in assessment compatible with an accountability system in which all interested parties are informed about, and informative to, student learning. The same issues and possibilities are likely to be evident in the development of other contextualized assessments, whether or not they involve portfolios.

Features of the Pittsburgh Portfolio Experience

Portfolio assessment provides especially useful illustrations for contextualized assessment because it is closely related to the everyday life of classrooms and so to views of learning and instruction. In Pittsburgh as in many other schools and districts, in fact, the impetus for portfolios of writing has come from an awareness that conventional approaches to assessment do not reflect or encourage views of writing compatible with forward-looking instruction (Camp, 1990). The development and implementation of portfolio approaches also provides opportunities for teachers to enter fully into the discussion of assessment in relation to curriculum, especially if they are closely involved in designing the portfolio, as they have been in Pittsburgh.

Teachers' Role in Developing the Assessment

The development of portfolios has occurred in Pittsburgh in the context of the Arts PROPEL project, in which sixth- to twelfth-grade teachers have been full partners in collaboration with supervisors and researchers from the beginning. Teacher discussion has influenced the course of the project and the design of the portfolios (Camp, 1990). In the early discussions of portfolio purpose and design, for example, researchers (the author included) asked teachers to consider two questions: "What do *we* want to learn from the portfolios about students' writing abilities and their development as writers?" and "What do we want *students* to learn about writing and about themselves as writers?" The discussion that followed quickly indicated the teachers' sense of priorities: for the teachers, the primary question for portfolio design was how the portfolios could promote students' learning; what others, including teachers, could learn about students and their writing was clearly a secondary issue. As a result, the portfolio was designed primarily to enhance instruction; assessment is secondary to instruction and intended to serve it.

All of the classroom activities associated with the Arts PROPEL portfolios were designed by teachers who had firmly in mind the conditions of their classrooms and the abilities of their students. Each activity was tried out first by a small group of teachers then by a larger group, then revised as a result of teachers' and students' experience. In the few cases in which a piloted activity did not fit well with the ongoing life of the classroom, teachers did not hesitate to point out problems. In important respects, the teachers' students were also part of the collaboration. When they agreed to engage with an activity they did not much like, for example, they asked teachers to indicate to the rest of the research team that they considered the design to be flawed and their work to be less than optimum as a result.

The activities developed for the portfolio were evaluated by looking closely at student work resulting from the activity. Teachers were essential to the discussion and analysis of student work, indicating where they saw evidence of learning they considered valuable, what the evidence suggested to them about students' learning, and what they would do differently to elicit better evidence. As the portfolios evolved in their classrooms, they evaluated folders and portfolios from one another's students, at once trying out procedures and frameworks for evaluation and contributing to the group's understanding of student learning and development.

Assessment Integrated with Learning and Instruction

The Arts PROPEL portfolio as it evolved from the collaborative explorations is designed around a series of experiences directed toward helping students learn about writing and about themselves as writers; the evidence in the writing that results from these experiences provides the basis for judgments about what students have learned and how they have developed. The assessment function is thus thoroughly embedded in the instructional purpose.

Students keep all of their writing in a folder, then engage in activities in which they go into the folder to make selections for the portfolio. Each time they write a major paper, which goes into the folder accompanied by the notes and drafts involved in creating it, students reflect on what they believe to be the paper's strengths and what they find least satisfying in it. Each time they make a selection for the portfolio—approximately five times—

they reflect on the selected paper in greater depth, indicating why they selected the piece and what they value in it, as well as something of the processes that went into creating it. Both kinds of reflective activities involve students in evaluation of their own work, in self-assessment; in many instances the reflective activities also lead students to engage in peer evaluation.

Because the questions given to students for each of these selection and reflection activities are open-ended, they invite students to apply and become aware of their own criteria and standards for writing. In this way, students are encouraged to exercise judgment not only about which piece of writing to select but also about what criteria to apply in the selection. The selection and reflection activities move gradually from least demanding to most demanding, from focus on a single piece of writing to discussion of change in the year's work; support is provided for each successive step. Through the progression of activities students are helped toward greater awareness about their writing and toward the exercise of increasingly independent judgments about its quality.

The emphasis in the portfolio design on students' making their own selections and applying their own criteria complicates the task of assessment because it means that portfolios vary from student to student and classroom to classroom. This variety in the writing tasks and in the conditions under which the writing is generated means that the sample of writing in the portfolios is not standardized in ways traditionally associated with assessment. But the variety allowed by the design creates a closer integration of the portfolio with learning and instruction. The portfolio is a genuine sampling of learning as it occurs in each classroom and as it is experienced by the student. Although the selection and reflection activities require classroom time, they do not require that teachers reshape their approach to curriculum, as a more standardized portfolio would. It is true that, through the portfolio activities, teachers discover and take advantage of opportunities for enhancing student learning that they were not previously aware of. From students' portfolio reflection, for example, teachers learn about aspects of students' understanding and use of writing processes that can be directly addressed in instruction. In this sense, involvement with the portfolio changes classroom climate and affects teaching strategy, sometimes significantly; but the changes are consistent with the view of learning and the goals for instruction already held by the teachers. The changes occur because the contextualized assessment information provided by the portfolio indicates possibilities for learning that teachers might not otherwise see.

The emphasis in the portfolio design on student choice also yields richer information about student learning than would be available from a more standardized approach. The writing generated as part of students' reflections, especially when it arises from genuine occasions for selection, makes visible much that is otherwise hidden in students' writing performance. The reflections indicate what students value in writing and what is important to them both in their work on a particular piece of writing and in the work of a semester or year. They reveal processes and strategies that students use in creating a piece of writing—brainstorming, consulting with others, revising to take advantage of opportunities not previously seen—as well as the extent of students' awareness of their own and alternative processes and strategies. All of this information, which is critical to learning and instruction, makes the portfolio assessment more useful than a more conventional approach.

Interestingly, then, the decision to allow for variety at the expense of standardization of performance, which occurred because the portfolio was designed primarily to serve learning and instruction, makes possible the gathering of information that represents better sampling of student behavior and more comprehensive assessment. The Arts PROPEL portfolio, as it turns out, is able to provide information more valuable to students themselves, to their teachers and parents, and to school- and district-level administration than information derived from more standardized approaches. Why? Because it was designed in collaboration with teachers and supervisors who knew from their experience with students and classrooms that freedom of selection in the portfolio would be essential to students' learning and necessary for the portfolio's compatibility with a diversity of teaching styles.

This is not to say that the measurement principles related to standardization are unimportant to assessment. Quite the contrary. Unless portfolio evaluation is to be entirely idiosyncratic to each pairing of teacher and student, some common meaning must be made of student performance from one portfolio to another and one classroom to another. If the performances exhibited in the portfolio are not to be standardized, then the burden of standardization falls on the process of portfolio interpretation and evaluation. In recognition of the need to establish a common basis for interpretation and evaluation of the Arts PROPEL portfolios, a number of procedures have therefore been developed that take into account the perceptions and concerns of several individuals and groups interested in students' learning.

Multiple Assessment Procedures Serving and Representing Multiple Audiences

Evaluation of the Arts PROPEL portfolios draws on the perspectives of a number of parties interested in students' achievements and development as writers—students themselves, the classroom teacher, parents, teachers from other classrooms, and district-level supervisors. The student work in the portfolio is examined by each of these parties, each of whom indicates what he or she sees and values in it. Through this process, the portfolio provides the basis for dialogue among multiple perspectives within the educational community and ensures that each perspective is represented in the public discourse about student learning.

The beginning of the assessment dialogue occurs in the classroom. The design of the Arts PROPEL portfolios requires, in fact, that procedures of assessment and self-assessment become part of classroom life. When students reflect on their writing and make selections for the portfolio, they engage in assessment; they make decisions based on their own and others' evaluations of their work. If the students write in the process of reflecting, they engage in the first step toward an assessment dialogue whose evidence is eventually carried beyond the classroom. When students respond to one another's writing, indicating what they see and value, they also engage in assessment. Teachers responding orally or in writing to students' work and to their reflections on their work are taking the second step in the assessment dialogue initiated by students' reflections. Teacher–student conferences, which occur while students are writing or when they are making decisions about portfolio selections, constitute yet another facet of classroom portfolio assessment.

One result of these classroom assessment dialogues is teacher's and students' collaborative development of a vocabulary of evaluation. Teachers sometimes collate students' reflections on a particular assignment or project for writing, presenting the group of reflections to students so that they can see the variety in their perceptions of writing. Discussion of the reflections helps students discover what qualities they as a group think are important to good writing. At the end of discussions, the qualities students have identified are posted in the classroom for consideration on subsequent occasions for writing, reflection, or discussion. Additional qualities are added to the list as a result of discussions that occur throughout the school term. Through this documentation of the vocabulary of evaluation, the classroom assessment contributes to both students' and teachers' sense of criteria and standards for writing.

Parents have been brought into the classroom assessment dialogue as reviewers of their child's writing folder. Students take the folder home and ask a parent (or surrogate for the parent) to read the writing in it and answer a handful of open-ended questions about what they see in the writing. The review procedure allows parents to participate in a nonthreatening way in the dialogue about the student's writing. Parents can get a sense of the classroom interactions around their child's work from the student's written reflections and the teacher's written comments on the writing. Since none of the questions asked of parents requires expertise on their part, they can enter the dialogue as readers and as individuals who bring a perspective on the student that is not always available from within the classroom. When the parent review is complete, students bring the folder back to the classroom and reflect on what they and their parents learned about the writing and the student's development as a writer. Thus the experience is brought into direct connection with the student's classroom learning.

The parent review procedure addresses an important assessment function within the school context. It informs directly an audience with a clear interest in student learning, and it provides opportunity for the views of that group to be expressed in the school environment. The evidence of student achievement and learning in the folder is more immediately intelligible to most parents than are traditional forms of assessment information. With time and experience in looking at student writing, parents are likely to enter fully into the discussion about what is to be valued and nurtured in their children's writing.

But the portfolio assessment dialogue also extends across classrooms. Teachers who have been working with their students to develop a shared classroom vocabulary for the evaluation of portfolios come together to exchange perceptions with other teachers. In groups of three to five, teachers from the same school or grade level examine duplicate copies of one student's portfolio. One teacher acts as recorder, facilitator, and timekeeper for the session. The teacher of the student whose portfolio is being reviewed listens while fellow teachers describe the qualities of writing and evidence of learning they see in the portfolio, then provides additional evidence from classroom observation that is relevant to the discussion. The recorder-facilitator reads back the notes he or she has taken on the discussion and helps the group come to consensus about the qualities observed in the portfolio. Finally each of the teachers offers suggestions about what next steps would be most likely to further the student's development as a writer.

The purpose of the session is not to evaluate numbers of portfolios, but rather to enlarge, reinforce, and refine teachers' perceptions of student writing—an important component of assessment conducted within the school context. The exchange of perceptions among teachers contributes to a shared cross-classroom vocabulary for interpreting portfolios and to the beginnings of consensus about evidence of learning. In addition, the suggestions for instruction developed at the end of the conference provide diagnostic information that teachers can apply directly to students' learning.

The expertise that teachers develop through discussion of portfolios within and across classrooms is further reinforced by conferences between supervisor and teacher. For these conferences, teachers are asked to select three to five portfolios, or folders if they like, representing the range of student writing performance in their classrooms (Doran, 1990). Using a set of questions asking for his or her perceptions of the students' strengths and development and of the teaching strategies used to bring about development, the teacher reviews the portfolios in advance. In conference the teacher and supervisor discuss the teacher's review of the portfolios, using them as the basis for a discussion of the teacher's program of instruction.

The teacher–supervisor conference gives teachers an occasion to refine their perceptions of student learning under the guidance of an experienced professional thoroughly familiar with the goals and curriculum of the district. It allows supervisors a view into teachers' pedagogical and assessment strategies, while allowing teachers to shape that view in terms of the context and rationale behind the strategies. The supervisor in turn is able to engage with the teacher in terms most likely to lead to more effective strategies where they are called for, thus contributing to the teacher's professional development on a one-to-one basis. In addition, the information gathered from the conferences helps supervisors allocate resources for professional development in the district as a whole. In these ways the teacher–supervisor conference based on portfolios effectively addresses a number of assessment functions in an arena critical to accountability.

Each of the portfolio assessment procedures described so far contributes to teachers' and students' awareness of qualities of writing and evidence of learning to be found in portfolios. In addition to serving accountability directly by keeping all parties informed about student learning, they also inform teachers' and students' perceptions—directly or indirectly—and thereby contribute to the ongoing assessment activities involved in classroom work on portfolios. They also lay the foundation for the interpretation of portfolios by contributing to a shared vocabulary for qualities of writing and consensus about evidence of learning. However, none of the assessment procedures described above gives evidence of students' achievement and development in terms that allow for systematic aggregation of data across classrooms. In this respect, although the procedures described clearly contribute to the information necessary for accountability, they would not be sufficient without an additional procedure yielding interpretable cross-classroom data on student performance.

For these reasons the interpretation and evaluation of portfolios by groups of teachers applying shared standards and criteria is critical to the Arts PROPEL portfolio assessment. This task is complicated, as suggested earlier, by the variety among portfolios from student to student and classroom to classroom. The pieces of writing that a student has selected for the portfolio may address several audiences and purposes for writing or a few; if they include only one or two types of writing they may show clear indications of growth, but if they include several the evidence of growth may be more difficult to discover. Some portfolios will contain abundant evidence of process, while others may contain less. Only the reflective activities and the pieces of writing resulting from them are constant from portfolio to portfolio.

What is needed for evaluation of such portfolios is a framework of criteria that is compatible with the portfolio design, one that allows for the variety among portfolios and takes advantage of the information provided in the reflections. In recognition of this need, the Arts PROPEL portfolio evaluation framework has been developed through examination of the data found in the portfolios and documentation of the perceptions of teachers and others examining them. It has emerged specifically from the vocabulary used by teachers, supervisors, and researchers in discussion of sample portfolios over a year's time; as a result it takes into account what teachers see in both the writing selected for the portfolio and the reflections that accompany them. The framework attends to three categories of evidence: accomplishment in writing, use of processes and resources for writing, and development as a writer. The evidence for the first category comes almost entirely from the pieces of writing selected, whereas evidence for the second and third come from both the selected pieces and the students' reflections. Each category calls for a holistic judgment based on the evidence in the entire portfolio. The result of the judgments in the three categories is a profile of the student as a writer, rather than a single score.

The evaluation of portfolios is conducted in sessions closely resembling those used in recent decades for the evaluation of individual samples of student writing, thereby taking advantage of existing procedures for assuring reliable judgment. Sample portfolios are presented, scored, and discussed to establish standards and illustrate the application of criteria. Where judgments differ, the differences are discussed in relation to evidence in the portfolio. When the group has developed sufficient consensus to establish a common basis for evaluation, the rating of portfolios begins. Each portfolio is rated independently by two teachers; discrepant ratings are resolved by a third reading. Sample portfolios are presented periodically to reinforce and refine teachers' understanding of standards and criteria.

Once the portfolio program is implemented districtwide, the portfolios rated at evaluation sessions will represent a structured sampling of portfolios from classrooms across the district. The results of the rating session will be aggregated to create district-level and school-level group profiles. This information will contribute to decision making at district and school levels. The portfolios not rated at this session will be evaluated by teachers in their classrooms using the same standards and criteria as were used at the rating session. They will be informed in their judgments by their experience at the group rating sessions and by exemplar portfolios as well as written discussion of the ratings assigned and the evidence for the ratings. The ratings by classroom teachers will be monitored through a moderation or auditing system, both as a means of supporting and guiding teachers in their judgments and to ensure commonality of standards and criteria across the district.

Implications of the Pittsburgh Experience

No doubt the portfolio approach developed in the Arts PROPEL project, including the portfolio evaluation procedures, will evolve as other assessments have in the history of Pittsburgh writing assessment. In the meantime, though, what the approach and the procedures demonstrate is that assessments deeply grounded in the classroom context for learning—whether or not they focus on writing and whether or not they are based on portfolios—can also be useful for purposes of accountability, especially if the definitions of assessment and accountability are expanded to take into consideration the whole of the educational system.

The procedures described in the Pittsburgh illustration are not meant to be seen as representing the best possible approach to assessment, or even the best possible approach to portfolios of writing. But they suggest that assessments can be developed that reflect enriched views of learning and serve the various parties involved in furthering students' learning. It may be, then, that assessment developed, refined, and implemented within the school context can serve both instruction and assessment, and can serve them well. At the very least, it is a prospect worth considering.

MOVING TOWARD ASSESSMENT GROUNDED IN A VIEW OF LEARNING

Assessment has the potential to either reinforce or undermine the goals for learning established in a school or district. Where curriculum is moving toward emphasis on complex performances drawing on interrelated knowledge and skills, on the thinking processes behind student products or performance, or on students' roles in shaping their own learning, in fact, assessment may be critical to the success of the transition. If this is the case, then an approach to assessment design that begins with goals for learning is clearly in order.

Admittedly, the exigencies of school life are such that attention to assessment in a school or district is most likely to be stimulated by a crisis or an immediate need having to do with particular and unpredictable circumstances. Nevertheless, a heuristic for looking at assessment design in relation to the school learning context may be a helpful point of reference for schools in the process of change, especially if it takes into account the ways in which assessment is most likely to affect the realization of goals for learning. Many of those factors are represented by the discussion in this chapter—in the questions raised early in the chapter as a starting point for thinking about assessment in relation to the educational context, in the characteristics seen as desirable for contextualized assessment in current discussions of assessment and accountability, and in the experiences with assessment in Pittsburgh. It seems possible, therefore, at this point to arrive at a heuristic based on what is currently understood about the relationship of assessment to goals for learning. What follows is a series of questions reflecting current concerns that can help guide the development of assessment compatible with new views of learning.

The first two questions are addressed to the primary task, which is to clarify goals for learning and instruction:

1. *What do we want students to learn?*
2. *What kinds of experiences do we think would be most appropriate for them to learn from?*

The question that follows, once the priorities for learning and instruction are set, addresses the overall issue for assessment:

3. *How would we know that students are learning what we want them to learn?*

Following upon this question are a series of questions whose answers help to shape the design of assessment:

4. *What kinds of evidence do we believe would be convincing?*
5. *From what sources and contexts can that evidence be gathered?*
   Observation and documentation?
   Projects combining instruction and assessment?
   Performances?
   Portfolios?
   Publications and exhibitions?
   Conventional tests or adaptations of them?
6. *Who should respond, observe, or evaluate in each case?*
   Student?
   Classroom teacher?
   Students' peers?
   Teachers in groups? In pairs?
   Parents?
   Supervisors or curriculum coordinators?
7. *What criteria should be applied? How might they be developed? How should they be made public?*
8. *What do we want students to learn from the assessment—the experience in which evidence is gathered and evaluated? How can we make it possible for them to learn from the experience itself and from the responses and perceptions of others?*
9. *What do we want teachers to learn from the experience of responding to and evaluating students' work? In what circumstances are they likely to evaluate most reliably? To learn most?*

10. What audiences need to know about students' achievement and development?
11. How much and what kind of information would be most useful for each of these audiences? What procedures would invite them to contribute in meaningful ways to the discourse about student learning?
12. What review processes would enable us to determine whether
    a) we're getting the kind of information we want
    b) the information serves the purposes most important to each audience
    c) the process of getting the information supports genuine teaching and learning?

No set of questions can guarantee the development of responsible and informative assessment, but an orientation toward primary issues, and particularly toward the relationship of assessment to the view of learning it is meant to serve, may help. In the transitions now experienced by students, teachers, and schools moving toward richer and more contextualized views of learning, this kind of focus on the relationship between learning and assessment—whatever the questions raised—may well be the impetus needed for genuine improvement in the learning environment provided by schools.

REFERENCES

Archbald, D. A., & Newman, F. M. (1988). *Beyond standardized testing*. Paper published by the National Center on Effective Secondary Schools, School of Education, University of Wisconsin-Madison.

Camp, R. (1990). Thinking together about portfolios. *The Quarterly of the National Writing Project and the Center for the Study of Writing, 12*(2), 8–14, 27.

Cole, N., & Moss, P. (1989). Bias in test use. In R. Linn (Ed.), *Educational measurement* (3rd ed., pp. 201–219). New York: Macmillan.

Cronbach, L. J. (1988). Five perspectives on validity argument. In H. Wainer & H. I. Braun (Eds.), *Test validity* (pp. 3–17). Hillsdale, NJ: Erlbaum.

Darling-Hammond, L., & Ascher, C. (1991). *Creating accountability in big city school systems*. New York: ERIC Clearinghouse on Urban Education and the National Center for Restructuring Education, Schools, and Teaching, Teachers College, Columbia.

Doran, J. A. (1990, November). *Portfolios for professional development: An administrator's story*. Paper presented at the annual meeting of the National Council of Teachers of English, Atlanta, GA.

Eresh, J. (1990, November). *Balancing the pieces: Content, teachers, tests, and administration*. Paper presented at the annual meeting of the Conference for Secondary School English Department Chairpersons, Atlanta, GA.

Gitomer, D. (in press). Performance assessment and educational measurement. In R. Bennett & W. Ward (Eds.), *Construction versus choice in cognitive measurement*. Hillsdale, NJ: Erlbaum.

Frederiksen, N. (1984). The real test bias: Influences of testing on teaching and learning. *American Psychologist, 39,* 193–202.
Frederiksen, N. (1986). Toward a broader conception of human intelligence. *American Psychologist, 41,* 445–452.
Frederiksen, N. (1990). Introduction. In N. Frederiksen, R. Glaser, A. Lesgold, & M.G. Shafto (Eds.), *Diagnostic monitoring of skill and knowledge acquisition* (pp. ix–xvii). Hillsdale, NJ: Erlbaum.
Frederiksen, J. R., & Collins, A. (1989). A systems approach to educational testing. *Educational Researcher, 18,* 27–32.
LeMahieu, P. G., & Wallace, R. C. (1986). Up against the wall: Psychometrics meets praxis. *Educational Measurement: Issues and Practice, 5*(1), 12–16.
Linn, R. L., & Dunbar, S. (1990, June). *Complex, performance-based assessment: Expectations and validation criteria.* Paper presented at the Educational Commission of the States/Colorado Department of Education Assessment Conference, Boulder, CO.
Messick, S. (1989a). Meaning and values in test validation: The science and ethics of assessment. *Educational Researcher, 18,* 5–14.
Messick, S. (1989b). Validity. In R. Linn (Ed.), *Educational measurement* (3rd ed., pp. 13–103). New York: Macmillan.
Mislevy, R.J. (in press). Foundations for a new test theory. In N. Fredriksen, R. J. Mislevy, & I. Bejar (Eds.), *Test theory for a new generation of tests.* Hillsdale, NJ: Erlbaum.
Mitchell, R. (1989, October). *A sampler of authentic assessment: What it is and what it looks like.* Paper presented for the California Assessment Program Conference, Sacramento, CA.
Shepard, L. A. (1991). Psychometricians' beliefs about learning. *Educational Researcher, 20,* 2–16.
Snow, R. E. (1989). Toward assessment of cognitive and conative structures in learning. *Educational Researcher, 18,* 8–14.
Snow, R. E., & Lohman, D. F. (1988). Implications of cognitive psychology for educational measurement. In R. Linn (Ed.), *Educational measurement* (3rd ed., pp. 263–331). Washington, DC: American Council on Education.
Wiggins, G. (1989). A true test: Toward more authentic and equitable assessment. *Phi Delta Kappan, 70,* 703–713.
Wolf, D., Bixby, J., Glenn, J., & Gardner, H. (1991). To use their minds well: Investigating new forms of student assessment. In G. Grant (Ed.), *Review of Research in Education, 17,* 31–73.

Chapter 10
Organizational Design and Teaching for Student Learning*

William A. Firestone

Rutgers Graduate School of Education

Teachers often see parallels between the way they are treated by higher authorities and the way they treat their students. Such parallels provide the link between policies that affect teaching and the quality of the student's experience. If one wants to move away from work-centered classrooms to learning-centered classrooms for students, as Marshall advocates in the introduction to this volume, it is necessary to help teachers think of themselves less as workers and more as professionals. Teachers' conceptions of themselves depend in part on how schools and districts are designed. Making schools more bureaucratic will encourage teachers and their students to act like workers; building professional organizations will encourage them to be more professional and learning oriented.

---

* This study is being conducted under a grant furnished by the Department of Education, Office of Educational Research and Improvement, Grant #OERI–G008690011–89. Research reports are issued by CPRE to facilitate the exchange of ideas among policymakers and researchers who share an interest in education policy. The views expressed in the reports are those of individual authors and are not necessarily shared by the U.S. Department of Education, CPRE, or its institutional partners.

Many reforms of the last decade included attempts to substantially change teachers roles in schools. However, there was a fundamental ambivalence on the direction such changes should take. The story of recent reforms is commonly divided into two "waves" (Passow, 1989). In the first, reformers' deep distrust of educators promoted an effort to make schools more bureaucratic. Teachers were treated largely as workers who could be expected to follow specific formulae and needed to be externally motivated to do so. The second wave viewed teachers more as responsible problem solvers who needed to be facilitated by professionalizing their work settings through improved working conditions and better training in order to improve. This story is in fact a simplification. The tension between bureaucratic and professional reforms occurred in many locations at many times. There is also considerable confusion; reforms were often proposed and justified as ways to professionalize teaching that, in practice, had the opposite effect (Popkewitz & Lind, 1989).

To help clarify the current situation, this chapter addresses four tasks. It first presents theoretical arguments that link views of learning with views of teaching and then with conceptions of organizational designs. Next, it examines two kinds of current reforms—job differentiation and teacher "empowerment"—in light of those theories to suggest how they are likely to affect teachers. Job differentiation varies the remuneration teachers receive to reflect either the amount or quality of their work. Rank distinctions may be introduced. Teacher empowerment includes teachers more in decision making outside the classroom. Third, it presents case studies of bureaucratic and professional reforms that show the link between structural change and teachers' behavior and orientations. Finally, it identifies three challenges that must be met to professionalize schools.

1. Professionalizing reforms will have significant costs, so funding must be found;
2. Professionalizing reforms will require teachers to become more tolerant of, and responsible in, implementing new roles for teachers; and
3. Professionalization alone will not create learning-centered classrooms. To that end, structural change should be accompanied by a vision of what modified teaching practice and learning-centered workplaces are like. That vision will require balancing priorities on empowerment and pedagogy.

LINKS AMONG CLASSROOMS, TEACHERS, AND ORGANIZATIONAL DESIGN

The educational system is hierarchical with individual students grouped in classrooms overseen by teachers. Similarly classrooms are grouped in schools overseen by principals, which in turn are grouped into districts.

Higher levels include the state and federal governments. Higher levels of the system define appropriate performance goals, monitor performance, set constraints, and provide resources to lower ones. The nature of those goals, constraints, and resources will affect the activity of the lower levels. The effects of higher levels are somewhat limited. Educational organizations are often viewed as loosely coupled systems (Weick, 1976) where those at lower levels have considerable autonomy from oversight and control. Nevertheless, a shortage of textbooks, the absence of support in maintaining an orderly environment, and a testing program that overemphasizes some topics at the expense of others or stresses rote memorization rather than thinking will affect teachers' performance even if they are never supervised, evaluated, or otherwise directed by administrators (Corwin & Borman, 1988).

Essentially my argument is that one's conception of classroom learning should be supported by congruent conceptions of instruction and by compatible organizational designs of schools. Organizational design may not dictate instructional practice or approach to learning; there is room in schools to buck the tide. Still, organizational arrangements make it easier to teach certain ways that in turn lead to certain kinds of student learning. Hence, learning-centered classrooms will not become prevalent unless congruent organizational arrangements also spread.

Classroom Metaphors

Marshall (this volume) identifies two metaphors: the student as learner, and student as worker. There are noticeable parallels between these metaphors and both paradigms for research on teaching, and images for organizational design (Table 10.1). At the student level, Marshall distinguishes between the role of the student as learner and student as worker. The learning metaphor is most conducive to the kind of higher order thinking that reformers believe will become increasingly necessary as America attempts to compete with the Japanese, the Germans, and other economic rivals (NCEE, 1983). In this view, students become problem solvers who do not focus on completing specific products to the teacher's specifications but rather on creatively addressing an issue where there may be more than one right answer. The student as learner is intrinsically motivated, because the tasks themselves are interesting and require active engagement. Students also take more responsibility for their learning.

The metaphor of the student as worker fits with basic skills instruction. Here the student is expected to learn discrete facts and skills in a teacher-centered classroom. The student is a passive recipient of teacher talk who is motivated by grades rather than an interest in the task. Exercises are given that only have one right answer, and teachers are the final arbiter of what is correct.

Table 10.1. Theories of Learning, Teaching, and Organizational Design

CLASSROOM METAPHOR	*Student as Learner.* Emphasizes the process of learning, the student as a thinker, intrinsic motivation, and errors as something to learn from. Students learn to solve problems and place facts in a complex web of relationships.	*Student as Worker.* Emphasizes the products of student work, the student as passive recipient, extrinsic motivation, and the suppression of errors. Discrete facts and skills are learned.
TEACHING RESEARCH PARADIGM	*Reflective Practice.* Sees teachers as problem solvers who plan, assess, and adjust. Teaching must take into account both content and student capacities. Teachers use complex theories about teaching to make judgements on what to do.	*Direct Instruction.* Sees teachers as executors of rules about effective instruction. Teachers should maximize time-on-task and manage instructional functions. These rules are general enough to cut across subjects and students.
ORGANIZATIONAL DESIGN	*Professionalism.* Assumes low certainty and need for workers to be problem solvers. Strategic decisions are decentralized. Work is coordinated through training and mutual adjustment. Intrinsic incentives are stressed.	*Bureaucracy.* Assumes high certainty, so experts know best. Strategic decisions are centralized. Work is controlled through direct supervision and standardization of work (curruculum guides) and outcomes (tests). External incentives are stressed.

Teaching Research Paradigms

Although much of this book provides visions of what learning-centered classrooms are like and factors that contribute to their creation, it is worth noting that there are obvious parallels between these two metaphors of students and the primary paradigms for research on teaching in the 1970s and 1980s. The older paradigm of direct instruction fits well with the student-as-worker metaphor. This paradigm is based on process–product research that identifies discrete variables through which student achievement can be increased (Brophy & Good, 1986). This research has identified three clusters of variables. The first is time. Students spend more time on some curricular areas than others, and more time is linked to increased achievement, especially when it is devoted to the skills tested (Brophy & Good, 1986). The second is teacher expectations. Teachers call on high-achieving students more often, praise them more and criticize them less, and give them more time to recover from failures. These differences in teacher responses exacerbate poor students' poor performance (Good, 1983). Finally, teachers who manage instructional functions appropriately increase achievement (Rosenshine, 1983). Appropriate management includes frequent review and checking of past work so errors will not go undetected; presentation of material in small steps with considerable modeling; frequent, guided practice to the point of "overteaching;" extensive monitoring; and designing problems or exercises so students get most answers right.

Although there have been some exceptions, direct instruction has been interpreted to mean that more is better: more time, higher expectations, more breaking material into small steps, and so on. Thus, direct instruction is used to establish a set of universals for teachers to follow. This research simplifies the task of teaching tremendously. Although thought may be required to apply these variables to different content areas or students with different backgrounds, the general direction is clear. Thus the teacher, like the student, becomes a worker whose tasks are externally defined. However, the teacher's own task is managing student workers who are expected to produce correct answers more efficiently.

At its popular apex, direct instruction was already being challenged by the reflective practice paradigm. In this view, there were no uniform rules about how to teach. For instance, direct instruction provided little information about how teachers should maximize the conditions that increased time-on-task (Carter & Doyle, 1989). Nor did it provide adequate information on how the subject matter determined what teaching tasks were important or what knowledge teachers needed to interpret classroom events or to establish and maintain a positive learning environment. Some teachers addressed these issues more effectively than others; and the more effective ones had developed explicit theories about learners, curriculum, subject matter, and the teacher's role. They had approaches to planning that were nuanced and automatic, but they also knew how to read the situation and when to deviate from the plan. They could analyze events and take corrective action (Clark & Peterson, 1986). This new paradigm moved from the regular application of externally observed principles to the teacher's internal problem-solving processes. It examined how teachers' rich, specific understanding of their work helps to interpret new problems (Carter & Doyle, 1989). Although direct instruction deemphasized the uncertainty in teaching, this new paradigm highlighted it. In effect it made teachers learners in complex settings and suggested that teachers were supposed to use a wide array of teaching strategies to make learners out of students as well.

Organizational Design

The link between teaching and organizational design comes from theories about how the certainty of a technology determines organizational structure (e.g., Perrow, 1970). In these theories, technology does not refer to hardware, like computers, but very broadly to the way work is done. Moreover, in many fields—like teaching, nursing, and law—technology is socially determined; it depends on the prevalent metaphors.

According to these theories, where the work entails few unusual problems and established theories guide the search for solutions, certainty is high. Where there are many problems and few established theories, certainty is low. Teaching is defined as relatively certain by those who view students as fundamentally similar, deemphasize the differences in subject matter, and believe there is a well-specified technology of teaching. Direct instruction appears to be such a well-specified technology because it suggests a firm science of instruction that reduces the number of solutions from which teachers must select—such as increase time-on-task, provide frequent drill-and-practice, and design lessons to maximize student success.

Teaching is viewed as uncertain by those who believe teachers must significantly adjust their approaches to reflect subject matter, students, and other contingencies. The reflective practice paradigm, with its emphasis on the range of factors teachers must consider and the complexity of problem solving required, highlights uncertainty.

Where certainty is high, efficiency is enhanced by a bureaucratic structure. Staff experts who have the firmest knowledge of the relevant theory are the experts, so work can be centrally controlled. Teachers are considered lower level functionaries whose work is directed and monitored by administrators and district staff. When certainty is low, a professional model is needed. In this model, people closest to the work best understand how to proceed, because tacit knowledge and an artistic feel for the situation are crucial. Management depends on lower level employees, and staff experts have little if any more knowledge than those workers. Organizations must be designed to let those who do the work use what they know. In this model, the teacher is a professional (Bacharach & Conley, 1989; Weick & McDaniel, 1989).

Three crucial issues separate the bureaucracy and the professional organization: (a) control over strategic decisions that affect the organization's overall operation—including questions of policy, work allocation, discipline, staff development, and evaluation; (b) control over operational decisions like what to teach and how to teach it (Bacharach & Conley, 1989); and (c) incentives. The bureaucratic design centralizes strategic decisions by monopolizing decision making, controls operational decisions by standardizing work activities, and features extrinsic incentives that are controlled by managers. The professional one coordinates both strategic and operational decisions by developing networks among workers at different levels, incorporating more people in decision making, and encouraging frequent interaction (Rowan, 1990). It also supplements extrinsic incentives with intrinsic ones that come from the work itself.

Strategic Decisions

In the bureaucracy, strategic decisions are centralized. The highest policy decisions may be made by an elected board or other entity, but top managers translate those broad policy directives into specific operational and allocation decisions (Weber, 1947). These are made without reference to workers' concerns, since managers and their staffs have the relevant expertise.

In the professional organization, strategic decisions are shared because managers and workers have different kinds of knowledge (Bacharach & Conley, 1989). The latter group understands work processes, challenges, and complexities better, while the former know more about the outside environment and have a broader overview of the organization. Furthermore, as carriers of special values, professionals will advocate critical concerns that might otherwise be ignored (Weick & McDaniel, 1989). Moreover, worker participation in decision making is said to build commitment to the decisions that result, so compliance will be easier (Berman & McLaughlin, 1975). It also promotes commitment to the organization more generally (Newmann, Rutter, & Smith, 1989).

Operational Decisions

The same distinction between centralized control in the bureaucracy and shared decision making in the professional organization is applicable to operational decisions, but the means are different. Mintzberg (1983) lists five ways to coordinate operational activity. The first two—mutual adjustment and direct supervision—involve face-to-face interaction. Mutual adjustment is informal, face-to-face discussion, often among equals. Much information can be communicated between two people, and everyone's judgment gets included. The interaction in mutual adjustment facilitates teacher learning, the implementation of new practices, and a greater sense of certainty in teachers' work (Little, 1982; Rosenholtz, 1989). However, it is time consuming and expensive. Also information does not travel well, so mutual adjustment can only coordinate the work of a few people.

With direct supervision one person oversees the work of others, issues orders to them, and monitors their progress. This process is quicker, less expensive, and ensures greater comparability of practice. It can include a few more people, but it limits the information exchanged and whose judgment is included.

The other three mechanisms standardize or prespecify different aspects of the work, namely, work processes, outcomes, and inputs. One can standardize work processes to control how tasks are done. Curriculum guides and textbooks standardize educational work processes. Standardizing outputs specifies results instead of how the work gets done. District and state testing programs standardize outputs. These kinds of standardization are even quicker and cheaper than direct supervision, and they can be applied on a very broad scale. However, they constrain even more the information exchanged, and judgment is exercised primarily when standards are set. They have the effect of turning students and teachers into workers assigned to achieve externally specified standards through externally specified means.

Finally, in labor-intensive work like teaching, one can standardize such inputs as skills and values by detailing the training workers should receive. Such training can include scientific knowledge and book learning, but it also features long hours of apprenticeship or supervised practice of the sort doctors receive in their internships and residencies. In addition to developing technical skills, standardization through training effectively socializes trainees to significant values of the group. This approach can be time consuming and expensive. Skills and values are often standardized where tasks are especially complex. However, with standardized skills, a great deal of discretion is left to the worker. This discretion allows the worker the opportunity for creativity and problem solving. In teachers it is conducive to continuous learning. Teachers themselves engage in activities compatible with the student-as-learner metaphor and so may expect the same from students. Whether they will depends on the specific skills and values developed through training.

Bureaucratic organizations use direct supervision and standardization of work processes and outputs to control operational decisions. Standardization works best in predictable situations where one can anticipate problems and know what solutions are available and when to apply them. Supervision often reflects the greater knowledge or organizational commitment of the supervisor. All three techniques remove judgment from the worker (whether that worker be teacher or student) and emphasize the production of a standardized product.

By contrast, professional organizations emphasize mutual adjustment and standardization of skills and values. A great deal of knowledge is needed to cope with uncertainty, and substantial information must be exchanged just to understand what is happening. With these techniques, the professional's discretion is channeled. Decisions made alone are influenced by extensive training, but they are often made after consultation with colleagues. There is more opportunity to treat students as learners in professional settings.

Incentives

Bureaucratic and professional organizations use different incentives and distribute them in different ways. The bureaucratic organization relies on extrinsic incentives, especially money but also externally conferred honors and prestige. Bureaucracies often use extrinsic incentives to reinforce standardization (Weber, 1947). Then, rewards are conditional upon compliance with external standards. A complete system for applying incentives will specify a standard, provide a means of observation, and link rewards to observed performance (Dornbusch & Scott, 1975). Extrinsic reward systems can be very effective controls over worker behavior (again whether those workers are teachers or students); but if improperly designed, they can lead to unanticipated consequences—like concentrating on measured performance at the expense of other valued activities—and be demotivating (Lawler, 1973).

Professional organizations supplement extrinsic incentives with intrinsic rewards from the task. Moreover, the incentives are not geared to shaping behavior to administrative ends so much as building worker commitment, which they do fairly effectively, at least in the private sector (Porter, Lawler, & Hackman, 1975). Intrinsic incentives include skill variety (engagement in many different activities using a variety of talents), task identity (the completion of an identifiable piece of work from start to finish), task significance (importance to the overall work or to others), autonomy (freedom in scheduling work and determining the procedures to use), opportunity to interact with peers or colleagues, and feedback (clear information on the effectiveness of one's work) (Oldham & Hackman, 1981). A sense of mastery of increasingly complex tasks can also provide intrinsic rewards (Ryan, Connell, & Deci, 1985). Moreover, designers of organizations can increase intrinsic incentives by removing barriers to task accomplishment (Staw, 1980).

Since intrinsic incentives come from the work itself, administrators cannot link them to performance. However, opportunities for job enlargement or enrichment that increase intrinsic incentives may be distributed as rewards. In the professional organization, peers should help distribute these rewards because technological uncertainty means that promotion decisions require the kind of judgment best exercised by the professionals themselves and because, as champions of key values, they are well placed to determine who should be rewarded.

There is a parallel between intrinsic rewards for teachers and the student-as-learner metaphor. Like professional teachers, student learners get their incentives in part from the growing sense of mastery that comes from accomplishing increasingly complex tasks. Professional teachers can work with student learners. Whether they do so or not depends on how they define task accomplishment. If they continue to hold to a student-as-worker metaphor, substantial change in teaching is not likely. Thus professionalized teaching contexts are conducive to the student as learner metaphor but will not automatically bring it about.

REFORM OPTIONS

The learning metaphor and the reflective practice paradigm view students and teachers as problem solvers in uncertain environments who are sensitive to intrinsic incentives. The professional model suggests that, as a result, teachers should participate in making strategic decisions; and their work should be coordinated through training and mutual adjustment. The work metaphor and the direct instruction paradigm view students and teachers as producers of fairly standardized products, through prespecified means, who can best be motivated through extrinsic incentives. The bureaucratic model suggests that teachers should not contribute to strategic decisions, and that their work should be controlled through direct supervision and standardization of work processes and outputs.

The effects of current proposals to redesign teaching can be predicted by examining their fit with these models. Some of the most discussed reforms of the 1980s included job differentiation and modified governance. Both of them could be professionalizing reforms, but job differentiation can also bureaucratize teaching.

States and districts have implemented many programs to differentiate teachers' jobs (Southern Regional Education Board, 1990). Two issues separate the various plans: whether the changes they make are based on merit or job enlargement, and whether they are permanent or temporary (Darling-Hammond & Berry, 1988; Malen, Murphy, & Hart, 1988). The first issue is the most fundamental. The merit principle assumes that all teachers do the same work, but that pay varies depending upon the quality of the work. The success of this strategy depends on finding means to measure teacher quality that are acceptable to teachers. Merit is fundamentally bureaucratic. Its popularity stems from its link to efforts to increase external accountability and discipline of teachers. Moreover, it assumes that teachers can be effectively motivated by extrinsic incentives (Rosenholtz, 1987); its primary effect is to increase such rewards. The theory is that teachers will conform to externally defined standards of excellence in order to reap the rewards.[1]

Job enlargement creates situations for some teachers to do more or different work from others. This work may include some combination of mentoring beginning teachers, providing training to all teachers, or developing new curricula. In this case, sorting good from bad teachers is secondary to changing the nature of teachers' work, although the question of which teachers should get enlarged positions still arises. The principle requires identifying tasks teachers can do, achieving agreement that such

---

[1] In theory, teachers could participate in setting these standards. If they did, the merit principle would be more professional. In practice, they rarely do.

tasks are worth additional reimbursement, and clarifying the relationship between the added work and regular teaching responsibility.

Job enlargement has two professionalizing features. First, it expands both intrinsic and extrinsic incentives. Those who receive special tasks get paid more for more varied work and opportunities to develop new skills. In addition, the results of their work should be available to others who benefit from enhanced training opportunities and enriched curricula. Second, teachers selected for enlarged positions have augmented opportunities for influence. Greater influence should increase the motivation of those involved and insure that a teacher perspective is better reflected in instructional decisions (Carnegie Forum, 1986). Such changes encourage teachers to be more reflective and can help them to elicit similar activity from students as well.

The permanency issue pits the conceptions of reformers against current norms of teacher equity. The hierarchy of teaching is quite flat, with teachers receiving their maximum salary increase within fifteen or twenty years of entry and with the top salaries not a great deal above those of beginners when compared to other occupations (Lortie, 1975). With salaries typically allocated on the basis of seniority and education, there is little incentive to maintain one's productivity. Many teachers reach their peak productiveness within five years of entering the field (Rosenholtz, 1985). Reformers have argued that teachers would be more motivated to improve their performance if they had a series of career milestones that involve some mix of increased remuneration and increased responsibilities to work toward (Carnegie Forum, 1986). This strategy assumes that generally acceptable ways can be found to identify improved performance so teachers could move to the next level when their work had progressed to a measurable extent. Teachers' concerns about equity and vulnerability suggest that judgments about progress will be so difficult to make that rotating positions is preferable (Malen, & Hart, 1987). The concept of progressive increases in money, status, and responsibility is lost; but abuses are avoided.

Taken together, these dimensions suggest four job-redesign alternatives (Table 10.2). Merit pay plans give teachers temporary bonuses for good performance. Before the recent interest in redesigning teachers' work, they were tried in the 1920s and 1950s and then faded from view (Johnson, 1984). In the 1980s, they were much criticized by teachers. Florida initiated, and later discontinued, such a program. Master teacher programs assess teachers' performance at one time and give good ones permanent increases in salary. Tennessee modified its initial merit pay program into one that emphasized master teachers. Generally, merit-based programs have been most popular with state legislatures (Malen et al., 1988).

Job enlargement programs are rarer although informal project add-ons have been part of teaching for many years. Any time a teacher receives

Table 10.2. Job Redesign Alternatives

Stability	Differentiation Principle	
	Merit	Job Enlargement
Temporary	Merit Pay	Project Add-Ons
Permanent	Master Teacher	Career Ladder

summer work to develop new curricula or teach summer school, it is a project add-on. In addition, state programs in Tennessee and South Carolina included this element (Malen et al., 1988).

Professionally oriented reformers like the Carnegie Forum (1986) have been the biggest advocates of career ladders. The Holmes Group (1986) model includes three career steps:

1. *Instructors* are first and second year teachers who have not yet made a career commitment to teaching and who lack practical experience. They are not given full responsibility for a classroom on their own, as beginning teachers now are, but are overseen by colleagues.
2. *Professional teachers* are in many ways like teachers found in most schools today. They have demonstrated a commitment to teaching and subject-matter knowledge. Their responsibilities would not necessarily extend beyond the classroom, although their input would be solicited.
3. *Lead teachers* continue to teach but are interested in broader educational policy issues and want to work formally with other adults. They could take on such instructional leadership responsibilities as supervising instructors, curriculum development, training and coaching all staff, developing testing and measurement systems, helping professional teachers who want it, or action research. They could also supervise and evaluate instructors and professional teachers and collegially manage school buildings.

Although the term *career ladder* is very popular and was adopted by several states (Southern Regional Education Board, 1990), few use this approach in its pure form. Moreover, career ladders can have a significant bureaucratic component, depending on how teachers are selected for promotion. When these decisions are made strictly by administrators using standardized criteria, they further centralize control over teachers' work in the classroom.

The most frequently discussed changes in governance professionalize schools by including teachers when making strategic decisions. The Carnegie Forum (1986, p. 2), for instance, advocates "a profession of well-educated teachers prepared to assume new powers and responsibilities to redesign schools for the future." How much power teachers should have over these decisions is not entirely clear. Some of the language of the Carnegie Forum suggests that schools should be totally run by lead teachers. Bacharach and Conley (1989) suggest that the critical question is how to increase teacher participation without sacrificing the ability of management to coordinate. Even though some decisions are clearly in the realm of administrative authority, they argue, teachers should have formalized opportunities to influence them.

One popular means to engage teachers in strategic decisions is site-based management, that authorizes schools to make decisions that previously had been made at the district level and involve teachers in the process. The kinds of decisions the school can control include curriculum, personnel—especially hiring—and budgets (Clune & White, 1989). Site-based management need not empower teachers; all these decisions could be made strictly by the principal. However, such changes usually include a school council or steering committee. Teachers are typically the dominant members of such committees, but parents and high school students can also be included. Teacher influence typically depends on the authority vested in the council and the proportion of teachers on it.

Teacher influence need not be limited to the school level; it can also include district decisions. The ABC District in Cerritos, California, uses a Curriculum Master Plan Council to design its curriculum. With a representative teacher from each school and overseen by the teachers' union, it is supported by a district-level "management facilitator," and detail work is done by ten districtwide subject area committees also made up of teachers. The Council has an annual budget of approximately $170,000 for a variety of purposes including paying teachers for summer development work. Its curriculum guides are reviewed by all teachers in the district, and final decisions are subject only to approval by the school board (Sickler, 1988).

TWO CASES OF REDESIGNED TEACHING

A more concrete sense of what redesigned teaching might look like is provided by case studies of two districts that did exemplary jobs of implementing state teacher reform policies. Mossville's[2] reform was extremely bureaucratic. It discouraged teacher reflection. By treating teachers explicitly as workers, it encouraged them to treat students the same way. Academy's program was more professional. At the school and district level,

---

[2] District names are pseudonyms.

it encouraged teachers to experiment and think about what they were doing. While evidence on changed classroom practice is limited in both districts, it appears that Academy created a context where movement towards the student-as-learner metaphor was possible. The description of each project first outlines the formal design and then the consequences for teaching practice and teacher sentiments.

Bureaucracy in Mossville

Mossville was one of fifteen districts participating in its state's pilot Teacher Development Program (TDP). The theme of that program as described by one principal was

> accountability. Teachers can't close their doors and do what they want. They're being looked at and inspected, and teachers have not had the kind of supervision and accountability we have now.

The program was a classic master teacher plan with permanent positions assigned on the basis of merit. Fully certified teachers could be promoted to two positions:

- *Career Status I* (CS I) for teachers who had completed three years of service and thirty hours of a state-designed effective teacher training program and who had been evaluated as at least "at standard" in all functions assessed through the state's teacher evaluation system.
- *Career Status II* (CS II) for CS I teachers who have completed four years of service, were judged "above standard or higher" on the teacher evaluation system, and had compiled a portfolio showing years of service, valid state certification attendance records, indicators of professional growth, unique assignments or leadership roles, and additional duties or responsibilities.

The primary reward for promotion was extrinsic: a pay increase of one step or about 5 percent for each rank achieved.

Although teachers could opt out of the TDP, they had to be evaluated by the state-mandated teacher evaluation system. Success on this evaluation system was necessary for promotion. The system specified eight criteria. Five were drawn from the research on direct instruction: management of instructional time and student behavior, quality of presentations, monitoring of student learning, and instructional feedback. The other three areas referred to out-of-class work.

Evaluations were based on four one-period, in-class observations conducted by the principal or an observer-evaluator (OE). OEs were teachers on full-time permanent assignment to the district office to help conduct evaluations and provide training on the evaluation system to teachers and principals. The principal made the end-of-year evaluation and promotion recommendation, but it had to be signed by the OE. About 80 percent of the teachers in the system achieved the CS I rating or higher, and over 40 percent achieved the CS II. Seventy-six percent of those who applied for the CS II received it. Those not recommended for promotion could appeal to a special board of teachers and administrators and then to the school board. In effect, this evaluation system influenced operational decisions through a combination of direct supervision and standardization of work.

To support the program, the OEs offered an extensive inservice program. In its first year, they concentrated on offering the state-mandated effective teacher training program to all teachers in the district. Later, it was offered only to new teachers, and OEs shifted to new training efforts. One provided more detailed instruction on how to improve each of the five classroom functions. Another introduced teachers to alternative instructional strategies like Socratic questioning and showed how they could be compatible with the classroom functions.

Mossville had two mechanisms that could provide teacher input to decisions about the TDP. The local steering committee was state mandated. It had twenty-six members, including four teachers. In addition there was a teacher development council with two members from each school. Although both bodies were used to assess teacher sentiments and provide information, decisions were essentially made by district administrators. Thus, teachers had no greater input to strategic decisions.

The main effect of Mossville's program was to standardize instructional approaches around the teacher evaluation criteria. This was especially apparent to principals:

> I find them [teachers] paying attention to research and time on task. People weren't slack, but they're better. Student management, presentation skills, monitoring. Theirs and mine are improving.

> Instructionally, teachers do a better job. They make better plans and are better prepared. They make more effective use of time. Their expectations are higher.

> Its made some teachers more organized in lesson delivery. Some practices are much more widespread now than they were. It's raised teachers' consciousness about those practices that we look for over and over again.

Teachers generally agreed with this assessment saying "[we] are all in the classroom trying to keep time-on-task." Other comments referred to general improvement in teachers' organization. Teachers said, "The strength is that teachers have been better prepared," or "the program made me better organized..." or "there's a focus. It's not hit or miss. There's a plan." While it is not clear what the implications of these changes were for students, they appeared to treat teachers as workers by emphasizing time-on-task and standardizing instructional strategies rather than leaving room for teacher reflection and variation in practice.

At the same time the program reduced their commitment to the district. In response to a survey of district staff,[3] teachers disagreed that the effects on the district had been positive (2.57 on a scale where 1 = strongly disagree and 5 = strongly agree) and that it provided incentives for good teachers to remain in the district (2.64). Interviews with teachers noted what was referred to interchangeably as "stress" or "pressure," as in the following comments.

> There's a certain stress, a burnout from trying to keep up with everything.

> We're frightened all the time. It has made good teachers neurotic. We are measurably more anxious than we used to be. Its our reality no matter how many times we are told not to be.

Professionalism in Academy

Academy's Career Enhancement Program (CEP) was locally designed within a broad state framework. The superintendent described how

> All we do focuses on improving teaching and learning. We'll do all we need to do, but the decisions should be made as close to the action as possible. Everyone is a professional. Everyone wants to be the best they can be.

The program itself had three parts. The extended day component paid each teacher for about ten days of preparation time when children were not in school. Most of these days were before school began. Teachers controlled half the days, and the other half were for district and building inservice. The state also required a small merit pay component that the district complied with during the year of the study by offering a bonus to all teachers who successfully implemented a district writing-across-the-curriculum program. It was locally designed to be awarded to all teachers.

The third component provided for selective job enlargement. Three positions were created:

- *Teacher leaders* who received approximately twenty-five days of summer work at their daily rate plus an $1,100 stipend primarily to mentor new teachers and provide additional assistance to all teachers.
- *Grade-level and cluster leaders* who received an $1,100 stipend and had an option to do summer curriculum development work at their daily rate.

---

[3] Methodological details are provided in Firestone and Bader (in press).

At the elementary level, one leader was responsible for coordinating curricular and instructional issues for each grade across all schools. At the secondary level, there was one cluster leader in each school for each subject area. The subject area teams were responsible for across-school coordination.
- *Curriculum specialists* who did curriculum development or other tasks in each building for an $1,100 stipend and no summer work.

To be eligible for a CEP position, teachers had to pass their annual principal evaluations, but this was a minimal condition. Once that was reached, teachers competed for positions. Teacher leaders were chosen in each building by the principal and two teachers elected by all teachers. Candidates had to submit to a "peer review" where their instructional and leadership qualities were assessed using an open-ended questionnaire by a sample of teachers who knew them. In some buildings, they also had to submit proposals. Specialists were to be selected by the principal, but in some buildings the same committee that selected the teacher leaders later chose the specialists. Grade-level and cluster leaders were chosen by teachers and district personnel. The emphasis in selection in Academy was on reaching consensus rather than strictly assessed merit on fixed criteria; voting rules and committee composition were set so administrators could not veto teacher decisions and vice versa.

Quotas for teacher leaders and specialists were set for each building. The program budget provided enough money so that about 40 percent of the teachers could be specialists, 10 percent could be teacher leaders, and an additional small number could be grade-level or cluster leaders at any one time. Since teachers were elected for fixed terms—one year for specialists, two years for other positions—many more teachers experienced CEP positions. After four years of operation, only 37 percent of all teachers had had no position, 29 percent currently were or had been only specialists, and 34 percent currently were or had been teacher, cluster, or grade-level leaders. Members of this last group may have been specialists, too.

Most of the work of teachers with special positions fell into two categories: training and curriculum development. Training included the mentoring of new teachers but also coaching on new instructional strategies including Principles of Effective Teaching, also direct instruction-based, and TESA, a program to raise teachers' expectations for low-achieving students. Curriculum development took many forms. At the more developed extreme was a districtwide, discipline-based, art appreciation program. One school used its curriculum specialist resources to develop itself as a building wide gifted-and-talented program for all students. More commonly, specialists in particular were "worriers" about their curriculum areas who constantly searched for new materials or teaching strategies and shared them with teachers. Districtwide coordination of curriculum development was enhanced by the grade-level and cluster leaders.

The job enlargement program increased extrinsic rewards by adding to teachers' income, but it also added intrinsic rewards. Those with special positions enhanced their work variety and had a chance to complete significant tasks, often tasks they chose. Task accomplishment also seemed to rise, because those with and without special positions believed they were more effective teachers because of the training and curriculum development offered. The program also increased the amount of mutual adjustment in the district because teachers with special positions interacted so much with other teachers and because all teachers had more time to work together and receive training together.

Academy had a districtwide task force chaired by the superintendent. It consisted of one teacher from each building, a representative from the teachers' association, and two principals. Its authority was established early in the planning for the CEP, when the superintendent proposed that the district implement a merit pay program. Teachers objected, and when they showed that their colleagues strongly agreed with them, the merit pay idea was dropped. Since then the task force has played a major role in the design, implementation, and modification of the CEP. Thus, teachers had substantial influence over strategic decisions. This influence was extended even more by the authority that teachers with special positions had over both curriculum and training.

The main effect of Academy's program was to diversify and enrich curriculum and instructional practice. Specific curricular changes that teachers listed included the new art program, one high school's first AP Spanish course, a program focusing on at-risk youth in a high school, a cooperative learning program and enriched offerings without formal programs in elementary music, science, social studies, writing across the curriculum, and critical thinking. Teachers found these developments very useful:

> The things they've provided are immeasurable. The art specialist did a presentation to my first graders on Monet. They understood it.
>
> I venture much further because I was able to go to in-service [on cooperative education]. It's wonderful to watch my "babies" meet in groups of five with one as a gatekeeper, one as a recorder.

While there is no direct evidence that students were treated more as learners, there was more room for teacher experimentation and learning than had existed in the past. In effect a context was created that was conducive to the student-as-learner metaphor, even though there were no overt steps in that direction.

The teacher-as-learner view was facilitated by the variety of training that was offered. New teachers said, "It goes easier. They assist you. I've had people come and help me. It helps in your weaknesses." More experienced teachers focused on specific training opportunities saying, "We are required to go through PET, [Performance Effectiveness Training] and that has improved teaching." Although PET was required, most curricular and instructional developments were presented as voluntary opportunities, and most teachers appeared to take advantage of them. Appreciation of training and support activities was strongest among beginning teachers. These teachers were cooler than their more experienced colleagues about special provisions to help them get started, but they were more enthusiastic about almost every positive feature of the program than older teachers.

Academy teachers were much more positive about their program than their colleagues in Mossville. In response to another survey, they agreed that the program improved morale (3.50 on the same scale where 1 = strongly disagree and 5 = strongly agree) and that it provided incentives for good teachers to stay in teaching (3.86). When interviewed about the important aspects of their CEP, Academy teachers often gave lists of positive aspects like this one:

> The students are getting a better education. The opportunities it gives teachers for growth. It always gets into more days and more pay which is important to other teachers. Building level personnel are more cognizant of district operations and vice versa. It has made a lot of difference in the feeling tone. Whenever someone has more time to prepare the job and take ownership, they're bound to do a better job.

To summarize, Academy designed a program to professionalize teaching. It did so by creating a job enlargement system that gave teachers opportunities to help their colleagues become more effective educators. They had both the time and the opportunities for collegial interaction necessary for more reflective practice. Academy also empowered teachers through its task force and the job enlargement positions themselves. Program effects included an enriched curriculum, improved pedagogical practice in a variety of directions, and a much more motivated staff. Teachers had become more professional; implications for students were less clear.

Mossville's orientation was much more bureaucratic. The district implemented a merit pay program rather than job enlargement. Although it established the forms to empower teachers, real influence stayed with the central administration. Additional training was provided, but it was delivered by district staff, so the teacher's role did not really change. The major effect was to treat teachers as workers by intensifying in-class supervision and manipulating extrinsic rewards. Teachers opposed these developments but were unable to change them.

CHALLENGES TO PROFESSIONALISM

Redesigning schools and districts to make them more professional will not be easy. At least three challenges must be met.

The Financial Challenge

Advocates of professionalization have not fully considered the financial implications of their ideas. In fact, some of the research supporting professional redesigns has led attention away from these issues. One recent impetus for professionalism has been criticism of merit pay programs. While popular, they have a long history of failed implementation (Johnson, 1984). Merit pay has two problems. First, it is hard to develop an evaluation system that teachers agree is fair. Second, merit pay reduces collegiality and increases competition among teachers (Rosenholtz, 1987).

The problems with offering teachers financial rewards displaced attention from the costs of reform. The research base used to criticize merit pay also suggested structural changes that would professionalize teaching by increasing teacher collegiality and the opportunity to learn from peers. Little attention was given to the cost of these reforms, and policy makers and reformers may have assumed that such costs would be negligible.

As part of its effort to professionalize, Academy created professionalizing arrangements. However, that district's experience illustrates that adequate arrangements cost money. The key to these arrangements was time. Teachers are conventionally paid for their contact hours with students. The amount of time they put into preparation varies substantially. Past experience at Academy showed that teachers would not put in the time for potentially intrinsically rewarding activities without being paid. Teachers explained that such activities were valued in substantial measure because they were money-making opportunities. When asked who benefits most from Academy's program, one teacher responded

> Teachers who are innovative, willing to develop things, and help with new courses. It's nice to know you can get paid for what you do. Before the CEP, we weren't paid for new ideas. It was expected. The bottom line is financial.

Another said, "The extra money is an incentive to start new programs that teachers wouldn't find the time to do." This is not surprising; teachers like everyone else have competing commitments in the form of family responsibilities and nonwork interests.

It is important to stress the financial dimension for two reasons. First, reformers who look at teaching and teachers' working conditions microscopically are likely to overlook this important requirement. Second, the need for financial support could be a major impediment to serious efforts to redesign teaching. The necessary financing will certainly come from tax money, probably from the state. In this era of substantial distrust of all public employees, taxpayer revolt, and (as this is written) both recession and financial crisis in more than half the states in the nation, the probability of obtaining the substantial increases in funds needed for the kind of professionalizing reform described here appears low.

The Challenge to Teachers

I have suggested that job enlargement effectively facilitates teacher professionalization. The difficulty with job enlargement, merit pay, and other forms of job differentiation is that teachers oppose any effort to introduce new criteria for differentiating rank and remuneration other than those that already exist—such as, years of service and degrees received. There appear to be two bases for this opposition. First, teaching is an occupation with strong norms of equity. Teachers have great difficulty in judging their success and that of their peers, so they question the efforts of others to do so. They doubt the validity of test scores and question the accuracy of performance assessments, whether made by peers or administrators. Even when different learning outcomes can be identified, they question how much these results are attributable to themselves and how much to their students (Johnson, 1989). Second, the industrial trade union model that predominates in teaching gives up control over work to protect job security and access to work. Moreover, it is based on the assumption that all workers should be treated equally, regardless of performance (Mitchell, 1989).

Opposition to differentiation was apparent in both districts. Mossville's evaluation system appeared thorough and well designed, including the provision of a check-and-balance in the form of observations by both the principal and the OE, a teacher temporarily promoted. Yet, as expected, teachers repeatedly questioned its fairness on four grounds. First, observers disagreed in their assessments and varied in their thoroughness.

> Principals list more strengths than OEs 'cause you have a relationship so you're seen as a person. The person knows you more than 30 minutes twice a month.

> We have someone who understands. She got to be an OE simply because she's so good. The assistant principals are not as knowledgeable.

Second, teachers questioned the expertise of some observers, saying "an English teacher can't judge a trig class" or that high school teachers could not assess kindergarten classrooms. Third, teachers cited examples of misuse of evaluative authority. These included decision that both punished enemies and rewarded favorites. As one said, "I wonder about the situation where some teachers are CS IIs. Had I been principal, they wouldn't have gotten it." Finally, promotion was based on a time sample that was too small to be a reliable measure of their work. Moreover, as expected, the whole selection process proved to be moderately divisive.

Academy's professional model incorporated a collegial selection process, but it created similar strains. Promotion decisions were made by committees where two out of three members were teachers. In addition, teacher leaders underwent a modified peer review where those who knew the candidate filled out a questionnaire evaluating leadership potential. The selection process remained stressful, however. According to one teacher, "When the selection process takes place... it is tooth and nail.... There is a two-month period of building tension." Some teachers still questioned the fairness of the process, arguing that administrators really made the selection decision. More prevalent though was the divisiveness that stemmed from the way colleagues of candidates used the peer review process. Teachers reported that

> The only bad thing is the peer review... Teachers don't sign their name. Some accountability is needed. Last year some people felt inadequate for the teacher leader job 'cause one person gave them a negative peer review.

Further movement towards professionalism will require teachers to take responsibility for selecting colleagues for differentiated positions and to exercise that responsibility in a civil way. This is a part of teacher empowerment that teachers themselves may be uncomfortable with. To learn better how to manage this selection task, it may be useful for teachers, working with school boards and administrators, to borrow from approaches already in place in law, where promotion to partnership is a major differentiation point, and higher education, where the key break points are promotion to tenure and then to full professor. These models will help develop procedures that are fair, accurate, and legitimate in the eyes of teachers and the public. However, even the best-designed systems will be stressful. Teachers must become more tolerant of such stresses in order to take the next step.

The Challenge of Combining Structures and Vision

Structural reforms alone are not likely to change teaching practice (Peterson & McCarthy, 1991; Timar, 1990). Job enlargement and empowerment create conditions that encourage reflective practice and treating students as learners, but they are insufficient to reach such objectives alone. When one assesses changes in Academy critically, one find a mixed bag. Teachers were clearly thinking more actively and deeply about curricular and training matters than they ever had before, and the curricular changes were apparent in the classroom. Still, many changes were an enrichment of past practice rather than a radically new way of working with students. A music specialist would find a box of instruments in a storeroom and share them with colleagues, or a high school teacher would start an AP course. Larger steps were also being taken, like trying to implement the new National Council of Teachers of Mathematics standards. Teachers clearly reported trying new approaches in the classroom, but it is hard to know how much these approaches accommodated to past classroom practices as happened in research reported by Cohen and Ball (1990).

We suspect that real changes in instructional practice and student roles will require the strong communication of a different vision of practice to teachers. The advocates of reflective practice have a fairly clear and sophisticated vision of what it should look like (Clark & Peterson, 1986). Such a vision is not likely to come from teachers themselves. Their own practice is heavily influenced by how they were taught. They also lack access to new ideas. Teachers spend so much time in class with students or preparing for the next day that it is hard to keep track of new developments. Even when access is provided, teaching is conservative enough an occupation that there is resistance to drawing on anything but one's own experience (Hargreaves, 1984; Lortie, 1975).

In most school districts these visions will come from administrators who have more time to follow national developments. Here administrators face a serious dilemma: how to balance their concerns with empowering teachers and a specific pedagogy. Mossville and Academy illustrate two patterns that will not be sufficient. The administration in Mossville was strongly committed to a bureaucratic, work-centered view of teaching and had no interest in empowering teachers. Its success in getting teachers to exhibit desired instructional behaviors was attributable in large part to its refusal to incorporate teachers into the district decision making. On the other hand, teachers' refusal to internalize the Mossville vision of effective instruction was also attributable to the top-down, centralizing strategy employed.

Academy's administrators were strongly committed to teacher empowerment, but although they supported professionalism in general, their vision of pedagogy was rather diffuse. The superintendent who initiated the CEP explained that

> My interests were in curriculum and instruction.... I'm interested in leadership of principals as instructional catalysts. I wanted fairly intensive training of principals. Instructional observation and analysis. Stimulating feedback from principals to teachers.

In fact, he relied heavily on training and evaluation programs based on direct instruction. It can be argued, however, that successful teacher empowerment in Academy depended in part on this diffuse pedagogical vision. Other case studies suggest that, if he had had a more specific pedagogical vision, he would have been tempted to maintain more control over strategic decisions in order to implement it (Firestone, 1980; Firestone & Bader, in press; Rossman, Corbett, & Firestone, 1988). In Academy, the superintendent's diffuse vision contributed to an environment with a rich variety of modest educational experiments but very few radical departures in the direction of reflective teaching or learning (as opposed to working) environments for students.

At this point it is easier to identify the problem than the solution. Professionalizing teaching and spreading learning environments for students will require job enlargement and teacher empowerment. These conditions facilitate the reflection and problem solving among teachers that will help them model learning behavior to students. Yet teachers currently lack images of the kind of reflective practice that accompanies professionalism and the learning environments that Marshall advocates in this volume. In the absence of such a vision, empowerment can become license to maintain old practices, and job enlargement can simply reinforce more of the same.

Advocates of reflective practice and learning environments for students—whether administrators or teachers—cannot be passive. They need to use the authority at their disposal to get their views a hearing and to provide the apparatus for the dissemination and implementation of their ideas. This includes provision for training, follow-up coaching, supplying needed materials and encouragement, and so forth. The reflective practice paradigm and student-as-learner metaphor cannot be forced on teachers. These ideas must be adopted voluntarily, but such adoption will require a good deal of training, support, salesmanship, and probably visionary preaching. This balance of empowerment and a particular pedagogical vision can only be spread by very proactive advocates.

SUMMARY

I have pointed out the parallel between metaphors of students as learners and workers, paradigms of teaching as reflective practice and direct instruction, and designs of schools as professional organizations and bureaucracies. My conclusion is that professional organizations are most likely to treat students as learners. A review of recent reforms suggests two that are likely to facilitate movement towards implementing the learner metaphor (teacher empowerment and job enlargement) and one (merit pay) that will probably work against it.

At the same time, I identify three challenges that must be addressed if professional workplaces are to become more prevalent. First, professionalism requires money to buy teachers time to act as problem solvers and feel rewarded for doing so. Second, teachers must become more tolerant of differentiations in rank, remuneration, and work. In professional organizations, they will help select those who get the "better" jobs so they will have to become more civil in carrying out that responsibility. Finally, structural changes are not enough. Advocates of the learning metaphor will have to sell new ways of teaching but do so in ways that do not undermine the new empowerment of teachers.

REFERENCES

Bacharach, S. B., & Conley, S.C. (1989). Uncertainty and decisionmaking in teaching: Implications for managing line professionals. In T. J. Sergiovanni & J. H. Moore (Eds.), *Schooling for tomorrow: Directing reforms to issues that count* (pp. 311–328). Needham Heights, MA: Allyn and Bacon.

Berman, P., & McLaughlin, M.W. (1975). *Federal programs supporting educational change. The findings in review* (Vol. 4). Santa Monica, CA: Rand Corporation.

Brophy, J.E., & Good, T. L. (1986). Teacher behavior and student achievement. In M.C. Wittrock (Ed.), *Handbook of research on teaching* (3rd ed., pp. 328–375). New York: Macmillan.

Carnegie Forum on Education and the Economy. (1986, May). *A nation prepared: Teachers for the 21st century.* New York: Author.

Carter, K., & Doyle, W. (1989). Classroom research as a resource for the graduate preparation of teachers. In A. Woolfolk (Ed.), *Research perspectives on the graduate preparation of teachers* (pp. 51–68). Englewood Cliffs, NJ: Prentice-Hall.

Clark, C., & Peterson, P.L. (1986). Teachers' thought processes. In M.C. Wittrock (Ed.), *Handbook of research on teaching* (3rd ed., pp. 255–296). New York: Macmillan.

Clune, W.H., & White, P.A. (1989). *School-based management: Institutional variation, implementation, and issues for further research.* New Brunswick, NJ: Center for Policy Research in Education.

Cohen, D.K., & Ball, D.L. (1990). Policy and practice: An overview. *Educational evaluation and policy analysis, 12,* 233–39.

Corwin, R.G., & Borman, K.M. (1988). School as workplace: Structural constraints on administration. In N. Boyan (Ed.), *Handbook of research on educational administration* (pp. 209–238). New York: Longman.

Darling-Hammond, L., & Berry, B. (1988). *The evolution of teacher policy.* Santa Monica, CA: The RAND Corporation.

Dornbusch, S.M., & Scott, W. R. (1975). *Evaluation and the exercise of authority.* San Francisco: Jossey-Base Publishers.

Firestone, W.A. (1980). *Great expectations for small schools: The limitations of federal projects.* New York: Praeger.
Firestone, W.A., & Bader, B.D. (in press). *Redesigning teaching: Professionalism or bureaucracy?* Albany, NY: SUNY Press.
Good, T. (1983). Classroom research: A decade of progress. *Educational Psychologist, 18,* 127–44.
Hargreaves, A. (1984). Experience counts, theory doesn't: How teachers talk about their work. *Sociology of Education, 57*(4), 244–253.
Holmes Group, Inc. (1986). *Tomorrow's teachers: A report of the Holmes Group.* East Lansing: MI: Author.
Johnson, S.M. (1984). Merit pay for teachers: A poor prescription for reform. *Harvard Educational Review, 54*(2), 175–185.
Johnson, S.M. (1989). Schoolwork and its reform. In J. Hannaway & R. Crowson (Eds.), *The politics of reforming school administration* (pp. 95–112). New York: The Falmer Press.
Lawler, E.E. (1973). *Motivation in work organizations.* Monterey, CA: Brooks/Cole.
Little, J.L. (1982). Norms of collegiality and experimentation: Workplace conditions of school success. *American Educational Research Journal, 19*(3), 325–340.
Lortie, D.C. (1975). *Schoolteacher: A sociological study.* Chicago: The University of Chicago Press.
Malen, B., & Hart, A.W. (1987). Confronting reform in teacher preparation: One state's experience. *Educational Evaluation and Policy Analysis, 9*(1), 9–24.
Malen, B., Murphy, M.J., & Hart, A.W. (1988). Restructuring teacher compensation systems: An analysis of three incentive strategies. In K. Alexander & D.H. Monk (Eds.), *Eighth annual yearbook of the American Education Finance Association 1987* (pp. 91–142). Cambridge, MA: Ballinger Publishing Company.
Mintzberg, H. (1983). *Structure in fives: Designing effective organizations.* Englewood Cliffs, NJ: Prentice-Hall.
Mitchell, D. (1989). Measuring up: Standards for evaluating school reform. In T.J. Sergiovanni & J.H. Moore (Eds.), *Schooling for tomorrow: Directing reforms to issues that count* (pp. 42–60). Needham Heights, MA: Allyn and Bacon.
National Commission on Educational Excellence. (1983). *A nation at risk: The imperative for educational reform.* Washington, DC: U.S. Government Printing Office.
Newmann, F.M., Rutter, R.A., & Smith, M.S. (1989). Organizational factors that affect school sense of efficacy, community, and expectations. *Sociology of education, 62*(4), 221–238.
Oldham, G.R., & Hackman, J. R. (1981). Relationships between organizational structure and employee reactions: Comparing alternative frameworks. *Administrative Science Quarterly, 26*(1), 66–83.
Passow, A.H. (1989). Present and future directions in school reform. In T.J. Sergiovanni & J. H. Moore (Eds.), *Schooling for tomorrow: Directing reforms to issues that count* (pp. 13–39). Needham Heights, MA: Allyn and Bacon.
Perrow, C.B. (1970). *Organizational analysis: A sociological view.* Monterey, CA: Brooks/Cole.
Peterson P., & McCarthy, S. (1991, April). *Reflections on restructuring in one school.* Paper presented at the annual meeting of the American Educational Research Association, Chicago.

Popkewitz, T.S., & Lind, K. (1989). Teacher incentives as reforms: Teachers' work and the changing control mechanism in education. *Teachers College Record, 90*(4), 575–594.

Porter, L. W., Lawler, E.E., & Hackman, J.R. (1975). *Behavior in organizations.* New York: McGraw-Hill.

Rosenholtz, S.J. (1987). Education reform strategies: Will they increase teacher commitment? *American Journal of Education, 95,* 534–562.

Rosenholtz, S.J. (1985b). Effective schools: Interpreting the evidence. *American Journal of Education, 93,* 353–388.

Rosenholtz, S.J. (1989) *Teacher's workplace: The social organization of schools.* New York: Longman.

Rosenshine, B.V. (1983). Teaching functions in instructional programs. *Elementary School Journal, 83*(4), 60–69.

Rossman, G.B., Corbett, H.D., & Firestone, W.A. (1988). *Change and effectiveness in schools: A cultural perspective.* Albany, NY: SUNY Press.

Rowan, B. (1990). Commitment and control: Alternative strategies for the organizational design of schools. In C.B. Cazen & S.M. Johnson (Eds.), *Review of research in education* (pp. 353–392). Washington, DC: American Educational Research Association.

Ryan, R.M., Connell, J.P., & Deci, E.L. (1985). A motivational analysis of self-determination and self-regulation in education. In C. Ames & R. Ames (Eds.), *Research on motivation in education. Vol. 2: The classroom milieu* (pp. 13–49). Orlando, FL: Academic Press.

Sickler, J. (1988). Teachers in charge: Empowering the professionals. *Phi Delta Kappan, 69*(5) 354–357.

Southern Regional Education Board. (1990). *Paying for performance—Important questions and answers: The 1989 SREB Career Ladder Clearinghouse report.* Atlanta, GA: Author.

Staw, B.M. (1980). Intrinsic and extrinsic motivation. In H.J. Leavitt, L.R. Pondy, & D.M. Boje (Eds.), *Readings in managerial psychology* (pp. 23–61). Chicago: IL: The University of Chicago Press.

Timar, T.B. (1990). The politics of school restructuring. In D.E. Mitchell & M.E. Goertz (Eds.), *Education politics for the new century* (pp. 55–74). London: Falmer.

Weber, M. (1947). *Social and economic organization.* New York: Oxford University Press.

Weick, K.E. (1976). Educational organizations as loosely coupled systems. *Administrative Science Quarterly, 21*(1), 19.

Weick, K.E., & McDaniel, R.R. (1989). How professional organizations work: Implications for school organization and management. In T.J. Sergiovanni & J.H. Moorc (Eds.), *Schooling for tomorrow: Directing reforms to issues that count* (pp. 331–354). Needham Heights, MA: Allyn & Bacon.

Chapter 11
Beginning with the Classroom: Implications for Redesigning Schools*

Carolyn M. Evertson
Joseph Murphy

Vanderbilt University and
The National Center for Educational Leadership

Preceding chapters have focused on expanded views of student learning and have shown how these look in classrooms. These chapters examine the issue of student learning from the classroom level. What remains unexamined is how the redefinition of learning and, subsequently, teaching in order to bring about learning for understanding, fits within the broader reform movement of restructuring schooling. In this chapter we bring together these two perspectives: The perspective of classroom research on teaching/learning processes, and the administrative and organizational perspectives.

---

* We wish to thank Judith L. Green and Catherine Randolph for their editorial comments on earlier versions of this chapter.
  Support for this research was provided by the National Center for Educational Leadership (NCEL) under U.S. Department of Education Contract No. R117C8005. The views in this report are those of the authors and do not necessarily represent those of the sponsoring institution nor the Universities in the NCEL Consortium—The University of Chicago, Harvard University, and Vanderbilt University.

The purpose of bringing these two perspectives together is to make visible factors from both that will support or constrain the new directions discussed in this volume.

The two bodies of work we propose to bring together are, first, the work on classrooms drawn from this volume and other complementary work in the field, and, second, work on the organizational level which embeds the classroom in the larger system. What we will argue is that we must understand both bodies of work if we are to bring about a transformation in learning experiences for students. Following a brief historical perspective of reform efforts, we will begin with an illustration of a study at the policy level that attempted to bring about changes in what occurs at the classroom level, and will draw on the work presented in this volume and related work to help understand why the desired changes in how teachers taught did not occur. Next, we will examine changes in definitions of learning, teaching, and studenting which are necessary in order to capture new directions. These changes will be placed in the context of a larger look at the reform effort to date to suggest some additional constraining factors at the systems level. Finally, we present five common assumptions about redesigned schools that must be addressed to extend the dialogue.

The order of the presentation from the classroom outward to the organizational levels is a deliberate attempt to do what political scientists and organizational theorists have called "backward mapping" (Elmore, 1979-1980). Before we go to the example, we will briefly describe what *backward mapping* means and where it comes from.

Forward mapping, according to Elmore, "begins at the top of the [policy implementation] process with as clear a statement as possible of the policy-maker's intent, and proceeds through a sequence of increasingly more specific steps to define what is expected of implementers at each level. At the bottom of the process, one states, again with as much precision as possible, what a satisfactory outcome will be, measured in terms of the original statement of intent" (p. 602). On the other hand, "the logic of backward mapping is the opposite of forward mapping. It begins, not at the top of the process, but at the last possible stage, the point at which administrative actions intersect private choices. It begins, not with a statement of intent, but with a statement of the specific behavior at the lowest level of the implementation process that generates a need for the policy" (p. 604).

Murphy (1991) applies this idea from policy implementation to teaching for understanding. He contends "that revisions in organizational and governance structures should backward map (Elmore, 1979–80) from the student. That is, fundamental discussions about how to restructure educational processes for more effective learning flow from rich conceptions of teaching and learning and should precede the restructuring of other aspects of schooling" (p. 74).

To understand the need for the application to educational reform of backward mapping from the point of view of the student, we need to look at the historical phases of reform as captured by Murphy (1990b, 1991).

HISTORICAL PERSPECTIVE ON RESTRUCTURING AND SCHOOL REFORM

> Few reform reports have touched on the heart of the educational processes, what is taught and how it is taught. (National Governors' Association, 1989, p. 1)

Reform has been a cyclical activity for educators for the past century and a half (see Cuban, 1984, 1990; Passow, 1984; Powell, Farrar, & Cohen, 1985). The latest round of reform dates from the late 1970s and early 1980s, when growing disenchantment with America's schools became crystallized in a series of highly visible reform reports (see Murphy, 1990a, for a review). Fueled by widespread dissatisfaction with educational outcomes and the underlying conditions of schooling, an array of initiatives was enacted to shore up the educational enterprise and thus, it was hoped, restore America to its preeminent economic, scientific, and technological position.

Collectively, the reform measures of the early and mid-1980s have been labeled the "standards-raising movement." Based on the belief that quality schooling had derailed, reformers set about repairing and righting the engine. Improvement strategies were sketched out by state-level policymakers and reform-minded businesspeople far removed from the local school. Teachers and administrators were thought to be largely responsible for the mess in which education found itself, and improvement strategies were designed to force them—and their young charges—to work harder. Rules and prescriptions to achieve this objective were promulgated in unprecedented numbers in nearly every state in the nation (see Murphy, 1990b, for a review).

Even as these standards were being sent down to schools, critics were wagging their heads in disapproval. These critics viewed schooling's problems quite differently from their colleagues in the standards-raising movement. They saw a changing world order—a shift from an industrial to a postindustrial society and a rapidly changing social structure on the home front—contributing to education's difficulties. They traced problems, not to the doors of teachers and administrators, but to the system of schooling itself. Since they saw little evidence that top-down reforms had worked in the past, they were skeptical that they would be successful now. They reached similar conclusions about the use of controls and prescriptions. These analysts pinned their hopes on bottom-up change strategies that empowered teachers, and often parents, to restructure (rebuild, reinvent, transform) education. (See Murphy, 1990b, 1991, for reviews.)

Buttressed by these criticisms of the standards-raising approach to reform, as well as by a number of influential reform reports released in the mid to late 1980s, school restructuring was pushed to the center stage of the reform movement. Under the rubric of restructuring, changes in four broad areas were highlighted: (a) *school-based management*—redistribution of authority for decision making from the district level to the school level; (b) *teacher empowerment*—development of strategies to promote professionalism within the teaching force (Firestone, Chapter 10, this volume), including giving teachers greater control over issues such as entry into the profession, improving working conditions, increasing collegial interaction, and providing teachers with more authority at the school site; (c) *choice/voice*—providing parents with additional influence in deciding which schools their children should attend and in determining what happens to them when they are there; and (d) *teaching for understanding*—a shift from teacher-centered to student-centered learning within the context of more coherent curricular programs and more flexible organizational structures (David, 1989; Elmore, 1989; Murphy, 1991).

As the chapters in this volume remind us, of these four areas, restructuring teaching for understanding has received the least amount of attention, both in the reform reports and in state-, district-, and school-level efforts to restructure schools. Rather than backward mapping from the student, the reform movement has approached change structurally, from the outside. We find this general absence of attention to teaching and learning in discussions of school reform to be troubling for three reasons. First, since teaching and learning are what we are about, it seems illogical to look elsewhere for improvement. Second, in the absence of linkages with teaching–learning processes, the other elements of restructuring are often treated as ends in themselves, pursued without being grounded in the essential purposes of schooling (Council of Chief State School Officers, 1989). Third, a number of researchers have been hard pressed to find any empirical connections between the other components of educational change such as those just described and improved educational processes and outcomes (Hawley, 1988; Malen, Ogawa, & Kranz, 1989).

Given this historical frame and the need to look from the classroom to the larger organization in which the classroom is embedded, we will return to the restructuring literature and will revisit this history to expand on the issue of restructuring from the inside.

FAILURE OF STRUCTURAL CHANGES TO ALTER TEACHING PRACTICE

An Example from a Study of Class Size

Substantive change in what is taught and learned and how it is taught and learned will require more than tinkering with structural changes at the organizational level. It will require an understanding of the interdependence of each element upon other elements in the system. In Cuban's (1990) words:

> Reforms do return again, again, and again. Not exactly as before or under the same conditions, but they persist. It is of even greater importance that few reforms aimed at the classroom make it past the door permanently. It is important to policymakers, practitioners, administrators, [parents, students, community] and researchers to understand why reforms return but seldom substantially alter the regularities of schooling. The risks involved with a lack of understanding include pursuing problems with mismatched solutions, spending energies needlessly, and accumulating despair. The existing tools of understanding are no more than inadequate metaphors that pinchhit for hard thinking. (pp. 11–12)

The problem of "getting past the classroom door" has been well documented. The literature on factors influencing the adoption of innovations designed to improve practice is extensive (McLaughlin, 1987; Fullan, 1991).

An example of a failure of single strategy approaches initiated from the outside comes from one of the studies in Tennessee's Project STAR, a study supported through funds from the state legislature to examine the effects of changes in class size—small (13–17 students) vs. regular (21–27 students)—and support (regular size class with an in-class aide) on the achievement of students in grades K-3. In one portion of this study, reading and math lessons in 155 second- and third-grade classes of all three types were observed. Teachers in 62 of these classes received inservice training in effective teaching practices. *Effective teaching* as used here represents a behaviorist, direct-instruction model of teaching and learning. Specifically, the training employed a teacher-change model (Richardson, 1990) such that certain practices deemed "effective" in research studies (such as questioning strategies to elicit higher order thinking) were presented in workshops prior to the beginning of the school year and changes in class size. When the school year began, these teachers were assigned to small or regular-sized classes, or to regular-sized classes with in-class aides. The hope was that the 62 trained teachers would adopt effective teaching practices in the coming year as their classes changed in numbers of students or in level of paraprofessional support.

Analysis of the narrative reports compiled by observers revealed a striking similarity among classes, regardless of class size or training condition. While there were some differences between the second and third grades, and large differences between reading and math lesson structures, class type (e.g., class size and support) and inservice training appeared to have little effect on teaching practices (Evertson & Randolph, in press). The lack of variation in teaching practices was attributed to factors not systematically accounted for in the study. We will explore some of these factors, clustered under key categories. While we separate them here, they are in fact interrelated.

Curriculum, Teacher Instruction, and Assessment

The first factor that may have contributed to the lack of change following reduction in class size was the pervasiveness of the state's mandated curriculum, known as part of the Basic Skills First program, on how the teachers taught. The Basic Skills First program encourages a convergent, fragmented, skills-based approach to the curriculum rather than an understanding-based approach that emphasizes thinking and problem solving. This supports a definition of learning as convergent and right-answer oriented, with a goal of eliminating errors rather than using them to make student thinking visible. Based on this curriculum, the state designed objectives and an assessment system in language arts and math, and local school districts are required to use either the state system or to follow state guidelines in designing their own. In one typical system, teachers are provided with a skills checklist for each student. They are to mark each skill for each student as "not covered," "exposed," or "mastered." Acquisition of skills is measured by frequent multiple choice tests. The demands of the program, both in terms of the quantity of material to be covered and the quantity of paperwork involved, encourage adherence and few deviations. Traditional methods for teaching reading and mathematics introduce few risks and accomplish the "objectives mastered" requirements of the district. In short, there are few incentives and many potential risks in changing practices substantially. Changes in class size and brief inservice training must be considered weak treatments under these conditions. Furthermore, the effective teaching inservice training did not address the Basic Skills First curriculum directly, and did not directly encourage change in existing instructional practices.

The Basic Skills First curriculum is accompanied by frequent objective assessment that emphasizes convergent thinking and right answers. These assessments form the accountability system for teachers while they measure student achievement. This type of assessment creates a press to practice items and formats similar to those that will be tested. Teachers wishing to diverge from the state curriculum may have been limited by this assessment system.

Classroom Organizational Patterns

The influence of the curriculum and assessment system extended to how teachers grouped students within the classroom. Of 153 reading lessons observed in both grades, only 5 were conducted in arrangements that allowed students to use one another as resources, and that opened up the curriculum to uncertainty. The remaining 148 reading lessons were conducted in whole group and traditional reading group formats, suitable for the convergent thinking encouraged by the curriculum.

Summary

Overall, the study revealed the enacted view of classrooms as work environments, where the emphasis was on products, rather than as learning environments, where the emphasis was on processes. Although teachers reported liking the small classes, it was clear that altering class size alone was a relatively minor innovation in the face of accustomed practice and in and of itself was impotent to change deeply held teacher beliefs and patterns of teaching (Evertson & Randolph, in press; Word et al., 1990).

The study illustrates as nearly as possible Elmore's (1979–1980) definition of *forward mapping*. Policy was developed at the state level and proceeded through specific steps to affect teaching practice in the classroom, from the top of the process. We will revisit these findings later in light of what previous chapters have shown, to suggest reasons that desired changes were not realized and to suggest factors that need to be considered in further work.

As this study implies, real change in classrooms will require transformation of the definitions of learning, of teaching, and of studenting. The following sections will address each of these new definitions and possible supports and constraints on change.

REDEFINING LEARNING

Efforts toward transforming schools to support student learning must begin with understandings about what learning is and what it "looks like." As Marshall and others (this volume) have illustrated, prevailing images of how students should be engaged in learning have taken several forms. (See

Bruner, 1985, and also see Elkind, 1987, for a humorous account of our images of learners over the history of schooling.)

As Marshall (this volume) describes, *the transmission model* of learning is built on the underlying assumption that knowledge is conveyed by discrete bits, and that the sum of the parts equals the whole. This model assumes that the student has no active role in his or her own learning, and does not allow for the fact that the group of students influences what gets learned. The transmission model assumes delivery of knowledge "from-one-person-to-the-next."

A second model, akin to the first, is *the additive model*. This model assumes that knowledge can be imparted in discrete bits like beads on a string, that the sum of the bits equals the whole, and that the summing of the bits and integration to a larger whole can be done by the student independent of contexts for when, how, or why to use the information.

The transmission model and the additive model were the models used by teachers in the class-size study. A third model, *the constructivist/interpretative model*, assumes that there is a purpose to learning, that students do perceive the purpose and actively engage in and construct the meanings to be gained. Several of the chapters of this volume employ this model (e.g., Chandler, Chapter 2; Collins & Green, Chapter 3; Peterson, Chapter 6; Weade, Chapter 4; Wood et al., Chapter 7).

In the interpretative model, students construct meaning. They use prior knowledge from a variety of sources to solve the problem that is created when new information is presented to them. The teacher's role of facilitator of knowledge construction requires more than the distribution of discrete bits of information. Once we take on this third approach to learning, we must consider different kinds of classroom organizational structure, which allow for constructing meaning within and across texts, tasks, and content, and which support purposeful learning. Students should not just be learning *what*, as in the first model, but learning *how*, how to problem solve. This requires that students have a problem to attack. Students should be learning to do something with the knowledge that they are constructing.

At least two issues are of concern: (a) the nature of what gets accomplished in classrooms, how it is defined, how it is evaluated, and what counts as content knowledge in reading, writing, math, science, and so on (e.g., right answers on worksheets, ability to add three place numbers vs. ability to solve complex problems); and (b) the nature of student participation in classroom events (e.g., raising hands and waiting to be called on vs. working with peers on a project).

In rethinking classroom and school organizational structure, we focus on certain central questions. We address the question of what factors support or constrain access to learning in school and other educational settings by asking how the actions and interactions of participants in the classroom influence (a) the opportunities students and teachers have to learn, (b) the assessment of performance and/or learning (i.e., what counts as learning), and (c) what is accomplished in classroom settings (i.e., curriculum). Each of these areas will be elaborated in the sections which follow.

Opportunities to Learn

The questions above are based on the notions that, over time, what students come to learn and know is constructed, and what we see when we look in classrooms is performance in a particular patterned way (see Weade, Chapter 4). The kinds of students we produce are a direct result of the kinds of teaching in which we engage students. In effect, we are constructing models of learning in the classroom inadvertently, if not overtly, in terms of the kinds of opportunities students have and the types of tasks they are allowed to perform. For example, consider chapters in this volume by Peterson and by Collins and Green. As the teacher in Peterson's chapter shifts her own values in thinking about appropriate teaching of math for her students, she moves from the scripted CSMP materials, which emphasize convergent right answers, to a student-centered, problem-solving approach. In Collins and Green, when a substitute comes in and moves students from a multitask to a recitation format, the definition of learning and what counts as learning is changed, to the confusion of the students. In both chapters, what students come to know and understand shifts, leading to a change in their opportunities to learn and display their knowledge.

The Influence of Assessment

As Camp (Chapter 9) and Weade (Chapter 4) remind us, a critical element in what is taught, how it is taught and what students learn is the method used to evaluate student learning. Madaus (1987) discusses the relationship of the assessment system to classroom teaching and student learning. He emphasizes the importance of beliefs about the power of the test results to affect participants. If important decisions are perceived to be related to test results, then teachers will teach to the test. Eventually, through the accumulation of past exams, the assessment defines the curriculum. When they are guided by this assessment-based curriculum, teachers pay particular attention to the form of the questions on the test (short answer, essay, multiple-choice) and adjust their instruction accordingly. Power over classroom instruction and curriculum is thus transferred to the agency that sets or controls the exam.

These principles illustrate the power of the testing program to drive what is taught and how it is taught. In effect, they insinuate a definition of learning that becomes value driven, based on the test. This criticism of testing is not new; the class-size study described previously is just one example of how the relationship between testing and curriculum can play out.

Curriculum

Chandler's chapter (Chapter 2) reminds us that all classrooms are learning settings. The issue becomes what is learned. In her view the curriculum is not merely a document, a potential, but is that which is constructed by teachers, students, and texts in the process of interaction. For Chandler, the critical element becomes whose knowledge is being learned and what values underlie the choices made. To return to the class-size study, clearly the values about what reading or math knowledge was of most worth, what was defined as reading or math, and how much time was spent in studying math or reading concepts were influenced to a large extent by what was to be tested and for what individual students and teachers were to be held accountable. The influence of the state's and district's values were not only felt in the classroom, they drove what was taught and how it was taught. Teachers responded by routinizing instruction in ways that left little room or incentive for deviation.

Madaus (1987) cites an example (LeMahieu, 1984) of a similar instance of narrowing the curriculum of the Chicago Mastery Learning Reading (CMLR) program in which a sequence of 273 separate subskills were to be mastered before the student could proceed. One teacher describes the effect on her teaching:

> Because CMLR is mandatory and accountability is emphasized with charts and reports about how many students have passed 80 percent of their tests, and because in many schools basal readers and other books are in short supply, or even nonexistent, CMLR becomes the central part of the reading instruction, and children never get a chance to read real books. CMLR crowds out real reading. (p. 105)

These examples illustrate the interaction among assessment, curriculum, and opportunities to learn in redefining learning. These factors must be recognized in any attempt to restructure teaching.

RELEARNING TEACHING

As we have stated, teaching for understanding will require a series of transformations that affect both teachers and students. If the student is actively involved in constructing, interpreting, and making and exploring meaning, the student must be in a more active role. A new role for students requires a new role for teachers. This requires considering how to help teachers make the transformation from a minimum competency curriculum with accompanying assessment, such as we have seen in the class-size study, to learner centered, multitask settings where students take charge of their own learning.

Teaching and the Teacher's Role

> Locating knowledge across the curriculum must include an analysis of the role of the teacher in making knowledge accessible to students. The teacher's role in mediating the content of the culture for students is complex. At the point where the students' learning, the broader cultural content defined as subject disciplines, and the organization of the school converge, school knowledge (or curriculum) is "located" within the dynamic interaction of which teachers are the center. (McNeil, 1990, p. 117)

Peterson (Chapter 6) provides an example of a teacher's redefinition of teaching based on the constructivist/interpretative model of learning. As Keisha, a third-grade teacher, began to think about learning in a different way, she began to move from reliance on the text, acknowledging only students' contributions that seemed to fit her "script" and orchestrating classroom discourse that was mostly convergent, toward unpacking mathematical ideas and thinking about new mathematical language by following students' thinking. Wood, Cobb, and Yackel (Chapter 7), too, have shown how a change in learning mathematics requires a change in teaching mathematics. They point out that "teaching is viewed as a process of encouraging children's individual constructions of mathematical ideas as well as acculturating them to the mathematics of the community by providing them opportunities to learn during social interaction."

In order to understand what is involved in relearning teaching, the complexity of the teacher's role must be understood. Figure 11.1 is a schematic diagram that shows the mutual influences of various elements on the selection and implementation of instructional tasks. Four dimensions are represented: (a) *nature and structure of knowledge;* (b) *what is worth knowing*; (c) *how a teacher thinks learners learn*; and (d) *the repertoire of strategies a teacher can use.*

As the overlapping of the circles suggests, these four elements interact as the teacher makes instructional decisions. Changes in any one element influence the decisions made regarding the other three. For example, perceptions about the nature of mathematics (dimension a) influence a teacher's beliefs about what is worth knowing (dimension b). A view of the learner as passive recipient of information (dimension c) implies teaching practices and strategies (dimension d) designed to transmit content from teacher to student. Influences may occur in any direction.

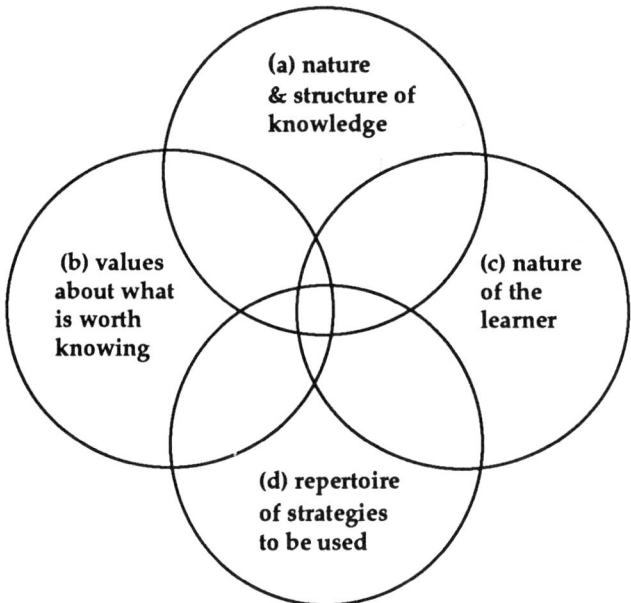

Figure 11.1. Elements to be considered in making instructional decisions.

When teachers take on new definitions of learning, new organizational structures, and new ways of bringing content to students, elements of practice must be relearned (Sizer, 1988). We would contend that, rather than relearning the whole of teaching, however, what is required is to expand repertoires. This may mean that teachers move through developmental stages in the process of refining, extending, and modifying their teaching. Because they are also relearning ways of bringing substance to students, students must also relearn teaching and studenting (Fenstermacher, 1986), a point to which we shall return later.

The culture of the classroom and the school must be rebuilt to support these new ways of seeing learning. Three areas which teachers must relearn in order to participate in the rebuilding of classroom and school culture are managing complexity, learning to see learning, and managing uncertainty.

Managing Complexity

Different classroom tasks have different implications for management (Bossert, 1979; Doyle, 1983). As teachers select one type of task, they are also selecting requirements for management depending upon the nature of the knowledge, the background abilities of the students, the nature of the learner, and what values are held about the worth of the task, as Figure 11.1 shows.

The relearning that teachers must do if classrooms are to change is demonstrated by the implications of a change in the metaphors for teaching (Petrie, 1990). For example, Cohen and Lotan (1990) provide a metaphor of the teacher as supervisor of complex technology. They make a distinction between the more common metaphor of the teacher as supervisor of factory workers and as manager of a complex technology. The latter assumes nonroutine tasks and the delegation of authority to the "workers" (students). Instead of being symbolized as assembly-line workers, students in this view are seen as scientists, who work in teams at a variety of tasks. Classrooms are thus highly differentiated, uncertain, complex environments, where direct supervision is no longer efficient or effective. Instead, teachers must learn to delegate authority and to allow students to use each other, not just the teacher, as resources.

Teachers' decisions about whether to choose complex tasks are frequently based on what they understand about the demands or requirements of the school system. As we can see from the class-size project, teachers did not open their classrooms to complexity. Teachers routinized and simplified classroom activity to meet management requirements. McNeil (1990) explains a standard response by teachers to administrators' inordinate attention to behavior controls and credentialing.

> One response... [as reported in previous ethnographic studies of classrooms by McNeil, 1984] has been to teach defensively. Apologizing for assignments and watering down content, teachers in several midwestern schools separated their personal, complex knowledge of course topics from the oversimplified content of course lectures in order to meet student resistance to demanding assignments. Teachers used specific instructional techniques to transform historical, political and economic content into "school knowledge," reducible to efficient and easy-to-grade fragments of fact. Like their teachers [students] came to view "school knowledge" as instrumental to schooling (learned for tests, for example) but not credible to appropriate into their own personal knowledge. The tendency to trivialize and "manage" complex social studies curricula in an attempt to achieve classroom control built walls between official social studies knowledge and students' personal knowledge and conceptions about how to learn. (p. 119)

Table 11.1 (McNeil, 1990) contrasts defensive teaching, described above, with what McNeil calls "empowering teaching." The characteristics McNeil lists under "empowering teaching" are consistent with the constructivist/interpretative model. "Defensive teaching," on the other hand, assumes a transmission or additive approach. It is also a response to a schooling context which does not support opening up the curriculum to complexity, uncertainty, and unpredictability.

Table 11.1. Models of Teaching as Locating Knowledge

	Defensive Teaching	Empowering Teaching
Teacher	Deskilled, personal knowledge separated from classroom knowledge	Professionalized, personal knowledge evident in course content and ways of knowing
Student	Passive role as client or consumer	Active role as participant, learner
Course Content	**Fragmented**, reductive information, often shaped by evaluation methods and "outcomes"	**Integrated**, coherent contextualized information
	Mystification of complex topics; reliance on experts to "know"	**Demystification** through exploration of multiple explanations, active participation in interpreting, solving
	Omission of controversy and complexity; distancing of students from topics	**Inclusion** of issues, conflicts, ambiguities, current topics, personal curiosities
Teaching Style	**Defensive simplification**, apologetic, undemanding presentations	**Teaching** with authority, teacher as model of learning

From: McNeil, L. M. (1990). Empowering students: Beyond defensive teaching in social studies. In C. Emihovich (Ed.), *Locating learning: Ethnographic perspectives on classroom research*, p. 129. Norwood, NJ: Ablex Publishing Corp. Reprinted by permission.

Learning to See Learning

Heap (1984) and Weade (Chapter 4) point up the difficulty in making the transition from what are taken for granted regularities of classroom life, the commonplaces (Sarason, 1982) and how what is seen manifests itself as evidence that students are learning what we want them to. Throughout this volume we see these tensions illustrated (Peterson, Chapter 6; Wood, Cobb, & Yackel, Chapter 7; Blumenfeld, Puro, & Mergendoller, Chapter 8).

The "look" of engagement can be deceiving. We can easily assume actual engagement with the substance of what is being learned, when, in fact, what students are exhibiting is procedural display and mock participation (Bloome, Puro, & Theodorou, 1989). *Procedural display*, as discussed by Bloome et al. (1989), is a phenomenon that occurs when students look like they are engaged in the task without actually acquiring the academic substance of the lesson.

The need to make learning visible is illustrated in a study by Weade and Evertson (1988). In this investigation, the academic and social task demands were examined for insights into how these demands co-occur in effective and less effective managers' classrooms. For one teacher, an effective manager whose students showed low achievement, management of the social tasks, the "how to do the lesson," was accomplished; however, it was clear that the students' understanding of the lesson was never made visible to the teacher. What counted for learning was the look of performance. The purpose of the academic tasks, and the reason for learning, were never made public. For another teacher, an effective manager whose students showed high achievement, learning was made visible by frequently requiring students to make their reasoning public, providing and asking for rationales, and providing logical scaffolding between the tasks. The Peterson, Weade, and Wood et al. chapters in this volume further illustrate this point.

In more complex classrooms, learning will look different. Teachers will not be able to depend on visual cues such as apparent on-task behavior (procedural display) to determine student understanding of material. Instead, they will have to learn new ways of seeing student learning. Peterson (Chapter 6) provides a helpful case study of the journey of one teacher in her attempts to take on new ways of making students' thinking visible.

Learning to see learning requires systematic and intentional inquiry. Teachers need to learn to look at the classroom events, their sequences, and how these build over time as knowledge is constructed, as opposed to counting discrete events. This will require intensive observation over time rather than occasional counts of students attending.

Managing Uncertainty

When the curriculum is opened up and students become resources for one another, it is no longer possible for a teacher to predict exactly what will occur. Peterson (Chapter 6) has documented what happens when students are allowed to construct mathematical concepts. As they make their thinking visible, the teacher may recognize areas of misconceptions that had not been predicted. The progress of the lesson must follow student thinking rather than the teacher's. Teachers learning to manage uncertainty will need support for their learning process, an issue which will be addressed later. Teachers must have permission, encouragement, and support to allow uncertainty into their lesson planning and classroom activity. In contrast, we have seen how teachers in the class size study had little incentive to open themselves up to uncertainty, given the prescriptive nature of the curriculum, the assessment system, and the expectations of the districts and the schools.

RELEARNING STUDENTING

While the rhetoric of the reform movement has focused on changing structures, which, it is assumed, will create conditions for student learning, the focus on students as active participants and mediators of what will be learned through instruction is absent. By forward mapping, policy makers have missed the focus on students as active participants and mediators of learning. This new conception of the roles of students is the central argument of this volume. While opportunities for learning may be extended, it is ultimately the students who, through engaging in the cultural life of the classroom over time, learn what it is possible to do as students and how to participate in the learning process (Chandler, Chapter 2; Collins & Green, Chapter 3; Weade, Chapter 4).

Studenting and the Student's Role

If students are actors along with teachers in the classroom culture, then the roles students are allowed to play vis-à-vis their own learning will determine in part their opportunities to learn. If, for example, a transmission model of learning is established, then one student role may be to listen and commit to memory. If a constructivist/interpretative model is implemented, then student roles may include commenting on others' ideas, providing explanations for the group, figuring things out for themselves, and making sense of concepts. Thus, as definitions of teaching and learning change, so will definitions of being a student. For students used to a transmission model of learning, being asked to explain their thinking may equate with being told they are incorrect.

Fenstermacher (1986) argues that the proper counterpart to teaching is not learning but studenting. He writes

> The concept of studenting or pupiling is far and away the more parallel concept to that of teaching.... There are a range of activities connected with studenting that complement the activities of teaching. For example, teachers explain, describe, define, refer, correct, and encourage. Students recite, practice, seek assistance, review, check, locate sources and access material. The teacher's task is to support... [the student's] desire to student and improve his capacity to do so. Whether and how much... [the student] learns from being a student is largely a function of how he students.... [W]e make the term 'learning' do double duty, sometimes using it to refer to what the student actually acquires from instruction (achievement), and other times using it to refer to the processes the student uses to acquire content (task). Because the term 'learning' functions in both a task and achievement sense, it is easy to mix the two and thus contend that the task of teaching is to produce the achievement of learning, when it in fact makes more sense to contend that *a central task of teaching is to enable the student to perform the tasks of learning.* (p. 39; emphasis in original)

Fenstermacher goes on to say that "the task of teachers is not necessarily to possess the content and convey it to the student, but is rather to enable the student to take possession of the content wherever it is found" (p. 40).

Students may resist opportunities to take on new roles and to respond in different ways to material. Change will require shifts in their own thinking about being students. Students must adapt to new roles and relationships, for example, what work structures are allowed (working alone as opposed to getting help from peers), how evidence of learning is produced (right answers in a workbook as opposed to extended explanations), and what social behavior is appropriate (listen and wait to be called on as opposed to explaining reasoning to a peer). Collins and Green (Chapter 3) show that, when a substitute teacher attempts a recitation format with students who have learned to participate in an interactive format, trauma results. Bossert (1979) also describes the difficulties of moving students from one activity structure to another. Gumperz (1986) describes the effect of sudden change on first graders' ability to make sense of their rights and obligations for participation.

In their study of how students perform writing tasks, Carter and Doyle (1982) report that, as tasks became more complex and uncertain, students negotiated with the teacher to provide more information. In the process, students reduced the task requirements to routine ones. This example demonstrates that, as we shift the kinds of demands we make on students away from routine performance and toward meaningful learning, we must be aware that students are also relearning their own definitions of what it means to be students.

Thus far we have examined schooling from the student outward, looking at new definitions of learning, teaching, and studenting. Now we will move on to the issues that must be addressed at the structural level in order to make such change possible.

THE PROFESSIONALIZATION OF TEACHING

Moving schools toward the vision of teaching and learning described in this volume will not be an easy task. As Marshall (1988, 1990, Chapter 1, this volume), Schlechty (1990), and others have shown, the factory model of education, the workplace metaphor of school activity, and behaviorist views of learning are dominant threads in the fabric of schooling in this country. For the rich conceptions of learning and teaching presented in this volume to replace them, important changes in the patterns of school activities and the texture of the school culture will need to occur. For the purpose of this chapter, we will now unpack the elements of these alterations under the headings of "the professionalization of teaching" and "new forms of school organization, governance, and management." While we acknowledge that there is a good deal of overlap in these categories—Wise (1989) goes so far as

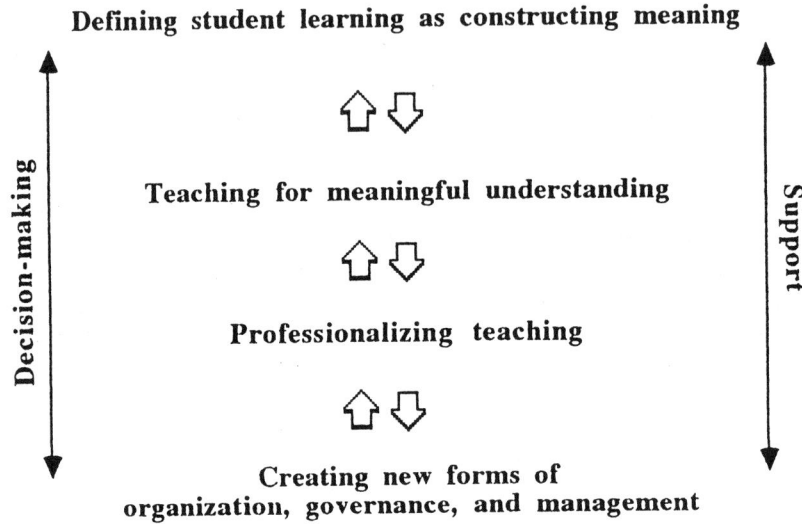

Figure 11.2. Dimensions in professionalizing teaching

to report that teacher professionalism is a new form of management—we believe that there is merit in trying to disentangle them for analysis. This is so because, in our model (illustrated in Figure 11.2), *professionalization of teaching*, as we define it, supports directly the development of a learning orientation in schools while new forms of organization and governance promote teaching for meaningful understanding indirectly through professionalization (see also Firestone, Chapter 10). As the model in Figure 11.2 shows, the potential exists for each of these elements to influence the others directly or indirectly; hence the arrows for direction of influence are double headed.

New metaphors of teaching help us begin to visualize the redesigned, professional conception of teaching needed to foster sustained student engagement and the active construction of learning. Metaphors provided by Barth (1988, 1989), McCarthey and Peterson (1989), Beck and Murphy (in press), and Schlechty (1990) are particularly useful (see also the spring 1990 issue of *Theory into Practice*). An overarching perspective on professionalization is provided in Barth's (1988) view of the school as a community of leaders. Conceptual detail on professionalization is provided by McCarthey and Peterson's (1989) metaphorical categories of teacher-as-colleague, teacher-as-leader, teacher-as-decision-maker, and teacher-as-learner.

For teachers to promote the development of a learning orientation in restructured schools—to help get teaching and learning beyond the workplace metaphor (Marshall, 1988, 1990)—they will need to engage in regular, and important, exchanges with their colleagues. Teachers will need to participate in decisions affecting the entire school and frequently perform leadership tasks—in Sykes and Elmore's (1989) terms, the managerial role of teachers will need to be institutionalized (see also Berliner, 1990). To perform in this fashion, they will need to be more collegial, to develop more interdependence with peers, and to share their knowledge with others in a variety of settings. In restructured schools, teachers will need to model a professional culture that can serve as an analog for classroom learning environments.

A professional work culture that fosters teaching for meaningful understanding will be one that supports the development of organizational structures that help "break down traditional teacher isolation in the classroom" (Bredeson, 1989, p. 11) and encourages "collegial interaction around problems of practice" (Elmore, 1989, p. 23). The professional culture in restructured schools will need to be one in which teachers are more concerned with the purposes of education than with implementing predetermined goals (Conway & Jacobson, 1990; Petrie, 1990). It is also one in which they will "exercise greater control over matters pertaining to curriculum and instruction and to the way in which the school's resources are employed to support teaching and learning," one in which there is "a decrease in control by authority and an increase in control through professional norms of performance, responsibility, and commitment" (Mojkowski & Fleming, 1988, p. 4).

In the service of promoting teaching for understanding, teacher professionalism recognizes and supports local control (Carnegie Forum, 1986), facilitates the redesign of teacher work by reconceptualizing the roles and responsibilities of the classroom teacher, and reinforces teacher efforts at continuous professional improvement.

Teachers attempting professional improvement in this new model of learning will also need a new model of professional development. If we revisit the class-size study, we can see that, although the teachers participated in training workshops, they did not make significant change in their teaching practices. The workshops weren't all that were necessary, and were not sufficient.

As we have argued, if learning is redefined within a culture of professionalism, the professionals will have to relearn teaching in light of the new definition. The relearning must not stop with the teacher; without full system support there will be resistance to change. This resistance may come from parents, administrators, or the teachers themselves. Therefore, as teachers relearn teaching, the relearning must include the variety of stakeholders in supporting the new actions. For the teacher to take on new practice takes time, and simultaneous change from the other actors. This model of professional development is a dynamic, transformative model as opposed to a linear model.

Supporting Opportunities for Teachers to Learn: Professional Culture

If teachers must relearn teaching (Sizer, 1988), several conditions must be present for administrators and for teachers. Schools must have a professional culture:

> we can no longer afford to conceive of the schools simply as distribution centers for dispensing cultural orientations, information, and knowledge developed by other social units. The complexities of teaching and learning in formal classrooms have become so formidable and the intellectual demands upon the system so enormous that the school must be much more than a place of instruction. It must also be a center of inquiry...a producer as well as a transmitter of knowledge. (Schaefer, 1967, p. 1)

If we accept the evidence that teaching is a process that involves judgments and decisions that lead to adapting specific behaviors to different contexts in ways that are most productive of student learning, then we are more likely to focus on different approaches to applying research to improve practice. Fenstermacher (1986) believes that teaching is a moral, purposeful activity, and that teachers' acts result from decisions and judgments grounded in premises and beliefs about teaching, learning, content, and the context of the classroom. According to this view, teachers cannot be viewed as mechanistic implementors of independent behaviors, and efforts to improve teaching cannot be viewed as ways to insert specific behaviors in the place of others deemed to be less productive. These premises suggest a professional development model that involves teachers and administrators as decision makers, knowledge users, and knowledge producers in local settings. The culture of the school must be developed to support professional growth (for insights about how this can come about, see Lieberman, 1988).

Learning opportunities for teachers and administrators are limited or extended by the culture of the school and what is valued there. If no one in a school talks to one another, that becomes the culture of teaching (Feiman-Nemser & Floden, 1986; Little, 1982; Rosenholtz, 1989), and teachers and administrators have few resources and little support for change. In a school where the value is on how teachers are able to explicate what they are doing and how they are doing it, then that norm will be carried over into the kinds of actions and interactions in which people will engage.

Agreement of Key Stakeholders

The professional development model must have coherence across elements. Without coherence, when there is a clash the element or elements perceived as dominant will win out. This dominance overrides changes in direction, training, and class organization. Bergamo, Green, and Ridgeway (1989) have shown that walls are built when key stakeholders are missing from the dialogue, as they were in the development and implementation of Columbus Instructional Model (CIM). This was a model for transforming learning for students and giving teachers voice. Its purpose was to bring about through dialogue the improvement of learning for children. It was built on the premise that all members had to engage in the process and the conversation involved in the process, and that this type of transformation of a system could not be brought about overnight. The district superintendent supported the development and implementation of the model and was committed to the long-term process required for lasting change. However, within 3 years, this superintendent assumed a new job. The incoming superintendent had different ideas about what was important for teachers and students to know and do. Without the support and vision from this very important policymaker, CIM came to a standstill and is no longer in operation. Because of the instability of the administration, and the resulting shift in key stakeholders, change was no longer supported.

NEW FORMS OF ORGANIZATION, GOVERNANCE, AND MANAGEMENT

Neither robust new conceptions of learning and teaching nor teacher professionalism are likely to flourish under prevailing forms of school organization and governance. "If the construction of a genuine profession of teaching is to succeed, schools will have to change" (Holmes Group, 1986, p. 67). In fact, a number of thoughtful scholars have concluded that, without meaningful restructuring of the way education is organized, very little improvement is likely to be seen in America's schools (Chubb, 1988; Greenfield, 1988). After extensive analysis of the literature on student learning and school management, it seems to us that changes in both the management and governance of school structures and classroom learning arrangements will be required to help teachers foster the vision of teaching and learning discussed earlier.

Management and Governance of School Structures

In terms of school-level conditions, analysts trace most problems to the bureaucratic infrastructure of schooling, with its emphasis on control, hierarchy, impersonality, line authority, and narrow job specifications (see, for example, Clark & Meloy, 1989; Chubb, 1988; Frymier, 1987; Giroux, 1988; McNeil, 1986; Sizer, 1984; Wise, 1978, 1988). The central argument of these critics is that bureaucracy is inconsistent with the nature of professional work and the needs and goals of a professionalized teaching force (see Firestone, Chapter 10). In nurturing professional judgment, hierarchical organizational structures have distorted educational processes, highlighted management issues at the expense of educational ones, and led to the creation of organizational arrangements that are at odds with the elements of active student learning presented throughout this volume.

The task of those involved in overhauling the organizational infrastructure of schooling to support a learning orientation is twofold: to insure the political and administrative decentralization of schools, and, within individual schools, to develop an alternative to the hierarchical model of school governance and management. On the first issue, a good deal of work is already under way to make the individual school site "the fundamental decision-making unit within the educational system" (Guthrie, 1986, p. 306), or, in Goodlad's (1984, p. 276) words, to insure that each school becomes "largely self-directing." Without the greater authority and responsibility for their own affairs that accompanies restructuring efforts such as school-based management and site-based decision making, it is difficult to transcend the factory/work metaphors of schooling.

The transfer of authority to the school site is an important but insufficient condition to insure the professionalization of teaching that we see as a necessary step in promoting teaching for meaningful understanding (see Firestone, Chapter 10). A new model of structuring learning, of managing the educational process, and of making decisions at the local level is also required. What appears to be needed is the replacement of hierarchically organized units with more organic systems. These new structures, labeled *heterarchies* by Maccoby (1989), are marked by principles quite distinct from the classic tenets of bureaucracy. To begin with, specialization of labor is no longer seen as a strength. In the more organic structures required to support personalized construction of knowledge, there will be a reduced emphasis on dividing responsibilities into an ever-increasing number of discrete roles. This principle of heterarchy is a core tenet in the Coalition of Essential Schools' efforts to restructure schools to support teaching for meaningful understanding (Houston, 1989). In a similar fashion, hierarchically based authority is replaced by professionally grounded authority. Authority is anchored less to specific roles and more to expertise. Leadership in turn is less a function of position and role than of knowledge and competence. Leadership becomes more densely distributed throughout the school. In structures designed to nourish a learning as opposed to a work orientation, impersonality (and independence and isolation) is replaced by a renewed focus on the human element. Integration of effort and cooperative work characterize heterarchical school organizations. Organizational adaptivity substitutes for the traditional concern for uncovering the single best model of work. The separation of management from labor, with administrators taking responsibility for planning and teachers for implementing—another element underscored by the factory/work metaphor—becomes meaningless in heterarchically organized schools. Roles, authority, responsibilities, and leadership are mixed together and assumed or exercised by all as needed to support the mission of knowledge construction.

Organization of School Learning Structures

The visions of teaching and learning developed throughout these chapters will require significant alterations in the structures in which the educational process unfolds. These changes must emphasize the centrality of human relationships in schools, replace program isolation with connectedness, and promote personal engagement in the teaching–learning process. They represent a fundamental reconceptualization of school climate—a shift from an emphasis on its physical factors such as smooth functioning of the parts of the system and toward a focus on its human elements. Schools have historically attempted to capture educational processes within impersonal, time-based, calendar-based arrangements. While this organizational motif is congruent with bureaucratically managed schools, it is inconsistent with the new principles of management just described. In heterarchically organized schools, time-, calendar-, and place-based systems give way to structures grounded in three powerful concepts: outcome-based learning, which recognizes learning processes as well as products; developmentally based learning, which considers student development as well as age; and the personalization of learning, which accepts diversity in student learning processes. These concepts reorient the organization of school learning structures toward student abilities and needs. In practical terms, these principles of organizing for meaningful learning play out in a number of ways that support this type of learning, such as broadened conceptions of how space can be used (including space away from the school), greater flexibility in grouping students for classes (e.g., multiage grouping at the elementary level, the use of houses at the secondary level), more creative scheduling patterns (e.g., the use of longer blocks of time than the traditional 50-minute class period), and alternate patterns of grouping students within classes (e.g., cooperative work groups). Structural changes will support change in schools when they are the product of backward mapping decision-making from broadened conceptions of student learning. As we have already said, "fundamental discussions about how to restructure educational processes for more effective learning should precede the other aspects of schooling" (Murphy, 1991, p. 88).

CONCLUSION

We contend that the first step in understanding the role of redesigned schools in supporting student learning, the kind of student learning that is the focus of this volume, must begin with a dialogue that focuses on the relationships among student learning, classroom processes, and schools as organizations. To do this will require hard thinking and action quite different from actions that have been taken in the past, actions that have relied on externally mandated changes. We suggest that the dialogue begin with five common assumptions about the requirements and processes for moving "beyond the classroom door." We believe that an initial step has been taken in this volume by pulling together research and examples from different fields. Beginning clues for thoughtful consideration of most of these assumptions have been suggested in the preceding chapters. It is clear, nevertheless, that many questions about these assumptions remain to be raised and discussed with a wider audience.

1. *Student learning will "look" different in redesigned schools than it does in nonredesigned schools.*
2. *The redesigned school will both conceptualize needs and propose and initiate solutions as opposed to merely implementing visions from outside.*
3. *Roles, relationships, and responsibilities among those with vested interests in schooling (teachers, administrators, parents, students, as well as the university) will change.*
4. *To accomplish these changes, mechanisms must be designed to support organizational relearning for all participants.*
5. *The process of improving learning in redesigned schools will look considerably different from a linear, incremental process.*

Although views regarding these assumptions have been suggested in the preceding chapters, more thinking and dialogue are needed if we are to begin with student learning and classroom processes in the redesigning of our schools. The dialogue must now extend to more of those holding a stake in educational reform.

REFERENCES

Barth, R.S. (1988). School: A community of leaders. In A. Lieberman (Ed.), *Building a professional culture in schools*. New York: Teachers College Press.

Barth, R.S. (1989). The principal and the profession of teaching. In T. J. Sergiovanni & J. H. Moore (Eds.), *Schooling for tomorrow: Directing reform to issues that count*. Boston: Allyn and Bacon.

Beck, L.G., & Murphy, J. (in press). *Understanding the principalship: A metaphorical analysis from 1920 to 1990*. New York: Teachers College Press.

Bergamo, H., Green, J.L., & Ridgeway, D. (1989, July). *Making professional development last: Issues and research, policy and practice*. Columbus, OH: Department of Educational Policy and Leadership, The Ohio State University.

Berliner, D.C. (1990). If the metaphor fits, why not wear it? The teacher as executive. *Theory into Practice, 29*(2), 85–93.

Bloome, D., Puro, P., & Theodorou, E. (1989). Procedural display and classroom lessons. *Curriculum Inquiry, 19*(3), 265–291.

Bossert, S.T. (1979). *Tasks and social relationships in classrooms.* New York: University of Cambridge Press.

Bredeson, P.V. (1989, March). *Redefining leadership and the roles of school principals: Responses to changes in the professional worklife of teachers.* Paper presented at the annual meeting of the American Educational Research Association, San Francisco, CA.

Bruner, J. (1985). Models of the learner. *Educational Researcher, 14*(6), 5–8.

Carnegie Forum on Education and the Economy. (1986). *A nation prepared: Teachers for the 21st century.* Washington, DC: Author.

Carter, K., & Doyle, W. (1982, March). *Variations in academic tasks in high and average ability classes.* Paper presented at the annual meeting of the American Educational Research Association, New York.

Chubb, J.E. (1988). Why the current wave of school reform will fail. *The Public Interest, 90,* 28–49.

Clark, D.L., & Meloy, J.M. (1989). Renouncing bureaucracy: A democratic structure for leadership in schools. In T.J. Sergiovanni & J.A. Moore (Eds.), *Schooling for tomorrow: Directing reform to issues that count.* Boston: Allyn & Bacon.

Cohen, E.G., & Lotan, R.A. (1990). Teacher as supervisor of complex technology. *Theory into Practice, 29*(2), 78–84.

Conway, J.A., & Jacobson, S.L. (1990). An epilogue: Where is educational leadership going? In S.L. Jacobson & J.A. Conway (Eds.), *Educational leadership in an age of reform.* New York: Longman.

Council of Chief State School Officers. (1989). *Success for all in a new century.* Washington, DC: Author.

Cuban, L. (1984). *How teachers taught.* New York: Longman.

Cuban, L. (1990). Reforming again, again, and again. *Educational Researcher, 19,* 3–13.

David, J. (1989). *Restructuring in progress: Lessons from pioneering districts.* Washington, DC: National Governors' Association.

Doyle, W. (1983). Academic work. *Review of Educational Research, 53*(2), 159–199.

Elkind, D. (1987). Action in the classroom: The Swiss movement. *Theory Into Practice, 26*(2), 383–387.

Elmore, R.F. (1979–1980). Backward mapping: Implementation research and policy decisions. *Political Science Quarterly, 94*(4), 601–616.

Elmore, R.F. (1989, March). *Models of restructured schools.* Paper presented at the annual meeting of the American Educational Research Association, San Francisco.

Evertson, C.M., & Randolph, C.H. (in press). Teaching practices and class size: A new look at an old issue. *Peabody Journal of Education.*

Fenstermacher, G.D. (1986). Philosophy of research on teaching: Three aspects. In M.C. Wittrock (Ed.), *Handbook of research on teaching* (3rd ed., pp. 37–49). New York: Macmillan.

Feiman-Nemser, S., & Floden, R. (1986). The cultures of teaching. In M.C. Wittrock (Ed.). *Handbook of research on teaching* (3rd ed., pp. 505–526). New York: Macmillan.

Frymier, J. (1987). Bureaucracy and the neutering of teachers. *Phi Delta Kappan, 69*(1), 9–14.

Fullan, M. (1991). *The new meaning of educational change*. New York: Teachers College Press.

Giroux, H.A. (1988). *Teachers as intellectuals: Toward a critical pedagogy of learning*. Granby, MA: Bergin & Garvey.

Goodlad, J.I. (1984). *A place called school: Prospects for the future*. New York: McGraw-Hill.

Greenfield, T.B. (1988). The decline and fall of science in educational administration. In D.E. Griffiths, R.T. Stout, & P.B. Forsyth (Eds.), *Leaders for America's schools*. Berkeley, CA: McCutchan.

Gumperz, J. (1986). Interactional sociolinguistics in the study of schooling. In J. Cook-Gumperz (Ed.), *The social construction of literacy* (pp. 45–68). New York: Cambridge University Press.

Guthrie, J.W. (1986). School-based management: The next needed education reform. *Phi Delta Kappan, 68*(4), 305–309.

Hawley, W.D. (1988). Missing pieces of the educational reform agenda: Or why the first and second waves may miss the boat. *Educational Administration Quarterly, 24*(4), 416–437.

Heap, J.L. (1984). Ethnomethodology and education: Possibilities. *The Journal of Educational Thought, 18*(3), 168–171.

Holmes Group. (1986). *Tomorrow's teachers*. East Lansing, MI: Author.

Houston, H.M. (1989, March). *Professional development for restructuring: Analyses and recommendations*. Paper presented at the annual meeting of the American Educational Research Association, San Francisco, CA.

LeMahieu, P.G. (1984). The effects on achievement and instructional content of a program of student monitoring through frequent testing, *Educational Evaluation and Policy Analysis, 6*, 175–87.

Lieberman, A. (Ed.). (1988). *Building a professional culture in schools*. New York: Teachers College Press.

Little, J.W. (1982). Norms of collegiality and experimentation: Workplace conditions of school success. *American Educational Research Journal, 19*, 325–340.

Maccoby, M. (1989, December). *Looking for leadership now*. Paper prepared for the National Center for Educational Leadership conference, Harvard University, Cambridge, MA.

Madaus, G. (1987). The influence of testing on the curriculum. In L. Tanner (Ed.), *Critical issues in curriculum* (pp. 83–121) (Eighty-seventh Yearbook of the National Society for the Study of Education). Chicago, IL: The University of Chicago Press.

Malen, B., Ogawa, R.T., & Kranz, J. (1989, May). *What do we know about school based management? A case study of the literature—a call for research*. Paper presented at the Conference on Choice and Control in American Education, University of Wisconsin-Madison, Madison, WI.

Marshall, H.H. (1988). Work or learning: Implications of classroom metaphors. *Educational Researcher, 17*, 9–16.

Marshall, H.H. (1990). Beyond the workplace metaphor: The classroom as a learning setting. *Theory into Practice, 29*(2), 94–101.

McCarthey, S.J., & Peterson, P.L. (1989, March). *Teacher roles: Weaving new patterns in classroom practice and school organization.* Paper presented at the annual meeting of the American Educational Research Association, San Francisco, CA.

McLaughlin, M.W. (1987). Learning from experience: Lessons from policy implementation. *Educational Evaluation and Policy Analysis, 9,* 171–178.

McNeil, L.M. (1984). Defensive teaching and classroom control. In M. W. Apple & L. Weis (Eds.), *Ideology and practice in education.* Philadelphia: Temple University Press.

McNeil, L.M. (1986). *Contradictions of control: School structure and school knowledge.* New York and London: Routledge & Kegan Paul.

McNeil, L.M. (1990). Empowering students: Beyond defensive teaching in social studies. In C. Emihovich (Ed.), *Locating learning: Ethnographic perspectives on classroom research* (pp. 117–140). Norwood, NJ: Ablex Publishing Corp.

Mojkowski, C., & Fleming, D. (1988). *School-site management: Concepts and approaches.* Andover, MA: Regional Laboratory for Educational Improvement of the Northeast and Islands.

Murphy, J. (1990a). Preparing school administrators for the 21st century: The reform agenda. In B. Mitchell & L. L. Cunningham (Eds.), *Educational leadership and changing contexts of families, communities, and schools.* Chicago: University of Chicago Press.

Murphy, J. (1990b). The educational reform movement of the 1980s: A comprehensive analysis. In J. Murphy (Ed.), *The reform of American public education in the 1980s: Perspectives and cases.* Berkeley, CA: McCutchan.

Murphy, J. (1991). *Restructuring schools: Capturing and assessing the phenomena.* New York: Teachers College Press.

National Governors' Association. (1989). *Results in education 1989.* Washington, DC: Author.

Passow, A.H. (1984). *Reforming schools in the 1980s: A critical review of the national reports.* New York: Teachers College, Columbia University, Institute for Urban and Minority Education.

Petrie, H.G. (1990). Reflections on the second wave of reform: Restructuring the teaching profession. In S. L. Jacobson & J.A. Conway (Eds.), *Educational leadership in an age of reform.* New York: Longman.

Powell, A.G., Farrar, E., & Cohen, D.K. (1985). *The shopping mall high school: Winners and losers in the educational marketplace.* Boston, MA: Houghton-Mifflin.

Richardson, V. (1990). Significant and worthwhile change in teaching practice. *Educational Researcher, 19*(7), 10–18.

Rosenholtz, S.J. (1989). *Teachers' workplace: The social organization of schools.* New York: Longman.

Sarason, S.B. (1982). *The culture of the school and the problem of change* (2nd ed.). Boston, MA: Allyn & Bacon.

Schaefer, R.J. (1967). *The school as a center of inquiry.* New York: Harper & Row.

Schlechty, P.C. (1990). *Schools for the twenty-first century: Leadership imperatives for educational reform.* San Francisco, CA: Jossey-Bass.

Sizer, T.R. (1984). *Horace's compromise: The dilemma of the American high school.* Boston, MA: Houghton-Mifflin.

Sizer, T.R. (1988, August). Creating a society that thinks: Re:Learning. *State Government News,* (The Council of State Governments), pp. 20–21.

Sykes, G., & Elmore, R.F. (1989). Making schools more manageable. In J. Hannaway & R.L. Crowson (Eds.), *The politics of reforming school administrations.* New York: Falmer Press.

Weade, R., & Evertson, C.M. (1988). The construction of lessons in effective and less effective classrooms. *Teaching and Teacher Education, 4*(3), 189–213.

Wise, A.E. (1978). The hyper-rationalization of American education. *Educational Leadership, 35*(5), 354–361.

Wise, A.E. (1988). The two conflicting trends in school reform: Legislated learning revisited. *Phi Delta Kappan, 69*(5), 328–333.

Wise, A.E. (1989). Professional teaching: A new paradigm for the management of education. In T.J. Sergiovanni & J.H. Moore (Eds.), *Schooling for tomorrow: Directing reforms to issues that count.* Boston, MA: Allyn & Bacon.

Word, E., Johnston, J., Pate-Bain, H., Fulton, B.D., Zaharias, J., Achilles, C., Lintz, M., Folger, J., & Breda, C. (1990). *Student/teacher Achievement Ratio (STAR) project technical report, 1985–1990.* Nashville, TN: Tennessee State Department of Education.

Author Index

A

Achilles, C., *318*
Adelman, C., 98, *118*
Adler, M., 40, *54*
Allington, R., 120, *148*
Alvermann, D.E., 125, *148*
Ames, C., 15, 16, *29*, 208, 209, 210, *238*
Ames, R., 15, *29*
Anderson, C.W., 210, *238*
Anderson, L.M., 6, *29*
Anyon, J., 41, *54*
Apple, M., 41, 42, *54*
Applebee, A.N., 126, *148*
Archbald, D.A., 240, 241, 242, 245, *260*
Archer, J., 15, *29*, 208, 209, 210, *239*
Ascher, C., 246, *260*

B

Bacharach, S.B., 268, 269, 275, *287*
Bader, B.D., 278, 286, *288*
Bailey, F., 37, *55*, 99, 104, *116*
Baker, C., 77n, 78, *83*, 119, 120, *148*
Ball, D.L., 153, 154, 170, *174*, 285, *287*
Barnes, D., 181, 185, *202*
Barr, R., 39, *54*, 199, *202*
Barrett, M., 21, *29, 30*
Barth, R.S., 308, *314*
Bartholomae, D., 128, 142, *148*
Battista, M., 182, *202*
Bauersfeld, H., 180, 188, *202*
Beauchamp, G.A., 40, *54*
Beck, L.G., 308, *314*
Bereiter, C., 8, 15, 16, *29*
Bergamo, H., 122, 144, 145, *148*, 311, *314*
Berliner, D.C., 40, *55*, 309, *314*

Berman, L., 37, 40, *55*
Berman, P., 269, *287*
Bernstein, B., 88, 97, 99, *116*
Berry, B., 272, *287*
Bishop, A., 189, *287*
Bixby, J., 96, *118, 261*
Blase, J., 21, 27, *29*
Bloom, A., 40, *55*
Bloome, D., 6, *29*, 36, 37, 54, *55, 57*, 62n, 69, *83*, 88, 91, 98, 99, 104, *116*, 119, 120, 121, 132, 133, 138, 143, *148*, 149, 304, *314*
Blumenfeld, P.C., 207, 208, 209, 212, *238, 239*
Blumer, H., 181, *202*
Bobbitt, F., 40, 41, *55*
Boggiano, A.K., 21, *29, 30*
Borman, K.M., 265, *287*
Bossert, S.T., 302, 307, *315*
Boyer, E., 40, *55*
Breda, C., *318*
Bredeson, P.V., 309, *315*
Brooks, H., 7, *31*
Brophy, J.E., 6, 8, *29*, 209, *238*, 266, *287*
Broudy, H.S., 41, *55*
Bruner, J., 7, 14, *30*, 192, 197, *202, 204*, 298, 315
Bull, G., 90, *116*
Burgess, R.G., 37, *55*

C

Camp, R., 250, *260*
Carpenter, T.P., 18, 22, 30, 32, 154, 159, 170, *174*, 210, *239*
Carr, W., 105, *116*
Carter, K., 267, *287*, 307, *315*

E

Eccles, J., 209, 210, *238*
Edelsky, C., 90, *116*
Edwards, A.D., 61, 62n, 65, 67, 68, 70, 72, 83, 127, *149*
Edwards, D., 6, 11, 26, *30*, 180, *203*
Eisner, E., 41, *55*
Elgas, P., 59, 62n, *83*, 138, *149*
Elkind, D., 298, *315*
Ellett, F.S., 92, *116*
Elliot, E.S., 209, *238*
Elmore, R.F., 3, 26, *30*, 292, 294, 297, 309, *315*
Emihovich, C., 62n, 83
Eresh, J., 249, *260*
Erickson, F., 39, 52, *55, 57*, 61, 77, *83*, 95, 100, *116*, 121, *149*
Ericson, D.P., 92, *116*
Evertson, C.M., 92, 100, *116*, 296, 297, 305, *315*

F

Farnham-Diggory, S., 7, 8, *30*
Farrar, E., 293, *317*
Feiman-Nemser, S., 310, *315*
Feldman, D., 88, *118*
Fennema, E., 18, 22, *30, 32*, 159, 170, *174*, 210, *239*
Fenstermacher, G.D., *116*, 143, *149*, 302, 306, 310, *315*
Fernie, D., 59, 61, 62n, 63, 64, *83*, 138, *149*
Fiedler, M., 92, *116*
Finney, R.L., 41, *55*
Firestone, W.A., 278, 286, *288, 289*
Fish, S., 128, *149*
Flanders, N.A., 172, *174*
Fleming, D., 309, *317*
Flink, C., 21, *30*
Floden, R., 310, *315*
Florio, S., 39, 52, *57*
Folger, J., *318*
Forman, E., 87, *117*
Forrestal, P., 87, *117*
Frederiksen, J.R., 244, 245, *261*
Frederiksen, N., 241, 245, *261*
Freire, P., 41, 42, *55*
Frymier, J., 311, *316*
Fullan, M., 295, *316*
Fulton, B.D., *318*

G

Gagne, R.M., 40, *55*

C

Cazden, C., 138, *148*
Chiang, C., 18, *30*, 159, *174*
Chubb, J.E., 311, *315*
Clark, C., 267, 285, *287*
Clark, D.L., 311, *315*
Clements, D., 182, *202*
Clune, W.H., 275, *287*
Cobb, P., 15, 19, *30, 32*, 178, 179, 181, 183, 186, 187, 188, 189, 191, 192, 198, 199, 200, *202*
Cochran-Smith, M., 36, 62n, *55, 83*, 88, *116*, 120, 122, 133, *148*
Cohen, E.G., 303, *315*
Cohen, D.K., 285, *287*, 293, *317*
Cole, M., 11, *31*
Cole, N., 244, *260*
Collins, A., 244, 245, *261*
Collins, E.C., 54, *55*, 60n, 62n, 64, 65, 68, 72, 79, 82, *83*
Collins, J., 63, 79n, *83*, 120, 121, 127, *148*
Conley, S.C., 268, 269, 275, *287*
Connell, J.P., 18, *32*, 271, *289*
Conway, J.A., 309, *315*
Cook, J., 87, *117*
Cook-Gumperz, J., 62n, 79n, *83*, 97, *116*, 120, 122, *148*
Corbett, H.D., 286, *289*
Corno, L., 211, *238*
Corwin, R.G., 265, *287*
Coulthard, R., 180, *204*
Counts, C.S., 41, *55*
Crawford, J., 92, *116*
Cronbach, L.J., 244, *260*
Cuban, L., 2, 8, 19, 23, 26, 28, *30*, 146, *149*, 293, 295, *315*

D

Darling-Hammond, L., 246, *260*, 272, *287*
David, J., 294, *315*
Davis, P.J., 178, *203*
Decharms, R., 28, *30*
Deci, E.L., 271, *289*
De Groot, E.W., 18, *32*, 209, *239*
Denzin, N.K., 36n, *55*
DeStephano, J.S., 53, *55*
Dewey, J., 7, *30*
Doran, J.A., 255, *260*
Dornbusch, S.M., 271, *287*
Doyle, W., 14, *30*, 40, *55*, 95, *116*, 170, *174*, 210, *238*, 267, *287*, 302, 307, *315*
Dunbar, S., 241, 245, *261*
Dweck, C.S., 15, *30*, 209, *238*

Gardner, H., 88, 96, *118*, 240, *261*
Geertz, C., 78, *83*
Gianconia, R., 16, *30*
Gilmore, P., 62n, *84*
Giroux, H., 41, *56*, 311, *316*
Gitomer, D., 241, *260*
Glatthorn, A., 62n, *84*
Glenn, J., III., 240, *118, 261*
Golan, S., 15, *30*
Golden, J., 120, 125, 128, 132, 147, *149*
Good, T., 6, *29*, 266, *287, 288*
Goodenough, W., 37, 38, 53, *56*, 61, 78, *84*
Goodlad, J.I., 26, *31*, 180, *203*, 312, *316*
Graham, K., 88, *117*
Graham, S., 15, *30*
Green, J., 8, 12, *30*, 36, 48, 39, 52, 52, 54, *56*, 59, 61, 62n, 63, 66, 67, 68, 68, 77, 77n, 81, *83, 84*, 88, 91, 95, 98, 99, 104, *116*, 120, 121, 122, 124, 132, 133, 143, 144, 145, 147, *148*, 311, *314*
Greene, D., *31*
Greenfield, T.B., 311, *316*
Griffith, P., 11, *31*
Gumperz, J.J., 38, 39, 52, *56*, 59n, 61, 71, 78, *84*, 104, *117*, 122, 124, *150*, 307, *316*
Guthrie, J.W., 312,*316*

H

Hackman, J.R., 271, *288, 289*
Hargreaves, A., 285, *288*
Harker, J.O., 12, *30*, 36, 38, *56*, 59, 62n, 77, 77n, *84*, 95, 104, *117*, 120, 132, 147, *149*
Hart, A.W., 272, 273, *288*
Harter, S., 209, *239*
Hawley, W.D., 294, *316*
Heap, J., 60n, 78, 80, 82, *84*, 91, 107, *117*, 120, 127, *150*, 304, *316*
Heath, S.B., 38, 61, *56, 84*
Hedges, L., 16*30*
Herasimchuk, E., 124, *149*
Hersh, R., 178, *203*
Hiebert, J., 154, *174*
Hilgard, E., 7, *31*
Houston, H.M., 312, *316*
Hoyle, R.H., 207, 209, 212, *239*
Hunter, M., 172, *174*
Hymes, D., 38, *56*, 138, *148*

J

Jacobson, S.L., 309, *315*
John, V., 138, *148*
Johnson, M., 7, *31, 70, 78, 84*

Johnson, S.M., 283, *288*
Johnson, V.G., 9, 20, *31*
Johnston, J., *318*

K

Kahn, J.L., 88, *116*
Kamii, C., 185, 197, 198, *203*
Kandal, I.L., 41, *56*
Kantor, R., *30*, 36, 53, *56*, 59, 61, 62n, 63, *83*, 88, 95, *117*, 122, 138, 143, *149*
Kemmis, S., 105, *116*
Kesner, J., 138, *149*
King, N., 37, 40, *56*
Klein, E., 59, 61, 62n, 63, *83*, 138, *149*
Klein, M., 42, *56*
Kliebard, H., 41, *57*
Knapp, N., 20, *31*, 155, *175*
Kranz, J., 294, *316*
Krummheuer, G., 179, *203*

L

Labinowicz, E., 188, *203*
Lakoff, G., 9, *31*, 70, 78, *84*
Lampert, M., 12, *31*, 153, 154, 170, *175*, 192, *203*, 210, *239*
Lather, P., 36n, *57*
Lawler, E.E., 271, *288*
Lepper, M.R., 8, *31*, 209, 211, *239*
Lemke, J., 77n, *84*, 91, 95, 113, *117*
Lemahieu, P.G., 249, *261*, 300, *316*
Lieberman, A., 310, *316*
Lind, K., 264, *289*
Linn, R.L., 241, 245, *261*
Lintz, M., *318*
Little, J.L., 269, *288*
Little, J.W., 310, *316*
Loef, M., 18, *30*, 159, *174*
Lohman, D.F., 241, *261*
Lortie, D.C., 273, 285, *288*
Lotan, R.A., 303, *315*
Luke, A., 77n, *83*, 119, 120, *148*

M

Maccoby, M., 312, *316*
MacDonald, JB., 41, *57*
Madaus, G., 299, 300, *316*
Maehr, M., 27, *31*
Malen, B., 272, 273, 274, 294, *288, 316*
Marshall, H.H., 2, 4, 7, 9, 10, 16, 17, 24, *31*, 40, 53, *57*, 60n, *84*, 152, *175*, 183, *203*, 208, 209, 210, *239*, 307, 308, *316*
McCarthey, S.J., 308, *317*

McCarthy, S., 284, *288*
McDaniel, R.R., 268, 269, *289*
McKenna, M.C., 90, *117*
McLaughlin, J., 26, *31*
McLaughlin, M.W., 269, 287, 295, *317*
McNeal, M., 179, 193, *202*
McNeil, L., 199, *203*, 301, 303, 304, 311, *317*
Mead, G.H., 181, *203*
Measor, L., 40, *57*
Meece, J.L., 207, 208, 209, 212, *239*
Mehan, H., 141, *150*, 180, *203*
Meloy, J.M., 311, *315*
Mercer, N., 6, 11, 26, *30*, 61, 62n, 65, 67, 68, 69, 70, 72, *83*, 127, *149*, 180, *203*
Merkel, G., 181, 185, 186, 187, 188, 191, *202*
Messick, S., 244, *261*
Meyer, C., 138, *149*
Meyer, L.A., 39, 52, *56*, 66, *84*, 133, *149*
Michaels, S., 79n, *84*
Midgley, C., 209, 210, *238*
Miller, J.W., 90, *117*
Mintzberg, H., 269, *288*
Mislevy, R.J., 241, 245, *261*
Mitchell, D., 283, *288*
Mitchell, R., 241, 242, *261*
Mohatt, G., 39, 52, *55*
Mojkowski, C., 309, *317*
Morine-Dershimer, G., 147, *150*
Morrow, L.M., 192, *203*
Moss, P., 244, *260*
Murphy, J., 292, 293, 294, 308, 313, *314, 317*
Murphy, M.J., 272, *288*

N

Neale, D.C., 20, 28, *31*
Newman, D., 11, 19, *31*
Newman, F.M., 240, 241, 242, 245, 269, *260, 288*
Nicholls, J.G., 15, *31*, 197, 198, *202*, 209, *239*
Nino, A., 192, *204*
Nolen, S., 15, *32*, 207, 209, *239*

O

Ogawa, R.T., 294, *316*
Oldham, G.R., 271, *288*

P

Paoletti, I., 78, *85*
Paris, C.L., 88, *116*
Passow, A.H., 264, 284, 293, *288, 317*
Patashnick, M., 15, 198, 209, *32, 204, 239*

Pate-Bain, H., *318*
Pearson, P.D., 90, *117*
Peddiwell, J.A., 33, *57*
Penna, A., 41, *56*
Pepinsky, H.B., 53, *55*
Perlwitz, M., 198, *202 203*
Perrow, C.B., 268, *288*
Perry, M., 170, *176*
Peterman, F., 20, 32
Peterson, P.L., 18, 20, 22, *30*, *31*, *33*, 155, 159, 170, *174*, 210, *239*, 267, 285, *287*, *288*, 308, *317*
Petrie, H.G., 303, 309, *317*
Petrosky, A.R., 128, 142, *148*
Philips, S.U., 39, 52, 53, *57*
Philips, S.V., 62n, *85*
Phinney, M.Y., 88, *116*
Piaget, J., 181, *204*
Piazza, C., 147, *150*
Pierce, C.S., 189, *204*
Pinar, W., 41, *56*
Pintrich, P.R., 18, 209, *32, 239*
Pokay, P., 209, *239*
Polkinghorne, D., 36n, *57*
Popkewitz, T.S., 264, *289*
Porter, A., 178, *204*
Porterm, L.W., 271, *289*
Powell, A.G., 293, 317
Prawat, R.S., 8, 14, 19, *32*
Puro, P., 6, *29*, 36, *57*, 143, *148*, 208, 212, *239*, 304, *314*
Putnam, R., 156, 157, *175*

R

Randolph, C.H., 296, 297, *315*
Rathmell, E.C., 188, *204*
Reid, J., 87, *117*
Reid, W.A., 42, *57*
Reineke, J., 156, 157, *175*
Remillard, J., 157, *175*
Richards, J., 200, *205*
Richardson, V., 183, *204*, 295, *317*
Ridgeway, D., 31, 122, 144, 145, *148, 314*
Robinson, J., 132, *150*
Robinson, R.D., 90, *117*
Rogers, T., *30*, *56*, 63, *84*, 88, 95, *117*, 122, 143, *149*
Rohrkemper, M., 17, *32*, 211, *238*
Rosean, C., *32*
Rosenholtz, S.J., 209, *239*, 269, 272, 273, 282, *289*, 310, *317*

AUTHOR INDEX 325

Rosenshine, B.V., 172, *175*, 178, *204*, 267, *289*
Ross, D., *175*
Ross, E.A., 41, *57*
Rossman, G.B., 286, *289*
Roth, K., *32*
Rowan, B., 268, *289*
Ruddell, R., 130, *150*
Rutter, R.A., 269, *288*
Ryan, R.M., 271, *289*

S

Sadow, M., 199, *202*
Salinger, J.D., 129, *150*
Sanders, T.S., 53, *55*
Sarason, S., 25, *32*, 304, *317*
Schaefer, R.J., 310, *317*
Schlechty, P., 91, 92, *117*, 307, 308, *317*
Schön, D., 9, *32*
Schubert, W., 42, *57*
Schultz, J., 61, 79n, *83*
Schutz, A., 178, 181, *204*
Schwarz, P., 138, *149*
Scott, J., 138, *149*
Scott, W.R., 271, *287*
Seymour, B., 108, *118*
Shannon, P., 199, *204*
Shea, J.F., 152, *175*
Shepard, L.A., 241, 245, *261*
Shor, I., 42, *57*
Shores, J.H., 40, *57*
Shulman, L.S., 152, *175*, 201, *204*
Shultz, J.J., 39, 52, *57*
Sickler, J., 275, *289*
Silliman, E., 96, *118*
Simpson, C., 209, *239*
Sinclair, J., 180, *204*
Singer, H., 130, *150*
Sizer, T.R., 302, 310, 311, *317*
Skemp, R., 185, *204*
Skinner, E., 18, *32*
Slavin, R., 8, *32*
Smith, B.O., 40, *57*
Smith, D., 20, *31*
Smith, E., 210, *238*
Smith, M.L., 20, *31*
Smith, M.S., 269, *288*
Snedden, D., 40, 41, *57*
Snow, R.E., 240, 241, 242, 245, *261*
Solsken, J., 77, *85*, 88, 97, *117*
Sowder, J., 173, *176*

Spencer, H., *57*
Spindler, G., 38, *57*, 62n, *85*
Spradley, J.P., 38, 42, *57*, 78, *85, 150*
Stanley, W.O., 40, *57*
Staw, B.M., 271, *289*
Steffe, L.P., 182, 183, 193, 202
Stevens, R., 178, *204*
Stigler, J.W., 170, *176*
Stodolsky, S.S., 180, *205*
Streeck, J., 178, *205*
Street, B.V., 120,*150*
Sykes, G., 309, *318*

T

Tannen, D., 96, 102, *117*, 141, *150*
Taylor, D., 88, *117*
Taylor, P.H., 40, *58*
Theodorou, E., 6, *29*, 54, *55*, 62n, *83*, 138, 143, *148*, 304, *314*
Thorndike, E., 7, *32*
Thornton, C., 188, *205*
Timar, T.B., 284, *289*
Todd, F., 181, 185, *202*
Trigatti, B., 198, *202*
Turner, D., 108, *118*
Tyler, W., 34, *58*

V

Voight J., 180, 187, 188, *205*
Von Glasersfeld, E., 178, 181, 183, *204*
Vygotsky, L., 7, 11, *32*, 192, *205*

W

Walker, R., 98, *118*
Walkerdine, V., 180, *205*
Wallace, R.C., 249, *261*
Wallat, C., 36, 38, *56*, 62n, 66, *84*, 124, 147, *150*
Weade, G., 88, 97, *117*, 120, 212, *150*
Weade, R., 62n, 69, 81, *85*, 88, 91, 92, 95, 103, 104, 114, *117*, 304, 305, *318*
Weber, M., 269, 271, *289*
Weber, R., 187, *205*
Weick, K.E., 265, 268, 269, *289*
Weinstein, C.S., 104, *118*
Weinstein, R.S., 4, 16, 24, *31*, 53, *57*, 209, 210, *239*
Wellborn, J., 18, *32*
Wells, G., 192, *205*
Wertsch, J., 7, 11, *32*
Wexler-Sherman, C., 88, *118*

Wheatley, G., 181, 184, 185, 186, 187, 198, *202*
White, P.A., 275, *287*
Wiggins, G., 240, 241, 245, *261*
Wilkinson, S., 96, *118*
Wilson, S., 170, *176*
Wise, A.E., 307, 311, *318*
Wolf, D., 111, *118*, 240, 241, 242, 245, *261*
Wood, T., 15, 28, *32*, 178, 179, 181, 185, 186, 187, 189, 198, 199, 200, *202*
Woolfolk, A., 8, *32*
Word, E., 297, *318*

Y

Yackel, E., 15, *32*, 178, 179, 181, 184, 185, 186, 187, 189, 198, 199, 200, *202*

Z

Zaharias, J., *318*
Zaharlick, A., 38, *58, 85*
Zuboff, S., 153, *176*

Subject Index

A
Achievement tests, 17–18, 20, 197–199; *see also* Assessment
Accountability, 17–20, 111, 197, 214, 240, 246–247, 250, 258; *see also* Assessment
Assessment, 17–21, 79–82, 109–111, 162–170, 239–260, 296, 299–301; *see also* Achievement tests
  as agent of change, 249, 251
  and enhancing learning, 251–156
  in context, 241–244, 248–258
  measurement issues, 244–246, 252–253, 256–257
  parent role, 254–255
  portfolio approach, 249–259
  writing, 245, 249–258

B
Backward mapping, 292–294, 313
Behaviorist views, 7, 17
  methods, *see* Methodology, behaviorist
  of learning, *see* Learning, behaviorist views
Beliefs
  about learning, 5–7; *see also* Learning; Teacher beliefs

C
Career ladders, 274
Class size, 295–297
Classroom
  continuity of classroom life, 67–76
  as culture, 37–39, 61–83
  management, 302–305
Cognitive engagement, 18, 172, 207–238

Community of learners, 154
Constructivist views, *see* Learning, constructivist views
Concept development, 215–218, 222–225, 234
Control strategies, effects of, 21–22
Curriculum
  integrated, *see* Subject matter, integrated
  as constructed, *see* Curriculum, sociocultural perspective
  as document, 40–41
  delivered, 34, 44, 47–51, 106, 114
  enacted, *see* Curriculum, delivered
  planned, 34, 44–45, 50–51
  received, *see* Curriculum, delivered
  sociocultural perspective, 33–54
  student-centered, 122, 128, 141, 143–144
  values, 300

D
Direct instruction, 266–267, 276; *see also* Learning, behaviorist views

E
Effective teaching programs, 172, 277, 295

F
Feedback to students, 218–220, 225–226
Forward mapping, 292, 297, 306
Frame clash, 75–76, 141

G
Goals, 15
  learning, 15–17, 208–209, 237
  performance, 15–17, 209

327

328 SUBJECT INDEX

Governance, 272, 274, 311–313; *see also* Organizational design

H
Heterarchies, 312–313
Holism, 66–67

I
Incentives (for teachers), 270–273, 276, 280; *see also* Merit pay
Instruction
  effective, 4
  decisions, 302
Intentions, situated, 104–113
Interactional sociolinguistic perspective, 59–62, 76–77, 81, 90, 104, 123; *see also* Learning, interactional sociolinguistic perspective
Intertextuality, 69, 129, 133–134, 137, 141

J
Job differentiation, 264, 272, 283
Job enlargement, 271—273, 278, 280–281, 283–284

K
Key ideas, 24–25
Knowledge
  value of, 301–302
  construction, 4, 17, 23, 62, 66–69; *see also* Learning, views of
Knowledge-work, 92–93

L
Language arts, *see* Literacy; Assessment, writing
Learning
  additive model, 298
  behaviorist views of, 1, 6–9, 16, 87–88, 115, 173, 178, 296, 306
  cognitive anthropological perspective, 77–79
  cognitive views of, 8
  collaborative, 185
  constraints on, 18–22, 46, 49–52, 139–141, 199
  constructivist views of, 2, 6–8, 11–16, 170, 173–174, 178, 181–201, 235, 306; *see also* Learning, for meaningful understanding
  social constructivist, views of, 68–70, 90–115, 120–121, 132, 145

definition of, 4–5, 51, 60–61, 76–82, 87
ethnomethodological perspective, 78, 80
interactional sociolinguistic perspective, 78, 80
interpretive model, 298; *see also* Learning, constructivist views
for meaningful understanding, 6, 18–28, 159, 162–168, 234–237, 294, 309, 313; *see also* Press for understanding
opportunities for, 44, 51, 60, 71, 145–146, 180–181, 183–184, 192–197, 299, 213, 236–238, 306
"procedural display," 6, 304–305
purposes, *see* Goals; Purposes of education
roots of dominant views of, 7–9
sites of, 99–100
situated definitions, *see* Learning, social constructivist
support for, 22–28, 46, 49–52, 200–201, 235–238, 214, 220, 237–238, 251–253; *see also* Assessment, and enhancing learning; Professional development
transmission model, *see* Learning, behaviorist views
Lesson construction process, 94
Literacy, 119–147; *see also* Literate action
  model of, 128–129, 142
  schooled, 122
  situated definition, 121, 132
  as socially constructed phenomenon, 120, 145
Literate action, 120, 122–130, 133–138, 142, 145

M
Master teacher programs, 273, 276
Mastery, 17; *see also* Motivation
Mathematics, 100–102, 108, 111–113, 153–174, 177–201
Merit, 272
  pay, 273, 281–283
Metaphors
  classroom as workplace, 1–2, 7, 9–10, 151–152, 297, 303, 307–308, 312; *see also* Motivation, work orientation
  classroom as a learning place, 10; *see also* Motivation, learning orientation
  student as learner, 265–266, 271, 286
  student as worker, 1, 265–266, 271, 303
  teacher as leader, learner, 308
  teacher as manager/supervisor, 1, 152, 303
  teaching as locating knowledge, 304

Methodology, 4
  behaviorist, 4
  observation, 80, 89; see also Methodology, qualitative
  qualitative, 5, 16, 123, 147
Moments
  in teaching, 105–115
  teachable, 97
Motivation, 212–238
  learning-orientation, 9–10, 15–17, 152, 198, 209, 308
  task-orientation, 15, 198
  work-orientation, 9, 17
Myths of teaching, 91–115

N

Negotiation of meaning, 181, 186–196; see also Social construction; Taken-as-shared meaning

O

Observation of learning, see, Methodology
Operational decisions, 268–269
  standardization, 269–270, 277–278
Organizational design, 263–287
  bureaucratic, 263–264, 266, 268–272, 275–278, 281, 311–313
  professional, 263–264, 266, 268–274, 275, 278–286, 308, 313
  technology, influence on, 267–268

P

Plans, see Teacher planning
Press for understanding, 214, 218–220, 229–237
Pressure, see Teacher, pressures on; Teacher stress
Professional development, 27, 122, 142–146, 156, 160–162, 200–201, 255–256, 309–310; see also Organizational design, professional
  school, 156, 174
Professionalism, 27, 266; see also Organizational design, professional
Process-product research, see Teaching research paradigm
Purpose of education, 3, 8, 41–42, 44–46, 265, 293–294; see also Learning

R

Reading, 36–37, 42–52, 130–132; see also Literacy

Reflective practice, 174, 266–267, 285–286
Referential system, 70–71, 76
Reform, 1–2
  bureaucratic, see Organizational design
  coherence of, 27, 311
  constraints on, 18–22; see also Learning, constraints on
  decentralization, see School-based management
  financial implications, 282–283
  historical perspective, 292–294
  professionally oriented, see Organizational design
  standards-raising, 293
  support for, 22–28; see also Learning, support for
Restructuring, see Reform

S

School-based management, 275, 294, 312–313
Science, 67–68, 100–102, 108, 111–113, 215–234
Shared understanding, 70–72
Social construction, 52–54, 61–67, 70–72; see also Curriculum, sociocultural perspective; Learning, social constructivist views
Social studies, 67–68
Sociolinguistic analysis, 123; see also, Interactional sociolinguistic perspective
Strategic decision, 268–269, 274–275
Subject matter
  integrated, 99–111
Student, see also Metaphors
  norms and expectations, 12–14, 37–40, 65–66, 71–77, 186–189
  perspective, 4–5, 12
  responsibility for learning, 25
  roles, 25, 38–39, 63–65, 92–94, 153–154, 177–181, 188, 248, 251–254
  views of self, 16
Studenting, 92–93, 306–307

T

Taken-as-shared meaning, 178, 181–182, 185, 189–191, 193–196
Teacher, see also Metaphors
  beliefs, 18–19, 23, 104–106, 170–174, 178, 181, 188, 199, 301
  commitment, 278
  empowerment, 264, 275, 281, 284–286

equity, 273, 283
evaluation of, 276–277, 279, 283–284
expectations, 13, 25, 37–40, 65–66, 72–76, 266
knowledge, 22
as learner, 281
planning, 106–114
roles, 38–39, 63–65, 92–94, 152–153, 177–181, 193, 248–253, 264, 301–302
pressures on, 19–21, 50, 52
stress, 278, 284
as worker, 270, 275, 278, 281
Teaching
defensive, 303–304
empowering, 303–304
for meaningful understanding, *see* Learning for meaningful understanding
moments, *see also* Moments, in teaching
as negotiation, *see* Negotiation of meaning
research paradigm, 266
uncertainty of, 192, 268, 303, 305
Text, 132
construction, 69, 132, 137
interactions with, 128–132, 136
interactions about, 132–136
interactions through, 128, 136–137
interpreting, 125, 132
oral, 133
Time, 282
Transmission model, *see* Learning, behaviorist views
Triangulation, 36

V

Vision, pedagogical, 285–286
Values, 42–48; *see also* Purpose of education